THE FIRES OF
PHILADELPHIA

THE FIRES OF PHILADELPHIA

PHILADELPHIA

Citizen-Soldiers, Nativists, and the
1844 Riots Over the Soul of a Nation

ZACHARY M. SCHRAG

PEGASUS BOOKS
NEW YORK LONDON

THE FIRES OF PHILADELPHIA

Pegasus Books, Ltd.
148 West 37th Street, 13th Floor
New York, NY 10018

Copyright © 2021 by Zachary M. Schrag

First Pegasus Books edition June 2021

Interior design by Maria Fernandez

Library of Congress Cataloging-in-Publication Data is available.

ISBN: 978-1-64313-728-5

10 9 8 7 6 5 4 3 2 1

Printed in the United States of America
Distributed by Simon & Schuster
www.pegasusbooks.com

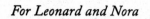
For Leonard and Nora

CONTENTS

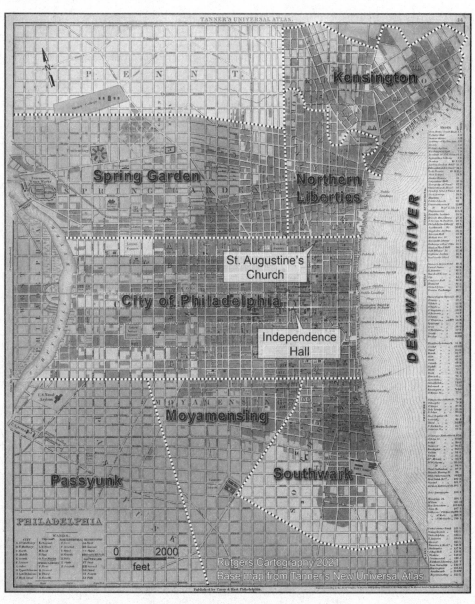

Central Philadelphia County

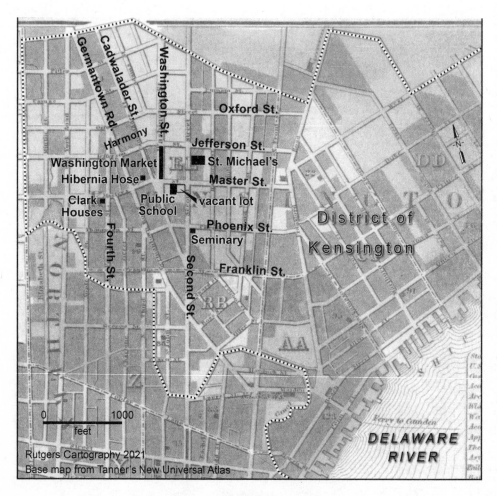

Kensington

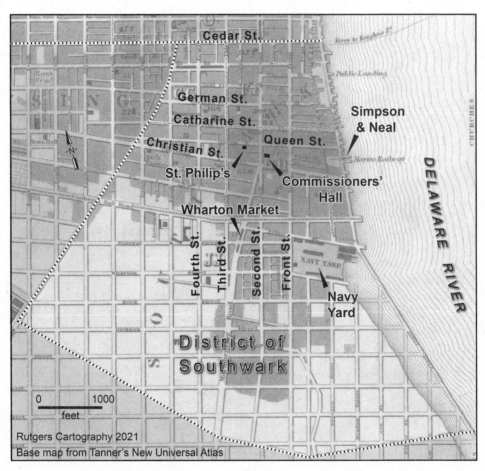

Cedar St.

Ferry to Knight P.

Public Landing

German St.

Simpson
& Neal

Catharine St.

Christian St.

Queen St.

Marine Railway

CHURCHES

St. Philip's

Commissioners'
Hall

DELAWARE RIVER

Wharton Market

NAVY YARD

Fourth St.

Third St.

Second St.

Front St.

Navy
Yard

District of
Southwark

0   1000

feet

Rutgers Cartography 2021

Base map from Tanner's New Universal Atlas

Southwark

Volunteers of the First Division, Pennsylvania Militia

Major General Robert Patterson

First Brigade

Brigadier General George Cadwalader
   First City Troop, Capt. John Butler
   First Regiment Artillery, Col. Augustus Pleasonton
      Junior Artillerists, Capt. W. H. Drayton
      State Artillerists, Capt. George Bumm
      Washington Grays, Capt. Jonathan McAdam
      Philadelphia Grays, Capt. George Cadwalader
      Cadwalader Grays, Capt. R. K. Scott
      National Artillery, Capt. J. K. Murphy
      Independent Guards, Capt. George D. Haswell
   102nd Regiment Infantry, Col. Joseph Murray
      Washington Blues, Capt. William. C. Patterson
      1st. Co. State Fencibles, Capt. James Page
      2nd Co. State Fencibles, Capt. Joseph Murray
      National Grays, Capt. Peter Fritz
      Hibernia Greens, Capt. F. Mullen
      Montgomery Hibernia Greens, Capt. J. B. Colahan

Lafayette Light Guards, Lt. J. M. Peirce
Union Fencibles, Capt. R. M. Lee
National Guards, Capt. Thomas Tustin
Mechanic Rifles, Capt. A. D. Mintzer
City Guards, Capt. Joseph Hill
Markle Rifles, Capt. T. L. Saunders

Second Brigade

Brigadier General Augustus Roumfort
    First State Troop, Capt. Thomas Betton. After May 11, 1844
    Capt. John Bavington
124th Regiment, Col. James Goodman
    Jackson Artillery, Capt. Jacob Hubeli
    Germantown Blues, Capt. John Miles
    National Blues, Capt. J. H. Perkins
    Mifflin Guards, Capt. Samuel Herkershimer
    Irish Volunteers, Capt. James Goodman
    Monroe Guards, Capt. William F. Small
    Marion Rifle, Capt. George Eberle
First Battalion German Volunteers, Major Frederick Dithmar
    Philadelphia Artillery, Capt. William Wicht
    Washington Light Infantry, Lt. A. Syberg
    German Washington National Guards, Capt. Jonathan Reiss
    German Washington Volunteers, Capt. Samuel Heintzelman
    Union Grays, Capt. Jonathan Streeper
    German Yeagers, Capt. Charles Ditmer
Volunteers attached to Militia Regiments
    Washington Cavalry, Capt. George Snyder
    Philadelphia Cadets, Capt. George White
    Washington Artillery, Capt. Henry Mallory
    Schuylkill Rangers, Capt. Jonathan Conny

Third Brigade

Brigadier General Horatio Hubbell
    Independent Rifles, Capt. Thomas Florence
    Wayne Artillery, Capt. Jonas P. Fairlamb

Sources: *Public Ledger,* June 6, 1844; *Daily Sun,* August 28, 1846; Gen. H. Hubbell testimony, *Public Ledger,* July 20, 1844; *North American,* July 25, 1844; List of General Staff, Regimental and Company Officers of the First Brigade, First Division, P.M., c. 1843–1844, box 1, Brigade Inspectors Returns, 1812–62, Pennsylvania State Archives; *Journal of the Select Council of the City of Philadelphia for 1841–1842* (Philadelphia: J. Crissy, 1842), 116. Companies are listed in the order in which they appear in the brigade inspectors' returns, with companies not shown on those returns added at the end.

A Note on Terminology

This is a book about intolerance, and it reproduces intolerant language. Mostly that consists of terms disparaging Catholics and Irishmen, but I have also quoted slurs against Protestants, Jews, African Americans, and soldiers. I hope my use of these words produces more historical understanding than discomfort.

The capitalized terms Native American and Native here refer to members or supporters of the various Native American associations and the American Republican Party, while the lowercased nativist refers to anyone who wished that native-born citizens would enjoy greater privileges than immigrants. Some Whigs and Democrats held such views, so while all Natives were nativists, not all nativists were Natives. And not all Natives were native, in that the movement attracted some foreign-born Protestants. On one occasion, Natives acknowledged that American Indians were the "genuine 'Natives'" and invited them to lead a Native procession, but most of the time they imagined most "Natives" to be American-born Protestants whose ancestors had emigrated from Europe—especially those whose families had come from Great Britain prior to the Revolution.[1]

The Americans of the 1840s were wildly inconsistent in their spelling and capitalization, and I could offer variant spellings of the names of many or most of the characters in this book, along with some for street names and other proper nouns, such as the name of the Philadelphia Grays, who were also the Philadelphia Greys. For readability, I have sought to be consistent in my spelling of these terms in the main text, while direct quotations and notes acknowledge more variation. Philadelphia street names have changed considerably since the 1840s. Following 1840s usage, "Independence Hall" refers to the room in which the Declaration of Independence was signed, in a building then known as the State House. The open space to the south of the building was called both the State House Yard and Independence Square.

"Attack by the Irish Catholics."
Courtesy of the Library Company of Philadelphia.

1

Hurrah for the Natives, and Kill the Damned Irish!

Monday, May 6, 1844

As Lewis Levin looked out over the rabble who had come to jeer at him, he did not see Americans. Yes, some of these Irishmen had attained papers—real or fraudulent—purporting to make them citizens of the republic, but Levin knew better. Five years' residence in the United States was hardly enough to make real Americans of men who had been raised since infancy to love kings and popes. Perhaps twenty-one years—the time it took for a native-born American boy to reach the age of majority—would be enough to effect the transformation. Or perhaps, Levin suspected, no length of time would do it. An Irishman would forever remain an Irishman, never truly knowing the love of liberty that men born in America instinctually possessed.[1]

Levin did not expect the Irishmen to agree, and he had not come to Kensington to win friends. He had come to teach these foreigners a lesson in manners. In his role as editor of Philadelphia's *Daily Sun*, Levin had spent the last half year working to convince his readers that Irish Catholic immigrants were a menace to American self-government, and that only the native-born were fit to hold office. In the pages of the *Sun*, he had published screed after screed, warning that Catholicism had left a track of "blood-prints; human victims; civil wars; tortures; burnings; fire; desolation," and that Irish immigrants wanted to bring papal power with them to American shores. In the evenings, he had repeated these messages in fiery lectures to eager listeners in churches and public halls. Thousands of native-born Philadelphians were now calling themselves Native Americans, or simply Natives. They had even formed a new political party—the American Republicans—to challenge the Whigs and the Democrats, the two established parties that they despised for pandering for Irish votes.[2]

To build their party, the American Republicans had held rallies throughout Philadelphia and its neighboring districts, meeting with success after success, the crowds growing ever larger. The rapidly growing district of Kensington, however, was a challenge. Though less than two miles north of Independence Hall, it lay outside the boundaries of the City of Philadelphia, and thus—crucially—outside the jurisdiction of its police. Kensington's Third Ward was especially rough, a place where the parks and townhouses of Philadelphia gave way to pigsties and cramped workers' dwellings. With the largest concentration of Irish Catholics in Philadelphia County, the Third Ward would be particularly hostile to the Natives' anti-Irish, anti-Catholic messages.

Only three days earlier, on Friday, May 3, some Third Ward Natives had tried to hold a rally in a vacant lot at the corner of Second and Master Streets, but the Catholics had heckled them and then charged, tearing down the improvised stage and chasing the nativists out of the ward. Once safely across the border in a Second Ward temperance hall, the Natives denounced the "vindictive, anti-republican spirit, manifested by a portion of the alien population of Third Ward Kensington" and resolved to try again after the weekend.[3]

Now on that Monday, May 6, the nativists were back in greater strength, around five hundred in all. From all parts of the county they had converged on Kensington, their eyes and ears filling with dust as they walked through the heat. With them came leaders of the cause, none more prominent than Levin. They knew they were not wanted, but that was the point. At stake, they claimed, was the right of a political minority to be heard rather than submitting "to the strong arm of numerical force."[4]

Levin and his allies had arrived a bit before four o'clock that cloudy afternoon, assembling at the same dirty, vacant lot from which the Natives had been chased on Friday. They gathered some lumber—probably from the same stage that had been dismantled—and erected a makeshift platform against the wall of the grammar school on the lot's western side, one of the few sturdy buildings in the ward. Cheering, they raised the American flag, its twenty-six stars representing the doubling of the Union since their forefathers threw off European tyranny.[5]

All this noise attracted attention, and, as they had on Friday, the Catholic Irishmen of Kensington gathered to gawk and to heckle. These were rough working men—weavers and spinners, carpenters and masons—who went outside in shirtsleeves, not the frock coats and top hats of Levin and his friends.[6]

Ignoring the Irishmen, or at least pretending to, the Natives settled down to the business of their meeting. They had a prepared a series of resolutions—the usual warnings about the need to protect the ballot box from "hordes of ignorant and degraded foreigners"—plus a few new lines about how "common courtesy, if no higher motive," should have deterred Irishmen from breaking up Friday's meeting. But before the resolutions would come the speeches, given by the Natives' most respectable representatives.

The first up was Samuel Kramer, editor of the *Native American*, the daily newspaper he had launched just three weeks earlier. "We object not to [immigrants'] seeking in this land the bread that is denied them at home," he had claimed in his inaugural editorial. "But we do object that they should in the course of so short time be entitled to that which is denied to the children of the soil for a period of twenty-one years—the right of suffrage." On May 3, Kramer had been ranting that immigrants hoped to "sell the country to a foreign power" when the crowd rushed the stage and chased him away. This time, Kramer was able to finish.[7]

Kramer was followed by Peter Sken Smith, who had abandoned a string of failed banks and a flagging political career in Florida to make a new start in Philadelphia. Smith gave a tedious speech about rescuing the ballot box from fraud and restoring purity to the electoral franchise, but he too finished without interruption. The third speaker, John Perry, was not so lucky. By the time he began, the nativists had been at it for an hour, and the Kensington Irish had readied a response. A carter, John O'Neill, pulled up in a wagon, driving his horse from Second Street onto the vacant lot, right into the crowd. O'Neill got within six yards of the stage, then pulled the pin to dump his load of yellow dirt. Nearby Catholics laughed and applauded. Natives were outraged. One grabbed O'Neill's horse and demanded to know if O'Neill was deliberately disrupting the meeting. O'Neill, possibly drunk, replied that he would return "as often as he damned pleased." Still other carters arrived, each with a small load of dirt to dump. Yet even then, with belligerent Irishmen dumping dirt on the boots of the native-born, everyone kept their hands to themselves.[8]

Finally it was time for Levin to speak. Unlike Kramer's *Native American*, his *Daily Sun* was officially nonpartisan. But over the previous three months Levin's furious editorials had made him the best-known nativist in Philadelphia. Here in the Third Ward, surrounded by the targets of his rage, he was on his guard. Just five days before, Levin had been walking in the city with his wife and children when he encountered several men teasing a Black man for being unable to vote despite his native birth. Levin interpreted the remark as an insult to all Natives, and he started beating one of the men, John Manderfield, a constable "quite advanced in years." Before bystanders pulled him off, Levin had given Manderfield a black eye and a cut lip, along with lesser scrapes. And that was just with his fists; had he had a knife, Levin later swore, "he would have cut the hog's throat." With hands still bruised from punching the old man, in Kensington Levin was now again ready for a fight. As he waited to speak and watched O'Neill drive his horse into the crowd, he leaned over to warn a friend, "This is evidently the signal for attack."[9]

The attack came, but from an unexpected direction: above. As Levin rose to speak, a sudden storm whipped through Philadelphia, with wind strong enough to tear awnings off buildings and limbs from trees. A drenching rain came with it, clearing the lot more effectively than any nativist rhetoric or Irishmen's carts of dirt.[10]

A more superstitious group might have taken this storm as an omen that it was time to go home, and a few nativists did wander off. John Carroll's tavern lay just south of the vacant lot, and at least one of Levin's intended listeners headed there for a dry seat and a wet drink. But most of the Natives ran for the shelter of the Washington Market, only about seventy yards away, shouting and hooting and laughing as they went. A few rolled a hogshead toward the market so that Levin would have a place to stand.[11]

This simple decision to seek shelter rather than go home changed everything. Up to that point, the Natives had been heckled and harassed, but not seriously threatened. A few cartloads of dirt was an insult, not an actual attack, and the Third Ward Irish seemed ready to let the Natives proceed with their rally on the vacant lot, shouting to the wind. The Irish had not physically harmed anyone; to the contrary, they had helped a nativist off the stage on Friday so that he would not be injured when they tore it down. All of this suggests that both sides had been working of a rough script that dictated how to disagree publicly in an election season. Now, however, by changing the scene from the vacant lot to the market house, the Natives were deviating from that script.

The covered market was the pride of the Third Ward. Opened just three years earlier, its publicly owned arcade sheltered a block of Washington Street, running about 250 feet from Master Street on the south to Jefferson Street on the north. Under its protection, farmers and victualers leased stalls to feed the families of the surrounding neighborhoods. It had also become a political center. The previous year, in January 1843, striking weavers seized the arcade, then brutally and successfully defended it against the sheriff and his posse, who had marched from Philadelphia proper.[12]

Now, fifteen months later, neighborhood men—probably including some veterans of the previous year's fight—faced a second invasion from the city. As the Natives arrived, one market worker rolled up his sleeves and grumbled to his mates, "Keep the damned natives out of the market house. This ground don't belong to them—this is ours." His listeners rolled up their sleeves as well. They were joined by hecklers from the vacant lot who had made it to shelter before the Natives did.[13]

When the soggy, high-spirited Natives arrived, they did nothing to placate the Kensington men. Still shouting and hooting, they tore into the market, climbed onto the stalls, jumped from one to another, then planted their American flag in the middle of the market. Levin, standing on a stall or perhaps the hogshead, tried to resume his speech. He managed only eight words—"Fellow citizens, we have reached an important crisis!"—before the trouble began.[14]

As Levin began to speak, Kensington residents faced off, Protestant against Catholic. Some of the men had been present for the meeting on Friday, and now they resumed their argument about whether the Natives should be allowed to speak in peace. "Now let's make a noise, so that he won't be heard," one man suggested, and he and a companion did just that. David Fields, a Protestant immigrant from Ireland, was not on bad terms with the Catholics he saw in the market, but he feared that they would repeat their attack of Friday. "For God's sake," he begged. "Let us be quiet and listen to the speaker." "You old rascal," John McIldoon replied, "You're always talking." One witness, who watched from the third-story window of the public school, at first saw only two men—possibly Fields and McIldoon—fighting, though another eighteen or twenty watched and egged them on. Another thought that groups of about eight or ten Catholic and Protestant Irishmen each started fighting before most of the nativists from the rally had even arrived.[15]

The fight escalated from fists to sticks, and then from sticks to stones, easy enough to find in the perpetual construction site that was Kensington. More brawlers, including the Native refugees from the storm, joined in. Men outside the building hurled bricks at the nativists, who picked them up and hurled them right back. Soon the market house was filled with Natives and their adversaries slugging it out, while others spilled into the surrounding streets, some of them throwing stones at the houses on Cadwalader Street to the west. Five Kensington Irishmen surrounded a young man from the city, snarling at him. The youth pulled out two pistols and threatened to shoot anyone who attacked him. A Kensington man dared him to shoot.[16]

Overlooking the western side of the market was the Hibernia Hose House, home to the newest, and perhaps roughest, volunteer fire company in Philadelphia County. Its members had been feuding with the nearby Carroll Hose, one of countless, pointless grudges among the county's engine and hose companies, and some authorities even suspected the Hibernia men of setting fire to the workshop of a Carroll member. That day, however, the Hibernia men had not planned a fight; rather, they had gathered to complete their elegant house by installing a new bell. But when the storm came up and the nativists rushed into the market house, the firemen noticed the commotion, just about fifty yards away across a half-vacant strip of land.[17]

One of the firemen, Patrick Fisher, decided to act. An Irish Catholic immigrant, he lived on the same block as the hose house and likely knew many of the men in the market. For a time he had served as constable of the ward, until a charge of wrongdoing in office forced his resignation. Now, though no longer a professional lawman, he thought he could bring peace, so he rushed across the vacant strip to the market. He seemed a bit unsteady as he went—perhaps he had swallowed some courage while toasting the new firehouse bell. But he managed to climb onto a market stall, where he started shouting for people to go home. Then everyone heard a gunshot, and Fisher collapsed on the stall, his face bloody.[18]

Joseph Wood, a reporter, saw the flash, and he understood at once that yet more unspoken rules had been violated. A brawl was one thing, a gunfight another. "My God," Wood cried, "they've got firearms!" As in many riots before and since, the first gunshot destroyed whatever restraint had previously held the crowd. "Hurrah for the Natives," shouted Fisher's assailant, "and kill the damned Irish." "Come," another cried. "Let's get some guns and give the rascals their due!"[19]

◆

Ex-Constable Fisher would survive, but the peace of Philadelphia would not. Instead, the marketplace brawl sparked the first great city riot in the history of the United States. Before the violence was over, dozens would die, hundreds would be left homeless, and two Catholic churches would burn and a third would be ransacked. Troops would seize the city, at first ineffectually, but eventually with deadly force, firing cannon down city streets on a dark July night.

American cities had seen fighting before, but not at this scale. Previous riots had been brief affairs, lasting just hours, or a day or two at most. Usually rioters and authorities fought with fists and clubs, not firearms, and certainly not with artillery. While Americans were shocked by the rising urban violence of the 1830s, nothing prepared them for the devastation of Philadelphia's 1844 riots. When, after two months of bloodshed, the city finally calmed, Philadelphians were left staring at one another with resentment and mistrust.

"I have long had an idea," noted diarist Sidney George Fisher late in May 1844, "that the present civilization of the world, Europe & America, is destined to be destroyed by the irruption of the dark masses of ignorance & brutality which lie beneath it, like the fires of a volcano, beneath the cultivated fields which they fertilize to destroy." Fisher was not the first or last to compare a riot to a volcanic eruption, for good reason. However unexpected, riots result from longstanding hatreds and frustrations. An eruption makes suddenly visible the rage that has been hidden. Even when the violence calms, that rage still flows hot and dangerous underground.[20]

The eruption of 1844 altered the landscape of both Philadelphia and the United States, but it may be even more important for the underground currents it revealed. Levin and the Native Americans championed a vision of American citizenship limited to white, male, native-born, Protestant men. In the tumultuous 1840s, believers in this vision faced challenges from abolitionists, American Indians, early feminists, Mormons, and, not least, from Irish Catholic immigrants, who, even in these years before the Great Hunger, were already crossing the Atlantic by the tens of thousands. As these immigrants sought homes, jobs, votes, and the right to practice their faith, they presented an alternative vision of America, defined not by birthright but by a willingness to embrace shared values of freedom and democracy.

To keep America in the hands of those they believed worthy, Levin and his allies hoped to restrict the new arrivals to worshipping in private and waiting twenty-one years for citizenship.[21] They took this campaign to the streets, where men orated, paraded, voted, and brawled. The Natives did all of these: holding mass rallies in the shadow of the State House, marching in patriotic celebration, swaggering into immigrant neighborhoods, carrying honored martyrs to their graves. With few professional police to stop them, such masses of men constituted both a physical and symbolic force, collectively asserting that the city belonged to them.

Only one other force could equal this power: the citizen-soldiers of the volunteer militia. At first, the militia was slow to act, both from a horror of shedding their fellow Americans' blood and from a sympathy with the Native cause among both commanders and the rank and file. Seeing the Philadelphia establishment's tolerance of a movement hostile to their faith, Irish Catholic immigrants had to ask if the United States was still the land of freedom and opportunity they had believed it to be.

Eventually the answer came when the militia took a stand against the mob. These Americans proved themselves ready to fight, to kill, and to die in defense of the rights of a minority. In doing so, they affirmed that America could embrace the immigrant as well as the native-born. The nativist cause did not disappear, and its cramped view of American identity persists even to our day. But for the moment, American democracy passed a crucial test. It would endure.

Lewis C. Levin.
Courtesy of the Frick Art Reference Library.

2

Brilliant and Unscrupulous

ewis Charles Levin had taken a long and twisted path to that Kensington market house. Only thirty-five in May 1844, he had lived in several states, pursued multiple professions, married twice, fallen into drunkenness and bankruptcy, emerged back into prominence, and changed his religion. His gifts as a speaker and writer were undeniable. His morality was less certain.

Levin was born on November 10, 1808, in Charleston, South Carolina. His father, also named Lewis, had emigrated from England and joined the city's seven hundred Jews, the largest such community in the United States. Despite his death in 1817, the family apparently had enough resources to send the young Lewis to attend South Carolina College in Columbia, where he joined the Euphradian Society, devoted to developing eloquence in its members. Starting in early 1826, he operated a dry-goods store in Columbia, selling everything from unbleached homespun to fancy lace goods imported from Liverpool. Levin seems to have left the college in 1827, after his sophomore year. By 1829, Lewis and his mother could be found sharing lodgings in Cincinnati, where Lewis found a new occupation: schoolmaster.[1]

Levin's "Cincinnati School for Practical, Scientific, and Classical Education" opened that May, promising to embrace "all the branches of learning usually taught in the most approved seminaries," but also to provide a "government of the school [that] is mild, consisting solely of moral influence." Though he claimed that the school was rapidly filling, it lasted no more than a year. By May 1830, Levin had abandoned it, making his way to Woodville, in southwestern Mississippi, where he started a new academy for both male and female students. In the confident, aggressive tone that would characterize all his writings, Levin denounced "the method pursued in most academies," which emphasized rote learning and the need to pass college entrance exams, calling it "as injurious to a boy's habits, as it is to his taste." Instead, Levin promised "to render study interesting to the pupil" and to encourage each student to "form his own conclusions, on whatever he may read, study, or observe, without being whipt into the face of any man's isolated conceptions." By June 1830, just a month after starting his school, Levin claimed to have enrolled fifty-five pupils and recruited a board of visitors that included several prominent men of the community.[2]

Alfred Bynum, who had graduated from South Carolina College, joined Levin in the spring of 1831. A few months later, Levin gave the July 4 oration at another academy. As Henry Foote, later a US senator from Mississippi, heard the story, Bynum claimed to have written the speech himself. And in Mississippi in 1831, a dispute over authorship was reason enough for two young men to find weapons and head to a convenient field for a duel. "Southern blood, owing we suppose to the temperature of our climate," a local newspaper had recently surmised, "is too volatile and inflammable to be confined to the same channels that it may in a Scotchman or even a New Englander." Though he lost some of his volatile Southern blood to Bynum's rifle, Levin recovered.[3]

One observer later remembered Levin as "a stout and well-built man, with a sonorous voice and a commanding and flowing diction." Foote thought him "a man of exceedingly handsome person." Most striking of all were his "bright eyes [which] positively almost seemed when he chanced to be a little excited, to be ready to fall from their sockets." Foote knew enough phrenology—that art of judging a man by the shape of his head—to know that those prominent eyes meant one thing: Levin's "organ of language," located in the front of his brain, was so large that his eyes no longer quite fit in his head. A man with eyes like that would be a talker. Congressman Alexander Stephens would later say that while Webster, Clay, and Calhoun all gave masterly speeches, "for genuine eloquence, for the spontaneous outburst of what may be called the native oratory," Levin had no peer. Foote thought that Levin rivaled William Charles Macready, Edwin Booth, and Edwin Forrest—the great tragedians of the day. But magnificent delivery could not always compensate for a lack of reasoning, and Foote judged that Levin "spoke in public with great fluency, but without much display of argumentative power." A later acquaintance agreed that Levin "presented a fine appearance, graceful in every action, charming in rhetoric and utterly reckless in assertion," calling him "one of the most brilliant and unscrupulous orators I have ever heard."[4]

Levin found his way to Vicksburg, where "his very impulsive nature got him into several serious personal quarrels," from which Foote extracted him. According to one report, Levin not only persuaded an African American barber to shave him on credit, but borrowed heavily from the barber, never repaying the hard-earned cash. Eventually, Levin moved on, no doubt to Foote's relief. He may have spent time in Louisiana and Kentucky before washing up in Nashville. There, he won the heart of the beautiful—and Christian—Ann Hays, daughter of a Nashville lawyer. At a time when American Jews were few and often scattered, intermarriage was fairly common. Still, the Charleston congregation in which Levin was raised expelled members who "married contrary to the Mosaical Law," and denied them burial in its cemetery unless they reformed. Thus Levin's marriage weakened or even ended his identification with the Jewish community. In any case, the pair was married on January 2, 1833, by the Reverend George Weller, most likely in Weller's new Christ Church, an imposing Gothic Revival structure consecrated just eighteen months earlier. Levin, it seemed, had married into Nashville society, and his future was bright. But barely a year after his marriage, Ann was dead.[5]

If we are to believe Foote, Levin decided to travel all the way to Baltimore to find a suitable tombstone for his late bride. While he pondered the selections, another customer came in: a lovely young widow, there to order a stone for her late husband. This was Julia Ann McCubbin Gist. In July 1832, at the age of twenty-two or so, she had married Thomas Hammond Gist, a man some twenty years her senior and a member of a prominent Maryland family. But Thomas died just eleven weeks later, the day after his forty-third birthday. He had lived long enough for Julia to conceive a daughter, Thomasina Hammond Gist, born on April 28, 1833.[6]

Besides his daughter and his name, Thomas left behind a significant estate, consisting of both slaves and real estate scattered around Baltimore. Administering this complex assemblage while caring for an infant girl cannot have been easy, and perhaps the idea of remarriage, as well as Levin himself, appealed to the young widow. In any case, on December 3, 1834—eleven months after Ann's death, and twenty-five months after Thomas's—Levin married Julia in Baltimore County. He was still new enough to town to be described in the newspaper as "L. C. Levin, Esq. of Tennessee."[7]

The "Esq." was not new; at some point before Ann's death, Levin learned enough law to style himself "esquire," and he may have practiced in Louisiana and Kentucky. Certainly in Baltimore he practiced law, but he also continued to make trouble. In 1834, he was indicted in Philadelphia for assault and battery with intent to murder Aaron Clement of the Indian Queen Hotel. Though he avoided prison, he was found guilty of one count and fined $75 and court costs. Two years later, Levin battled fellow Baltimore lawyer Henry Stump, slashing him in the head and ribs with a bowie knife. His enemies would later charge that Levin "is said to have been a resident of four or five different States, in the criminal records of every one of which his name may be found coupled with some heinous offence against the laws." Levin himself later described his Baltimore years as "a world of storm, and tempest, and excitement." "During my habits of dissipation," he explained, "I indulged in broils, fights, and at times was reckless to a degree." Yet perhaps his hot temper appealed to Julia; years later, she would herself face charges for cowhiding a young gentleman while her footman restrained him.[8]

Despite the occasional knife fight with other members of the bar, Levin found he liked Baltimore's courts enough to stay there, becoming an effective defense lawyer, representing clients with "brilliancy and power." By 1837, Levin was listed as an attorney at law with an office on Baltimore's Hanover Street. That same year, he and Julia received $5,500, a significant amount of capital, against Julia's dower interest in Thomas Gist's real estate. Whether the amount reflected a mortgage or an outright sale with the right of repurchase became a matter of some dispute in later years. John Iglehart—the lender or the buyer, depending on who you believed—later claimed that the Levins used the money to discharge Lewis's old debts.[9]

In January 1840, the Levins had a daughter, Louisa. Around that time, for reasons yet unexplained, the growing family moved to Philadelphia, a city not unlike Baltimore in its general appearance. Along the Delaware River waterfront, source of the city's original wealth, steamboats, ferries, and oceangoing sailing ships took on passengers and cargo or supplies from the shipwrights, chandlers, sailmakers, and other maritime concerns. A bit inland sat the city's major banks as well as the Exchange, from whose cupola clerks could peer through a telescope to spot arriving vessels and figure out what cargoes needed trading downstairs. Surrounding these great structures were humbler buildings with sloping brown roofs. Most rose to four or five stories, forming, depending on one's taste, a scene of harmony or "mediocrity personified in brick and mortar." Within, noted a journalist, were "silk button manufactories, taverns, fancy toy shops, auction stores, China-shops, fishing-tackle establishments, clothing stores, jewelry, stoves, drugs, boots and shoes, and every conceivable variety of shops," which were "interspersed here and there with islands of rich green foliage that refresh the soul."[10]

Once settled, Levin apparently tried to continue his career as a lawyer but without success. An acquaintance later accused him of borrowing a gold watch, claiming he needed to keep time while arguing a case in front of an alderman, then immediately pawning the watch and pocketing the money.

Whatever law Levin practiced in those early years in Philadelphia, he did so unobtrusively enough to escape notice by the newspapers. Perhaps he could not find legal work; he later warned young men that "there are near 400 lawyers, old and young, hanging about the courts of Philadelphia, and actually not business enough for more than one-fourth the number." Rather than scrounge for cases, Levin reinvented himself again as a man of public affairs.[11]

Had Levin remained in his native south, he might have ended up a fire-eating defender of slavery, interspersing his verbal attacks with occasional brawls. Levin was violent and impetuous enough, and while still in Nashville, he had won attention with a passionate defense of South Carolina's doctrine of nullification. But north of the Mason-Dixon Line, Levin needed a different cause. He found it in temperance.[12]

Americans had been drinking since the dawn of European settlement, but only after the Revolution did they begin to perceive liquor as a major social problem. Partly this was because Americans, especially men, were drinking more, as inland farmers flooded the seacoast with cheap whiskey. Moreover, in the growing cities drunkenness disrupted work and social life more than it did on the farm. By the 1830s, Philadelphia County was home to thousands of "tippling houses, oyster cellars, and gambling houses." Here, young men of the town could play games, sing songs, and generally enjoy the company of fellow workers. Civic functions, like Fourth of July parades and elections, were equally wet. In addition to such cultural factors, poverty was both a cause and effect of alcoholism. Some lost employment when they turned to drink, while others turned to drink when their businesses failed. When they drank to excess, some were taken to hospitals for treatment of delirium tremens, the withdrawal pains and madness suffered by a heavy drinker when he could no longer stomach alcohol or ran out of the cash to pay for it. More were hauled before the mayor, who might dole out fines to as many as half a dozen men in a single morning.[13]

Like so many of his generation, Levin succumbed. Foote recalled being invited to Levin's hotel room once to find "wine and hot whisky-punch flowing there in abundance." Levin's enemies later painted a vivid, if possibly libelous, portrait of Levin's early years in Philadelphia. "Bloated with drink" and dressed in rags, with "swollen cheeks and sunken eyes," they imagined him being carried home in a handcart, howling after enemies with a knife, playing at cards and dice, and letting loose speech "of that blasphemous and revolting kind which makes the soul sicken at the sometime picture of humanity." Levin himself later described his days as a drunkard, if in less vivid terms. In 1841, he later admitted, he could have been found "in an obscure tavern . . . enslaved and fettered, bound hand and foot by the power of Alcohol." He eventually lost his fortune to "dissipation and prodigality." Some of this account may have been exaggerated; the more degraded Levin's account of his days as a drinking man, the more impressive would his later conversion appear. That said, Levin did have a record of violence, and in March 1841, the newspapers announced his application for state bankruptcy protection, listing his address as the Moyamensing Prison.[14]

But there was hope. Starting in the mid-1820s, clergymen, public officials, and other reformers began arguing that alcohol was more of a curse than a blessing. In 1840, they were joined by the Washingtonian movement, founded by Baltimore workingmen, which emphasized sobriety as the key to self-improvement. While this "temperance" movement at first tolerated moderate consumption of beer, wine, and cider, by the mid-1830s, reformers increasingly argued for total abstinence from both fermented and distilled liquors as the only true form of temperance, especially for drunkards like Levin. They called on Americans to pledge "to drink no ardent spirits, except as a medicine; and also to use their influence totally to abolish the drinking of ardent spirits." By March 1841, reformers claimed that around seventeen thousand residents of Philadelphia County had taken the pledge, one quarter of them in the previous ninety days. One was Lewis Levin. As he would later explain, that spring he "cast off the damning yoke, *and with his pledge against future bondage*, HE STANDS A FREEMAN IN THE LIGHT OF HEAVEN!"[15]

Levin's rescuer was probably the Reverend John Chambers, who later became his frequent companion on the lecture-hall circuit, and perhaps a friend as well. Born in Ireland in 1797, Chambers had come to America as an infant. His father, a follower of the Irish nationalist Wolfe Tone, was a wanted man who hid under a load of cabbages until the ship was safely out of port. Though raised a Presbyterian, Chambers was denied ordination when he rejected the Westminster Confession of Faith, instead regarding the Bible as the only infallible guide. Rather than compromise his beliefs, Chambers sought ordination as a Congregational minister, and under his leadership what had been the Ninth Presbyterian Church of Philadelphia became the First Independent Church. In withdrawing from the Presbyterian Church in the United States in this way, Chambers was following the lead and the advice of the Reverend John Mason Duncan of Baltimore, who later would marry Levin and Julia Gist. Perhaps Duncan provided Levin with a letter of introduction to Chambers, or simply served as a common reference point. Alternatively, in his search for souls, Chambers may have stumbled across a drunken Levin slumped across a table in the corner of a foul tavern.[16]

Chambers steered his flock away from cards, dancing, and theater, and he was so firm a temperance man that once when summoned to a funeral, he stood outside in the rain and demanded that the corpse be brought to him rather than enter a house where liquor was being served. That same determination led him to vilify hotel keepers and anyone else whom he saw as an obstacle to reform. The *Daily Chronicle*, while expressing sympathy with the temperance movement, included Chambers "among the wildest, most bitter, and bigoted of [the] rabid lecturers" who believed the purity of the cause justified "malice, falsehood, and wrong."[17]

By the time he encountered Chambers, Levin had already married two Christian women in ceremonies performed by Christian clergy, and it is likely that at some point he formally adopted the Protestant Christian faith, quite possibly under Chambers's guidance. Some evidence for a formal conversion is Levin's later swearing an oath "on the Holy Evangely of Almighty God," presumably meaning the New Testament. Regardless of Levin's exact religious status, his writings suggest a general appreciation for Protestantism, as when he wrote that in its capacity to prevent evil, "the temperance cause is next to the Christian religion; and . . . one of its legitimate fruits." Temperance, he boasted, "has brought ministers and laymen of all sects together, and bound them in a holy brotherhood; it has taught the world that the great business of Christ, of christians and of churches on earth is to do good." When a group named the Levin Washington Society excluded clergymen from membership, Levin asked them to change the rule, or to change their name. In 1843, he would write that to achieve reform, men "must possess a portion of that holy spirit which prompted the Son of God." He would "regard the Saviour as the leader of the Native American party," write fierce defenses of Protestant practices, and advocate for "Christian Republican Government."[18]

Not all were convinced by the temperance cause or its converts. One Fourth of July, Colonel Augustus Pleasonton snickered that "the Temperance people" would "drink iced lemonade till they all shall have the stomach ache," while he toasted Independence with good wine. Critics were especially inclined to mock "men who acknowledge themselves intimate with every species of profligacy and corruption" yet "deliver Popular Lectures on the highways upon the subjects of morals and politics." But those more sympathetic to the cause saw such men not as a hypocrites but rather as converts who from personal experience could proclaim the value of giving up drink. Levin embraced this role, occasionally styling himself "L. C. Levin, Esq., of the Jefferson Society," which was composed of "reformed drinkers."[19]

In July 1841, Levin combined his skill as a writer and speaker with his newfound rejection of alcohol by embarking on a fourth career as an editor and activist. His initial platform was the *Temperance Advocate and Literary Repository*, a biweekly temperance newspaper published in Philadelphia. According to Levin's critics, "those who converted him from Judaism to Christianity and from constant bestial inebriation to sobriety placed a newspaper press under his control." Mostly, the *Advocate* published repetitive stories—reprinted from other periodicals—of good men ruined by drink. In a typical tale, two young men celebrate the acceptance of their marriage proposals to beautiful and wealthy girls. Intoxicated, one fatally stabs the other, and, though acquitted of murder by reason of insanity, flees the country, leaving both ladies to die young. Less commonly, subscribers could read of drunkards who, having pledged abstinence, had become clean, healthy, prosperous citizens, ready to lend a hand to the next drunkard ready to reform.[20]

In a movement divided between those who believed that moderate use of alcohol was acceptable and those who insisted on total abstinence, Levin sided with the latter, counseling absolute avoidance of alcohol as a drink, except for medical purposes. Moderate drinking, he warned was the first step to disaster. Sacramental communion ought to use grape juice. Even root beer was suspect. Levin once found himself outdone when, while staying at a temperance hotel, he was denied a warm lemonade with which to nurse a cold, apparently on the principle that any beverage other than cold water was the first step toward the tavern.[21]

Levin spread the word with his voice as well as his pen. In Philadelphia as elsewhere, lecturing was a popular form of public entertainment, which reformers viewed as a more wholesome alternative to the theater. "Lectures on Shakespeare, are infinitely better than Shakespeare on the stage," Levin assured his readers. And unlike taverns, they were suitable for ladies, thus adding to their wholesomeness. Discriminating Philadelphians could hear some of the day's greatest thinkers: physicist Dionysius Lardner, geologist Charles Lyell, historian Jared Sparks, or writer Edgar Allan Poe. Levin could not claim such stature, but he lectured frequently, often in the company of clergy, sometimes as often as twice in three nights. An admirer called him "one of nature's true orators, and whose experience in drunkenness is of a truly thrilling character." In January 1842, Levin gained further notice, winning election as president of a state temperance convention in Harrisburg. There he called for the state legislature to empower wards, boroughs, and townships to deny liquor licenses. Pass the law, he told his listeners, and the "monster" of alcohol would be cast "into that lasting perdition which his malignity has prescribed for man."[22]

Despite this attention, and for all his warnings about the ruin awaiting drunkards, Levin found the life of a temperance editor hardly more financially secure. In August 1841, he had boasted of over a thousand subscribers. At the annual subscription price of $1—designed to be "within the means of the many"—he should have been grossing $1,000 per year. In reality, while it was easy to start a newspaper, it was hard to turn a profit. "The country is flooded with periodicals," one Philadelphian griped, "the one containing in great measure the ditto of the other." Such competition, Alexis de Tocqueville had observed, "discourages people with great business acumen from embarking on this kind of venture."[23]

Levin's lack of such acumen caught up with him on Friday, January 28, 1842. That evening he addressed a "Great Temperance Meeting" at the Methodist Church in Camden, New Jersey, just across the river from

Philadelphia. He spoke freely of his past bankruptcy, but "he had now, he believed, thoroughly redeemed his reputation from reproach, and, by the blessings of Heaven, would soon be able to discharge every obligation under which he rested." To the contrary, a sheriff's officer stepped up and arrested him on a civil charge for debt.[24]

Fortunately for Levin, Congress had recently enacted a federal bankruptcy law that proved wildly favorable to debtors, who rushed to file. One European observer watched insolvent men "sworn to their schedules by platoons of some ten, or twelve at a time, or as many as can conveniently place their hand upon the Sacred Volume at the same moment." On April 6, 1842, Levin joined the crowd. He listed debts of at least $6,728, a fortune for most Philadelphians. Against these debts, Levin claimed just the furnishings of his rented house (including a tea set held in trust for his daughter, Louisa), some books, the clothes worn by himself and his wife, and the subscription list of the *Temperance Advocate*. The bankruptcy assignee eventually judged Levin's property worth only $70, and even those few items he found necessary for Levin and his family. As was common, Levin's creditors would get nothing. After a summer of following all the routines of advertising the impending bankruptcy and notifying the luckless creditors, Levin's debts were discharged.[25]

Levin remained a prominent spokesman for the temperance cause. In April, even as he begged readers for funds, he had the honor to speak to a temperance procession, likely numbering thousands, in Independence Square. On July 4 in Westchester, New York, he gave the oration to four thousand people, though the heat forced him to abbreviate his remarks. "His eloquence," claimed a temperance reporter "is enough to melt the stoutest heart and convince the most stubborn hearer. . . . His sarcasm, when brought into play, is of the most withering and blasting description." In October, the *Public Ledger* praised his address to a temperance meeting of firemen, calling it "one of those beautiful, highly wrought and philosophical efforts for which he is so remarkable."

In January 1843, Levin embarked on a two month "Southern Tour" to Baltimore and Washington. In Baltimore he spoke for an hour and, claimed the *Baltimore Patriot*, "enchained his audience with tones of eloquence, bursts of passion and touches of tenderness, which pierced every heart."

Much like a preacher calling for souls, Levin called drunkards to come forward for all to witness their conversion. "The scene here beggars description," wrote one observer. "The first who advanced was a poor tattered drunkard—he approached the table a slave—he retired a freeman. Others followed, among them was the friend of my early youth; and as I beheld him sign the pledge, which act lightened up many a face with joy, I uttered a prayer mingled with my tears." Levin made special efforts to redeem Baltimore's firemen in the hopes of transforming them from drunken rowdies into guardians of property. The grateful fire insurance companies of the city—which presumably would pay fewer claims if the firemen were sober enough to extinguish blazes—later bought Levin a silver pitcher as a token of their thanks. In August 1843, he spoke outdoors in Chester County, Pennsylvania. "It is astonishing how the people rushed toward the stand when he commenced to speak," wrote an awed listener. "Never was he so eloquent as when, under the shade of the forest, he engaged the attention of the spell-bound listeners; and when he gave his experience every eye moved and every heart sympathized with the speaker."[26]

Levin's true financial salvation came not from newspaper subscriptions or ticket sales, but from Samuel Atkinson, publisher of the *Saturday Evening Post*. In February 1843, Atkinson, a teetotaler, purchased the *Temperance Advocate* but retained Levin as editor, and left him at least some financial interest in the newspaper. Then, in August 1843, Atkinson purchased another newspaper, the *Daily Sun*, and installed Levin as editor of that paper as well. This choice would change Levin's life, and Philadelphia's history.[27]

George Cadwalader.
Courtesy of the Library of Congress.

3

The Best Amateur Officer in the United States

While Levin was gulping whiskey in a dark tavern, George Cadwalader was sipping port in one of the finest parlors in Philadelphia. At a time when a fortune of $10,000 was enough to afford servants and a fine home, and when perhaps 4 percent of Philadelphians commanded half or two-thirds of the wealth in the city, Cadwalader was very, very rich, with an estimated worth of $150,000. Philadelphians of Cadwalader's generation could get that rich in one of three ways. They could inherit money from their fathers, marry a wealthy widow or an heiress, or earn their money through manufacturing, trade, or finance and real estate. Cadwalader did all three. By his midthirties he had become a gentleman of breeding, polish, wealth, and fame. Yet refined as he was, he was also ready to kill.[1]

George Cadwalader was born on May 16, 1806, into a family whose history paralleled that of Philadelphia itself. In the 1690s, his great-great-grandfather had been among the Welsh Quakers recruited by William Penn to help populate the new colony of Pennsylvania. His great-grandfather, Dr. Thomas Cadwalader, was a pioneering physician and a friend of Benjamin Franklin, and a member of both the Common Council of Philadelphia and the Provincial Council. Thomas's son John abandoned the family's Quaker pacifism to command a brigade of Pennsylvania militia in support of George Washington's New Jersey campaign. And in 1814, John's son Thomas, George's father, was chosen to command a force of thousands of militiamen who—in the wake of British attacks on Washington and Baltimore—had assembled to repel a possible attack on Philadelphia. That attack never came, but Thomas had sufficiently proven his worth as a brigadier general to retain the post, and he later ascended to divisional command. George Cadwalader thus grew up as both the son and grandson of generals.[2]

George followed his father and grandfather to the University of Pennsylvania, graduating in 1823, and, like his father, studying law. He then joined his father in service to a particularly rich client: the Penn family, whose ancestors had founded Pennsylvania and who still owned land in Philadelphia and around the state. Overseeing their American holdings kept Thomas busy and flush, and in George he found a hardworking, trustworthy aide with whom to share both the work and its rewards. They collected rents, traded mortgages, and paid taxes on a broad portfolio of properties in a partnership George later described as "uninterrupted harmony."[3]

"Though there is no titled nobility or hereditary aristocracy," noted an English visitor to Philadelphia, "there is a decided aristocracy of family connexion as well as of wealth; and of the two, the first are the most fastidious about the rank and station of their associates." George Cadwalader belonged fully to this untitled aristocracy, both by connection and wealth. In his spare time, he might organize a dancing party or entertain visiting French nobility. He himself was related to a British peer; his aunt—Thomas's sister—had married the British minister to the United States, who in 1823 became the second Baron Erskine. As if a name and fortune weren't enough, George was quite handsome. "His person is tall and soldierly," an admirer later wrote. "He has dark hair and eyes; a bold aquiline nose, and a mouth indicative of great resolution. The expression of his countenance is martial, yet highly pleasing." By his midthirties he had framed his features with full, silky whiskers at a time when such growths were considered fine ornaments, especially for a military man. "With large and naturally glossy black whiskers we always associate honesty of mind and firmness of purpose," facetiously observed one student of "whiskerology." If he was right, George was one of the most honest, firm men of his age. To the end of his life, he would keep those honest whiskers as well as long, often wild hair, parted to sweep over his forehead, offering a hint of animal passion however careful his dress.[4]

With his wealth, name, and looks, George could have enjoyed an extended bachelorhood. Instead, in late 1829, at the age of twenty-three, Cadwalader became engaged to Frances Butler Mease, known as Fanny. Her father, James Mease, was a polymath who had edited a multivolume encyclopedia and authored *The Picture of Philadelphia*, which covered everything from the city's system of inspecting shad and herring to the "spirit of toleration" of religious differences. Fanny's maternal grandfather, Pierce Butler, had been born in Ireland, the third son of a baronet. After marrying a South Carolina heiress, he became an American patriot and a South Carolina politician, serving that state as a delegate to the Constitutional Convention and then as a US senator.[5]

The betrothal surprised George's friends. One intimate recalled a recent ride at which both Fanny and another young lady had been mentioned, and George had "betrayed more emotion" in speaking of Fanny's rival. "Your sangfroid is really admirable," he teased. But that sangfroid might have indicated a real lack of passion. In later years, when she traveled without George, Fanny would write tender letters about missing his whistle and his black eyes, and begging him to write her more frequently. For his part, George would earn some notoriety with the elaborate provisions he made for a mistress. But for a gentleman of the era, marriage could be less about love and sex than about connections and capital, and Fanny had both of those. "From my wife's property I am in easy circumstances," he explained to a correspondent a decade later, "but from habit and education have been used to a life of occupation and business, which it is my intention to continue, having a great aversion to an idle life in this country."[6]

The couple was married in May 1830. Aside from a daughter who died as an infant, they had no other children. But they enjoyed the comforts of their combined fortunes, with carriages built to order in New York, furniture sent from Paris, and walls decorated with frescoes by Italian artist Nicola Monachesi. They rode through the country together on impressive mounts and hosted some of Philadelphia's finest parties at their town house a on shady, genteel stretch of Chestnut Street. Diarist Sidney George Fisher described their rooms as "very sumptuously furnished [and] decidedly the handsomest in town." Better still, judged the snobbish Fisher, the Cadwaladers "have been accustomed to this thing all their lives, and do it with ease, propriety & grace. Very different from the gaudy show, crowded glitter and loaded tables of certain vulgar people here, who by mere force of money have got into a society to which they are not entitled by birth, education or manners."[7]

When not managing property or entertaining guests, George might be found yachting, hunting ducks, or traveling to Europe. He kept two carriages and eventually stabled horses worth tens of thousands of dollars. His favorite was Ned Forrest, described by the awestruck Fisher as "the fastest trotter in the world, and a steed of matchless beauty." In an early portrait, George stands in riding boots, leaning comfortably against the saddle of a magnificent mount, while a seated dog stares reverently upward. Lest he find himself alone in such pleasures, in 1834 he helped found the Philadelphia Club for the "encouragement of social intercourse," serving as the club's first chairman and welcoming fellow Philadelphia gentlemen as well as distinguished visitors and diplomats passing through the city on their way between New York and Washington or the south.[8]

"He is a man of the world," wrote Fisher, enviously. "A man of pleasure, shrewd, practical, with much business ability, no education, but a good deal of experience in life, very gentlemanlike & easy in his manners, cautious & close in conversation, and either from sagacity or wonderful good luck, or both, the most successful & fortunate person I know of in all his undertakings. By speculating in real estate he has made a large fortune in a few years, and lives with more splendor & expense than any man in town." Cadwalader could enjoy anything, it seems, except inaction. After boasting of the tranquility of a Long Branch farmhouse where she was lodged, Fanny conceded, "*You* would not like this place even for an hour."[9]

Like other Philadelphia aristocrats, the Cadwaladers had devoted time and money to the city's hospitals, colleges, and learned societies. But George had no interest in literature or politics. Instead, like his grandfather and father before him, he would serve the public and make his name as a commander in the Pennsylvania Militia.[10]

American militias were the institutional descendants of the *fyrd* of Anglo-Saxon England—an assemblage of all able-bodied, freeborn men between the ages of sixteen and sixty, who were required to bear arms against invasion or disorder whenever called upon to do so. Britons took care to distinguish their militias from the standing armies of the European continent, which they saw as instruments of despotism. Starting in the 1650s, English radical Whigs warned that a professional army would be more loyal to the king—who paid its salary and promoted its officers—than to the people. Moreover, the expense of maintaining an army meant higher taxes. By contrast, these thinkers argued, militias composed of landowning citizens were liberty's guarantors. These locally organized, part-time soldiers, they believed, would remain loyal to their communities rather than to a despotic monarch. A militia composed of the people would not act against the people.[11]

English colonists brought these ideas with them across the Atlantic. By the early eighteenth century, most of the British North American colonies had organized militias composed of more or less all free white men, regardless of property, who were required to muster periodically, bringing weapons with them. Because of its Quaker origins, Pennsylvania was something of an exception, but even there men formed armed companies at times of war with France. Then, as tensions with Britain increased in the winter of 1774–1775, the colonies reorganized their militias under locally elected officers, who could be expected to uphold traditional liberties. As the Revolutionary War progressed, however, the disappointing performance of state militias led Congress to rely more and more on Continental troops—often poorer men, lured by large bounties into long enlistments.[12]

In the aftermath of war, the framers of the Constitution had new concerns about weak or disloyal militias to complement their old fears of standing armies. They resolved these doubts by establishing a hybrid system that divided responsibility for the militia between the federal and state governments. Congress would "provide for organizing, arming and disciplining the militia," while the states would be responsible for appointing officers and training the men. Still, this was too much for the Anti-Federalists, who feared that the shift of power from the local to national governments would replace law enforcement based on "affection to the government" with enforcement by a standing army. The result was the passage of the Constitution's Second Amendment, which guaranteed "the right of the people to keep and bear Arms," ambiguously linking that right to the need for a "well regulated Militia."[13]

By the 1820s, with the threat of European invasion diminished, compulsory militia muster seemed less a patriotic duty and more an obsolete ritual that deprived working men of a day's wages. Those who could afford them paid fines for delinquency or bought bogus certificates of exemption from unscrupulous surgeons. Poorer men grudgingly attended muster, then did everything they could to express their annoyance. Some reported for duty armed with pitchforks or umbrellas rather than muskets, or threw eggs at their officers. In Philadelphia, a regiment elected a deformed ostler as colonel, then dressed him in an absurd uniform and armed him with a rusty sword. In later years, some companies stopped holding elections entirely, leaving regiments without the required number of officers. "The fact is undeniable," a Philadelphia newspaper lamented, "the trainings of ununiformed militia have gradually sunk the military pride of our citizens to so low an ebb that nothing short of the actual breaking out of a war seems likely to revive it." Another suggested abolishing the annual musters entirely: "nothing can be more farcical than to suppose them ever capable of putting the people in a posture for defence."[14]

As in previous decades, however, some men actively enjoyed their militia service. Rather than serve alongside malcontented conscripts who only mustered when required, these enthusiasts joined more selective units. Some of these companies dated back to the colonial era, others from the War of 1812, while others were newly organized despite general peace. The

Marquis de Lafayette's tour of the United States in 1824, during which he met the young George Cadwalader, inspired men in several cities to organize companies to receive the great hero; a New York battalion even called itself the National Guards in reference to Lafayette's command in the early days of the French Revolution. (Eventually, the name spread, until by the twentieth century the nation's entire organized militia became known as the National Guard.) And just as Lafayette was preparing to return to France, Americans began celebrating the fiftieth anniversary of their own revolution, leading additional patriotic citizens to form volunteer militia companies.[15]

Old or new, these companies took pains to distinguish themselves from the bands of militiamen who appeared only for compulsory muster, calling themselves "volunteers," "uniform companies," "independent companies," or "active militia," as opposed to the "common," "ordinary," or "undisciplined" militia. "The volunteer militia are generally the most efficient," wrote Major General Cadwalader (George's father) in 1826. "Some of the corps are scientifically trained by frequent drillings, and are always fitted for immediate service, and the rest of them may be considered so, under proper instruction, in a few weeks." "Having a great fondness for military pursuits," agreed some Maryland officers in 1846, "the members of these associations provide themselves with uniforms, colors, music, and all other necessary preparations. It is an agreeable recreation for them to spend a day, or part of a day occasionally, in practising military manoeuvres; and, when the system is in active operation, some of these corps attain such a proficiency in discipline as to be equal to any company in the regular army."[16]

Whether or not the last claim was true, these volunteer militiamen believed themselves the nation's prime defense against invasion by a European power. In the 1830s and 1840s, they could still meet a few old veterans of the first war against Great Britain, and plenty of middle-aged veterans of the second. A third war was plausible in an age of boundary disputes from Maine to Oregon. "We may, in all probability, soon have a War with England," warned Pennsylvania's adjutant general in March 1840. "We should be ready!" At other times, France seemed the more likely invader. Whatever hostile force arrived, it would face a US army of scarcely ten thousand regulars, spread out across the country too thinly to defend any one spot against a determined enemy. "We should place the country in an attitude of complete defence, so as to be ready at any time to resist invasion," wrote the *New York Military Magazine* in 1841. Unless the nation wanted "a large standing army; ruinous in it's expenses, and tyrannical in it's power," that meant a disciplined volunteer militia. Volunteers also served in expeditionary forces; in 1837 and 1838, 510 Pennsylvania troops, including six companies from Philadelphia, fought the Seminoles in Florida.[17]

While preparing for war, volunteers also enjoyed the pleasures of peacetime: camaraderie, flashy uniforms, and the excitement of parades and military balls. "Take great pains to procure a uniform that will fit your person neatly," warned one officer. "A soldier who has not taste in dress is hardly worth having." Taste in dress could be expensive; even in a relatively "economical" company, the uniform would cost the volunteer $13, and a rifle another $7, at a time when $20 represented more than two week's wages for an artisan. In addition, volunteers were expected to pay dues, and perhaps make donations. The money went to hire musicians, rent armories, and print documents. For officers and commanders, expenses could be even greater. A fine uniform—beaver chapeau, swan plume, silk sash, gold-fitted sword—could run close to $100, and on top of that they might be expected to contribute, according to rank, to a common regimental fund. Yet such funds subsidized the expenses of less affluent members, and volunteer militias enlisted clerks and mechanics as privates and noncommissioned officers. Enjoying at least nominal equality within their companies, volunteers took pride in both defending and embodying American democracy.[18]

Though given the independence to choose their names, set their training schedules, collect their fines, and elect their officers, volunteer militia companies remained part of the official state militia, and service in them excused members from ordinary militia musters. Some states abandoned compulsory service entirely, choosing to rely instead on the volunteers. Others, including Pennsylvania, spent millions to equip their volunteer companies with weapons, musical instruments, tents, and colors, though the volunteers themselves remained responsible for their uniforms and other expenses. Such a well-drilled militia was a matter of civic pride, and Philadelphia paraded its volunteer troops to mark key occasions—the visit of Lafayette in 1824, the deaths of Thomas Jefferson and John Adams in 1826, and France's July Revolution of 1830—as well as annual holidays. Such occasions could unite a city divided by ethnic and political rivalries. In February 1844, for instance, George Washington's birthday was celebrated by German and Irish units, among others.[19]

Not everyone trusted the volunteers. One Virginia colonel complained that the wealthy young men who joined the volunteer companies had "notions of superiority . . . that unfit them for military subordination" along with "hot-bed constitutions, vitiated palates, and enervated limbs." A political pamphlet mocked a candidate for missing the War of 1812 yet performing an "arduous tour of duty" required of a peacetime militia general. "These troops," a European observer snickered, "turn out on all public or gala days; their gay dress—their strange variety of costume, tending to inspirit and enliven the scene; indeed they would seem as if organized and drawn together for no other possible or earthly purpose, their military skill and capabilities being strictly confined to marching and countermarching in subdivisions and sections, through the streets and principal thoroughfares of their towns and cities for the edification of the boys and young children of the neighbour-hood, and the delight of their female friends and acquaintances, to the dis-cordant sound of some three or four wind instruments and a half-strung bass drum, discoursing boisterous music." Some cynics crashed ceremonial ban-quets or disrupted parades with forged orders calling for the immediate dispatch of troops. At times, the confrontations could become violent. In 1838 in New York City, a half-drunk cartman whipped his horse and crashed full speed into a body of troops, injuring several. "This so exasperated the troops," reported a newspaper, "that they fell upon the wretch and nearly despatched him with sabre cuts and bayonets. He was taken almost lifeless to the hospital." Similarly, in 1841, a crowd of civilians confronted a Phila-delphia militia unit returning from a sham fight. The soldiers were pelted with brickbats, and they responded with their swords and bayonets, wounding two men and a boy, and killing a horse.[20]

George Cadwalader entered the world of the volunteers on July 24, 1826, not long after his twentieth birthday. At first he rode with the storied First City Troop, the same unit his father had joined as a youth. Cadwalader progressed slowly, rising only to the rank of fourth corporal by 1828. Per-haps eager for more authority, in 1831 he won election to the captaincy of a younger company, the Philadelphia Grays. Founded in April 1825—during the militia boom that marked the half-century anniversary of the battles of Lexington and Concord—the Grays had dissolved the following year. Under Cadwalader's leadership, however, they revived, and by 1835 numbered close to a hundred men, most of whom were "contributing members" whose only participation was to pay a $2 annual fee. The remaining thirty or forty would drill about once a week in their armory at Chestnut and Eighth streets, a short distance from Cadwalader's elegant home.[21]

The company was among the city's smartest. The full equipment of a member ran $36, most of which went for a dress uniform whose gold and scarlet trimmings and careful tailoring cost more than $25, twice the total cost of the uniform of an ordinary volunteer. Moreover, Cadwalader spent heavily from his own purse on the horses, drivers, and ammunition needed for the complex, precise "flying artillery" drill that thrilled Philadelphia crowds, which gathered to watch as four galloping horses drew each cannon from one side of the field to the other in a careful dance that would allow the company to advance or retreat as needed. He spent as well on the calfskin sword belts, with gilded mountings, that would make his officers shine on parade. (Eager to order, he was not always prompt to pay his bills.) According to a later account, the command of the Grays earned Cadwalader "the reputation of being the best amateur officer in the United States." Yet even the Grays were vulnerable to the contempt of citizens not persuaded of the militia's value. Cadwalader was livid when the driver of a mail stage drove through his column—purposefully, George was sure.[22]

In addition to the Grays' captaincy, Cadwalader secured a series of posts that put him in contact with senior officers. By 1834, he was one of two brigade secretaries. In 1835, he won election as a battalion major. Cadwalader was not hostile to the idea of a small regular army, and one of his most regular correspondents was his cousin Samuel Ringgold, a West Point graduate and regular army officer who was revolutionizing US Army artillery tactics. But he still embraced the citizen soldier's creed that the militia was essential to liberty, and he coauthored a report asserting that "a large standing army, in time of peace, is not only regarded as dangerous to public liberty, but is objectionable on the score of expense," and that the

American people should "mainly depend for their defence and safety, upon the National Guard, her citizen soldiers."[23]

Two events of the early 1840s thrust George into greater responsibilities. First, on October 26, 1841, Thomas Cadwalader died, just short of his sixty-second birthday, having been in poor health since the summer. The day following his father's burial, George sent letters to their chief clients—family members included—to tell them that his father's last wish was that George take over the accounts, and the accompanying fees.[24]

The second event followed within months. The militia's First Brigade, which was drawn from Philadelphia City, had to choose a new brigadier, and George sought to become the third General Cadwalader to command Pennsylvania troops. He was not the obvious choice. Still only a thirty-five-year-old major in the spring of 1842, he was junior in age and rank to several officers of the brigade. Indeed, the forty-seven-year-old Colonel James Page—a former president of the Common Council, War of 1812 veteran, and the commander of the State Fencibles since 1819—was the preference of some of the brigade's senior officers. Only after Page's appointment as county treasurer disqualified him from the race did they seek out Cadwalader.[25]

Though Cadwalader would benefit from his family name, the election was no cinch. He faced two serious opponents: Peter Fritz of the National Grays and Robert M. Lee of the Union Fencibles. To win command, he would need a plurality of "those citizens liable to perform military duty," that is, all white men between ages eighteen and forty-five. He would also need friends to monitor the election; in 1835, supporters of each candidate had accused their rivals of forged votes and double voting. On the day of the election, June 6, 1842, partisans of each candidate marched through the streets and hitched fine teams of horses to any vehicle—a wagon, omnibus, furniture car, or even a sleigh mounted on wheels—capable of carrying a band of musicians. Fifes, drums, trumpets, and trombones all contributed to the racket, while flags and placards made a grand spectacle. Beneath the pageantry ran hints of real rivalry, as Fritz's backers called him "the poor man's friend," distinguishing the stonecutter captain from the aristocratic Cadwalader. In the end, though, Cadwalader finished with 45 percent of the vote to Fritz's 39, with Lee a distant third. Cadwalader was too sick with varioloid smallpox to greet the band and supporters that marched to his house after the results were announced, but one of his brothers offered refreshments and an appropriate address, after which the band marched away to play, more delicately, for Cadwalader's recently widowed mother.[26]

The following summer, Cadwalader was invited to command a militia encampment in Easton, Pennsylvania, about fifty miles north of Philadelphia. Over seven hundred men mustered from eastern Pennsylvania and New Jersey, along with twenty-seven musicians. For men used to drilling in small units in local armories, the tasks of forming regiments with strangers and sleeping in white tents in a farmer's field must have been disorienting. But Cadwalader got them through it, seeming to be everywhere, "at regiment drill, at company drill, at morning parade, at evening parade, directing at all points," so that the men would leave the encampment better soldiers than they had arrived just days before. He also embraced the festive nature of the occasion, and out of his own pocket paid for an evening of fireworks by Samuel Jackson, a pyrotechnist from Philadelphia.[27]

For Cadwalader, Easton was a triumph. The local Whig newspaper praised his "strict discipline and watchful care," which allowed hundreds of troops and as many as fifty thousand spectators to gather "without running into riot, disorder and immorality." The rival Democratic newspaper was just as enthusiastic. "If all military officers were as capable, as active, and as gentlemanly as General Cadwallader [sic]," it observed, "the severities of military life would be by one half diminished, and Florida wars would not remain unfinished for five years, as they have done." Governor David Porter, himself a major general in the militia, told Cadwalader that the encampment "was decidedly the best thing of the kind he had ever seen." Away from his wife and mother, and among his brother officers, Cadwalader was at home.[28]

Cadwalader's military celebrity kept growing. One militia company, the National Rangers, renamed itself as the Cadwalader Grays, ostensibly in honor of George's father and grandfather, but taking care to seek the approval of the new General Cadwalader. Composers wrote marches in his honor and artists printed lithographs destined for the walls and albums of Philadelphia's finer parlors. When President John Tyler visited Philadelphia in 1843, Cadwalader led the grand military procession that escorted him to his hotel. Though often reluctant to sit for a portrait, the new general did allow artist John Sartain the time to capture his likeness. The result was an engraving that painstakingly captured all the finery of Cadwalader's new position, from the embroidered oak leaves on his cuffs to the brigadier's paired buttons on his tunic to the drooping plume of swan's feathers on his shako, all carefully crafted to US Army standards by Cadwalader's New York tailors. Cadwalader himself looks more dreamy than fierce, his long fingers seemingly more suited for the keys of a piano than the sword on which his left hand rests.[29]

For whom was that sword meant? Cadwalader's father and grandfather had defended Pennsylvania against redcoats whose hostility to the American republic was simple and direct. General Cadwalader would face a more subtle threat: a domestic clash between Irish immigrants who came to build the republic and white, native-born Americans determined to deny them that chance.

Thomas Grover.
Courtesy of the Library of Congress.

4

American-Born Citizens

I n May 1844, Samuel Finley Breese Morse would gain immortality by tapping on an electrical apparatus in the United States Capitol while his partner, Alfred Vail, sat before a similar device in Baltimore, forty miles away. As the long and short pulses produced by Morse's taps reached his machine, Vail decoded them as a line from the Bible: "What hath God wrought!" When Vail sent the same message back as confirmation, witnesses knew they had seen the invention of a marvel: the magnetic telegraph. A decade earlier, however, Morse was devoting his energies not to invention but to the fight against popery and immigration.[1]

Early in 1834, while sick in bed with an illness that may have added to his bitterness, Morse began writing a series of essays entitled *Foreign Conspiracy Against the Liberties of the United States*. "Are not the Catholics of this country the subjects of the Pope," Morse asked. "Do they not owe him an allegiance superior to any due to our laws?" Irish Catholics, he ranted, "keep alive their foreign feelings, their foreign associations, habits and manners," thus threatening "American character, and national independence." After publishing his essays as a book in 1835, in 1836 he ran for mayor of New York City as a "Native American." Though he finished last in a four-man race, others would succeed in turning nativism into a powerful political movement.[2]

Morse's 1834 essays were just the latest expression of a hatred that stretched back to Europe's wars of religion. Following the Reformation, English Protestants in particular had argued that Catholics could not be loyal subjects. "Treason in Papists is like original sin to mankind," wrote English clergyman Abednego Seller in 1688. "They all have it in their Natures though many may deny it, or not know it." While not all Britons were Protestants, and not all Protestants were British, a century of warfare with Catholic France reinforced the belief that a united kingdom of Englishmen, Welshmen, and Scots, of Anglicans and nonconformists, could still share a common identity as British Protestants.[3]

The same logic shaped laws in Britain's colonies. In 1701, for example, New York banned Catholic priests, threatening them with life imprisonment or death. Even Maryland, founded by a Catholic proprietor and intended, in part, as a haven for English Catholics, was seized by Protestants in 1689. They restricted Catholic worship and fined ship captains "to prevent too Great a number of Irish Papists being Imported into this Province."[4]

Pennsylvania was something of an exception. Though founded as a Quaker refuge, from its start in the 1680s the colony had granted religious liberty to all who believed in one God, and political privileges to all Christians. For a time, it was the only British colony to permit Catholics to worship publicly. Even so, in 1728, the Pennsylvania legislature considered limiting "the importation of Irish Papists and convicts" before contenting itself with a tax of twenty shillings on "Irish servants," papist or not. In

1757, during the French and Indian War, the colony ordered the confiscation of firearms and ammunition from any "Papist or reputed Papist."[5]

As British Americans moved toward independence, they scrambled old fears of the pope with new fears of the king. Samuel Adams railed against "popery," and Alexander Hamilton warned of "arbitrary power, and its great engine the Popish Religion." Yet once Americans took up arms against King George III, most welcomed Catholic patriots into their ranks. More significantly, the old enemies—Catholic France and Spain—became America's new allies against Britain, enabling an otherwise impossible victory. With independence secured, American Catholics claimed a place in the new republic. In 1790, the new president, George Washington, assured his Catholic constituents that "I hope ever to see America among the foremost nations in examples of justice and liberality." The Constitution of 1787 made no mention of God, and it banned religious tests for public office. The First Amendment of 1791 further prohibited an official creed while guaranteeing free exercise of religion. These provisions restricted only the federal government, but most states followed suit, and in 1833 Massachusetts became the last state to disestablish its church.[6]

Although they would no longer support their churches with tax revenues, many Americans still expected their governments to reflect Protestant values. In 1824, the Pennsylvania Supreme Court ruled that "Christianity, general Christianity, is, and always has been, a part of the common law of Pennsylvania," but it clarified that this was "Christianity with liberty of conscience to all men." Judge Joel Jones of Philadelphia's District Court regarded "Martin Luther as the forerunner of George Washington in the great cause of civil and religious liberty." Supreme Court Justice Joseph Story agreed that "the Protestant religion is far more congenial with the spirit of political freedom, than the Catholic."[7]

Nativism was never merely anti-Catholic or anti-Irish. Nativists sincerely believed that they were working for a positive goal: building American identity and American democracy. They claimed, at times, to oppose attachments to any other country, not just Ireland. "When men, whether Dutch, German, Irish, English, Scotch, or anything else," proclaimed one nativist newspaper, "come into this country and assume to become citizens, they should at once forget their lingo or their brogue, and glory to be called

Americans." Others joined the nativist cause out of despair with the Whig and Democratic parties, both of which could seem more eager to reward supporters with jobs and contracts than with efficient government. Of course, to blame all corruption on immigrants required a fair amount of imagination and prejudice. And in pledging to hire only native-born men for government jobs, or to trade only with fellow native-borns, they were merely proposing to replace one clan with another.[8]

Calling opponents of immigration "nativists" may give too much credit to their own branding. As a Catholic newspaper explained, "There is no disguising the fact at this moment, that the soul, and *animus*, of the Native American party is hostility to the Catholic citizens, whether of native or foreign birth." In 1838, one group of nativists from Washington County, New York, openly voiced what many other nativists were thinking when they petitioned Congress to ban Catholic immigration. Another slip would take place in 1846, when William Baker, a prominent Philadelphia nativist, suggested, "Let the doors of our Native American Associations be thrown wide open, that all may enter, Natives, Irish, Germans, Scotch—all who are opposed to the insolent demands of the Court of Rome." Officially, at least, nativists claimed that they supported freedom of conscience, but for Catholics they offered only the freedom to worship behind closed doors, while enduring all manner of insult in the public realm.[9]

In theory, nativist screeds against Catholic immigrants could have applied equally to arrivals from Germany, France, Spain, or Quebec. In the 1840s, however, Catholic and Irish immigration seemed synonymous. In the space of just over thirty years, from 1780 to 1821, Ireland's population had risen from four to seven million, outpacing the island's economy. In the hopes of greater freedom and prosperity, between 1815 and 1845 as many as one million Irish—most of them Catholic—crossed the Atlantic to Canada or the United States. Some sailed straight from Londonderry to American ports. For many, the great journey started instead with an eastward passage to Liverpool: fourteen to thirty hours on the crowded open deck of a steamer, trying not to vomit or fall overboard. Then days or weeks in Liverpool, seeking passage on an ocean ship while avoiding the snares of "sharpers" and "man-catchers" aiming to separate bewildered migrants from their money. Those who held onto enough cash to buy an authentic ship ticket then endured anywhere from eighteen to sixty days at sea, much of it in the crowded, dark hold. There they faced the perils of the sea—seasickness and storms—and of their fellow passengers, who could be screaming children, belligerent adherents to a different sect, calculating thieves, or unhappy carriers of cholera, dysentery, or smallpox. If 300 passengers left Liverpool, perhaps 295 would live to see Philadelphia, along with however many babies were born mid-ocean.[10]

Appalled by these numbers, some Americans who felt no animus toward immigrants still hoped to dilute their concentration. Philadelphia gentlemen organized a new Irish Emigrant Society, designed in large part to steer new arrivals out of crowded Philadelphia as quickly as possible and on their way to the "immense vacant territories of America, the rich and beautiful savannahs of the South, the fertile prairies and woodlands of the West, and the vast wildernesses which only require the hand of industry to make them blossom as the rose." But while some immigrants heeded that advice, thousands more found homes in Philadelphia County, especially the inner districts of Kensington, Moyamensing, and Southwark. Moreover, many of the county's most prominent Catholic clergy were Irish-born, further linking nationality and religion. To men like Levin, the Irish Catholic community represented a unique threat: a community large, homogeneous, and organized enough to change the character of Philadelphia and the United States.[11]

The nativists' journey toward forming their own political party began in New York City in June 1835, when a group of "American Born Citizens" established a "Native American Democratic Association." At first they pledged to oppose immigrants in both major parties—Democrats and Whigs. But Whig-leaning nativists seized control, making the association appear to be a branch of the Whig Party. In 1837, following Morse's defeat, the nativists endorsed Whig Aaron Clark, who won election as mayor. Clark, in turn, formally approved of the Native American principles. Rather than compete with the Whigs for nativist support, Democrats saw a chance to lock in the immigrant vote. Irishmen, Democrats argued, far from being monarchists, had left their native land "to escape from political oppression," and thus embodied the "love for liberty" that would make them great Americans. From the 1830s on, Democrats generally welcomed immigrants, while nativists would vacillate between joining the Whigs or striking out on their own.[12]

Events in New York would set the pattern for the nation. In the years after Clark's election as New York's mayor, native-born Americans in other cities and states began organizing nativist associations of their own. The Washington, DC, organization, founded in 1837, initially attracted some prominent Catholics—including descendants of old Maryland Catholic families who had lived in North America for generations. But within its first few months, Catholic members resigned over what they perceived as anti-Catholic prejudice, and the organization began its decline. A Germantown, Pennsylvania, Native American Association, apparently inspired by the Washington group, did not explicitly denounce Catholics, instead accusing European immigrants of being "filled with all the requisite materials to spread among our citizens anarchy, radicalism, and rebellion." That was not enough, and the new group apparently vanished within weeks. Perhaps the only lasting nativist group that avoided anti-Catholicism was the Louisiana Native American Association, which hoped to woo Catholic Creole families. Even then it took a swipe at an Irish Catholic hero, referring to "the beggarly agitator Daniel O'Connell." To build their movement, nativists needed a Catholic enemy.[13]

While New York nativism mostly attracted Whigs, in Philadelphia the movement initially lured Democrats frustrated by the growing Irish presence in their party. Indeed, some of the fiercest nativists would emerge from the county's Democratic stronghold: Southwark.

In the 1840s, "Philadelphia" could mean either of two entities. The City of Philadelphia, founded by William Penn, occupied a two-square-mile rectangle stretching from the Delaware River on the east to the Schuylkill on the west. The 1840 census counted 93,665 residents in this rectangle, the Cadwaladers and their fellow gentry among them. Beyond the city lay the remainder of Philadelphia County, a 129-square-mile jurisdiction with a total population of 258,037, including the city. Much of that was farmland, but the areas nearest to Philadelphia City—both to the north and south—were nearly as urban as the city itself. Four jurisdictions—the Northern Liberties, Spring Garden, Southwark, and Kensington—counted among the fifteen largest cities in the United States and functioned as "districts" governed by boards of commissioners. A fifth, Moyamensing, came in at twenty-seventh, still larger than such old colonial ports as New Haven or Savannah. Like other less populated parts of the county, it was formally a township.[14]

The oldest of Philadelphia County's independent districts, Southwark lay directly to the city's south. By the 1840s, its Delaware River frontage featured two public landings, a marine railway, and Philadelphia's Navy Yard, as well as more than a dozen smaller wharves, while ropewalks, shipwrights, and a shot manufacturer clustered nearby. Just inland lay the shops and dwellings of the district's merchants, giving way to mostly residential blocks west of Fifth Street. In the 1820s, William Heighton, an English-born cordwainer, contrasted the workers' "small, delapidated, half furnished dwellings, their wretchedly clad children, and their coarse, if not scanty supply of human subsistence" with "the richly canopied and lofty halls of the great; the splendid furniture; the sumptuous and superabundant provision; the trains of domestics; the rolling chariot and the gilded equipage." He concluded that the American republic had failed to deliver true liberty and equality. Though the Workingmen's Party he inspired did not long survive as an independent movement, the Democrats adopted several of its positions. Thanks to workingmen's votes, Southwark became a solidly Jacksonian jurisdiction, "the cradle of Democracy."[15]

Thomas Grover was reared in that cradle. Born in Delaware County in 1788, Grover had arrived in Southwark as a child, and he personified its gritty ambition. Apprenticed to a house carpenter, he later joined his maternal grandfather in the business of building wharves, winning lucrative contract after contract from the Southwark government. Grover also entered politics, first winning election to Southwark's fifteen-man Board of Commissioners in 1818, and then, in 1829, being chosen by his fellow commissioners as board president, a post he would retain for most of the next seventeen years. As national party divisions emerged, working-class Southwark gave Democrats nearly 70 percent of the vote in the local elections of 1836. Grover joined the wave and was toasted in 1834 as "a Democrat, firm and unflinching in every trial." This party loyalty—his enemies claimed—kept the government contracts coming, and made him rich. But Grover failed to rise in office. Over the years, he made efforts at a state assembly seat and was spoken of as a candidate for state senate, coroner, or sheriff. None of this came to anything, and Grover remained a local Southwark politician, only occasionally found in a board meeting in the city or a party convention in Harrisburg. He accumulated grudges.[16]

Even a loyal Democrat had to choose sides in the late 1830s, as the party divided into conservative and radical wings, largely on the issue of banking. Opposition to the Bank of the United States was a central Democratic principle, and Grover as much as any Democrat warned that the "Bank party" threatened to "reduce old Southwark to a state of vassalage." But in 1838, Grover—who himself had helped found the Bank of Southwark—was among the relatively conservative Democrats dismayed by an amended version that would require state banks to pay the US Treasury in gold. This may have been the start of Grover's gradual departure from the Democratic Party. In 1840 and 1841, candidates of the "Amalgamated" or "Reform" ticket won the Southwark elections. Facing reelection for a three-year term in 1842, Grover joined the Reform ticket as well. But he had gambled badly. "Where is the reform?" asked one voter. "Is the District better governed? Are the streets better lighted or kept in better repair? Are the TAXES reduced? Are the police officers more efficient?" Unable to answer such challenges, the Reform ticket lost by hundreds of votes. Though uncharacteristically out of office, Grover still had friends on the board of commissioners who, perhaps as a sop, appointed him as the Southwark representative to the Board of Guardians of the Poor, and in 1843 he was named to a three-year term as president of the board of health.[17]

Grover's closest associate was Lemuel Paynter. Born in Delaware in 1788—the same year as Grover—Paynter moved to Philadelphia and served in the same militia unit with Grover during the War of 1812. The two men continued serving together in the Democratic Association of Southwark and in various civic efforts, from a committee to build a monument to George Washington to the board of a fire-insurance company. By 1825, Paynter had established himself as a German Street grocer. That same year, he gained election to the Southwark Board of Commissioners, for the first of many terms, and in 1833 he was elected to the Pennsylvania Assembly.[18]

Into the 1830s, Grover and Paynter remained on good terms with the Irishmen and Irishmen's sons who joined the Southwark Democrats, sharing stages with James Campbell, John Keefe, Thomas McCully, Joseph Doran, and John McCoy. In 1834, Paynter even served on the Democrats' Southwark Committee of Naturalization, devoted to helping immigrants become citizens and, presumably, voting Democrats. Over the next several years, however, both Grover and Paynter picked fights with some of the leading Irish Democrats of Southwark. First, they tried to purge Keefe from the party leadership, antagonizing immigrant voters. Then Paynter defeated Doran, the Southwark district solicitor, to win the Democratic nomination for Congress in 1836.[19]

Whigs denounced Paynter as the "unknown, illiterate, and presumptuous superintendent of the streets of Southwark." One paper mocked him for spelling "cabbage" as "kabbitch" and assuring a constituent, "We this aftirnoon Succeded in gitten before the house yeur Police Bill and giving the Commessinors power to Borrow ten thousand dollars." Democrats shrugged off such snobbery, lauding Paynter as "a *practical mechanic* and working man." "He is a friend of the poor man, and, being one of the people," they promised, more likely "to watch carefully over their interests as a Doctor, a Lawyer, a Judge, a President of a Rail Road Company, or a speculator in public lands." Such appeals worked, and in October the voters of Southwark chose Paynter.[20]

After two terms in Congress, Paynter declined to seek reelection. But in 1843, Pennsylvania reapportioned its congressional districts, requiring new elections, and Paynter decided he would like to return to Washington. His opponent was Thomas McCully, the former state senator who had taken over as president of the Southwark Board of Commissioners during Grover's brief absence from it. Though he himself had been born in Pennsylvania, McCully was known for steering public works jobs to Irish immigrants. The contest soon grew nasty. When McCully tried to speak at a Southwark meeting, he was shouted down with cries of "Liar!" and "Cabbage-head!" Outside, a gang led by Paynter's son, "Young Lem," found an Irishman employed by McCully on the Catharine Street culvert. They beat and kicked the worker, then fled. Three weeks later, still under bond for the assault on the culvert worker, Lem got into a scrap at another Southwark meeting, ending up with a severe knife cut over his eye.[21]

Despite this violent opposition, McCully won the district nomination, even getting a majority in Southwark. But rather than rally behind the nominee, Paynter's supporters backed a rival from Passyunk, the township west of Moyamensing, thus splitting the Democratic vote in an otherwise "invincible" Democratic district. Irish Americans saw bigotry at work, accusing the Southwark Democrats of opposing McCully "because of the Mc in his name." By the time of the election, the split was so bitter than when it became clear that McCully's Democratic rival could not win, McCully's detractors began voting for Whig candidate Edward Joy Morris, handing him the seat. Still running as Democrats, Paynter and Grover regained seats on the Southwark Board of Commissioners, though Grover narrowly lost the presidency of the board.[22]

While the Southwark Democrats bickered themselves into defeat, nativists in New York City were thriving. No longer content to function as a faction of the Democrats or Whigs, in August 1843 they formed an entirely new party: the American Republican Party. The new name may have signified an effort to get beyond the "Native American" label of the 1830s. If so, it was a failure, in that newspapers and even official party materials continued to refer to the new group as the Native Americans, a practice that would continue throughout the organization's existence.[23]

Members of the new party claimed to want efficient, honest municipal government, and they blamed the failure of reform on the tendency of the old parties to buy votes by offering more jobs and market licenses to German and Irish immigrants. Yet Catholicism remained their most prominent grievance. "Although I do not war against the Catholic Church," claimed one American Republican speaker that autumn, "it is anti-democratic. Ask any Irishman who he has to obey, and he will tell you the priest. Well, the priest must obey the bishop, and the bishop the archbishop, and the archbishop the old Pope of Rome on his seven hilled city." His listeners responded with groans, hisses, and cries of "no popery!" In the November elections for state offices, the American Republicans finished behind the Democrats and Whigs, but the thousands of votes they received suggested that the new party was a contender.[24]

Philadelphians were watching. On December 5, 1843, less than a month after the New York elections, Oliver Cornman gathered Spring Garden nativists to a hall on Ridge Road, hoping to form an American Republican Party in Philadelphia County. Other wards followed: Locust Ward, North Mulberry Ward, and Cedar Ward—all in the City of Philadelphia itself—and the Third Ward of Southwark. By late January, the ward-level associations were beginning to coalesce. Around this time, Paynter and Grover abandoned the Democratic Party entirely and joined the American Republicans. Their defection in the face of Irish competition added to the American Republicans' reputation as the party of disappointed political hacks.[25]

Yet such men appealed to thousands of voters and ward leaders, some of whom were nursing their own frustrations. Many of them, like Grover and Paynter, represented Philadelphia's respectable mechanic class, neither professional men nor unskilled laborers, but small businessmen or craftsmen: dry-goods dealers, grocers, printers, builders, shipwrights. Cornman, who organized the first meeting, was himself a painter. Philadelphia's American Republicans, one claimed, "were the 'bone and sinew' of the country—the mechanic, the operative, the laborer—men who earn their bread by the sweat of their brows." Such men might regard immigrants not as brother workers but as rivals, especially during the hard times that hit the country after the financial collapse of 1837. "I utter not one word of complaint against these poor men," wrote one Kensington workman, "who, pursuing the advances of nature, seek the best conditions for themselves." But he feared that "competitors from the Old World" could drive him into an impoverished old age.[26]

Philadelphia's American Republicans also attracted more educated, well-born men who saw in the new party a chance to rise after failing as Democrats or Whigs. One was Peter Sken Smith, whose unusual middle name derived from the Oneida name Skenondough. The forty-eight-year-old son of a wealthy New York landowner, Smith was known as "General" thanks to his 1820s command of a division of riflemen in the New York militia. In the 1830s, he had turned to politics, unsuccessfully running for Congress as the nominee of both the anti-Jackson and anti-Masonic forces in his home town of Oswego, New York. He also started drinking heavily, ruining his health.[27]

Smith moved to St. Augustine, Florida, where he invested his inheritance in railroads, canals, an insurance company, and real estate. He also sought political office, but the prominent abolitionism of his younger brother, Gerrit, cost him support among Florida's slaveholders, who denounced him as "a broken down politician [who] left his home to retrieve his broken fortunes in Florida. . . . He will profess himself any thing, whenever his convenience or interests require the change." Thanks to such attacks, Smith narrowly missed election to the territory's first constitutional convention, losing out to David Levy, who had been born in the Danish West Indies. Disgusted to lose to an immigrant, Smith left for Pennsylvania, leaving a string of failures behind.[28]

Like Smith, Charles J. Jack hoped to ride the new movement to heights that had so far eluded him. Born in 1798, and claiming descent from the "Heroes of the Revolution," Jack had by 1827 begun styling himself "Col. C. J. Jack," having won election as lieutenant colonel in the unorganized militia. In the 1820s, Jack edited the short-lived newspaper the *Jackson Democrat* in support of Andrew Jackson's cause. By 1832, however, Jack had turned against Jackson, and he spoke at large public meetings designed to rally support behind a single opposition candidate. In 1837, Jack himself had run for Congress. Though he was unsuccessful in that effort, he remained a popular speaker and a reasonably prominent member of Philadelphia's civic life. Jack also maintained a militia career, and in 1842 made a fairly hopeless bid to become brigadier general, the post ultimately won by Cadwalader. Undaunted, in 1843 he was elected captain of the Monroe Guards.[29]

While still a Democrat in 1829, Jack had joined Irish Americans to celebrate Catholic emancipation in Ireland. But when he abandoned the party, he grew angry that Irish immigrants continued to support it. Democrats, he believed, set tariffs too low for Pennsylvania's manufacturers, and he watched in disbelief as Pennsylvania's Irish-born dyers, spinners, and weavers voted for the Democrats they should have recognized as "their bitterest enemies." Moreover he believed that newcomers had not shared the sacrifices made by more established families. Writing in a family Bible in the 1830s, Jack had carefully recorded the military service of his own ancestors and of those of his wife, as well as their sufferings at the hands of a callous national government that had failed to pay his father for provisioning Washington's army at Valley Forge. But he remained a patriot. "My children are all descended from a gallant, patriotic and distinguished race," he wrote. "May they ever defend the glorious inheritance, the Constitution of their Country—against every domestic traitor and foreign foe."[30]

Finally, there was that greatest of climbers: Lewis Levin. Levin's first efforts at denouncing Irish Catholics came in the fall of 1843 with a series of attacks on Daniel O'Connell, the Irish statesman then trying to win Irish autonomy within the British Empire. Because such autonomy would require the repeal of the 1800 Act of Union, O'Connell's cause became known as Repeal. As a temperance man, Levin might have been expected to say a kind word about the O'Connell who had described teetotalism as "a foundation stone of the edifice of Irish liberty." Instead, Levin denounced O'Connell as a seditious monarchist whose secret goal was nothing less than "a *Roman Catholic King.*" Far from being his country's George Washington, O'Connell was, Levin suggested, just another lackey of Catholic despotism. Eventually, Levin developed a full conspiracy theory, claiming that the Repeal movement never intended to change Ireland's political status. Rather, its primary goal was "*to reach the United States*—pollute our ballot boxes—disrupt our Union—light the flame of civil war in the States—and *combine the Irish Catholic vote*, for the purpose of extending the Romish denomination of his Holiness the POPE."[31]

Levin drew closer to the nativist cause in February 1844. Early in that month, he picked up the *Daily Chronicle* to find two attacks against his first cause—temperance—and perhaps himself personally. On February 3, "A Teetotaler, but no Washingtonian" mocked temperance societies that honored those who, like Levin, who could make "the most bold and barefaced avowal of previous transgressions of the laws of morality, honor, and even decency." Three days later, another writer claimed that Protestant temperance efforts were less effective than those of Catholic clergy, and it also condemned "the formation of societies of reformed drunkards, of the very lowest orders of the Protestant community."[32]

An apoplectic Levin responded with a series of editorials as bitter as anything he had penned against O'Connell. He claimed that the pope opposed temperance, since "Catholic '*Distilleries*' . . . constitute the fountain head of the power of the Catholic church." "His Holiness of Rome," Levin concluded, "aspires to carry out his *pious* intentions, through the

American ballot-boxes, by calumnating all Protestants as drunkards." And he accused the *Chronicle* of a "ferocious and malignant assault upon the Protestant churches . . . under the cloak of all the evil passions engendered in such brooding exuberance by the ambitious and domineering spirit of the church of Rome." He deduced that the second author was "a *Foreigner* and a *Catholic*" since "*no American* would degrade himself by composing a tissue of such stupid falsehood and bitter defamation."[33]

The reference to his antagonist as "a *Foreigner*" suggested a new line in Levin's thinking. As of November 1843, Levin had established himself as anti-Repeal and anti-Catholic, but he was not yet wholly anti-immigrant. By January 1844, however, Levin had begun to distinguish between Irish Catholic immigrants and the native born. A native-born Repealer was "a wanton renegade from the most sublime system of freedom ever invented." But "foreign monarchists" were even further beyond redemption, since their "love of kings and popes" derived from "early associations, the prejudices of the nursery, the lessons of their mothers, and the examples of their sires."[34]

Some of Levin's bile may have been exaggerated to keep the newspaper lively amid fierce competition, since Levin knew that fury sold newspapers. According to later reports, his screeds gained so many subscribers that, even with eighteen-hour days, his pressmen struggled to print enough copies for all who wanted them. Though angry on the page, Levin appeared cheerful in person. An office boy at the *Sun* knew that the best time to ask him for a favor was when "he was in a good humor, having just pitched into foreigners to his own entire satisfaction."[35]

A trip north led Levin further into the nativist camp. In February 1844, he traveled to New York to address American Temperance Union's grand celebration for Washington's birthday. While there, Levin thrilled to watch the city's American Republicans erect a "Liberty Pole," reminiscent of those raised by the Sons of Liberty in the lead-up to the Revolution. He praised New Yorkers for defending "the purity of our ballot boxes from the polluting touch of the priest-kings of Europe," and he predicted that "the American Republican party of this city forms a nucleus from which will spread the wholesome moral opinions destined to rescue our proud Republic from the thraldom of Romish power."[36]

As Levin watched the erection of the Liberty Pole, he took note that some American Republicans had decorated its base with a tin box containing various items of symbolic significance. One in particular captured his attention: "part of a Bible *once* used in the public schools of this city, which had been defaced and obliterated by order of the Jesuit Trustees!" Here, he now understood, was the issue that could alert complacent Americans to "the grappling irons of papal power." Levin was not ready to stop complaining about Daniel O'Connell's efforts at Irish autonomy, but now he linked the Liberator to a local threat, claiming that the Bible had been excluded from New York's common schools "because the followers of *O'Connell and the Pope* object to it as '*dangerous*' to the Roman Catholic religion." "The Bible forcibly dragged out of the hands of American children by a Romish priest," he marveled, "at the instance of the Pope, at the head of a gang of rum-soaked voters . . . under the Irish Catholic banner!"[37]

In the ten years from Morse's illness to the start of the 1844 political season, New York City's nativists had shown the potential for independent nativist party, centered on hostility to Catholics and reliant on the symbolic power of defending the Bible. Philadelphia nativists, Levin chief among them, watched and learned.

Morton McMichael.
Courtesy of the Library Company of Philadelphia.

5

The Mob Shall Rule

W hile Levin thrived on conflict, Morton McMichael wanted to believe that everyone could be friends. Even as angry men rioted in the streets of his Philadelphia—his America—he kept looking for common ground.

A descendant of Irish Protestants, McMichael was born on October 2, 1807, in New Jersey, but his family moved to Philadelphia while he was still a boy. He attended the University of Pennsylvania and gained admission to the bar at age nineteen. Despite this training, McMichael's first calling was journalism. Still in his teens, he began publishing works in Philadelphia's periodicals, and in 1826 he became editor of the *Saturday*

Evening Post, the first of several editorial posts he would hold. Such achievements won him the attention of Philadelphia's elites, or at least a place in what a later critic described as "a juvenile *coterie* of mutual-admiration penmen." Edgar Allen Poe praised one of McMichael's poems, either from true admiration or from gratitude for McMichael's assistance in Philadelphia's literary scene.[1]

McMichael was short, smart, and energetic. "He has a quick, jerking motion, as he walks," wrote a critic. "He seems all life, all motion. Yet he is by no means indiscreetly hasty in his temperament. Notwithstanding the bilious-sanguine and nervous energies that appear to control his nature, he is a tolerably cool and generally a shrewd politician, a circumspect writer, an amusing and self-possessed speaker, and (where he chooses to be) a sociable, agreeable, earnest, though always self-complacent and selfish individual." In an early photograph, his hair is sandy, his face clean shaven, and his eyes more quizzical than confident. His lips are slightly parted, as if McMichael wants to ask a question but cannot yet find the words to do so. His head is large relative to his shoulders, and his fingers appear to have been fidgeting.[2]

Eager to make friends, and reluctant to make enemies, McMichael gained early success in politics. In 1831, just barely twenty-four, he was appointed a director of public schools. The following year, he gained the Democratic nomination for a seat in the state assembly. He came in fifteenth in a field of sixteen, but no one seemed to hold it against him, and in 1833 he was named alderman and police magistrate for Spring Garden. In 1836, as a public school controller, he toured Boston and New York to examine schools there, and that fall some even speculated he might gain the Democratic nomination for Pennsylvania's Third Congressional District, which covered Spring Garden, Kensington, and other northern portions of Philadelphia County.[3]

As police magistrate McMichael had to contend with Philadelphia's culture of violence, particularly attacks on the Black community. In August 1834, while white mobs roamed parts of Philadelphia and Moyamensing in what became known as the "Flying Horses" riot (because it began with a white mob's attack on a carousel), he prepared to defend Type Alley, a predominantly African American lane in Spring Garden. No attack came, but the following month, McMichael was appointed to a committee to investigate the causes of the August riots throughout the county. Perhaps hinting that men suffering under tyranny might legitimately revolt, the committee denied any such legitimacy for American mobs. "Where the People are sovereign," it explained, "and the Laws are made by of their own choice, the Government and People are equally and eminently bound to ensure that every man shall dwell safely under his vine and his fig tree, from Dan even to Beersheba, and there shall be none to make him afraid." In the mid-1830s, that was fantasy.[4]

Throughout the 1830s, Americans watched in astonishment and dismay as their cities erupted in riots of unprecedented frequency and ferocity. After a period in which at most a handful of mob actions won national attention each year, two dozen did in 1834, and at least three dozen in 1835. These were in addition to more than a hundred lesser riots that attracted merely local notice. Each riot increased the likelihood of the next as Americans began to get used to the idea that this was a way in which groups could assert their grievances. "The state of society is awful," lamented *Niles' Weekly Register*. "Brute force has superseded the law, at many places, and violence become the '*order* of the day.' The time predicted seems rapidly approaching when the mob shall rule." National leaders agreed. "This spirit of mob-law is becoming too common and must be checked," wrote President Andrew Jackson in 1835. Three years later, a twenty-eight-year-old lawyer named Abraham Lincoln warned that "whenever the vicious portion of population shall be permitted to gather in bands of hundreds and thousands, and burn churches, ravage and rob provision stores, throw printing presses into rivers, shoot editors, and hang and burn obnoxious persons at pleasure, and with impunity; depend on it, this Government cannot last."[5]

Some riots were just larger versions of the drunken brawls that scandalized respectable Philadelphians trying to get a decent night's sleep before another day of productive labor. Males between the ages of sixteen and twenty-one, known as "half-grown boys," seemed particularly inclined to fight. "The real actors in these disreputable proceedings," the *Pennsylvania Inquirer* reassured its readers, "are, after all, but comparatively few in number, and chiefly composed of idle boys not yet arrived at years of discretion."[6]

For men and youths who liked a predictable routine of fighting, the volunteer fire companies beckoned. At first, the companies fought one another for the chance to extinguish fires. Only the earliest hose carriages and engines to reach the site of a fire would be of any use, so companies competed to arrive first, then fought for access to fire plugs and the honor of fighting the blaze. Eventually, companies began brawling even without the excuse of a fire. Each fire company owned or rented a house that served as a clubhouse for the men of the company and sheltered its equipment, whether an elaborate hand-pumped engine or a simpler, but still treasured, hose carriage. Many companies attracted auxiliary gangs with colorful names like Hornets, Snappers, Rockboys, Skimmers, Scrongers, and Revengers whose only purpose was to fight other firemen and their accompanying gangs. "We're the saucy Hyena boys of George's street as all knows," sang one gang. "We can whip the Penn and Globe, likewise the Carroll Hose."[7]

Other riots had deeper causes. As a new political party system emerged in the 1830s, election days, which could be held twice a year, became increasingly unruly. Men were freed from both work and from the presence of women, and they took the opportunity to drink, fight, bark like dogs, and roar like bulls. Whigs and Democrats battled over polling places, using fists, knives, and rocks to keep rival voters away from the ballot boxes. The boxes themselves were usually protected inside courthouses, town halls, stores, or saloons. Voters were supposed to cast ballots at designated windows, which meant climbing a short platform and voting in full public view. Party volunteers swarmed around these windows, eager to hand printed tickets with their nominees to arriving voters, and often as eager to block their opponents from reaching the platform and window with tactics ranging from shouts and curses to physical force. Shoving was only considered a violation of normal practice if had been enough to dissuade a "man of ordinary courage" from voting.[8]

In the Philadelphia elections of October 1834, so many men crowded around polling places that a person's best chance of voting lay in crowd-surfing to the ballot box or wielding a knife to clear the way. One knife-wielding man, hastily fleeing a scrap, slashed the femoral artery of William Perry, a young carpenter, who had been peacefully watching the battle. Perry bled to death early the next morning. Ten days later in

Moyamensing, partisans began feuding with relatively benign tactics: Jacksonians tearing down electioneering bills and Whigs cutting down a hickory pole erected in honor of "Old Hickory." But when Jacksonian reinforcements arrived from the city and from Southwark, they used their advantage to ransack the tavern serving as Whig headquarters. When the Whigs inside defended themselves with blank cartridges and buckshot fired from the upper stories and the roof, the Jacksonians set the building on fire, then prevented firemen from extinguishing the blaze. By the end of the night, three men were dead, and more than a dozen more severely injured.[9]

Other riots targeted religious minorities. On July 12, the anniversary of the 1690 victory of Protestant King William III, Prince of Orange, over Catholic King James II at the Battle of the Boyne, Protestants known as Orangemen marched through the towns of Ireland, often provoking fights with local Catholics. On July 12, 1831, some Philadelphia Protestants tried an Orange march of their own, mixing songs and symbols of Irish Protestant supremacy with patriotic American emblems. That provoked a bloody but nonlethal brawl with Irish Catholic immigrants, and members of both groups faced criminal charges as well as a scolding "that the banks of the Delaware or Schuylkill would never be visited with those scenes which had taken place on the Boyne or the Shannon."[10]

Three summers later, Sister Mary John left the Ursuline Convent in Charlestown, Massachusetts, in a state of some anxiety, then returned to the convent at her bishop's urging. Nearby Protestants exchanged rumors that she and others were being held captive in the convent's dungeons, and the town's selectmen insisted on searching the premises on August 11. The search came up empty, but that evening, a crowd of two thousand or more gathered, some of whom smashed the convent's doors and windows and set it on fire. Fire companies watched passively, apparently sharing the mob's conviction that such convents "ought not to be allow[e]d in a free country." The nuns fled to Canada. In 1839 in Baltimore, another nun fled her convent, leading to similar anxiety. For three days, city officials held off the crowds with a mix of oratory and armed force until physicians diagnosed the woman as a "perfect maniac" whose complaints should not be taken seriously.[11]

Nationwide, the most common cause of rioting was hostility to efforts to abolish slavery, which throughout the country sparked attacks against abolitionist speakers, their property, and African American homes and businesses. Lincoln's warnings about the shooting of editors and the drowning of presses, for instance, referred to the November 1837 mob murder of abolitionist editor Elijah Lovejoy. Philadelphia was no exception. In the "Flying Horses" riot, which had brought McMichael out to defend Black homes, a hundred or so white boys and men ransacked the houses of Black families while whites hung lamps to signal that the mob should pass them by. At least one African American perished in the violence, which lasted for three nights. The following July whites again attacked, this time targeting a group of Black-owned houses called the Red Row while again sparing those white-owned buildings identified by candles in their windows. At least one of the African Americans wounded two attackers with musket fire, but the mob pressed forward, setting fires and cutting the hoses of the firemen trying to extinguish the blazes. The following night, city officials had to personally negotiate the withdrawal of a few dozen armed Black men who had barricaded themselves against an anticipated assault by a white mob numbering in the hundreds.[12]

In May 1838, a group of antislavery activists inaugurated Pennsylvania Hall, a magnificent meeting space on Sixth Street, just south of Franklin Square and well within the confines of the City of Philadelphia. The opening series of lectures included a speech denouncing mob violence in Charlestown, Baltimore, Vicksburg, and elsewhere, and calling for "virtuous men and good citizens, to yield a hearty obedience to the laws." But on the hall's very first night of official operation, a brick crashed through a window. The following evening, as abolitionist William Lloyd Garrison spoke, thousands of people gathered outside, some smashing more windows, others briefly invading the lobby. Then, on the evening of May 17, only the fourth day of the hall's operation, a large mob battered down its doors, building a bonfire of antislavery literature, fine furniture, construction debris, and tar and turpentine brought in from the waterfront. As if this were not enough, someone cut the gas lines that had helped illuminate the vast hall, adding that fuel to the fire. Firemen rushed to the scene, but the crowd kept them from trying to save the hall, which may have been beyond saving in any case. As many as fifteen thousand people watched the building burn.[13]

Hungry for more action, the next day antiabolitionist mobs roamed the streets, looking for another abolitionist meeting to attack. Someone spread the rumor that the abolitionists would be using the school room of a large, four-story brick building, just erected by a group of Quakers and intended as an asylum for about forty "destitute colored children," none of whom had yet moved in. Neither the children nor the Quakers were abolitionists, but that hardly mattered to the mob, who set the building on fire. The building lay a short distance north of Philadelphia's northern border, outside of the jurisdiction of the city police. Instead, responsibility fell to Spring Garden's police magistrate: Morton McMichael.[14]

With no professional police force in Spring Garden, McMichael had to rely on his own stern voice and whatever volunteer aid he could find. Rushing to the threatened Quaker asylum, he scanned the faces in the mob, but saw no one he knew. Then help arrived in the form of the Good Will Engine Company, dashing up from its house at Race and Juniper Streets. Despite their benevolent name, the Good Will men had a reputation as brawlers. But under McMichael's direction, the firemen put their aggression to good use, chasing away the mob and then suppressing the fire. The bricks were scorched, and the shutters and window frames burnt. Yet the orphanage survived. McMichael credited the firemen, who, he wrote, "notwithstanding the menaces and attacks of a ruffianly mob, bravely persisted in discharging their duty as firemen," and whose "gallant and intrepid conduct" saved the building. Ignoring such modesty, the newspapers credited McMichael himself, "the efficient and spirited police magistrate . . . whose deportment on the occasion is spoken of in the highest terms by all who witnessed it."[15]

By 1844, significant Philadelphia riots had taken place in 1828, 1829, 1831, 1834, 1835, 1838, 1840, and 1843. Philadelphia was becoming the most riotous of America's cities—something of a distinction, given the competition from Boston, New York, Baltimore, and Cincinnati. The capping indignity came in August 1843, when New York lithographer H. R. Robinson released a print ironically entitled *A View of the City of Brotherly Love*, showing the spirit of William Penn frowning down on every kind of disorder. Some of the violence is personal, from the ragged women—one Black, one white—brawling in the foreground to the gentry more discreetly stabbing and shooting each other indoors behind glass windows. But most of the scene is of public violence. Pennsylvania Hall and a church burn, while Smith's Beneficial Hall (destroyed in 1842) is already in ruins. Members of the Fairmount Engine, dressed in their parade capes, attack the Good Will Engine, depositors make runs on defaulting banks, weavers strike, and Kensington residents—men and women together—tear up a railroad. In the background, the common militia celebrates July 4 with its own melee. Not a constable or sheriff is to be seen. The *Daily Chronicle* denounced the "filthy caricature . . . evidently calculated to fasten a stigma upon our beautiful city," and insisted that "there is a portion of this disgraceful publication grossly libellous." But only a portion.[16]

"The City of Brotherly Love."
Courtesy of the American Antiquarian Society.

Despite their frequency, these riots left relatively few corpses in the street, which was especially surprising given the widespread diffusion of firearms. Since 1790, Pennsylvania's constitution had guaranteed "the right of the citizens to bear arms, in defence of themselves and the state." However ineffective mandatory militia drills might be at preparing the country for invasion, they did teach many white men the basics of loading and firing a musket. And while not every home had a gun, they were common enough that corner groceries sold powder and shot. Some Philadelphians kept shotguns for hunting excursions; others used them to exterminate rats. Newspapers carried ads for weapons and ammunition in between those for schoolbooks and bread, and on Tamarind Street, Henry Deringer Jr. manufactured rifles for hunting and warfare; only later would he develop the pocket pistols that would immortalize his name (misspelled with two Rs). These guns killed; both children and adults regularly shot themselves or loved ones while mishandling weapons. Yet, for the most part, when Americans marched to a riot, they left their guns at home.[17]

While the body count remained low, the riots did considerable damage to property. In an effort to spur Philadelphia officials to greater efforts at preventing riots, in 1836 the Pennsylvania legislature passed an act making the county treasury liable for riot damages, an idea enshrined in English law since 1714 but new to the United States. Unfortunately, responsibility for keeping law and order was as divided as the county itself. In Philadelphia City, the mayor was supposed to keep the peace, helped by two lieutenants, forty-five police officers, and 129 night watchmen whose duties also included lighting the streetlamps. Mayor John Swift, who served as mayor from 1832 to 1841 (with the exception of one year), occasionally showed considerable physical courage, repeatedly leading police forces against mobs. But even he could value political loyalty over competence; in 1834, he fired half of the city's police force for voting Democratic.[18]

Beyond the city's boundaries—Vine Street to the north, Cedar Street to the south—the law was even weaker. Most outlying districts employed just one or two police officers and a handful of watchmen. The exception was Kensington, which employed none at all. There, and in other districts, elected ward constables earned fees for serving civil process at the direction of aldermen, but they received no pay for keeping the peace, and therefore tended not to. "The weakness of the net of criminal justice in Philadelphia is so notorious," the grand jury complained in 1840, "that our comfortable city has become the favorite haunt of rogues of all sorts and sizes." Worse still, because each force had jurisdiction over only its particular city or district, they could not combine to keep order. "A rogue may be chased by a constable to the southern side of Cedar street," lamented the *Public Ledger,* "and then turn around and laugh in the law's face, secure in the territory of a *foreign country!*"[19]

Philadelphia County as a whole—which included both the city and the districts—came under the jurisdiction of the sheriff, who was elected for a single three-year term. While the sheriff had the power to cross Cedar or Vine at will, he would be lucky to find anyone to follow him. True, the sheriff was legally empowered to summon any male above age fifteen to join a posse comitatus. But as riots continued, posses became harder to form. By 1843, the *Chronicle* warned that the sheriff "might as well call upon the stones in the street to rise and aid him, as upon a promiscuous assemblage, unorganized, undistinguished from the mob by any outward badges, and unprepared for such an emergency."[20]

Nowhere was the weakness of the posse system more obvious than in Kensington. In the summer of 1840, residents there rioted to protest the extension of a railroad that, they feared, would disrupt their neighborhood for the benefit of wealthy travelers passing between Philadelphia and New York and whose right of way had been granted by the state legislature over the objections of every representative from Philadelphia County. When the Supreme Court ruled against them, hundreds of angry Kensington residents—including significant numbers of women—insisted that track workers stop their work. The sheriff then assembled a posse of over a hundred men, gathering them in Emery's tavern, owned by the president of the railroad. The posse then waded into the crowd, cracking some skulls with maces and making several arrests. But the much larger crowd counterattacked with "ground apples" (paving stones), injuring some officers and chasing the rest out of Kensington. That evening, the crowd took further revenge. Egged on by adult men, some teenage "boys" smashed the doors and windows of Emery's, where some of the posse were recovering. They then set fire to the building and, as the police inside escaped through a back door, threw stones at arriving fire companies until assured that the tavern was beyond saving. Only then did the mood of the crowd change to one of peace and satisfaction. "Women and children mingled fearlessly and freely in the crowd," noted one observer, "as the consummation of the outrage was going on." Here was an old-fashioned, orderly riot, in which a community, denied relief by the courts, found another means of justice. Eventually, in 1843, the railroad was removed.[21]

Two years after the railroad riot, in November 1842, weavers in Kensington and Moyamensing went on strike and—according to their employers—attacked master weavers, threatening to pull down one's house, beating the wife and breaking the furniture of another, stealing guns from a third, and mutilating the looms of two more. When master weaver Hugh Clark, in his capacity as alderman, attempted to arrest a weaver named Edward Develin, he was "severely maltreated" by a mob that liberated the prisoner. For their part, the weavers disavowed any violence, and insisted that master weaver Charles White had beaten his wife with his own fists. In January, the violence intensified. On January 9 and 10, 1843, hundreds of weavers in Moyamensing and Kensington attacked dwellings where men were working for lower rates, seizing the chains of their looms and destroying them in the streets. They even threatened to burn a large factory and Clark's home.[22]

At the start of the strike in November 1842, the county sheriff was Henry Morris, a respected man, though slowing at age sixty-five. In early December 1842, however, Morris dropped dead of a sudden heart attack. To fill the vacancy, Governor David Porter appointed his own son, William, a twenty-one-year-old lawyer. On January 11, young Sheriff Porter assembled two hundred special constables in the Kensington Commissioners' Hall, then marched them to the Kensington market, a covered arcade, where an estimated three or four hundred men waited with pistols, muskets, clubs, and brickbats torn up from the neighboring sidewalks. As Porter and his men approached, a few guns were fired at them, but Porter pressed on. When they arrived within a hundred yards of the market, the men inside began throwing brickbats and stones, then shouted a loud huzza and charged the posse.[23]

As the *Chronicle* described the affair, "Some few of the constables stood their ground and brought off four prisoners, armed with bludgeons, but the majority took to their heels and ran off as hard as they could scamper." Deserted by most of his posse, Porter tried to make do with the authority of his office. "I am the sheriff!" he cried. "Holy Jasus—you're the one I wanted!" shouted an Irishman, who then clubbed Porter to the ground, hitting him more once he was down. Porter was so badly injured that some days later he remained unable to stand, perhaps because doctors had applied more than a hundred leeches to his wounds. Confined to his bed, he turned his duties over to a deputy and wrote to George Cadwalader, newly installed as brigadier general, formally alerting him that "the civil authorities are no longer able to preserve the peace" and requesting military aid. Exactly what form that aid would take would be Cadwalader's decision, but, Porter suggested, "these measures ought to be of the most decided character."[24]

Cadwalader accordingly summoned six companies of volunteer militia, more than 250 men in total. While most of them saw no action, at least one was present for the peaceful arrest of three rioters. And that seemed to have been sufficient, for by January 14, the *Chronicle* reported that Kensington "was in a perfect state of quietude during the whole of yesterday. . . . The weavers have all returned to their work." The lesson, it seemed, was that a determined mob could fight off a sheriff's posse, injuring the sheriff in the process, but a major show of force by the militia would so intimidate the rioters that the worst of them would submit to arrest. Only a man confident of his peacemaking ability would now want to be sheriff.[25]

By the late 1830s, Morton McMichael's ties to the Democratic Party were weakening. At first a Democrat, he had won election as Spring Garden alderman as a nonpartisan candidate. In 1840, a group of disaffected Democrats nominated McMichael for the Third District's seat in Congress, and when the incumbent Whig decided not to seek reelection, the Whigs nominated McMichael as well. He had no hope of winning the general election against the regular Democrat, but he did what he could, giving "fearless and ardent" speeches in favor of Whig presidential candidate William Henry Harrison. Two years later, not long after Cadwalader's election as brigadier general, McMichael was appointed quartermaster for the First Division, giving him a place in the county's militia structure. Then, in 1843, he ran for sheriff.[26]

The post was lucrative; the sheriff collected fees worth an estimated $20,000 per year. But by 1843, the sheriffalty had become a dangerous line of work. "In times of turbulency and danger," noted the *Daily Chronicle*, "when the law and its ministers are boldly defied in open riot, and the lives and property of citizens placed at the mercy of a reckless and vindictive mob, then personal energy and unflinching determination are requisite to quell disturbance, and prevent open acts of violence and destruction."[27]

Confident he had these qualities, McMichael ran as a Whig. In a county with a Democratic majority, that was a liability, but not a fatal one; a strong candidate could overcome the party loyalties of a fair number of voters. And McMichael was strong. The nominally independent *Daily Chronicle*, whose editor knew McMichael well, called him "a man of active business habits, sterling talents, unquestionable integrity, and a generous combination of the social virtues." Thanks to his "conciliatory disposition" he had "few, if any enemies among either Whigs or Democrats." Calling on "the owners of property—the friends of order—and the enemies of lawlessness and disorder." Regardless of party allegiance, to choose "a man in whom the public have confidence." The *Chronicle* reminded readers of McMichael's defense of the orphans' asylum in 1838, which it considered "ample evidence of the manly and determined spirit which made him a terror to evil doers." "The choice of a Sheriff," it warned, "may be an issue between public order and disorder—a supremacy of law or mobs."[28]

McMichael also appealed to Irish Americans, traditionally a Democratic voting bloc. He had embraced his ancestry, joining the Hibernian Society for the Relief of Emigrants from Ireland. (Democrats groused that he sought Irish votes "on the strength of the Mc. to his name.") A more significant factor may have been Irish American bitterness over the failure of the Democratic party to elect Irish-born candidates to major office. "Thus excluded," warned a writer, Irishmen "cease to be American citizens; and if not citizens, what are they but slaves! or if not slaves, at best reduced to a political level with the free colored population." McMichael's Democratic rival, James Hutchinson, was rumored to have once called on a mob to "lick these God damned Irish sons of bitches."[29]

On election day, Hutchinson did carry several of the outlying districts, beating McMichael by more than six hundred votes in Southwark, and by narrow margins in the Northern Liberties, Moyamensing, Kensington, and even McMichael's Spring Garden. But these margins were too small to overcome McMichael's 3,253 margin in the Whig-dominated city, giving McMichael a countywide victory of 1,587 votes. On his first day in office,

McMichael "made a clean sweep of all the old clerks and deputies, down even to the bill poster," replacing them with his own men. Disappointed native-born Democrats denounced McMichael as the winner of the "naturalized vote," and blamed the Irish for the damage they had done.[30]

Beyond distributing the spoils of office, the new sheriff made plans to return Philadelphia to a state of order. In late November, he proposed a "permanent Volunteer *Posse*, for the suppression of disturbances of the public peace." He recruited about three or four hundred like-minded men, who recommended that the sheriff keep a list of names of volunteers who would be ready "at the shortest notice" to help the sheriff restore order. Some of the men who volunteered as captains of posse companies also held militia commissions. But the posses themselves would not be militia companies; they would not wear uniforms, save for "some distinctive badge or ribbon by which we may be known from the rioters." And rather than carrying muskets, they would be issued, "if thought proper, such maces as are ordinarily used by officers of the peace." "The effort of such an organization once brought to bear in a riot will be conclusive," the *Daily Chronicle* assured its readers, "and prevent the recurrence of such acts."[31]

Around the same time, McMichael asked the Pennsylvania legislature for an English-style riot act. Under his proposal, if "twelve or more persons were assembled together in a riotous manner," the sheriff, mayor, or any justice of the peace could demand that they go home or be treated as felons. If "it became necessary to kill, maim or wound, any person or persons," the civil officer and anyone assisting him would be held harmless; indeed, the bill also assured that they would be paid for their services. The provision for lethal force spooked legislators, and the bill got nowhere. If McMichael were to face future riots, he would do so with uncertain authority and resources.[32]

Augustus Pleasonton.
Courtesy of the National Gallery of Art, Washington.

6

Bayonets and Ball Cartridges

At the start of the upsurge in rioting in the 1830s, city authorities sought to contain the violence with the traditional tools of watchmen and civilian posses, lightly armed. In New York in 1834, the mayor himself tried to quell a riot, bringing with him police officers, constables, and about forty watchmen. But the rioters were unimpressed, and at least a dozen watchmen and police officers were wounded. One captain suffered a fractured skull, and a watchman died of his wounds. The following year, Baltimore's mayor initially resisted calling out the militia in response to attacks on bank officers and their houses. Believing that "the peace of our cities was preserved in ordinary troubles by the ordinary police; that the

64

constable was not armed with a musket but a baton," he summoned citizen volunteers and armed them with two-feet-long sticks of poplar or white pine. This "Rolling Pin Guard" held back the crowd for a while, but after they were showered with stones, the mayor relented and issued firearms.[1]

As the violence persisted, authorities increasingly turned to the volunteer militia, which offered both more lethal weapons and a better sense of discipline than companies of watchmen or posses of civilians. For example, after four years without riot duty against canal workers, militia intervened in six canal riots in 1834 and 1835. But no one was entirely sure what the militia was supposed to do when summoned to a riot. Organized to repel a foreign invasion, the volunteers armed themselves for the battlefield, with muskets, cavalry sabers, and cannon issued to each state by the United States Ordnance Department. And they trained as soldiers preparing to fight off an invader, not as police readying to face a mob. The military magazines published by volunteers likewise featured US Army drill instructions, biographies of Revolutionary War officers, and accounts of battles of the Napoleonic Wars. They offered no analyses of militia actions against rioters.[2]

Some officers hoped that merely showing up would be enough. In 1841, Cadwalader coauthored a report asserting that the "frown of disapprobation" of their fellow citizens would demoralize a mob more surely than "being threatened with the bullet or the bayonet." That was a nice thought, but not one borne out by experience. In practice, militia called for riot duty typically used some blend of intimidation and actual physical force.[3]

In July 1834, a colonel in New York City drilled his men in both bayonet and firings, then refused to march against rioters until his men were issued lethal ammunition. After some debate, the mayor and aldermen acceded to the request. Once on the street, the men were stoned and spat upon, and—recorded the unit's history—"were with difficulty restrained from opening fire at will on their assailants." Yet restrained they were, and they relied only on their bayonets—and the locust-wood clubs of accompanying police—to chase away a mob. At the end of the day, the colonel boasted of "a victory, without firing a 'shot!'" Impressed by this performance, in 1836, the New York state legislature specifically empowered the mayor of New York City to summon troops to his aid "whenever their services shall be required in aid of the civil authorities to quell riots, suppress insurrection, to protect the property or *preserve the tranquility of the city.*" In Baltimore, Boston, and Washington, men organized new companies specifically to keep domestic order.[4]

Nor did troops merely disperse crowds; acting with law enforcement officers, militia officers sought to arrest rioters, sometimes by the dozen. Militia eventually learned that mass arrests might not be worth the trouble. In Indiana, they arrested more than a hundred Irish canal workers before realizing they had no place to detain them. The troops settled for eight men suspected of leading the violence, threatening them with bayonets until they reached Indianapolis.[5]

To subdue mobs, a threat needed to be credible, and troops would kill if they must. In September 1831, the sheriff of Providence County, Rhode Island, tried to stop a two-day riot with the constables and watchmen of the town of Providence. When they failed, the governor ordered out the volunteer militia, which was met with hisses and stones. On September 24, a particularly aggressive mob tried to seize the soldiers' muskets. The sheriff shouted warnings, then the soldiers fired into the air. Still the crowd pelted them with stones, until, in desperation, an infantry captain ordered his men to fire into the crowd, wounding eighteen, four of whom died from their wounds. An official committee sanctioned the action. "The men could stand the pelting no longer," it concluded. "Surrounded as they were, no effectual use could be made of the bayonet. They were obliged to fire, or suffer their ranks to be broken. Had their ranks been broken the lives of many if not all of the soldiers would have been sacrificed, and their arms fallen into the possession of the mob." For the rest of the 1830s, this remained the sole case of militia firing into an urban crowd, but officers prepared for further lethal combat.[6]

No militia officer was more ready—perhaps even eager—to fire into a mob than Colonel Augustus Pleasonton. Born in Washington, in 1808, Pleasonton had graduated from West Point at age seventeen and had spent four years in the army before resigning his commission to study law in Philadelphia. In 1835, still in his twenties, he had been elected to command the Pennsylvania Militia's First Regiment of Artillery. Though slightly younger than Cadwalader he resembled him in appearance, with flowing dark hair and impressive whiskers.[7]

No doubt Pleasonton was as ready as any militia officer to repel a foreign foe. As a small boy, he himself may have witnessed the British raid on Washington in September 1814, during which his father, a state department clerk, had spirited away the Constitution and the Declaration of Independence before enemy troops could burn them. But Pleasonton was equally ready to defend American government against its domestic enemies. He despaired that military inaction permitted riots to continue until "the mob have satiated their appetites for violence and outrage, [and] order is restored by the exhaustion of the rioters; and lasts just until some new cause of excitement produces similar consequences in a little while after." When his fellow officers debated the rightness of using volunteers against fellow citizens, Pleasonton concluded that "a great part of the disinclination of the volunteers . . . to fire upon a mob, proceeds . . . from sheer cowardice, and these same men would behave ill in the presence of an enemy. . . . To the devil with such officers and such soldiers!"[8]

If Pleasonton was going to fight, he would be ready to kill. In June 1838, for example, Sheriff John Watmough summoned troops to suppress an anticipated race riot in Moyamensing, directing that each soldier be issued two rounds of ball cartridge. Thinking this insufficient, Colonel Pleasonton (who happened to be Watmough's brother-in-law) issued at least ten rounds per man, then sent his quartermaster to the state arsenal to get two cannon ready if needed. The next day, on the advice of Major General Robert Patterson, Pleasonton borrowed 1,700 more cartridges from the US Army.[9]

Pleasonton was not alone in wish for such forceful responses. Marylander Roger Taney—soon to become chief justice of the United States—probably spoke for many when he wrote of the 1835 Baltimore riot that "there ought not have been a moment's hesitation about the use of fire arms, the firm and free use of them the moment that force was attempted by the mob." A New York newspaper alluded to Napoleon's claim that blank cartridges only emboldened a mob, and that it was best to shoot real ammunition first, and resort to blanks only when the crowd was on the run. The newspaper concurred, arguing that "a few well-directed vollies, in the memorable Sixth Ward election riots, and the abolition riots which followed soon afterward, would have at once put an end to the disturbances, and taught a salutary lesson." Such a lesson came in 1842 as Cincinnati mobs formed in response to bank failures. Rather than protect the fraudulent banks that had ruined them, most militiamen declined to muster. Captain O. M. Mitchell of the Citizen's Guards marched with just twelve men, each supplied with only two rounds of ball cartridge. When they were about to be overwhelmed by the mob, the sheriff ordered them to wheel and fire. They did, wounding at least three.[10]

Mitchell's actions showed that the militia could kill, but the refusal of so many Cincinnati volunteers to muster also reflected the truth that troops—either as individuals or as whole companies—might follow their own sympathies and prejudices rather than the directions of elected officials. In 1835, members of a volunteer company in Vicksburg, Mississippi, led a lynch mob that hanged five men without trial. A few months later, the ladies of the town presented the Vicksburg Volunteers with a flag, in part to praise their "gallantry and courage" in the mob action. In 1837, Boston militia units insulted a primarily Irish company, which was then attacked by a mob. And in 1838, the distinction between mob and militia faded as armed men in Missouri sought to expel Mormon settlers. When militia units marched against him, Mormon leader Joseph Smith complained, "the Governor is mob, the militia are mob, and the whole state is mob." Following some bloodshed, the Mormons fled east to Illinois, but Illinois governor Thomas Ford also proclaimed his helplessness. "The militia may be relied upon to do battle in a popular service," Ford explained in a posthumously published memoir. "But if mobs are raised to drive out horse thieves, to put down claim-jumpers, to destroy an abolition press, or to expel an odious sect, the militia cannot be brought to act against them efficiently. The people cannot be used to put down the people."[11]

The Pennsylvania Militia faced its own test of political neutrality in an event later recalled half-humorously as "the Buckshot War." In October 1838, a close election between supporters of Governor Joseph Ritner (a coalition of Whigs and Anti-Masons) and Democratic challengers was made all the more fraught due to proposed amendments to the state constitution that would reduce the governor's power. Returns showed a majority for Democrat David Porter, leading Democrats to try to block the new constitution from going into effect, thus preserving the power of the office for Porter. Both sides claimed a majority in the state's house of representatives and elected rival speakers, each backed by crowds of angry spectators. Philadelphians hauled one of the speakers off the platform, and three senators escaped manhandling by jumping out a window. [12]

The Buckshot War.
Courtesy of the Library of Congress.

Ritner declared that a "lawless, infuriated, armed mob" had made it "unsafe for the Legislative bodies to assemble in the Capitol," and he ordered General Patterson to bring his First Division from Philadelphia to Harrisburg to restore order. Patterson was willing, to a point. "It is the highest privilege, as it is one of the most important duties, of the citizen soldier to sustain the civil authority whenever the emergency occurs which renders necessary a resort to armed force," Patterson told his men. "The spirit of misrule must be instantly, energetically, and effectually suppressed." But some Pennsylvanians suspected Ritner of a coup d'etat. Smelling partisanship, Colonel James Page, a Democrat, tried to get his fellow officers to disobey the order to march. When they refused, he told them that he would take his company to Harrisburg but "would in no event order his men to fire upon those who might be creating difficulties there." And when the troops (Captain George Cadwalader among them) arrived in Lancaster,

Democrats greeted them with groans and hisses. In Harrisburg, Democrats were more subtle, wooing the soldiers with gifts of poultry and pies, along with newspapers denouncing Ritner. In return, they asked the troops for buckshot cartridges as souvenirs, gradually disarming some companies.[13]

Patterson responded with deliberate political neutrality. He asked his men "to carefully abstain from all political discussion, or from doing or saying any thing calculated to produce unpleasant feelings, or collision with citizens. A soldier belongs to no party." When Governor Ritner sounded out Patterson on his willingness to obey orders, the general explained his limits. "I said that I had not come for any political purpose and would not sustain any party in the wrong," Patterson later recalled, "that my command was composed of both parties, nearly as many of the one as the other." He would not take orders from any claimant to the speakership of either chamber. He would not order his troops to fire, except in self-defense. And while he was prepared to take orders from the governor, he would only obey proper orders. A command to clear the capitol would not count. Moreover, Patterson insisted that every order from Ritner be in writing. Ritner took this as a lack of "proper subordination," and he contemplated sacking Patterson and taking direct command of the troops.[14]

Pleasonton, who just months before had expressed his disgust with his fellow officers' disinclination to fire on a mob, was now "much disturbed at the entire want of preparation at Head Quarters of the Division, for a struggle that may be near at hand." Patterson, he believed, had thought through neither the legal questions of which civil officers might appropriately claim his aid, the leadership questions of which of his officers and companies were most reliable, nor the tactical questions of how one might clear a senate chamber. On this last question, Pleasonton offered an elaborate plan in which some of Patterson's best men would be equipped with axes to chop down the senate doors, and another group would be given ladders with which to storm the windows, while double-shotted cannon fired at the capitol's northern facade in the hopes of scaring the mob into fleeing through the southern exits. Somehow, Pleasonton imagined that this plan would minimize bloodshed.[15]

Patterson ignored the plan and was able to keep his troops out of the capitol and out of the political process. The legislative leadership, he insisted, "must be settled by the Senators and Representatives themselves." No mob stormed the senate chamber, and Ritner's order dismissing Patterson remained in the governor's pocket. A week after the troops' arrival, three Whigs caucused with the Democrats, allowing the latter to decisively elect the speaker of the house and install Porter as governor. Patterson had successfully avoided both outright disobedience to orders and charges of interference in politics. He described his troops as men who would leave their homes quickly, at great sacrifice, and with plenty of ammunition, but who would never threaten American democracy.[16]

With Americans uncertain about the proper role of the militia, Philadelphia authorities avoided summoning them to riot duty. Philadelphia mayor John Swift was himself a militia officer, having risen to the rank of colonel and almost to brigadier general. Yet he used the military as little as possible. On the third night of a serious race riot in 1834, Swift ordered two militia companies to arms, but they remained in their armories while a posse confronted the mob. Four years later, when a mob threatened Pennsylvania Hall, Swift calmed the crowd briefly, boasting "We never call out the military here! We do not need such measures!" But though the mob cheered Swift's pronouncement, it also proved him wrong, for it soon burned down the hall while Swift's police watched helplessly. Swift's friends defended him, arguing that calling out the militia would have violated "the spirit of the people, and the genius of our institutions." Not everyone agreed. "Let our Mayor, who never *flinches* from duty because danger is in its path, call upon the military to aid the civil arm," thundered the *Public Ledger* in 1838. "Let our volunteer companies, under direction of the civil authority, be upon the spot, with bayonets and ball cartridges. Better is it that all the ruffians in our city, even were they a hundred thousand instead of three thousand, should bite the dust, and leave their blood knee deep in the streets, than that the great principle of freedom of speech and the press be surrendered."[17]

After that disgrace, Philadelphia authorities began to call on troops more frequently. In August 1842, once his outnumbered posse had been chased away from a race riot, Mayor John Scott sought military aid "as the last and only means of restoring quiet and order." With the newly elected Cadwalader summering at Saratoga Springs, it fell to Colonel Pleasonton to muster sixteen companies—506 men in all, including twenty cavalrymen and crews for two six-pound cannon—and deploy them at key points. Preparing for the worst, Pleasonton issued five rounds of ball cartridge to each man. Despite his belief that some mobs needed shooting, in this case he never felt the need to order a volley. Two years later, he would judge differently.[18]

Bishop Francis Patrick Kenrick.
Courtesy of the Catholic Historical Research Center of the Archdiocese of Philadelphia.

7

The Gospel of the Devil

W hile Pleasonton and his fellow officers pondered how they would subdue trouble if it started, Levin and the Natives sought an Irish Catholic villain a bit closer to home than Daniel O'Connell, the champion of home rule for Ireland. They found Bishop Francis Patrick Kenrick. While the gentle bishop would seem an unlikely foil for Levin, he shared some of Levin's eloquence and his firm convictions, especially when it came to educating the next generation. That was enough for Levin to twist Kenrick's image into the antagonist he needed.

Kenrick was born in Dublin, Ireland, on December 3, 1796. His uncle, the parish priest, guided both Francis and his younger brother, Peter, into the priesthood. At the College of the Propaganda in Rome—dedicated to training missionaries for work in non-Catholic lands—Kenrick studied Scripture, philosophy, and theology, as well as Greek, Hebrew, French, Italian, and Latin, which he mastered so completely that he began to use it for correspondence and even his diary. In 1821, just as Kenrick was finishing his studies, Bishop Joseph Flaget of Bardstown, Kentucky, asked Rome to send a good theology professor. Kenrick seized the opportunity, writing his mother of his eagerness to labor in "an abandoned part of the world." Four and a half months later, he arrived in Bardstown, where he met Flaget's every expectation. Tall and handsome, with dark blue eyes, the young priest tended to the needs of Kentucky's few and scattered Catholics while amicably sparring with the local Protestants he regarded with a mix of pity and amusement. If Flaget had had his way, Kenrick would have remained in Bardstown as his successor. But Rome had a bigger job for the young prodigy.[1]

The diocese of Philadelphia—which covered all of Pennsylvania as well as Delaware and western New Jersey—had a long tradition of Catholic worship. By 1829, Philadelphia County alone housed perhaps twenty-five thousand Catholics, making it the second-largest Catholic community in the United States after Baltimore. Yet the diocese had become an embarrassment to the Church. For nearly twenty years, its bishops, priests, and lay trustees had been bickering over control of the diocese, especially its property. Nominally the man in charge was Irish-born bishop Henry Conwell. Already in his seventies at the time of his consecration in 1820, the learned Conwell had proven unable to resolve the spat, and in 1828 he had been summoned back to Rome. Against instructions, he returned to Philadelphia the following year.[2]

Needing a man in Philadelphia with unquestioned energy, intelligence, and loyalty to Rome, Pope Pius VIII chose Kenrick. Old Conwell would be allowed to retain his title as a kindness, but Rome named Kenrick coadjutor, with the expectation that he would run the diocese. "What a charge to fall on so weak & worthless a being as myself!" Kenrick lamented to a friend. But orders were orders, and on June 6, 1830, in Bardstown's St. Joseph's Cathedral, Flaget consecrated Kenrick and gave the young bishop—who was nearly penniless—a hand-me-down miter. "A tinge of modesty suffuses countenance, but he is never agitated," exulted a Catholic journalist about the new bishop. "His reasoning and arguments are cogent and powerful; his diction chaste, his language copious, his figures striking and appropriate, and his appeals to the heart irresistible."[3]

Despite Rome's instructions, Kenrick and Conwell struggled over power, and even the house they shared. At one point, Kenrick ordered Conwell's furniture moved from a parlor into the hall, then changed the locks. Conwell waited until Kenrick departed on a visitation to Pittsburgh, then retaliated by ordering Kenrick's belongings removed to a warehouse. Only in August 1831, when Pope Gregory XVI confirmed that Kenrick would have the full authority in the diocese, did Conwell accept his diminished role.[4]

Kenrick also needed to subdue the troublesome trustees of St. Mary's Church, which served the wealthiest of Philadelphia's Catholics and functioned as cathedral-church. "A different order of things prevails in this country," one congregant explained in 1820. "The opinions and wishes of the people require to be consulted to a degree unknown in Europe." They hoped to create, in Philadelphia and the United States, a Catholic church that reflected American ideals of separation of powers and democratic self-government. Kenrick saw only laymen overstepping their bounds, and in April 1831 he took the awful step of suspending all divine services at St. Mary's. After four weeks of brinkmanship, the trustees finally disavowed "all right to interfere in the spiritual concerns of the Church," and Kenrick reopened St. Mary's on his terms. To solidify his victory, he took American citizenship, which allowed him to insist that all church property be transferred to him. By the time of his thirty-fifth birthday, in December 1831, Francis Kenrick had broken the troublesome diocese to harness.[5]

Secure in power, Kenrick could plan for the future of a diocese rapidly filling with his fellow Irish Catholics. To serve them, he launched an ambitious building plan. Between 1830 and 1843, Kenrick began construction on nine new churches in Philadelphia County, compared to only four that had greeted him when he arrived. The most magnificent was a new cathedral: the Church of St. John the Evangelist, whose Thirteenth Street facade boasted an impressive Gothic doorway flanked by two towers, while buttresses and arched windows on the side walls continued the Gothic theme. As Father John Hughes boasted, "as a religious edifice, it will be the pride of the city. The leading Protestants and infidels proclaim it the only building that is entitled to be called a church, inasmuch as its appearance indicates its use, and there is no danger of mistaking it for a work-shop." Other churches were more easily mistaken, for Kenrick was happy to dedicate a simple structure whose cellar and foundations had been dug by the worshippers themselves, so long as it served the parishioners and God. Indeed, he would dedicate an unfinished building, with prayer now and plaster later. But those churches would only endure if Philadelphia's Catholic children retained their faith. And that meant finding a way for good Catholics to attend school.[6]

In the early part of the nineteenth century, Pennsylvania schools had been private institutions, with townships paying tuition only for the children of parents who could not afford school fees. In 1834, however, the legislature established a system of common schools, free to all children. Though Philadelphia's system became the county's largest budget item by far, it was also its pride. By the 1840s, Philadelphia's grammar schools were educating more than thirty thousand children, though only 350 boys, ages twelve and up, could attend its central high school. The *Chronicle* called the school system "the pet of the people," and noted "its effects upon the happiness and prosperity of the people, and the permanency of our system of government, are unparalleled in the history of the world." Moreover, explained the paper, the schools were crucial training grounds for republican virtue, where "the child of the wealthy and of the indigent sit side by side, enjoy the same equality, and the same opportunities of intellectual advancement; they mingle together in classes, and after school hours, forming a congeniality of thought and sentiment, which may attend them through life."[7]

From the start, the designers of the public schools sought to teach morality to their charges as armor against the vices they might encounter on the streets. Yet they also hoped to keep schools out of debates over religion. In 1827, for instance, Massachusetts required that school committees "shall never direct any school books to be purchased or used in any of the schools under their superintendence, which are calculated to favor any particular religious sect or tenet." Those two imperatives clashed as Protestants and Catholics agreed that schoolchildren should read the Bible, yet disagreed about what a Bible was.[8]

Such disputes dated back to the early sixteenth century, when Martin Luther emphasized the doctrine of *sola scriptura*—by Scripture alone—meaning that the written Bible was the sole source of divine teaching. To encourage laypeople to read the Bible themselves, rather than rely on the teachings of priests, Luther translated the Bible into German. This was no great novelty; since the development of the printing press in the 1430s, printers had issued translations of the Bible in several modern European languages. But all of these translations had started with the Vulgate: the Latin version first compiled by St. Jerome in the fourth century. By contrast, Luther started with the extant Hebrew and Greek texts of the Old and New Testaments. He was followed in this by others, including William Tyndale, who devised an English version, only to be strangled for heresy by Catholic authorities. [9]

After King Henry VIII's break with Rome, English Catholics fled to Douai, a university town in the Spanish Netherlands, where they produced their own English-language Scriptures, which became known as the Douay Bible. Unlike the Protestant versions, which, following Luther and Tyndale, had relied on Hebrew and Greek texts, the Douay was a translation of the Latin Vulgate. English Protestants responded with yet another version based on Hebrew and Greek texts, which became known as the King James Bible for its sponsor, King James I of England. [10]

While a casual reader might regard the Douay and King James Bibles as similar, a more careful inspection revealed significant divergences. "Take heed to yourselves, and to the whole flock, wherein the Holy Ghost hath placed you *bishops*, to *rule* the church of God, which he hath purchased with his own blood," admonished the Douay version of Acts 20:28. The King James disagreed. "Take heed therefore unto yourselves, and to all the flock, over the which the Holy Ghost hath made you *overseers*, to *feed* the church of God," it commanded. Likewise, where Catholic translations had *priests*, the King James spoke of *elders*. In the Douay Bible, Christians *did penance*; in the King James, they *repented*. Experts could point out hundreds of such differences, each with some significance for religious beliefs or practices. Reprintings of Reformation-era theological tracts, and sometimes daily newspapers, alerted nineteenth-century readers to the divergences between the translations. Moreover, Protestant Bibles omitted seven of the forty-six books that Catholics considered canonical portions of the Old Testament. A final, crucial distinction was that Catholic bishops believed that Bibles should include "notes drawn from the holy fathers of the Church, or from learned Catholics," while Protestants offered many of theirs "without notes or comment," believing the divine text sufficient. [11]

By the early nineteenth century, Protestants and Catholics promoted their rival Bibles as tools to win converts and maintain the faith of their existing adherents. Founded in 1816, the American Bible Society (ABS) devoted itself to the distribution of Bibles "without note or comment." In 1843 alone, the ABS reported printing 215,605 Bibles and Testaments in nineteen different languages and distributing them to needy seamen, boatmen, immigrants, prisoners, and hospital patients. The Philadelphia Bible Society, which remained separate but had a similar mission, distributed thousands of volumes as well. [12]

Initially, the ABS welcomed Catholics as partners in a great cause, working with Catholic clergy to distribute French, Spanish, and German Bibles (all translated from the approved Latin) to Catholic congregations in the United States and Latin America. But the society refused to distribute Douay Bibles, insisting on the King James Bible for English speakers. Comparable efforts in Europe led Pope Leo XII to warn of societies working "to translate—or rather to pervert—the Holy Bible into the vulgar languages of every nation." The result, he feared, would be "that, by a perverse interpretation, the Gospel of Christ be turned into a human Gospel, or, what is still worse, into the Gospel of the Devil." Thus prepared, European Catholics were wary of American Protestants bearing gifts. One ABS agent tried handing Bibles to immigrants arriving in New York by ship, only to have Irish arrivals push away his proffered gifts. "If you give one to me," an Irishwoman snapped at an American Protestant, "I will take it with me and *burn* it." [13]

Protestants could not, or would not, believe that the King James Bible served any one denomination over another. "An imperfectly translated Bible is better than none," one reasoned. Through malice or ignorance, some Protestants circulated the false rumor that the pope had forbidden all reading of Bibles in vernacular languages, thus excluding it from most family and civic life. In fact, Catholics agreed about the importance of translated Bibles, but they rejected Protestant claims about the King James version which, if they were going to be blunt, they considered "a perverted translation of a *fragment* of the Bible."[14]

In both Europe and the United States, Protestants and Catholics carried their disagreements over Bibles into debates over children's education. In 1811, the Society for Promoting the Education of the Poor of Ireland claimed "to afford the same facilities for Education to all classes of professing Christians, without any attempt to interfere with the peculiar religious opinions of any," even as it insisted that "the Scriptures without note or comment shall be read; but all Catechisms and books of religious controversy excluded." In effect, that meant requiring Protestant Bibles and banning Catholic versions. Eager for the funding yet reluctant to impose the Protestant practice on impressionable children, some Catholic teachers devised such stratagems as reading the Bible without note, without comment, and without students, admitting their pupils only when the danger had passed.[15]

In 1820, Irish Catholic champion Daniel O'Connell offered a more open challenge. "The Bible never can be received without note or comment by the Catholic persuasion," he explained while Protestants heckled him. "Gentlemen hissers, we believe that the entire word of God has not been preserved in writing," he continued. Catholics "must have *tradition,* which we also call the word of God." O'Connell had lost that argument in 1820, but following his successful achievement of Catholic Emancipation in 1829, the British government proposed a national system in which Bible reading would be limited, and some schools would be managed by Protestants, others by Catholics. This alarmed some Presbyterian clergy who insisted on Bible reading throughout the day. With mobs of Orangemen behind them, some threatened or even attacked schoolhouses, smashing objects and painting "P" for "popery" on doors and windows. For their part, Catholic clergy continued to complain of Catholic children forced "to attend at proselyting schools, there to learn heresy from a Protestant Bible, expounded by a Protestant teacher." Officially, however, children were guaranteed the right to absent themselves from any religious instruction their parents found objectionable.[16]

The same dilemma faced Americans: how to provide moral education when believers disagreed over what that meant. Some Protestants expected schools to function as explicitly religious institutions. In his 1841 address assuring listeners that Catholicism posed scant threat, Presbyterian minister Thomas Brainerd noted that "Every common school in our land where the Bible is read, as well as every Sabbath-school, is a tower of strength to our cause." Some years later, a Presbyterian would taunt Catholics: "We have a mill, of which the common school is the nether, and the Bible and its institutions the upper stone; into this mill let us cast the people of all countries and forms of religion that come here, and they will come out in the grist Americans and Protestants." Other Protestants argued that the King James Bible belonged in schools as a civic, rather than a religious, text. "There can be no reasonable doubt that the Bible is the basis of our civil government," argued a Baptist newspaper, "and if it is to be rejected from our public institutions, they must all fall." For their part, American Catholic bishops recommended that scriptures "be found in the houses of the faithful," not in public schools, where, they complained, the Bible was "too often made the subject of a vulgar jest, it sinks to the level of task-books, and shares the aversion and the remarks which are generally bestowed upon them by children."[17]

New York City's schools were run by the Public School Society, a nondenominational group of Protestants supported by state funds. Rather than rely on schools they considered Protestant, Catholics established free schools without state support, which, by 1840, educated about three thousand children citywide. Failing that, they kept their children home. In part as a result, less than 60 percent of city children ages five to sixteen attended common schools, compared to a statewide average of 96 percent. Describing Catholic immigrants' hostility toward the Public School Society system, Bishop John Hughes—himself an Irish immigrant—explained that "they would no more trust their children to it than to that tyrannical system of British mis-government which their fathers knew so well, and from which they derived the sad legacy of ignorance and poverty."[18]

Frustrated, Hughes tried electoral politics—a bold intervention of a Catholic clergyman into temporal matters. As the 1841 legislative election approached, he carefully endorsed only ten of the thirteen Democratic nominees for New York City. When those ten won election and the remaining three lost to their Whig rivals, Hughes had shown his power to swing elections. In April 1842, a chastened legislature worked out a compromise, shifting power from the Public School Society toward an elected board of education that would treat each city ward as the equivalent of an upstate town, and thus in control of its own school. Moreover, the new law denied funds to any school "in which any religious sectarian doctrine or tenet shall be taught, inculcated or practiced." Hughes still hoped to find the funds for a system of Catholic schools, but for the moment he was glad that poor Catholics would have some place to learn until then. Conversely, staunch Protestants fretted about a "High Priest . . . standing before the *ballot box*, the citadel of American liberties, dictating to his obedient followers the ticket they must vote."[19]

Three days after Governor William Seward signed the bill into law, New York voters chose a new council and mayor. On the afternoon of election day, Protestants—both native- and Irish-born—hunted Catholics in the Sixth Ward, leading to a street fight witnessed by thousands. The Protestants trashed the Sixth Ward Hotel, then proceeded to St. Patrick's Cathedral, whose grounds also included Bishop Hughes's house. Hughes was in Philadelphia at the time, but the frail seventy-seven-year old bishop John Dubois lay bedridden inside, listening in terror as stones and bricks crashed through the windows. Mayor Robert Morris arrived accompanied by police, and they were soon reinforced by a body of Irish women, who prayed as they put themselves between Dubois and his assailants. Though the bishop and the cathedral survived, the incident showed how debates over schoolbooks could escalate into violence.[20]

Like their counterparts in New York, Philadelphia school officials struggled to define the appropriate role of religious texts in classroom. By the 1840s, the city and county of Philadelphia, which together composed School District Number 1, was divided into eleven sections. The city and each district or township appointed directors for the sections, and each section named some of its directors to the board of controllers for the entire district. From the start, Catholics served as both directors and controllers, and by the early 1840s they estimated that about five thousand Catholic children attended the public schools.[21]

County officials struggled to reconcile the public's wish for moral instruction with the constitutional mandate to separate church and state. At some point in the early 1830s, a Catholic school director was troubled to find that one school had purchased copies of an anti-Catholic biography of Martin Luther to distribute as prizes to its best students. To avoid such awkwardness, in 1834, the board resolved to limit the public-school curriculum to "the ordinary branches of elementary education," leaving parents to supplement whatever religious instruction they wished during the Sabbath. It forbade "the introduction or use of any religious exercises, books or lessons into the public schools, which have not been adopted by the Board." That last clause, of course, legalized any religious books that *had* been adopted by the board, and from the start this included the King James Bible. State policy was equally ambiguous. A February 1838 report by Thomas Burrowes, superintendent of public schools, prohibited any *"catechism, creed confession, or manual of faith"* on the grounds that "sectarian instruction" was the business of a child's parent and spiritual teacher. Yet the same report recommended that "The *Old and New Testaments*, containing the best extant code of morality, in simple, beautiful and pure language, shall be used as a school book for Reading, without comment by the Teacher, but not as a text book for religious discussion."[22]

Bishop Kenrick doubted that the Burrowes compromise would work. "The Protestant bible is put into the hands of all the children, and used as a reading book," he complained. "Thus our religious rights in the education of our youth are seriously infringed." But the "venom of bigotry" against Hughes's efforts in New York led Kenrick to seek a quieter path in Philadelphia. Kenrick never endorsed political candidates the way Hughes had. Nor did he have reason to; Philadelphia already had what Hughes had worked so hard to achieve: a system of schools under the control of locally elected directors. But Pennsylvania's compromise proved fragile.[23]

In April 1842, the District of Southwark fired two Catholic school-teachers for refusing to read the Protestant Bible to their students. Then, in neighboring Moyamensing, a Protestant teacher whipped a Catholic girl for refusing to read the King James, telling the whole class that "all those who loved God" were as good as any priest. The following day, according to the *Catholic Herald*'s sensational account, the same teacher demanded that another student read from the same Bible:

"Why do you grow pale?" asked the gentle hearted inquisitor.

"I'm delicate ma'am, and afraid of being whipped," answered the child.

"And would bear a whipping rather than read the Bible?" asked Miss M.

"Yes, ma'am," sobbed out the young martyr.

"Sit down you little fool," rejoined the Teacher, and the poor trembling child sat down with all the merit, but without the punishment of martyrdom.

In yet another school, a child heeded her father's instructions to bring a Douay Bible to school for use when the Bible reading was required. Though she escaped a whipping, the teacher detained her after school hours as punishment. With both teachers and students under attack, Catholics feared they would be driven out of the public schools entirely while still being taxed to support them. "Catholics are anxious to avoid agitation in which Religious divisions might be mixed up in any way with political strife," insisted one. "But they would be unworthy [of] the privileges of freemen, if they tamely acquiesce in this flagrant violation of their constitutional rights."[24]

In the long run, Kenrick wished that "good Catholic schools could be multiplied throughout the state." But few Catholic parents could afford to pay for teachers, and religious orders could educate a relatively small number of pupils. For the foreseeable future, most Catholic children would remain in the public schools, and Kenrick needed to do what he could for them. Another option would be to remove the Bible from public schools entirely. In the spring of 1842, George Washington Biddle—George Cadwalader's first cousin and a member of one of Philadelphia's leading families—used his position as a school director to broach the idea that using a Bible not acceptable to every denomination constituted "a violation of the civil and religious liberty guaranteed by the Constitution to every individual." The board heard him out, but in the end only five other members on the thirty-six-member board voted with Biddle.[25]

If a no-Bible solution did not appeal, perhaps a two-Bible solution could. In March 1839, the commissioners of Baltimore's young public-school system had instructed teachers to let parents choose between the Douay Bible and the King James. Might this work in Philadelphia? On November 14, 1842, Kenrick wrote to the board of controllers, noting that Catholics regarded the King James translation as both inaccurate and incomplete, and asking that Catholic children be provided a Catholic Bible, as was the practice in Baltimore. "We do not ask you to adopt the Catholic version for general use," he wrote. "But we feel warranted in claiming that our conscientious scruples to recognise or use the other, be respected."[26]

None of Kenrick's proposals were likely to appeal to Philadelphia's more ardent Protestants, who believed two apparently contradictory ideas. First, that the Bible was powerful enough by itself to convert nonbelievers, even the occasional Catholic priest or Jewish rabbi who received a Testament from a missionary and just started reading. And second, that the Bible was so innocuous that Catholic parents were silly to fear that its presence in the schools would influence their children's beliefs. The American Protestant Association—a group of Philadelphia clergy formed in November 1842—accused the Catholic church of "efforts to destroy the religious character and influence of public Protestant education." That statement effectively conceded the association's own hopes that public education would be Protestant.[27]

The board sought to appease all sides. In January 1843, it responded to Kenrick, noting that the existing rules already prohibited religious exercises, such as the singing of hymns. As for the Bible issue, it resolved that children whose parents were conscientiously opposed to reading the King James Bible be furnished "any particular version of the Bible, without note or comment" that they preferred, or even to skip Bible reading altogether. Since all Catholic Bibles included commentary, the first option did nothing for Kenrick's congregants. Yet the bishop did not complain publicly. Instead, he preached a sermon on "charity towards enemies," warning Philadelphia's Catholics to prepare for the kind of violence suffered by their coreligionists in Charlestown and New York. "You must forgive even the midnight incendiary who applies the torch to the unprotected mansion of meek virgins," he told worshippers. "You must pardon even the assassin who fancies he renders God service when he points the poniard at your breast." Kenrick let himself vent in a letter Cardinal Paul Cullen, rector of the Irish

College in Rome. "Education here is in a sad condition," he wrote. "The Public Schools are everywhere conducted in a way to leave the children without any religious impression, or to impress them with sectarian views. The Bible is the symbol and watch-word of the sects."[28]

The January 1843 compromise held for the rest of the year, but both Protestants and Catholics understood the compromise as a Protestant victory. The American Protestant Association did accuse Catholic bishops of "attempting to drive the Holy Scriptures from our systems of public education," but it noted in November 1843 that "the practice of the public schools is substantially as it was prior to the effort to remove the bible from them." Catholics complained that "the tender minds of five thousand Catholic youth are daily subject to perversion by having a false and mutilated version of the Scriptures presented for their belief and reverence as the word of God," and that Catholic teachers were denied promotion because of their faith. "There is an anxiety on the part of Catholics here," grumbled the *Catholic Herald*, "to hush up these things, lest like scenes of political excitement as in New York, should grow out of them; but in the meantime conscience is forced, intolerance is rampant, and bigotry stalks abroad without shame."

Meanwhile, teachers and students muddled through. In one school, Catholics claimed, when Catholic children avoided the Bible readings, a vindictive Protestant teacher marked them absent, putting them at risk of suspension or expulsion. Another school was taught by a mother and daughter team, both Catholic. "The old lady refuses to read the Bible at the opening of the school," read one account of their practice, "but places the sacred volume in the hands of a child to read, and then the mother and daughter, and the host of Catholic children, make a desperate rush for the doorway and leave the room. The child who is selected to read the book has such a poor knowledge of reading, that no one can understand it . . . The noise, uproar and confusion, which is the inevitable result of such proceedings, can be imagined as well as described." By late 1843, the Bible debate had dragged on for nearly six years without any workable compromise. In 1844, it would become part of a larger debate about the role of Catholic immigrants in Philadelphia, one defined by politics as much as religion.[29]

The Native American.
Courtesy of the American Antiquarian Society.

8

Arouse, Native Borns!

The year 1844 began in bitter cold. In January, both the Delaware and Schuylkill froze, closing the city to navigation. When the militia paraded for the funeral ceremonies of Commodore David Porter, a trim, shivering Colonel Pleasonton envied his fatter brother officers, who claimed not to suffer. Indoors, in greater comfort, members of the American Protestant Association continued to complain about Kenrick's requests. "Were our privileges to be surrendered to those born on our own soil," argued one Protestant clergyman, "there would be *some* consolation in their loss, but to resign them to a foreign potentate is the last degree of calamity and shame."[1]

Throughout January and February, nativists met in private homes and fire houses to form American Republican ward associations. At the Philadelphia Museum, nativists engaged in public debates with their opponents. According to one nativist account, those opponents included "several blustering and exceedingly noisy Irishmen" who, in thick brogues, threatened to maintain their rights "with the bowie knife and rifle."[2]

Then something went wrong at the Master Street Girls' Grammar School in Kensington's heavily Catholic Third Ward. Some children—presumably Catholics—began complaining that one of the teachers, Rebecca Jackson, was denying them the chance to excuse themselves from daily Bible reading. Using either force or threats, she had chased them out of the small classroom where they had gone to wait out the ritual. When confronted by two assistant teachers, Jackson apologized. She had not known why the children had been gathering in the classroom during Bible reading, and she regretted having "wounded their feelings." That could have been the end of the story, but later that month the school got a chance visit from Hugh Clark.[3]

Clark personified both the opportunities open to Irish immigrants and the limits facing them. Born in Dublin in 1796, he sailed to the United States around 1818 and found his way to Philadelphia not much later. He spent some time driving a Conestoga wagon between Philadelphia and Lancaster, but by 1827 he was settled in Philadelphia and listed among the thirteen "of the most extensive and respectable" weavers surveyed by the Pennsylvania Society for Promoting Domestic Manufactures. He served as a captain in the unorganized militia and helped sponsor balls held by fire companies and clubs. In 1833, Governor George Wolf, a Democrat, appointed Clark as one of four aldermen for Kensington, a position he held for the rest of his life. By 1838 he had been elected police commissioner for Kensington, and by 1841 had been chosen as one of the district's twelve school commissioners. Later, he was chosen as a water-works commissioner as well.[4]

Clark was, however, unable to win office beyond Kensington. Democrats were eager for Irish votes, but they had proven themselves so unwilling to nominate immigrants for office that in 1838, a bloc of Irish voters boycotted the party. The resulting election losses taught the intended lesson, and in 1841 the Democrats nominated Clark for Philadelphia County treasurer.

Even so, some Democrats sought—unsuccessfully—to get him off the ballot. And in the general election, Clark lost to the Whig candidate even as his fellow Democrats took other county offices, suggesting that many voters had cast Democratic ballots with Clark's name "spotted" rather than voting for an Irishman. The slight majority he won in the outlying portions of the county could not make up for a crushing defeat in Philadelphia City, the Whig stronghold. Two years later, after seven hours of contentious balloting, Clark narrowly lost the Democratic nomination for the same office, much to the disappointment of hundreds of his assembled supporters.[5]

Though Clark had failed in his bids to win countywide office, he remained a Kensington alderman and one of the controllers of the public schools. In that capacity, he was showing off the Master Street school—just a few blocks from his own house—when he heard about the Bible incident from Louisa Bedford, the principal of the girls' school. "How are you getting along with your charges?" he asked. "I cannot say very well," she replied, explaining that the departure of Catholic children from the classroom continued to cause "considerable confusion."[6]

Clark himself had been "very much annoyed by constant complaints by Catholic parents" about Bible reading, and the "breach of discipline" caused by children's absenting themselves in the classroom gave him further reason to act. He made two suggestions. First, let the children have whatever version of the Bible they wished, and second, "if the bible could not be read in the school without producing confusion and disorder," Bedford should dispense with it altogether. "Perhaps," he remarked, it would "be the better course to desist for a season from having the Bible read." When they met again the following day, Bedford pointed out that she had long read the Bible in school, and found it "strange I should now be required to lay it aside." "I suppose I am being censured by the Catholics," she lamented. "You might be by some," Clark assured her. "But not by the more intelligent Catholics." Bedford acquiesced to his suggestion that she stop reading the Bible, though perhaps without making her true feelings clear; later she would speak publicly of "the invaluable privilege of reading the Bible in our public schools . . . to impress on the youthful mind the fear and love of God." For his part, Clark did not tell her to discontinue the practice, but he did promise to take responsibility if she did.[7]

While Clark had avoided directly ordering any teacher not to read the Bible, his proposal ignored the delicate compromise worked out by the school controllers—Clark included—in January 1843. The board had specifically limited Bibles to those "without note or comment," that is, Protestant translations, and it had allowed children to avoid the Bible readings if their parents wished it. By suggesting that children bring their own preferred Bibles (presumably including Catholic versions with notes and comments) and ruling that conscientious absence produced disorder, Clark was breaking the peace he had helped craft.[8]

And that is Clark's version of the story. John Painter, the secretary of the board of controllers, was convinced that Clark had not merely suggested that Bedford suspend Bible reading but ordered her to do so, and that Bedford, in the best tradition of Protestant martyrdom, had pledged to resign as principal before submitting to such an order. Clark accused Painter of misrepresenting the events, and the two fell to "high words" and threats. As the story spread, the details got wilder. In one version, Clark ordered a teacher to throw the Bible out the window. When she refused, he snatched it from her hands and threw it into the street himself. "The Pope reigns in Philadelphia!" warned Presbyterian minister Chauncey Webster. Popery had "rudely and insolently snatched God's holy Book from the hands of our defenceless children, and committed it to the flames, that it may reduce them also to the wretched condition of the ignorant, brutalized 'rum soaked' vassals, in whose bodies and souls it now traffics."[9]

Lewis Levin sniffed an opportunity. While he had mentioned Bible reading as an issue, he had never given it much prominence. Now, on February 23, Levin warned his readers of "a violent effort . . . now being made in Kensington to exclude the Bible from the Public Schools" by "the enemies of the Bible." Eventually, Levin would try to steer debate back to his own obsession with O'Connell, claiming that "the effort to bring the Bible into contempt is a part of the Repeal movement." But the Bible, not O'Connell, drew Philadelphia crowds.[10]

On Monday, February 26, angry Protestants gathered to discuss the situation. Organizers had summoned citizens to the Odd Fellows' Hall in Kensington, but on seeing the crowd, they adjourned to the larger Methodist Meeting House, which itself then filled so rapidly that the organizers were relieved that no one was injured in the crush. A few of Clark's supporters even managed to crowd in, but once identified they were hustled out the door. The star of the show was Painter, who repeated his claims about Clark and Bedford, and implored his listeners to stand up to the "minions of His Holiness the Pope." Another speaker, William Baker, denounced the Catholic Church as "that foul mother of harlots," and, for good measure, condemned Repeal as a plot "to establish the Roman Catholic religion in the British dominions." "There are no Protestant Irish Repealers!" his listeners assured him, suggesting that the crowd included some Irish Protestant immigrants. For this was not a nativist meeting, much less an American Republican meeting. Baker still considered himself a Democrat, and the meeting chair likely did as well. A follow up meeting on the afternoon of Monday, March 4, was even wilder. Again, far too many people showed up to fit in the chosen building—Kensington's Commissioners' Hall. Rather than leave hundreds of people disappointed, the organizers moved the meeting to an outdoor space behind the hall, despite the ground being soaked from the previous night's rainfall.[11]

A third mass rally took place on March 11 in the State House Yard, or Independence Square, which had long served as a place for rallies too large for any Philadelphia building. On this March afternoon, perhaps six thousand people from all over the county packed the square. "Never have we witnessed a more orderly and well behaved assemblage," a sympathetic reporter noted. And yet, Levin had warned in that morning's *Sun*, the crisis was "without any parallel in history," even the American Revolution. After all, "George the III never ventured to deny the reading of the *Bible* to our children!" Though held only days before a round of local elections, the rally was officially nonpartisan, and the speeches were more hostile to Catholics than to immigrants. "Every man who loves his country, his Bible, and his God," thundered Rev. Joseph Berg, editor of the *Protestant Banner*, "is bound by all lawful and honorable means to resist every attempt to banish the Bible from our public institutions." As the crowd cheered, he continued. "As an American citizen, and as a lover of my country," he declared, "I will resist anti-Christ." Lest anyone miss the connection between Catholicism and immigration, Elihu Tarr—a

Northern Liberties lawyer—spelled it out. Catholics, he argued, "might come to this country and enjoy all the rights of Americans, provided they did not interrupt us; but if, however, they did do so, they might expect to be told that they were welcome to take their departure—to go quietly away from these hospitable, free, and happy shores."[12]

Philadelphia's Catholics were troubled by such statements, but they consoled themselves with the thought that not all Protestants agreed. "The whole number of genuine bigots of the city and county of Philadelphia does not probably exceed 500," one hopeful Catholic estimated. The rest of the nativist movement, he guessed, was composed of "religious and political gamblers" seeking money or power, or zealots who might join any exciting cause. On Kenrick's instruction, Philadelphia's Catholics avoided public meetings. Instead, they petitioned the Board of Controllers of the Public Schools, complaining of discrimination of the January 1843 resolution excluding the Douay Bible and of the schools' failure to adhere to the 1834 resolution prohibiting "any religious exercises, books or lessons." Catholic children were being denied their own Bible and required to sing Protestant hymns and recite from the King James.[13]

The day after the State House Yard rally, the board of controllers heard from both sides. On the one hand, they had the memorial from the Kensington meeting, demanding Hugh Clark's resignation and a Bible reading in every school, on every morning. On the other, they had the Catholic petition and a letter from Kenrick. "I do not object to the use of the Bible," wrote Kenrick, reiterating his stance from November 1842, "provided Catholic children be allowed to use their own version." For its part, the board believed that the crisis would be solved if everyone would just adhere to its January 1843 policy—Bibles "without note or comment" for those children whose parents wanted them, no compulsory attendance or Bible reading for parents who declined. It reaffirmed its previous policies. If keeping the King James Bible in the public schools had been the real goal of the nativists, the board's March 12 action might well have sufficed. Moreover, the investigation into Hugh Clark's actions at the Master Street school was still continuing, and the teachers there would soon confirm his claim that he had not ordered them to end Bible reading. But the anti-Catholic ministry of the city used Kenrick's letter as an opportunity for fresh outrage, asking, "Must Popery then be taught at the public expense in our Schools?"[14]

In any case, by this point, nativists had moved past this single issue and had committed to following New York's example of converting a nativist movement into a nativist party. Toward this end, the nativists staged yet another rally on Thursday, March 14, the evening before the wards of the city and the districts held elections for minor offices, the most significant of which were assessors and the judges for the fall presidential election. These were the pettiest of elections, but they would serve to test party strength, and nativists from New York arrived to encourage Philadelphians to follow their example. One advised Catholics that "if they do not like our Schools, let them build schools of their own, and teach their children just whatever they please." As the cheers subsided, a heckler spoke up: "and we pay for your child!" Amid shouts of "turn him out! turn him out!" the man was dragged off, clutching desperately at the collars of his assailants.[15]

Despite cold, wet, windy weather the next day, voter turnout was higher than usual in several wards and districts. In the Second Ward of Spring Garden, the birthplace of the party, the Native Americans won the ticket, and countywide they attracted at least 1,300 ballots. It was, observed one newspaper, "for so young a party, a very respectable vote." Meanwhile, Southwark's Democrats widened the split that had begun in 1843, with rival regular and reform candidates facing off for minor offices. The regular Democrats won the Third Ward, but reform took the remaining four. The Democrats, one Whig newspaper claimed, "have been completely disorganized and crippled in Southwark, heretofore their strong hold." Meanwhile, even more dramatic shifts were disorganizing New York.[16]

Having built strength throughout the winter of 1844, New York City's nativists decided in March to nominate their own candidate for mayor rather than endorse a Whig as they had in 1837. The man they chose, James Harper, brought instant respectability. One of the founders of the Harper & Brothers publishing company, Harper was known for his philanthropy and his advocacy for temperance. And though he was also known to have been a Whig, his aldermanic running mates came from both Whig and Democratic backgrounds, signaling that the American Republicans were not just a rebranded Whig Party. They ran largely on the issue of municipal reform, promising to "abolish all unnecessary expenses [and] abolish all unnecessary officers and offices," as well as to remove all foreigners from government jobs. This promise likely drew votes from not only Protestant supremacists but also from some who took them at their word on reform.[17]

Notwithstanding Harper's own decorum himself, both his supporters and detractors turned violent in the days leading up to the election. In New York City itself, Irishmen lounging outside of a Democratic tavern jeered a passing nativist procession. Hearing the hisses, the Natives wheeled and smashed every window in the building. In Brooklyn, still an independent city, a group of nativists strolled past a Catholic church, which—the Irish claimed—they threatened to burn. Then, according to nativist accounts, the Irish began throwing bricks and stones and even firing coarse shot at the Natives, who fled. The mayor summoned the militia, but the fight was over before they could arrive. The following day, April 5, nativists swarmed New York City gun shops for muskets, revolvers, and any other weapons they could find. The afternoon before the election, American Republicans rallied to hear speakers denounce "Papal domination" and claim to have been attacked by Irish women with brickbats in their aprons and paving stones in their stockings. One called for "our American brethren, one and all, to join with us in the great work of Reformation." From the rally point, the nativists marched through streets, accompanied by bands and carrying "highly inflammatory" banners. "As well may the Pope attempt to put the Bible from the school," read one, "as the school book from the school boy." According to one account, the procession stretched for two miles and was met by cheering crowds and ladies waving silk handkerchiefs.[18]

The following day, on the night of the election itself, a thousand American Republicans marched through the city's Irish Catholic wards, yelling and waving banners reading "No Popery," while armed Catholics gathered to prevent a rumored attack on the cathedral. If the nativists had hoped to provoke another riot, they failed. But the nativists did win the election. Harper outpolled his two rivals combined, and the American Republicans captured two thirds of the city council and lesser offices in twelve of seventeen wards. The new party, marveled the *New York Republic*, "strides forth with the irresistible power of a giant."[19]

Astonished Philadelphians tried to make sense of the results. "The New York election has cast a bomb into the political ranks," wrote the *Daily Chronicle*, "which has spread disorder and dismay on both sides," especially in a presidential election year. "Each party is looking upon the movements of the Native Americans with jealousy, and yet both are afraid to touch them, for sagacious men know full well, that it is but a meteor which will soon reach its zenith, explode, and disappear." Levin was thrilled. "Nobly have the people of New York met the crisis," he wrote. "They organized their strength on the true principle of *opposition to foreign interference* in *the American ballot-boxes*; proclaimed by O'Connell to be the great desideratum of the Romish Church; and they have triumphed."[20]

The New York victory electrified Philadelphia's nativists. On the very evening of New York's election, hundreds gathered at the corner of Ninth and Spring Garden Streets to hear speakers proclaim the necessity of a Native American party. Two days later, on April 11, one of those speakers, printer Samuel Kramer, published the first issue of a new daily newspaper, the *Native American*, as an explicitly partisan nativist organ, unlike Levin's nominally independent newspapers, the *Temperance Advocate* and the *Daily Sun*. Officially, the *Native American* was nonsectarian, even tolerant. "It has never been the endeavor of this paper to excite any especial prejudice against the Roman Catholics in particular," it assured its readers, "because we will not adopt any course that can be construed into a religious persecution." Later, Kramer described Levin's *Daily Sun* as "somewhat notorious for the violence with which it has handled the Catholic church." "The true Native American party know nor care not for religious distinctions," he assured a reader. "The anti-Catholic spirit is assuredly pseudo-American."[21]

Despite the disclaimers, the *Native American* frequently castigated Catholics. It called on American Republicans to "redouble their efforts to shut out, in the only constitutional way, the power of this church from the ballot boxes," and would go on to write contemptuously of Catholic leaders. To emphasize Kenrick's Irish nativity, the paper would refer to him as "Bishop Patrick." And Kramer was happy to run letters to the editor that explained how "the debased minions of Popery" were unfit for republican self-government, and that "there is something in freedom particularly obnoxious to Papist principles." Nor did swearing off religious bigotry limit

Kramer's chances to disparage immigrants on other terms. "Two more vessels arrived at this port from Liverpool and Londonderry," he would report in early June, "filled to the very decks with the lowest, poorest, and most filthy kind of Irish. . . . The stench which arose from these people, as they came upon the shore, was of the most offensive and disgusting kind." Later, Kramer would assert that native-born Catholics opposed the nativist movement on orders from their "unnaturalized, alien priesthood."[22]

In his inaugural editorial, Kramer—a former Whig himself—accused the city's other newspapers of fearing to challenge naturalization policies lest they alienate naturalized voters from their preferred party, Democrat or Whig. The *Native American*, he pledged, would declare what most native-born citizens already believed: that naturalization came "too cheap." Immigrants did not take such sentiments kindly. According to the newspaper, when an "Irish cabman" encountered a newsboy selling the paper, he bought the entire stock, then burned them in the street. The newsboy and the editor were delighted with the sale.[23]

Both the *Daily Sun* and the *Native American* ran advertisements encouraging readers to shop at stores owned by other Natives, making the nativist movement an economic as well as a political force. It made a certain sense, since anti-Catholicism accorded with workingmen's concerns about other forces that would rob them of their self-mastery: monopolies, depression, and demon rum. As local organizations of skilled workers, small proprietors, and petty professionals concerned about maintaining their independence, nativist associations resembled fraternal lodges and temperance societies, and Levin's shift from temperance to anti-Catholicism was not so great a leap. By supporting one another's businesses, Natives could hope to regain the very independence that they feared the pope meant to seize. "The Tailors, the Carpenters, the Shoemakers, and all other mechanics," one boasted, "whipped their foe in by-gone days, and . . . it can be done again in in the present time."[24]

Whatever economic hopes the nativists entertained, electoral politics was never far beneath the surface. On April 15, six days after Harper's victory in New York, the *Native American* summoned its readers to a mass celebration in front of Independence Hall. Thousands of nativists from throughout the county arrived to hear speeches and resolutions, interspersed with music and cheers for a late-arriving delegation from Southwark, which had been firing salutes on the Queen Street wharf. In the wake of the meeting, the *Native American* did note that "several attempts were made by some *foreign* ruffians to create a disturbance, but the good sense of those present soon prevented any difficulty." On April 16, Spring Garden held a special election to fill three commissioners' seats left open by resignations. As voters tried to cast their ballots, Native Americans battled their opponents in the streets around the schoolhouse that served as the polling station. For a while it appeared they would prevail, but in the final count, the Democrats beat them by eighty-five votes out of nearly three thousand cast. On the other hand, the Native Americans had beaten the Whigs by three hundred votes, so in Spring Garden, at least, they were technically no longer even a third party. "Although we have not attained our desires," crowed the *Native American*, we consider it none the less a triumph." Moreover, the Democrats and Whigs had each attracted hundreds votes fewer than they had in the special congressional election of 1843, suggesting that the Natives were pulling support away from both of the older parties.[25]

April brought Philadelphia a lovely spring, one that drew so many people into the streets that the *Daily Chronicle* called for the city's four large public squares to be opened early, instead of waiting for May 1, as was customary. The ladies of the city showed off the latest fashions: Neapolitan bonnets and the newest style of parasol. However delightful the sunshine, Lewis Levin cannot have been in a good mood that spring. He and Julia were fighting in a Maryland court against John Iglehart, who had given them $5,500 back in 1837. They claimed that they had paid back almost all of the loan, but Iglehart denied that and claimed the dower rights with which the Levins had secured the loans. A Maryland court denied their request for an injunction, and the case would drag on for years. Still, Levin remained active, speaking at Native gatherings in Southwark. He would have spoken in New Market Ward as well, but the American Republicans there could not find a room large enough, so he spoke just across the street in Moyamensing.[26]

The one place that Native Americans were not triumphing was the Third Ward of Kensington, the site of the Master Street school controversy. Compared to the city of churches and museums where Lewis Levin and his friends were used to speaking, the ward was a rough frontier. As many as 80 percent of its residents were foreign born, mostly Catholic and Protestant Irishmen. In 1828, off-duty Kensington watchman Stephen Heimer had sought refreshment in a tavern and was told to keep his voice down; a woman was dying in a back room. Rather than quieting, Heimer loudly disparaged the "bloody Irish transports" around him. The Irish transports beat him to death. Irishmen dominated the handloom weaving trade, the source of bitter strikes in 1842 and 1843. In April 1844, that memory of these strikes was still fresh, as hundreds of weavers marched through the streets with music, flags, and banners and met to raise money for the legal defense of a weaver charged with attacking a rival who had accepted low wages. For the most part, the marches were peaceful, but nativists were suspicious. "These men are now parading our streets in large number," warned the Philadelphia correspondent of the *New-York Tribune*. "Acts of violence are looked for in Kensington."[27]

Physically, the Third Ward was a tough neighborhood as well, at the northern edge of metropolitan Philadelphia's dense settlement. By 1844, formal maps showed several new, larger streets, but many residents opened their doors to smaller alleyways or "courts," so narrow that the roofs of the buildings on each side almost touched. Some of its residents, especially along Master Street, occupied sturdy brick houses with fine wooden furniture and feather beds. Others made do with cheap, simple frame buildings, as little as twelve feet wide. In 1839, when Philadelphia City boasted almost 1,700 private baths, a committee found a single private bath and water closet in all of Kensington. Many buildings served as both residences and workplaces, whether shops, offices, or, most commonly, workshops with looms for carpets and other textiles. Parents, children, and employees crowded together; a married couple might share a bedchamber with an employee, though not the same bed. Other workers labored in separate buildings behind their homes, or erected dye houses and other outbuildings. A few lots were strictly business: warehouses, stables, a blacksmith shop, and, to the north, more rural elements, such as garden nurseries, pigsties, and a slaughterhouse. Interspersed with all of these were a number of vacant lots, giving the neighborhood a patchwork feeling and sight lines that shifted as one walked.[28]

The president of the Native Born Citizens of the Third Ward Kensington was William Craig, a Presbyterian, a temperance man in his twenties, and the owner or manager of a flour store on Second Street. In April, Craig had watched as American Republicans held rallies around Philadelphia, including one in the Fourth Ward of Kensington, just half a mile east of his home. A least three hundred people had gathered there, most of whom pledged to support the American Republican Party, or so boasted the *Native American*. After formally joining the movement on April 29, Craig wanted to host a similar meeting in his own Third Ward, but he was having trouble finding a suitable place. One potential host received threats that his house would be burned down if he welcomed the Natives. The threats likely came from Catholic neighbors who muttered to each other that "the Orangemen" were behind Craig's plans for a meeting, and "all they wanted was to make Orangemen of the Natives." As for John McManus, the secretary of the ward's Native American Association, one exclaimed that he "is a turncoat, a profligate, a thief" who "deserved to be hung up in the air by the heels and the flesh to be eaten off his bones by fowls." If such men came to their part of Kensington, the Catholics vowed, "they would not as many go away alive as came."[29]

Wary of violence, Craig invited the Natives of the Third Ward to meet farther south, in the Second Ward. The *Native American* excused the action, assuring its readers that the "the men of Kensington" were not themselves afraid of "ruthless savages," but they would hate to see "the vengeance of the untamed aliens . . . visited on the innocent landlord." But the retreat must have been humiliating to Craig, who found that he could not get leading nativists to speak to his fledging group so long as it could not meet in its own ward. And so in early May, Craig called for a meeting at six o'clock in the evening of Friday, May 3, in the Third Ward itself.[30]

Craig tried to reserve the brick house of his neighbor, ropemaker John Gee, on Second Street. But Gee canceled the meeting after receiving more threats of arson, as did another building owner. So Craig gave up trying to hold a meeting indoors. Instead, he summoned his fellow nativists to a vacant lot, at the southwest corner of Second and Master Streets. The lot—roughly 100 by 150 feet—was just a couple of blocks away from Craig's own home on Phoenix, and on the same block as Gee's house. On the west side of the lot stood the public school, a substantial brick structure, and on the south end was a tavern. "AROUSE, NATIVE BORNS!" Craig's notice exhorted readers. "Take the scales from your eyes—take a peep through the curtain, and behold the sun arise."[31]

Sometime before six o'clock in the evening of Friday, May 3, Craig and his group arrived and assembled some borrowed boards into a stage on the west side of the lot, against the schoolhouse wall. They had at last secured a prominent speaker: Samuel Kramer, editor of the *Native American*. Kramer was joined by John Perry of Kensington's First Ward, who had recently retired as a Universalist minister to become a printer and nativist activist. They had also attracted listeners, many of them neighborhood residents simply interested to know what the fuss was—perhaps another meeting of striking weavers? In the crowd of a hundred, the "very small component" of nativists from other parts of Philadelphia were outnumbered by Kensington residents, most of them hostile.[32]

Undeterred, Kramer delivered a rant against immigrants. One witness reported his telling the crowd "that there was a set of citizens, Germans and Irish, who wanted to get the Constitution of the United States into their own hands, and sell the country to a foreign power." Some cheered him on with cries of "down with the Papists!" But as Kramer continued, more skeptical residents came to listen, and the ones already there got ever noisier and angrier as Kramer explained their unfitness to vote. "You're a liar" shouted a naturalized citizen. "Come down here, you old crocodile," shouted Patrick Lafferty. "I am a better citizen than you, for I am sworn to the country, and you may turn tory as soon as possible." Kramer took the heckling in stride, telling the "turbulent persons" that they had just proved him right by showing themselves unfit to be citizens. Craig, the organizer, knew some of the men who were harassing his meeting, either by name or by sight. He called out Lafferty, warning him not to get into trouble, but Lafferty and those around him just interrupted more, until Craig and Perry waded into the crowd, offering to debate naturalization law with anyone who wished.[33]

Finally, the Kensington crowd could take no more. "Down with the stage!" someone shouted. "Down with the bastards!" Men rushed at the rostrum, tore up the stage, and then chased Kramer and his friends away, though they did not catch any of them. The hecklers seemed to regard their charge as a game—"like skylarking," one witness recalled—not as a serious fight. And the speakers suffered more insult than injury. Two had time to jump off the stage, while a third, an elderly man, was helped down. But the insult was real enough. The outnumbered Natives withdrew to the George Fox Temperance Hall. It was only three blocks south, but, lying one block south of Franklin Street, it was in the Second Ward. The "turbulent persons" had again chased the Natives out of the Third Ward. The furious Natives adopted a resolution complaining of "this flagrant violation of the rights of American citizens," and calling "upon our fellow citizens at large, to visit with their indignation and reproach, this outbreak of a vindictive, anti-republican spirit, manifested by a portion of the alien population of Third Ward Kensington."[34]

None of this was terribly unusual for the day; attacks against political rallies or speeches were about as common as election-day fighting at polling places themselves, though typically less violent. Moreover, it made sense that a third-party rally would collapse into violence more readily than one organized by one of the two established factions, the Whigs or the Democrats. New parties attracted men not yet familiar with the unwritten rules of electoral sparring while spooking established parties into more violent reactions. One of the reasons the elections of the 1830s—such as the fatal Moyamensing election of 1834—had been so bloody is that Americans were still feeling their way from the old Jeffersonian consensus into the new two-party system of Democrats and Whigs. By the 1840s, members of those parties might despise one another enough for some shouting and trickery, but they wielded fewer knives and guns.[35]

The American Republicans did not belong to this club, not yet. And they seemed to be following a different playbook, the one deployed so effectively by Ireland's Orangemen: Provoke the enemy to attack first, and thus win themselves the mantle of innocent martyrdom. In that sense, the May 3 fracas was, as Kramer had suggested, a Native American victory, since they had achieved their objective of showing the "aliens" of Kensington to be a violent threat to American liberty. They even hinted at a Catholic conspiracy. The *Native American* reported that "a popish priest was seen to leave the vicinity within an hour of the riot." But the victory was not complete, for the Native Americans had yielded the battleground. Even as they regrouped in the temperance hall, they vowed to return to Second and Master the following Monday afternoon.[36]

On Monday morning, May 6, Kramer's *Native American* summoned nativists to reassemble in the vacant lot at Second and Master. This time, they would start earlier, at four o'clock rather than six. And the call was not just for nativists from Kensington's Third Ward. Friday's assault on Kramer had been an attack on nativism itself, and now he sought the aid of all the American Republicans in the city and county. The meeting, Kramer pledged, would be "a practical test of the doctrine, long doubted by aristocrats, that the people are able to govern themselves." At stake was the right of a political minority to be heard against a "doctrine of submission to the strong arm of numerical force."[37]

"We are the friends of peace," he asserted. "We would do everything right to preserve it—but if we are to be assaulted by a horde of foreigners, when assembled for peaceful purposes, why let them find that blows can be given as well as taken." Kramer faulted the Kensington nativists of the previous Friday for arriving in small numbers "instead of assembling in force, to beat off the foreign rabble." This time, American Republicans were "to take the necessary steps to prevent a repetition" of Friday's outrage. *"Natives be punctual and resolve to sustain your rights as Americans, firmly but moderately."* Kensington's Catholics prepared as well. One neighborhood woman heard gunfire on Monday morning, and in the afternoon was startled to see a neighbor sharpening a large knife against the side of his house. "It makes one sick," she murmured to a friend.[38]

That afternoon, the nativists arrived. They built their stage, raised their flags, and gave their speeches, even as John O'Neill dumped his wagonload of dirt. Next came the rainstorm, the frantic, laughing run to the shelter of the market house, and Levin's abbreviated remarks: "Fellow citizens, we have reached an important crisis!" And then the first gunshot, followed by cries as ex-constable Fisher collapsed. "Hurrah for the Natives, and kill the damned Irish."[39]

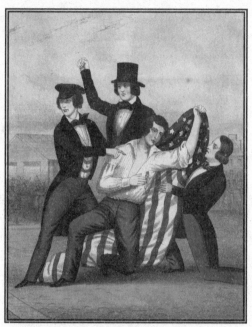

"Death of George Shifler in Kensington."
Courtesy of the Library Company of Philadelphia.

9

A Band of Armed Ruffians

At the sound of the first gunshots in the market house, William Craig, the local organizer, hustled Levin to safety, leaving younger men to smash the doors and windows along Cadwalader Street. Isaac Hare, twenty-three, led a gang of nativists, demanding of passersby if they were native born. Unlike many of the Natives, he lived in the neighborhood, on Third Street, close to Craig. The Hares were well-known for their Native American sympathies, and some blamed those "hot-headed set of fools" for the effort to hold a nativist meeting in the Third Ward. Referring to Isaac's Protestant father's having been born in Ireland himself, a man complained that the ward's nativism "was got up by a party of Irishmen and Irishmen's bastards."[1]

Though the firemen would deny it, Hare was rumored to be a former member of the Independence Hose Company, headquartered at Germantown and Second, about a quarter-mile south of the vacant lot at Second and Master. Another account, recorded decades later, suggests that Hare's companion George Shiffler, a nineteen-year-old apprentice leather worker, was one of those "saucy Hyena boys of George's street," who would accompany the Independence Hose to fires and help out with the fighting. The evidence is thin, but the claims are plausible. The Natives were rumored to include large numbers of firemen, who may have hoped that the party would deregulate firefighting, and the Natives of Kensington's Second Ward met at the house of the Globe Engine, a Hibernia Hose rival. Having young men—often described as half-grown boys—as unofficial volunteers gave fire companies more power to fight but also the chance to deny that their official members had battled. Since both Hare and Shiffler lived within a few blocks of the Independence Hose House, they would have been attractive candidates, and Independence Hose would have needed all the muscle it could get.[2]

Like Hibernia Hose, Independence was a particularly violent company, with an ongoing feud with the Northern Liberty Hose. In September 1842, for instance, the Independence had seized all three fire plugs near a burning stable. When they could not get their hoses to play water on the fire, they let the building burn rather than allow the Kensington or Globe Engine companies access to a plug, then seized the Kensington engine and made an effort to seize the Northern Liberty hose carriage as well. In December 1843, both the Independence and the Northern Liberty companies had arrived at a massive fire in a Kensington lumber yard. Seeing nothing they could do, the men retired to a nearby tavern, where they got to arguing. "From words they got to blows," a newspaper reported, "beating each other in the most brutal manner, and smashing every thing in the bar. Seven large baskets of broken glass were swept up after the belligerents had left the house." A second Kensington fire on the same day sparked another clash between the two companies, during which one fireman bit off another's ear. The following month, after another spectacular fire at a soap, oil, and candle works in Kensington, the Independence Hose men had again tried to seize Northern Liberty's carriage. In the ensuring fight—ferocious even by the standards of a fireman's riot—the rival companies used "bludgeons, spanners, shot slings, horns, pistols, &c, &c," and several were severely injured, one close to death. Only the personal appearance of three aldermen, including Hugh Clark, allowed the Northern Liberty men to get their carriage safely back to its house.[3]

The weekend prior to the Kensington riot had taken a typical toll: three firemen badly hurt in brawls, and two "auxiliary firemen" (youths, like the Hyenas) arrested for pulling old vehicles "at a furious rate through the streets." Thus, if Hare and Shiffler were connected, however informally, with the Independence Hose, it would help explain their aggression, which seems to have combined the Orangeman's hatred of papists with the fireman's disregard for danger and love of a good fight.[4]

"Here is the house of another damned Papist," Hare now cried, using a club to smash open the doors of his neighbors. He threw a brick through the window of the Master Street home of Patrick Wall, who took the assault calmly. "It is only Ike Hare cutting up some of his devilment," Wall reassured his frantic wife as the gang moved on. As the fighting intensified, Hare cheered his unarmed comrades. "Come on boys, don't be afraid," he encouraged them, flashing a pistol. "I'll shoot the first damned Irish Papist I meet." He did try, aiming the pistol and pulling the trigger, but he could not get it to fire. He was reduced to hurling bricks at his antagonists. Hare may have regarded the whole event as something of a sport. Months later, while awaiting trial, he would tell one visitor that the Kensington riot had been "a general shooting match, and it was the best man got the best shot."[5]

Perhaps so, but it was not an even match. The Natives had come to Kensington for a rally, not a battle, and they had only those weapons they had brought with them, plus whatever bricks, stones, and other debris they could snatch up from the street. Kensington's residents, by contrast, were just yards from their homes, so they could run inside and grab more firepower. One resident walked by with his gun, muttering, "we will kill all the damned sons of bitches we come across." Constable Saunders Gavit saw John Paul throwing stones early in the fight. The next time he looked, Paul was with three or four other men, all with guns. These men fired toward the market, then took up positions behind a fence to the south of the hose house. The nativists were thus both outgunned and exposed.[6]

The first fatality was George Shiffler, the Hyena. At the corner of Germantown and Master, he was hit by a "heavy charge from a musket" in the right arm and chest. He staggered against a fence, then collapsed. He survived just long enough to be carried south one block to a drug store. Undeterred, or perhaps spurred to greater frenzy, Shiffler's comrades held the corner and kept hurling sticks and stones. Several more were hit; a reporter estimated at least a hundred gunshots, of which about a dozen found their targets. Henry Temper, a young journeyman barber, was hit in the hip and leg as he climbed over a fence toward safety. Joseph Cox, age twenty-three, was a member of the Globe Engine Company, whose engine house lay just two blocks south on Germantown, and which had brawled with Shiffler's Independence a year and a half previously. That rivalry did not make the Globe allies of the Hibernia Hose, however, and—though he would deny it—Cox may have joined the attack. In any case, a musket or pistol ball slammed into his right hip, tunneling through his pelvis. Someone carried him away on a settee. Not everyone was so young; an elderly man was wounded in the neck. But most of the wounded, and likely most of the nativists doing the fighting, were young men, in their late teens or early twenties. This is not surprising—across cultures, it is the young men who fight.[7]

The battle remained uneven. Other than Fisher—shot in the market at the very start of the fighting—it is not clear that any Catholics were seriously wounded by gunshots that day. But that did not mean they were safe. Nativists scoured houses on Master and Cadwalader, looking for the men who were shooting at them. Whether or not they found them, they smashed doors, windows, and furniture. Elizabeth Brown told her husband to close the door. He had just done so when a pistol ball smashed through, hitting his leg, though apparently without hurting him much. Another man ran down Cadwalader Street and dove through the door of weaver Edward Devlin, closing it with his feet just in time to elude his pursuers. Other civilians were caught out of doors. A woman had the misfortune to be driving a milk wagon down the street when her horse spooked at the sight of retreating Natives coming toward it. The panicked animal overturned the wagon, spilling the woman and two children into the road.[8]

A few brave souls tried to stop the violence. "For God's sake, men, what are you about?" Edward Sherridan asked his neighbors. "Are you crazy?" But with both sides using firearms, the violence was already more serious than most Philadelphia riots. Combatants moved east and west along Master Street, with each group taking turns chasing and being chased. One man fled east, loading his pistol as he ran, then wheeling to fire at his pursuers. Another ran with a new musket at his shoulder, chasing the nativists past Second toward Front.[9]

So far, the battle had raged without intervention by the authorities, except for a futile attempt by former city high constable Willis Blaney, who was shot in the heel for his trouble. Someone hauled him off to a nearby drug store, which also received Pat Fisher and another wounded man. Kensington's current police force consisted of its five aldermen, a police magistrate, and five constables, one for each ward. Two of those constables—Saunders Gavit of the First Ward and John Blair of the Third—made it to the market, but they were clearly outmatched. Gavit had been at the market when the fighting started, and he warned some combatants that "they had done enough to send them to the gallows—that they ought to take their guns and leave." When they told him they would be damned if they did, Gavit gave up. Trying to arrest anyone would only get him killed. Blair thought the same. "I was by myself," he later explained, "and it was of no use to interfere." For emergencies like this, one needed the county sheriff, charged with keeping the peace outside the limits of the City of Philadelphia. So two nativists went looking for Morton McMichael, Esq.[10]

Barely six months into his term as sheriff, McMichael was in the city on the evening of May 6 when the messengers arrived to tell him of the bloodshed in Kensington. Even if he had been willing to march to the same Kensington market where his predecessor had been severely beaten, he could not hope to raise a posse. As a newspaper later explained, "no one manifested an inclination to face, empty handed, a band of armed ruffians, under the cover of night, and the shelter of houses,—who could fire their guns, and elude capture with impunity." So McMichael started knocking at armory doors, hoping to find a militia company that happened to be drilling that night. When this failed, he sought out Brigadier General George Cadwalader.[11]

Cadwalader had endured a dreadful winter. Early in the year, his beloved brother Thomas had fallen ill and died at age thirty-five. Exhausted from the effort and anxiety, George himself fell ill, and only in late March was he himself again. Now, in May, he had been looking forward to taking his Philadelphia Grays to New York City for a round of parades and banquets. Instead, he faced the prospect of the first real combat in his eighteen years of militia service. Yet, as Kensington bled, it was not Cadwalader the general but Cadwalader the lawyer who reacted first. What, he wanted to know, was the militia's legal duty?[12]

The answer was far from obvious. Cadwalader thought back to an 1834 letter from Judge Edward King to his predecessor, Brigadier General Andrew Prevost. King had acknowledged that militia intervention might occasionally be necessary, but stressed how extraordinarily bad things had to be before the troops should act. Volunteer troops would be a "dernier resort," acting only "in the last emergency" and when "absolutely necessary." Civil forces must have proven themselves unable to handle the violence. And if the violence had calmed by itself, only "unequivocal manifestations" of renewed fighting would justify intervention. Recalling all of this, Cadwalader expected censure if he acted at all aggressively. On top of this, the legislature had not promised to pay militiamen for riot duty, and—some speculated—this made them unwilling to take on the task. Unpersuaded that the violence in Kensington warranted military intervention, Cadwalader declined to order out his brigade.[13]

Having failed to secure military aid for that evening, McMichael himself, possibly accompanied by Cadwalader, went to the Washington Market to try to calm people down. By the time he arrived, the worst of the fighting was over, but the neighborhood was still occupied by angry nativists who wanted his sanction to go into the neighboring houses and arrest peace breakers. Instead, McMichael told them to go home; he would make any home inspections himself. For a moment, the Third Ward was peaceful. "From about seven o'clock . . . until after eight in the evening," one nativist later recalled, "the most profound silence prevailed in the immediate vicinity of the riots." The streets were nearly empty.[14]

The nativists withdrew, but they did not go home. Instead, they retreated to Second and Franklin, at the southern edge of the Third Ward. There, they built a bonfire and muttered about how to avenge the evening's losses. Some called for an attack on "Pope Clark's"; the home of Alderman Hugh Clark, was just a few blocks away at Fourth and Master. Others proposed an attack on the Hibernia Hose Company, perhaps by starting a fire that would lure the men from their house. At about ten o'clock a party raided a house on Second Street that, they thought, had housed a gunman that afternoon. They smashed the doors and windows and destroyed much of the furniture on the lower story, tossing the wreckage into the street.[15]

Then someone shouted, "Go to the nunnery!" "Kill the damned papists and burn them out!" another agreed. Constantine B. F. O'Neill, a Catholic lawyer who was stealthily observing all of this, concluded that the crowd comprised both Irish-born and American-born Protestants. Their vocabulary differed; the Americans were more likely to denounce "Catholics" while the Irish detested "Papists." But they could agree on a convent as a target.[16]

The "nunnery" was a complex at Second and Phoenix, just one block to the north of the bonfire. Opened in 1838, it housed the Sisters of Charity of the Blessed Virgin Mary, a religious school, and a school for boarding and day students. Father Terence Donaghoe had established both the religious order and the school without Kenrick's approval, leaving the sisters without clear status in the church or the diocese. The awkwardness lasted until 1843, when Donaghoe received an appeal from the bishop of Dubuque, Iowa, for "four or five sisters." Donaghoe counter-offered with a proposal to move all nineteen of the sisters, and himself, to Dubuque, leaving behind Kenrick and Philadelphia. By early 1844, the move was almost complete. The school had closed, with only Sister Mary Baker, an English widow, remaining as a caretaker until the Kensington property could be sold.[17]

Thus the "nunnery" was nothing more than a defunct school, overseen by a widow with the help of two girls. Still, it was a convenient symbol of popery, and there the mob marched. A boy warned Baker in time for her to lock the doors and shutter the windows, but these proved feeble defenses. Shouting abuse, men tore down the convent fence, threw stones through the windows, and riddled the walls with musket balls. One managed to splinter the door enough to throw blazing sticks inside. Fearing that she was about to be burned alive, Baker begged to be allowed to flee. A nativist responded by picking up a stone and knocking her unconscious. When she awoke, everyone had gone. Baker took a candle and stayed outside for the rest of the night.[18]

While she lay senseless, Baker had missed her own rescue; other men, presumably Catholics, counterattacked, hitting the vandals with a volley of musket balls and buckshot. Nineteen-year old William Wright fell dead, a musket ball through his heart, while twenty-one-year-old Nathan Ramsey lay gasping from a shot through the lungs. Ramsey, a member of the Native American Party, was carried away alive to an apothecary store, where friends summoned his wife and mother, but the wound appeared fatal. O'Neill heard that two others, never identified, had been killed as well. With at least two more casualties, the nativists had had enough, and they retreated. Nearby, John McAleer, was in agony. He had loaded his gun and fired at the nativists, only to have the weapon explode, tearing off his thumb. By midnight, Kensington was quiet. About two dozen Irishmen with muskets and sticks patrolled in front of St. Michael's Church, keeping strangers away. It had been a dreadful day. Shiffler and Wright were dead, Cox and Ramsey were seriously wounded, and others were nursing less severe wounds. But worse was to follow.[19]

"The Philadelphia Riots."
Courtesy of the Collection of the New-York Historical Society. Photography © New-York Historical Society.

10

I Have Got My Man!

Touring the Third Ward on the morning of Tuesday, May 7, a reporter witnessed a "sad and solemn" landscape: "streets strewn with the fragments of broken bricks and stones—houses with their windows, window shutters, and doors battered in—furniture destroyed—women engaged in removing their goods—groups of men standing at the corners of streets, deploring the events of the previous night, and evidently in a state of feverish anxiety, at the thought that the same scenes might recur again." George Roberts stared at the steps of a neighbor's house near Cadwalader Street. They had been hit at least twice with gunfire; one-ounce musketballs, he guessed.[1]

Among the debris near the seminary were the remnants of McAleer's burst gun, as well as his thumb, with a length of tendon dangling from it. Three men secured a warrant to track the trail of blood to the house of John Daly, at the corner of Second and Master. There they found Owen Daley, John O'Connor, a loaded gun, and some bloody sheets and pillowcases. The three men seized Daley and O'Connor and hauled them through the streets to an alderman's office while furious observers—presumably nativists—shouted "Kill them, kill them! Blood for blood!" Alderman Isaac Boileau released Daley for lack of evidence and set bail for O'Connor, who was escorted home by public officers as another crowd threatened to lynch him. The next day, McAleer, minus his thumb, made it to the hospital.[2]

Throughout Kensington, residents traded rumors, while downtown, men crowded around newspaper offices for a chance to read the boards where bulletins were posted every hour. The *Public Ledger* denounced the attack on the Natives' meeting, calling it "as gross an outrage as was ever perpetrated upon the rights of any body of free citizens." The attackers, it argued, had failed to show proper gratitude for the "political equality" America had offered them as immigrants. Finally, the paper warned, "Unless prompt measures are taken to prevent a recurrence of the scenes of yesterday, the most terrible consequences, the end of which it is impossible to foresee, must inevitably ensue, and the streets of our city be filled with bloodshed and all the horrors of a civil war."[3]

Augustus Peale, secretary of the Locust Ward Native American Association, did not want to see the Natives lose the momentum they had gained. Peale was a member of one of Philadelphia's most colorful families. His grandfather, Charles Willson Peale, had worked his way from being an orphaned saddler's apprentice to becoming one of the leading portraitists of British North America, whose subjects included George Washington (who posed for Peale seven times over the course of twenty-three years) and John Cadwalader, George's grandfather. Some of Augustus's uncles—Raphaelle Peale, Rembrandt Peale, Rubens Peale, Titian Ramsay Peale, and Benjamin Franklin Peale—became prominent artists, naturalists, and inventors themselves. Charles Linnaeus "Lin" Peale, Charles Willson Peale's thirteenth child, was less lucky. The least successful among his brothers, he tried soldiering, politics, manufacturing, and farming, and he even got a commission as an officer in the navy of Simón Bolívar. When Bolívar could not pay him, Lin considered becoming a pirate, but instead he returned to Philadelphia to take up taxidermy, as part of the family museum business. He died of apoplexy in 1832, leaving seven living children, including a twelve-year-old, then named Augustin.[4]

In December 1837, Augustin, who had just turned eighteen, was arrested for violent assault and battery against the family of Ralph Brown, which had been assailed on Market Street by "a gang of gentleman ruffians." According to the complaint, Peale, described as "a man of middling size, with sandy hair and whiskers, and striped pants," grabbed the heavily pregnant Mrs. Brown by the waist and "flung her around with a violent jerk," endangering "the life of the unborn innocent, and its mother." Six years later he had yet to find a calling. "There is nothing doing Here among my commershal frends and little prospect of any change," he wrote his uncle Titian in March 1843, hoping for Titian's help in getting a commission as a lieutenant or, barring that, work arranging taxidermied birds in cases. Instead, by 1844, according to one account, Peale was working as a dentist.[5]

In his letter to his uncle, Peale had boasted of connections to prominent Democrats, but the American Republicans had given him a chance for a faster rise. Now, in May 1844, the twenty-four-year-old Augustus, as he now styled himself, was prominent enough to suggest a way for the Natives to respond to Monday's violence: a mass meeting in Independence Square. Samuel Kramer opposed the idea, but his *Native American* ran an extra edition with Peale's call for the meeting. At the last minute John Gihon added the words, "let every man come prepared to defend himself." Around 11 A.M., the *Native American* and the *Sun* inserted the call into their latest extras, and others passed around handbills with the news. The natives would gather at three o'clock.[6]

Bishop Kenrick tried to calm things down with a message to the county's Catholics. "I earnestly conjure you all to avoid all occasion of excitement," he begged, "and then to shun all public places of assemblage, and to do nothing that in any way may exasperate." By noon, men were posting his message on corners throughout the city and its suburbs, especially in Kensington's Third Ward. Boys peeled off some of them to make ribands and cockades, but Kenrick had printed enough for his message to be well distributed. Whether anyone would heed it was another matter. Up on Cadwalader Street, William McDonough remarked to his neighbor, John Paul, "This is going to be a rough day, I presume." "Yes," Paul replied. "And I only wish to God Almighty they'd send us a few more guns." A few hours later, he got his wish. Three men in a wagon appeared at Paul's house with a bundle, the muzzles of flint-locks sticking out of one end. Together, Paul and one of the men from the wagon carried the heavy load inside.[7]

Back in the city, George Cadwalader was also preparing for combat. That morning, in the course of a debate that lasted nearly two hours, he persuaded his subordinate officers that the brigade should put itself at the sheriff's disposal. At noon he and his staff met with Sheriff McMichael. Francis E. Brady, an Irish-born court official and the first cousin of Alderman Hugh Clark, offered an update. Brady had seen the Natives gathering around a torn flag, and he knew there what that meant. "There will be great destruction at Kensington," he warned Cadwalader, "if the mob is not stopped."[8]

McMichael summoned a civilian posse, but he doubted it would suffice, so he also made out a formal request for military assistance. "The peace of the city and county is seriously threatened under existing circumstances," he wrote, "it being impossible for the civil authority without assistance to sustain itself. I beg leave to call upon you to order out the Military force under your command, to be places forthwith at my disposal." With the sheriff's formal request in hand, Cadwalader could act, and at one o'clock, he ordered the whole brigade to assemble. But that would take time. First, messengers would need to spread the word for each company to assemble in its armory by three o'clock. There, they were to be equipped with weapons, including thirteen rounds of ball cartridge per man, while Colonel Pleasonton readied two artillery pieces. Next, the companies would need to form into regiments by four, and by five o'clock Cadwalader could hope to have the regimental commanders at his home, ready to receive his orders. Thirty years earlier, when George's father was put in command of a brigade to defend Philadelphia from British attack, a five-hour mobilization would have been both impressive and sufficient. Even in 1838, the brigade had been given about twenty-four hours' notice before leaving for the Buckshot War in Harrisburg. But now, in 1844, the American Republicans were due to gather at three o'clock. Cadwalader had given the Natives at least a two-hour head start.[9]

As Cadwalader and McMichael conversed, the Natives marched through city streets with a large, tattered American flag, along with a banner reading, "This is the flag trampled under foot by the Irish Papists." Not everyone believed the claim; one witness later testified that the nativists had themselves damaged the flag by dragging it along the pavement in their hasty retreat the previous day. But for many the torn flag was an effective emblem of the danger of Irish immigration.[10]

By three o'clock, a large crowd had gathered in the State House Yard. Mayor John Scott was alarmed to see one man sitting with a double-barreled gun between his legs, and he directed a police officer to confiscate it. Most of the crowd was not carrying weapons, at least not openly. Some of the speakers even tried to calm the assemblage. The president of the meeting was Thomas Newbold, publisher of the *North American* and a member of the city establishment. "Do not let your feelings carry you too far," he begged his listeners, "but act as peaceable citizens. When we adjourn let us go home and trust to the laws for redress." "No!" they shouted back. "No!" This crowd wanted action.[11]

They might have gotten it from Levin, who, along with Peale and Gihon, was listed as one of the secretaries for the meeting, but he declined to speak. Instead, the hothead of the day was an otherwise obscure lawyer named William Hollingshead. "What was the duty of the Native American party?" he asked the crowd. "It was to prosecute with renewed ardor and energy the operations in which they had been engaged." Pointing to the torn flag, now hanging from a window of the State House behind him, Hollingshead urged the natives to return to Kensington. John Perry, who had been interrupted by O'Neill's cart the previous day, offered a compromise. He suggested that the Natives return to Second and Master, but not until Thursday afternoon, presumably to give tempers a time to cool.[12]

Had the crowd heeded Perry, the Kensington fight of May 6 might have remained a one-day affair. To be sure, it would still have counted as an unusually bloody riot, with more gunfire and death than the typical affray. But Philadelphia would have recovered, and the affair of the market house would have joined the list of atrocities somewhere below the burning of Pennsylvania Hall. But just as they had departed from the script when they invaded the market house the previous afternoon, the nativists standing outside of Independence Hall again defied expectations, and chose to turn their battle into a larger campaign. Shouting "this afternoon!" and "adjourn to Second and Master streets now," they voted to return to Kensington that very hour.[13]

And so they marched, five or six abreast, as many as three thousand strong, in a column stretching a quarter mile. They tramped north to Callowhill in Spring Garden, turned east to Second Street in the Northern Liberties, and then north along Second into Kensington. At the head scampered some half-grown boys, followed by somewhat older men. Isaac Hare, who had spent the previous afternoon battering homes on Master Street, now bore the torn flag and its accompanying banner denouncing Irish papists. They made good time, covering the two miles in about half an hour. Their numbers increased as they went, and some of the new men were carrying guns.[14]

C. B. F. O'Neill, the Catholic lawyer, had witnessed the scene in the State House Yard, and now he hurried ahead of the column to warn his Kensington neighbors that the Natives were coming. The families of Kensington had spent the morning debating rumors that the nativists would return and destroy their homes. Some, on hearing of the meeting in the State House Yard, fled their neighborhood with only what possessions they could carry. Manufacturer Francis Brady was in his Germantown Road home when John Taggart, a weaver in his employ, appeared, wearing his finest clothes and a look of terror. "Clear yourself, they are coming!" Taggart warned. Brady immediately understood who "they" were. He gathered his family and fled. Others remained, and now they lined Second Street and turned pale as they stared at the invaders. William Buck—who had seen plenty of bloodshed the night before—begged the marchers to stop. "For God's sake don't go up to that market," he pleaded, "as there will be a heap of you killed and the balance will have to run away!" The Natives gleefully dismissed the warning. "Oh, they'll be afraid to do anything; see what a crowd we have got."[15]

By around four o'clock, the marchers arrived back at the vacant lot on the corner of Second and Master; it was the third nativist meeting there in five days. They cheered and set the torn flag, with its placard, against a house on the south side of the lot. But although this was their official destination, some of them paused only briefly. Shouting, "to hell with the Pope; damn the Papists; down with the Papists!" "Come on, Natives!" and "Let us go to the market!" they moved west. Watching all of this, the pale men on the pavement conferred. "Now the women and children in the houses," they agreed, "and every man to his gun." They ran north up Germantown Road, shouting, "Get the guns!"[16]

In theory, the Natives had marched to Kensington to continue the earlier meeting that had adjourned in the State House Yard, and a handful of them even performed some of the motions of a political rally. Once in the market, Peale, who had helped organize the State House gathering, tried to call a meeting to order. But who would speak? The leaders of the movement—Levin, Kramer, Perry—had remained in Philadelphia City. Even William Hollingshead, who had urged the return to Kensington, seems not to have marched himself.[17]

Aside from Peale, perhaps the only American Republican of any prominence to have made it to Kensington was Charles Jack, who had spoken earlier in the State House Yard. Jack would later insist that he had tried to persuade the crowd to stay in the city, but when "that vast assemblage of most respectable citizens" insisted on marching to Kensington, he agreed to march with them. Now, at the prodding of Thomas Harris, a Southwark Native, Jack reprised Levin's role of the previous day. Over the objections of the clerk of the market, Jack climbed onto a stall to give a speech. All of this was something of a farce, since no one was going to listen to another oration. While Peale, Harris, and Jack may have sincerely believed that they had marched all the way to Kensington to bellow, others had come to avenge Native blood.[18]

It does not take many to start a fight. The unruly "boys" who had led the march into Kensington had ignored both the vacant lot and the market, and charged directly to Cadwalader Street. They began throwing heavy stones at women and attacking the same stretch of doors that Hare and his gang had attacked the previous afternoon. One tried to knock in a door by running at the house and then leaping so he slammed both feet into it.[19]

In the middle of this assault, some of the invaders attacked the Hibernia Hose House, compounding the violence of religious brawl with that of a

Philadelphia firemen's fight. Men raiding a fire house could be expected to target the engine or hose carriage inside, at once an expensive piece of equipment and the symbolic treasure of the fire company. For their part, any company members in the house at the time of attack would defend their house and carriage, with firearms if they could. So the men and youths who had marched from the State House likely knew that attacking a fire company could lead to bloodshed. As if this were not enough of a deterrent, some of them had read in Levin's *Sun* that the Hibernia Hose belonged to Irish Protestants, and thus was not a valid target.[20]

Hibernia Hose Company.
Courtesy of the Museum of Fine Arts, Boston. Photograph © 2021 Museum of Fine Arts, Boston.

But there was the Hibernia Hose House, right on Cadwalader Street, and some of the Natives found it irresistible. Its doors had been barricaded, but members of the mob started battering them with large stones. Harris watched as "a young man, pretty stout built, whom I thought crazy," hurled himself against the small door of the hose house, forcing it open. Once inside, he opened the larger door so his companions could seize the prized carriages. They grabbed two: an old carriage belonging to the Washington Hose Company, and the green and gold Hibernia Hose carriage, barely two weeks old. Then they pulled them east, along Master, toward the vacant lot where the nativists had met the previous afternoon.[21]

Then gunshots, from the west of the market. "The guns were very deeply loaded," recalled one witness, "and sounded more like field-pieces." Some nativists would later swear that the gunshots came first, and thus provoked the attack on the Hibernia Hose House, but most witnesses testified that the gunfire was a response to the attack on the buildings on Cadwalader Street, including the hose house. Most likely, it came from Hibernia Hose members, possibly firing from upper-story windows, trying to pick off the men stealing their carriage. They failed, and the raiding party pulled it further east, where they overturned it and started smashing it with stones. Eventually, they were able to set it on fire, and to use the remaining metal parts as improvised weapons.[22]

The Hibernia Hose men exacted a steep revenge, hitting around half a dozen of the raiders or those standing nearby. The firemen were likely joined by residents of Germantown Road and Cadwalader Street, though in the confusion it was hard to tell, and armed men mingled with women and children. "Boys," one resident warned, "take care of yourselves, or you may shoot one another." No survivor of the riot ever admitted having helped steal the hose carriage, but George Young, who had walked all the way from Southwark, conceded that he had been near the stolen carriage when he was shot. A small bullet ripped through Young's right shoulder blade and left lung, then lodged in his waistband. He fainted but regained consciousness as friends carried him to safety.[23]

John Wesley Rhinedollar, a youth of nineteen with an arrest record for larceny, had arrived in a foul mood. Earlier that day, while eating dinner at the home of a former employer, he had snapped a crisp piece of lamb in his fingers and boasted, "If I had the pluck of a damned Irishman in my hand, I would break it like this." As a teenaged member of the United States Hose of the Northern Liberties, he may have had experience stealing an apparatus. Now he helped pull the hose carriage by its tongue. But this was his last raid, for he collapsed as a musket ball or slug tore through his velveteen jacket, into his back, and through most of his torso, lodging in a rib. Given its trajectory, Rhinedollar may have been shot by his own comrades. He managed to regain his feet and stagger back to his fellow Natives on Cadwalader Street, who momentarily revived him with brandy. But the projectile had severed his aorta, and he was dead or dying as they carried him off on a borrowed settee. His was likely the first death of the day.[24]

Augustus Peale, after his futile efforts to hold a political meeting in the market, had retreated to the open lot at Second and Master. But now he walked back toward the market in an effort—he claimed—to direct others to safety. He made it as far as Cadwalader Street before coming under fire. For a while, he seemed charmed. The first bullet missed his head; the second went between his fingers. A third one hit his palm, but it was a spent ball, causing little injury, and he bent to pick it up. Then his luck ran out, for a fourth shot slammed into his upper left arm, shattering the bone.[25]

Charles Stillwell, a twenty-three-year-old ropemaker, had come up from Southwark, where he was rumored to be a member of the Hope Fire Company. Like Peale and Rhinedollar, he was a young man with an arrest record. Five years earlier, when he was in his late teens, he had been arrested with five others for riot, assault, and battery against a woman. He and his co-defendants had been acquitted, but here he was again at the corner of Washington and Jefferson Streets, in the middle of a riot. According to one witness, he was just standing there, one hand in a pocket, idly looking south toward Master. He fell, shot through the chest by a sniper concealed in a yellow house.[26]

Someone rushed back to the nativist base at the vacant lot. "You that have guns are wanted there." Some that had guns, and some that did not, moved west, toward the sound of gunfire. Once at the market, nativists searched for the shooters, some of whom were firing from behind boards and then retreating to reload. Spotting a man in a stable, a group rushed at him, knocking down the muzzle of his gun as he pulled the trigger. The musket failed to fire, and a gray-headed old man grabbed him by the throat before he could try again. They had nabbed John Taggart, the weaver who had warned his employer to flee. "Kill him!" some cried. "By the holy Virgin you may kill me," Taggart snarled, "for I've had the pleasure of shooting three of you damned Natives."[27]

They came close to killing him—beating him with sticks, stones, and clubs—then dragged him to Alderman Isaac Boileau's Second Street office, kicking him more along the way. By the time he was thrust before the alderman he was so dirty and bruised that, Boileau later explained, "he could hardly be told from a colored man." Boileau took custody of Taggart's musket, still heavily loaded with twenty-six slugs, then formally arrested Taggart and ordered him taken to the Northern Liberties watchhouse. On the way another mob seized him. One man looked for a cleaver with which to decapitate the wounded man. Others figured hanging would be easier, and they pulled the rope off a nearby awning and looped it around the neck of Taggart, who now lost his earlier bravado. "For God's sake don't kill me," Taggart begged, but the mob dragged him through the streets before leaving him for dead on a market-house stall. Surprisingly, Taggart survived and was taken to the Northern Liberties Hall where he was treated with the best medicine of the day: more bleeding. This, too, he survived.[28]

"Scene of the Conflagration."
Courtesy of the American Antiquarian Society.

11

A Rush of the Soldiers

As the fighting intensified, Peter Albright stormed onto the scene. At first glance, Albright—a thirty-six-year-old former constable of the Northern Liberties and a former militia officer—might seem just the man to restore order to the neighborhood. In fact, he was more of a force for chaos.[1]

Albright had a curious background. Though his Catholic father and Protestant mother had married at Christ Church, the Episcopalian church where George Cadwalader worshipped, they brought two sons, Jacob and later Peter, to be baptized by the Catholic priests of St. Augustine's. In his twenties, Albright had joined the Democratic Party in the Northern

Liberties, gaining appointment as a justice of the peace. He even served on the Democrats' local committee of naturalization. By 1837, however, he shifted to the Whigs, whom he likely helped by importing hundreds of illegal voters from New Jersey in one election, and stuffing ballot boxes in the next. In the aftermath, a Pennsylvania legislative committee found him to be "an individual of a bad reputation notorious for the commission of frauds at elections." But Albright grew disenchanted with the Whigs as well, perhaps because he felt he had been denied higher office in favor of an Irish candidate. By 1844, he was reputed to be a nativist.[2]

Though Albright's neighbors still addressed him as "colonel," his efforts as a militia officer had been to mock the institution. In 1833, he had paraded his company of ordinary militia in "fantastical dress," with men variously outfitted in five-foot-wide caps, fire buckets, and animal skins and armed with umbrellas and broomsticks. After facing a court-martial and spending some time in jail, Albright reappeared in the uniform of a Revolutionary War officer, with shoe polish on his face as a sign that he thought that militia officers were mainly adept at brownnosing. While his antics infuriated senior militia commanders, they delighted working men who hated the choice between mandatory militia service and the stiff fines for avoiding it. "If found guilty, and deprived of his commission," commented one newspaper, "the persevering and praiseworthy Colonel Albright has a chance of becoming the most popular man in the district." Though he despised military service, Albright could be personally belligerent. In 1841, as a tavern keeper who made his living on liquor sales, he had broken up a temperance meeting near his home, first with "the most abusive language that was ever uttered by man," and then with his fists. Even so, some men were willing to swear that Albright had helped suppress earlier Kensington riots.[3]

Albright had been passing through Kensington on Monday, May 6, the first day of the violence, and he had helped carry Patrick Fisher, wounded in the market, to an apothecary. He returned on Tuesday in time to see George Young fall and helped carry him to safety as well. "Colonel," a neighbor asked. "Must we stand for this?" If Albright was going to lead, he needed more than umbrellas and broomsticks. He returned to his house to get a gun, and told others to arm themselves and gather around him. Some of them raided

Northern Liberty Hall, where a German militia company kept fifty stand of muskets. Militiamen and Northern Liberties police snatched back most of the weapons, but the Natives made off with twelve or fifteen muskets.[4]

Albright later claimed that he meant only to have an armed force ready for Sheriff McMichael. He would, he said, neither act without the sheriff nor obey the sheriff's command to intervene without weapons, "as I had been beaten and stoned before in attempting to serve him." Others were less sure of Albright's intentions. They heard him muttering that he would "give the bloody rascals their due." Whether Albright himself fired his weapon would later be a matter of some dispute. But he did acknowledge gathering seventeen armed men, at least one of whom was to die in combat. With his help, it seems, the Natives improved their firepower.[5]

The most intense gun battle lasted for about two hours, from 4 to 6 P.M. The Natives established a rear base along Second Street. Most of them, and they may have numbered thousands, were unarmed and sensibly avoided coming within musket range of the market. Some remained at the vacant lot at Second and Master, others by the seminary one block south, at Second and Phoenix, and still others another block south, at Second and Franklin, the site of their bonfire the previous night. Second Street was far enough from the main fighting that the Natives could safely welcome reinforcements heading north from the city and distribute weapons, and combatants could regroup. Moreover, the Second Street home of Dr. A. E. Griffith, south of the convent, served as a field hospital where doctors and surgeons could try their hands at emergency military surgery. They received men with wounds from smooth musket balls and irregularly shaped slugs, the latter of which left larger, more dangerous wounds. Apparently Griffith and his colleague Dr. Bethell knew their business, since they saved the lives of both Augustine Peale and George Young though both had been expected to die.[6]

Second Street was still close enough to the market that natives gathering there could hear gunfire from the west and listen in shock as runners bore news of more men being shot. Those still eager to fight—and there were fifty or more—could move west along Master to the market house or the open lot between the market and the Hibernia Hose House, where they could fire northwest along Cadwalader. The Natives were well armed, but they had trouble finding targets. Men were shooting at them from alleys, houses, or rooftops, then disappearing before the Natives could return fire. By contrast, the Natives lacked cover. They could hide behind a brick house at the corner of Jefferson Street or crouch behind a pile of gravel in the open lot. Solomon Vickers—conspicuous in a green jacket and white hat—won the admiration of one reporter with his display of military expertise. "Sometimes, like a regular tirailleur, he would lie on the ground and let the fire of his enemy pass over him—then rise to his knees load, take aim, and fire," noted the *Daily Chronicle*. "At other times he would fire stooping or lying on his face. Upward of twenty shots were fired at him, but not one took effect, he escaped unhurt—without a scratch. His conduct would have done honor to the bravest soldier on the battle field."[7]

Others were less lucky. Charles Orte was shot in the head. Later, he showed off the hat he had been wearing, with the bullet hole through the crown. Lewis Greble, a thirty-two-year-old father of two, was also shot through his hat, but just above the hat band. Peter Albright pulled him away, but Greble died before Albright could get him home. Later, Albright lifted Greble's hat and saw his brain protruding from the wound. Lewis's brother, Edwin, had joined a friend to watch the procession. They staked out a spot some ways to the north and stood in their wagon to observe the combat. After seeing several men shot and carried off, Edwin Greble had had enough. "I am sick now," he told his friend. "Let's go." He likely did not realize that his brother had been killed.[8]

The Natives' opponents held a better position. Though roughly dressed—most fought in the shirtsleeves and caps they wore for weaving, not the more respectable coats and hats—they were surprisingly well armed, toting "handsome, brass mounted rifles." Moreover, they had better cover. Their rear base was Germantown Road, which ran parallel to Cadwalader, one block west. Women and children could find some shelter there, while men could reload and then return to the fight. A key resource was Patrick Murray's grocery, on the southeast corner of Germantown Road and Jefferson Street. As a large, three-story brick building, it could serve as a fortress, providing both cover and good sight lines for those inside. More importantly, while Murray did not sell guns, he did stock both gunpowder and shot. According to some witnesses, that afternoon he was willing to let his neighbors load their weapons with his supplies, not caring too much if they paid.[9]

To fire down Cadwalader, men could cut along one of the several courts—something between a street and an alley—that connected Germantown to Cadwalader. Harmony Court, just forty-eight feet north of Jefferson, was particularly well positioned. Harmony was lined with frame houses, some of which offered clear fields of fire down Cadwalader Street toward Jefferson and the market. One witness, William Friheller, could see no signs of organization among the men. "They did not appear to have any commander," he later recalled. "they appeared straggling, fighting on their own hook, here, there and everywhere." Yet they did begin to work out some basic tactics. Three or four boys, ages twelve to sixteen, served as scouts, running back and forth and beckoning the men to shoot east, toward Cadwalader Street. Smaller ones carried baskets of ammunition to the fighters. And small squads of men might venture a block or two away, only to return to reload. Men took cover where they could, firing over fences, piles of gravel, and carts. The ones in houses, especially in upper-story windows, had the best advantage. They could snipe at Natives in the market house without being seen themselves. But staying indoors was no guarantee of safety; some of the bullets were powerful enough to smash through walls. One shooter was injured when his gun exploded, but he found another and kept shooting. Another broke his ramrod and retreated to make a new one. "I'm sure I've shot five or six," he boasted to a neighbor. "The Lord is with me."[10]

Back on the Native side of the street, Matthew Hammitt, the nephew of a prominent Kensington shipwright, was moving north, firing a fowling piece better suited to shooting songbirds than for street combat. At thirty-seven, Hammitt was older than most of the combatants, and he looked older still, perhaps due to heavy drinking. Yet he was as determined as any. At one point, he had been among the group led by Albright, and Albright and another friend said they begged him to withdraw. Hammitt shrugged them off, vowing to "stick to them." He had just stepped off the curbstone into Jefferson Street when his hat flew off and he fell backward. A musket ball had drilled into his left ear, passed through his brain, and got part of the way into the other ear before stopping. John M'Leary and another man ventured into the gunfire to drag him away, waving their hats at the gunmen in a plea for mercy. Receiving none, they pulled Hammitt out of the street while under fire themselves, only to find that he was already dead, his brain oozing out from the entry wound. A man from Harmony Court came down and snatched Hammitt's little gun.[11]

Some residents enjoyed the spectacle, at least at first. Martha Longshore, a widow, lived in an alley dwelling and could have taken shelter. Instead, she later testified, "I insisted on going out," and did so in time to see about a dozen of her neighbors firing down Jefferson Street at the nativist invaders in the market house. "There were so many guns fired off it was impossible to hear," she would recall. "The women were busy helping their husbands and throwing stones," Longshore later testified. "I saw ten old women, with caps, very busy." Another woman roused her boarders and urged them to take up arms against the nativists. One old man simply walked down Cadwalader Street, oblivious to the battle around him. Some nativists cried "shoot him!" but a doctor among them rushed out to escort the man to safety and to scold him for his imprudence.[12]

Other residents did all they could to stay out of the fighting. John Steele, whose house on the east side of Cadwalader was directly in the crossfire, wisely shut his door and locked it behind him. George Friheller's wife opened her door on Germantown Road in order to let her husband in just as a group of combatants came around the corner. To her surprise, a "respectable looking man," seeking the quickest shelter, jumped into her arms. As bricks pounded against their walls and windows, women closed shutters and comforted sobbing children. Others hauled trunks, furniture, and bedding north to relative safety. By the time the refugees had reached Mud Lane, just a few hundred feet to the north, they felt safe enough to climb to the roofs of houses and watch the destruction from there. C. B. F. O'Neill found himself torn between his identities as a lawyer and a Kensington Catholic. "This is bad work, a day of retribution will come," he told his neighbors. "There is still law in the land." But he was losing faith in that premise, and he later told a court that his neighbors would have been murdered, their town burned, "but for the interference of ten or twenty men."[13]

Isaac Hare, one of the more violent nativists of the previous day's fighting, was back on the open lot between the market house and the hose house. On Monday he had been armed only with a club and a faulty pistol;

now he had musket and possibly a bayonet. He also had his gang with him, egging him on. "Go it, Ike!" they cried when he stepped into Cadwalader Street for a better shot. To the east, some Native raiding parties moved north from the lot at Second and Master. One group, spotting a face in a window on Washington Street, shot at it, then broke in the door. There they found Mary Mallon, an Irish-born Catholic in her mid-thirties. They grabbed her arm.

"Do you have any guns in the house?"

"We never had any guns, either here or in Ireland," she replied.

"Are you Catholic?"

"Yes."

"Would you die for your religion?"

"If you think it proper to shoot me, I would."

"We would not kill a woman," they assured her. "But if we had your husband, we would shoot him to inches." Then, telling her she was a decent, truthful woman, they left. All the while, Mallon's husband had been hiding silently in the cellar. At Washington and Jefferson, Joseph Fow led a band of armed men who broke into a home and found Patrick Magee lying on a sickbed, unable to rise. Finding no weapons, the men shook Magee's hand and left.[14]

Around five o'clock, the Natives made another assault on the Hibernia Hose House. After seizing the firemen's tools—they could serve as weapons—the Natives dragged the house's new bell into the street, where they shattered it. Then they turned to a classic rioter's tactic—arson—setting fire either to the hose house itself or the house on the corner of Cadwalader and Master Streets. The flames jumped from one frame building to the next, and soon multiple buildings on both streets were burning. The Natives now commanded the street, and they were able to fire at anyone trying to douse the flames.[15]

Even as the fire spread, the gunfire wound down, with pauses between volleys. Joseph Rice, a weaver in his late fifties; his wife, Bridget; and their two children had spent most of the afternoon in their Cadwalader Street home, the door fastened behind them. But at some point their neighbor knocked on the door to warn them that the Hibernia Hose House was on fire. Thinking, perhaps, that the shooting was over—it had been quiet for about fifteen minutes—Joseph went to investigate, leaving Bridget inside with the two crying children. As he peered over his fence, Hare and Vickers, on the east side of Cadwalader, took aim and fired. One slug hit the doorjamb of the blacksmith's shop behind Rice's house. The other drilled a perfectly circular hole into Rice's forehead, dropping him instantly. "By God!" his shooter exclaimed, slapping his thigh. "I have got my man!" When her husband failed to return, Bridget opened the door. Her neighbor Jane Develin gave her the news: "Joe's shot!" He was still breathing, but unconscious. Risking further gunfire, the two terrified women carried him inside, where neighbors put wet cloths on his head and gave Bridget the rather hopeless reassurance that he would recover. Instead, after an hour, he died. Bridget found the family Bible and wrote the date, "so as to let the children know the day upon which their father was killed."[16]

The fire that Rice had given his life to see continued to spread. From his vantage point at Cadwalader and Jefferson, C. B. F. O'Neill could see one house rapidly burning, while another had already been destroyed. He later recalled, "I calculated on the whole row being burned down that night." It was a good guess. The Natives had just destroyed the nearest fire company, and others nearby dared not drive into the crossfire. With no one to fight it, the blaze spread from house to house on Cadwalader, as well as to the market across the street. Residents seized what possessions they could, some risking gunfire to do so. Carpet-maker Ashton Hutchinson was shot in the face as he carried what he could from his burning manufactory. The bedridden Patrick Magee, who had endured the armed search of his house, now faced death as adjoining houses caught fire. When his daughter was unable to lift him, a neighbor pulled him to safety, but Magee's home and possessions were destroyed. Jane Develin, who had helped carry the dying Joseph Rice inside, now gathered her child and fled to the woods, where she remained all night.[17]

"A great sea of fire raged," wrote one reporter, "the roaring noise of which was heard at a considerable distance, mingled with the crash of falling timbers or tumbling walls." "In a short time," wrote another, "the whole row of buildings were in flames, the Irishmen still continued firing at intervals from their houses, even after they were set on fire, and as fast as they were driven out of one house by the heat of the flames and the falling rafters, they took refuge in another; They fought with a desperation becoming madmen." Not all of them were able to outrace the flames. Days later, a charred body would be found in a Cadwalader Street house, likely one of several people who were wounded by gunfire and remained to perish. Two miles to the south, residents of Philadelphia City could see the glow in the sky. Natives considered it a victory. They had seized the market house, from which they had been chased the previous day, and raised the "tattered banner" that had become the symbol of their cause.[18]

Throughout the afternoon, both sides had fought with almost no interference by any kind of authority. Constable Saunders Gavit was back on the scene, but he again knew he was outnumbered. When someone suggested that he try to break up a fight between nativists invading a house and Irishmen defending it with bricks, Gavit replied, "there is not enough of us—there's no use of us going to have our brains dashed out." Meanwhile, General Cadwalader stayed in the city, hoping to assemble his brigade in Washington Square by 5 p.m., and messengers had spread out through the city with his orders. But not until seven o'clock was Cadwalader's brigade ready to march north.[19]

When it did, it was an impressive sight. At least two hundred foot soldiers, accompanied by cavalry and two cannon, moved together to the beat of a drum. To show that he was ready for battle, Cadwalader had chosen an undress uniform rather than his most elegant finery. Sheriff McMichael and his posse marched alongside. Only forty or fifty men had answered his call for a posse, but at least their presence could show that the brigade embodied the civil law, not military tyranny. As the body moved north, sidewalk crowds heard the drums and then gaped as the soldiers themselves appeared.[20]

When Cadwalader reached Master Street around eight o'clock, he deployed his troops for action. He ordered Colonel Pleasonton's two cannon loaded with grape and canister—ammunition that would turn them into enormous shotguns, killing anyone in the general direction their muzzles pointed. One faced along Jefferson Street, toward the area from which most of the Irish gunfire had come. The other faced toward the now-burning market, where the Natives had established themselves. If either side resumed hostilities, Cadwalader's men could kill them instantly. He then dispatched two companies to the north end of the market. The arrival of the troops had an immediate impact. Merchant George Martin had been watching more or less continuous gunfire around the market house for hours; it only ceased when the troops came into view. A few of the boldest members of the crowd snatched at the soldiers' bayonets, shouting, "you dare not fire—you know us!" Cadwalader sought to calm the crowd with a short speech. He "knew neither friend nor foe in the matter," he explained, "and was determined at all hazards to see the majesty of the law vindicated." Apparently the speech had something for everyone, since the *Sun*'s reporter thought that Cadwalader "made a very handsome speech to the Native Americans" acknowledging that the wrongs against them "were great, very great indeed." The Natives shouted their approval.[21]

McMichael's constables were now confident enough to start searching houses. When they found John Holmes (said by Catholics to be an Orangeman) in a room with a heavily loaded rifle, they arrested him and turned him over to the troops. Better still, the troops provided protection to several fire and hose companies, which now began to play water on the burning market house and the twenty or thirty burning houses. "They went quietly to work, and did immense execution," wrote a reporter, and managed to confine the fire to the rows of houses on Cadwalader Street, north and west of the market.[22]

A reporter for the *Sun* described a hellish scene. "There is now an alarm of fire, which it is said is near the field of battle, and the confusion attending upon it, the vociferation of the firemen, and ringing of bells in the upper districts, the carrying away of the dead, the groans of the dying, the shouts of the Americans, and the yells of their enemies, the rolling drums of the military, will conspire to render a scene at once exciting and terrific to the stoutest heart." "Dark red clouds are lighting up with a horrid glare the blue and quiet sky," wrote another reporter. "Rolls of bright smoke taking fantastic shapes thicken in the air, while here and there thro' the dense crowd the flame-tongues of living light may be seen licking with fire some new building preparatory to its destruction. . . Hark! a shot! a scream! a rush of the soldiers! and another victim is borne away for surgical assistance."[23]

Under the protection of the troops, the inhabitants of the nearby blocks crept out of their shelters and salvaged what possessions they could: pillows, chairs, beds, and tables. One man was fortunate enough to find a horse and cart to carry his furniture, his wife, and three sobbing children, but he had lost his home. "The toil of 20 years gone in one moment," he exclaimed. "My God! have I deserved this?" Law student Isaac Mickle encountered an Irishman trying to persuade his pig to evacuate. "The game was completely blocked," Mickle wrote that evening. "The Irishman looked at the hog and the hog at the Irishman with mutual wonderment and despair." Eventually, Mickle and a companion were able to drive the pig in the direction its owner wished. "Sad business this!" lamented the Irishman as he departed. Gradually the flames died down, and the firemen rang the bells that signaled it was time to go home. Until around 11 P.M., a few stray shots rang down Master Street, apparently without hitting anyone. Unsurprisingly, militiamen wandering the unfamiliar, dark alleys and courts of Kensington failed to find the gunmen.[24]

While the calm was welcome, Cadwalader had arrived hours too late. Rhinedollar, Greble, Hammitt, and Stillwell were dead, Young, Peale, and several others grievously wounded. The *Public Ledger* would list Wright Ardis with a "dangerous wound," William Hillman with a "serious" one, James Whitaker with a splintered thigh bone, and John Lusher with a chest wound, which looked fatal. After Dr. Bethell extracted the slug from his arm, Augustus Peale made it home to the city, where he collapsed, both from loss of blood and from having not eaten all day. Around midnight, Dr. George Washington Norris arrived and examined Peale's splintered humerus, deciding on immediate amputation near the shoulder. The operation was successful, and Peale would recover relatively soon.[25]

Joseph Rice was the only Kensington Catholic who could be positively identified as having been killed on May 7, but the *Chronicle* suspected there were others. "An Irishman named Johnson was killed," it reported "and three others were seen lying dead in the yards at the rear of the buildings. It is thought that many bodies were burnt in the houses set on fire; but it was impossible to ascertain any thing positive in relation to them; for, though constantly firing guns and muskets, their persons could not be seen." Another account reported that an unnamed Irish gunman had shot two or three Natives by popping out from behind the corner of a house on Jefferson Street. That cover saved him from Native fire until a boy crept up behind him, pulled a pistol from his pocket, and shot him through the back of the head.

If there was any consolation, it lay in the fact that Kensington's Catholic institutions—the seminary and St. Michael's Church—remained standing. By 1 A.M. on the morning of May 8, Catholic men were said to be inside most of the county's Catholic churches, "armed and equipped, ready for attack." Cadwalader's troops, along with McMichael's posse, guarded St. Michael's, the most obvious potential target. Wednesday morning's *Daily Chronicle* warned that it could not yet count the dead. "Enough is known, however, to show that two of the bloodiest days Philadelphia ever witnessed have just closed—but to be renewed, in all probability, on the third, to-day. We trust, however, that the worst is over."[26]

It was not.

"Burning of St. Michael's Church."
Courtesy of the American Antiquarian Society.

12

How Can We Fire on Our Own Citizens?

By the morning of Wednesday, May 8, the Third Ward of Kensington had become a battlefield. Brick houses stood gutted; frame houses were left only charred timbers and tottering chimneys, looking, wrote one reporter, "like blackened monuments of anarchy." Some houses that had escaped the fire were perforated with bullet holes. Families that had once inhabited these ruins, or those that feared further violence, packed furniture and other belongings into cabs, carts, drays, or whatever other vehicles were available and fled the neighborhood, the women and children riding on top of the household goods. Others remained, the men vowing vengeance, the women weeping and tearing at their hair or handing weapons to their menfolk so they could avenge the dead. Farmers looking for the market house found only desolation, so they improvised stands to sell their offerings.[1]

About 7 A.M., two hours after sunrise, the Native Americans reoccupied the corner of Second and Franklin, at the southern edge of the Third Ward and the site of Monday night's bonfire. Again they raised their tattered flag, along with the placard blaming "Irish Papists" for the damage.[2]

Even as they gathered, most of the troops that had arrived the previous evening went home, having been awake all night. They were relieved by just two companies of the Second Brigade, composed of troops from the outlying areas of Philadelphia County, rather than the city troops of Cadwalader's First Brigade. Along with the smaller Third Brigade, these composed the First Division, under the command of Major General Patterson. Patterson himself remained downtown in the State House, where express riders arrived every half hour with reports from Kensington. But he did not send reinforcements, leaving only a few dozen men at most to try to keep the peace.[3]

The troops guarded the corpse of Joseph Rice, shot in the head while peering over the fence the day before. Eventually, around noon, coroner Francis Brelsford arrived, found the spot where Rice had been shot, and rather bravely peeked over the same fence. No one sniped at Brelsford, but he did see fires still burning, troops on patrol, and "considerable confusion." No one could be sure who was an agent of law and who was a vigilante mob. Gunsmith Edward Tryon handed a hundred muskets over to men he took to be a legitimate patrol; months later, he would be denied payment by the county on the grounds that the men had lacked any authority.[4]

With the tacit approval of the militia, some of whom joined in, nativist search parties roamed along Kensington streets searching houses for weapons. One search party discovered a stash of half-melted gold and silver in the ruins of one of the burned houses. The troops intervened, but not before the looters had made off with much of an old woman's life savings. Other searchers probed closets, sheds, and pigsties, finding about a dozen muskets, shotguns, and pistols. One of the weapons was in the hands of an Irishman, Oliver Cree, whom they beat severely before turning him over to the mayor of the Northern Liberties, who tried to protect the bruised man by locking him up in a cell in his office. Next door lay George Young—shot through the lung the previous day and thought to be dying. Young's sister sat on the steps outside "in an almost frantic state," surrounded by an excited crowd.[5]

Aside from Cree, no Irish Catholics seem to have put up serious resistance that morning, choosing instead to evacuate with as many of their possessions as they could cart off. By around noon, the mob grew even bolder. After searching a house for suspected weapons, they would set it on fire. Troops extinguished a blaze set near the ruined market house, but were too late to save a house on Washington Street and a row of houses in Harmony Court. Elsewhere, troops guarded fire companies as they fought the flames.[6]

Of all the buildings in the Third Ward, St. Michael's Church stood out as a likely target for arson. Churches had burned before. In 1831, in New York City, St. Mary's Church burned under mysterious circumstances. In 1834, in a much clearer expression of anti-Catholic rage, the mob in Charlestown, Massachusetts, had torched the convent there and threatened the town's Catholic church. Following the destruction of the convent, insurance companies refused to cover a new Catholic church in Roxbury unless it was sheathed in brick for improved fire resistance. In 1842, following the ban on religious instruction in New York's schools, a mob had attacked the New York bishop's residence, on the grounds of that city's cathedral, dispersing only when a troop of cavalry arrived. And just the previous month, in April 1844, Brooklyn nativists had threatened to burn a Catholic church there before they were driven away by armed Irishmen.[7]

Philadelphia had its own history of threatened and actual attacks on churches. During the Orange riot of 1831, Protestants claimed to have heard Catholics threatening to burn the Southwark Baptist Church after Rev. William Ashton gave an anti-Catholic sermon. In August 1834, just days after the destruction of the Charlestown convent, a white mob destroyed the First African Presbyterian Church, though they used stones and bricks rather than fire. In 1842, anti-abolition mobs burned the Second African Presbyterian Church on St. Mary's Street. Now Catholic churches faced the same danger.[8]

St. Michael's was both the nearest Catholic church to the Kensington battlefield and a symbol of Kensington's Irish Catholic community. Not quite ten years old in 1844, it had been built in part through the efforts of three Irish-born Catholics: Bishop Kenrick, Alderman Hugh Clark, and Father (later Bishop) John Hughes, all of them targets of nativist anger. So right from the start of the May agitation, Kensington residents had traded rumors that St. Michael's would be attacked. Nativists claimed that on May 6, armed men had marched from the church to defend the seminary, killing William Wright and wounding Nathan Ramsey. On Tuesday, May 7, Levin's *Sun* reported that "large stacks of fire arms and men are secreted in St. Michael's Church," and by Wednesday morning, nativists could be heard vowing to burn every Catholic church in Philadelphia.[9]

Father Terence Donaghoe, who had pastored St. Michael's from its dedication in 1834, was by this point well into the process of moving to Dubuque along with the Sisters of Charity of the Blessed Virgin, and he had spent several months in Iowa getting things ready. Returning to Kensington in the early spring, he had fled to the countryside after the violence of May 6, missing the chance to watch wounded nativists carried past his windows on Tuesday the seventh. He returned in time to celebrate Mass on the morning of May 8, the Feast of the Apparition of St. Michael, the church's patron saint. He next went downtown to visit Kenrick, then decamped for the village of Haddonfield, about nine miles outside of town.[10]

This left Father William Loughran in charge of the church, but at around 10 A.M., Captain Jonas Fairlamb of the Wayne Artillery Corps (which included at least one Catholic member) gently advised Loughran to depart as well. The priest complied, gathering some especially valuable books and departing in a cab, leaving keys to the church and the parsonage with Fairlamb. Fairlamb searched the church for weapons, finding nothing but a fowling piece. The captain then locked the church, handed the keys to his commander—Brigadier General Horatio Hubbell of the Second Brigade—and gave his men a break for lunch. Then, with the twenty-four men under his command, he resumed patrolling the area.[11]

Around 2 P.M., Fairlamb got the report that buildings on one of the courts west of the market was on fire and went with his troops to investigate.

Just as they arrived, they heard that a mob was stoning St. Michael's and Donaghoe's parsonage next door. The Waynes hurried back and stopped the stoning, only to be distracted by yet another call of a fire to the west. When they left to check on this second fire, the mob swarmed again. General Hubbell remained at St. Michael's, and he himself ordered three young men down from the fence, but a larger group was behind the church, smashing one of the back windows. Someone got word to Fairlamb, and he ordered his men back to the church at double-quick time, but he was too late. The church's enemies had set the building ablaze.[12]

The fire burned quickly, showing through the church's Gothic window, while smoke, and then flame, shot through the roof. People surrounded the church, some trying to save it, others cheering its destruction. Someone in the crowd played a fife: perhaps "Yankee Doodle," or perhaps "Boyne Water," that old Orange anthem. Others sang and danced. One report claimed that even amid the chaos, a grieving couple held a funeral for their infant in the churchyard. The sturdy church stood for more than an hour, its wooden crucifix standing, wrote one reporter, "amid the living fire like a monument of unyielding faith." But at last it shook and collapsed, to the cheers of the crowd below.[13]

Meanwhile, other half-grown boys were ransacking Donaghoe's parsonage, a three-story brick building just across a small open space from the church. They tossed Donaghoe's belongings out the windows. "Here comes a carpet waving in the wind as it falls," noted a reporter, "and now demijohns, a crucifix, some sacred images are flying through the air, tossed by the infuriated multitude, and carried away by the spectators. A Catholic Bible produced some contention, but it was at length gotten by one individual who ran off with it." The boys salvaged some loot for themselves; in a tavern that evening, they would pass around cigars from Father Donaghoe's supply and show off a passbook from a nearby grocery, snickering at the priest's purchases of brandy. Other possessions they destroyed out of spite. When Donaghoe's copy of Shakespeare landed at Philip Banks's feet, Banks wanted to read it, but the boys snatched it away and tore out all the pages. Whatever the boys did not loot was doomed anyway, for soon the parsonage was burning, its roof having caught fire from the blazing St. Michael's. The fire also spread to adjoining houses and a weaver's factory. Terrified residents threw their furniture and belongings out of windows, then ran out themselves, clutching their children.[14]

Fairlamb's Wayne Artillery tried to impose some order; when two nativists appeared with muskets, the soldiers seized the weapons. By charging back and forth along Second Street, Fairlamb's men were able to clear a path for the fire engines that soon arrived. But two dozen militia had scant chance to control a crowd that may have numbered in the thousands. Mostly they watched as the church burned down to its walls. The mob even tore up the surrounding shrubs and trees.[15]

With St. Michael's and its parsonage burning, the mob moved south on Second Street to the Sisters of Charity complex, which had survived the attack on Monday evening. It would not be so fortunate this time. Men tore down the fence (hastily repaired after Monday's attack), battered down the door of the school house, and smashed the windows. One group started a fire in the vestibule, while another ran upstairs to the cupola, setting a second fire there. "At the same moment," a reporter noted, "the lower stories are filled with the Natives who are tearing, pulling, smashing and destroying everything. The spirit of demolition is active. Windows, doors, fences, the trees in the garden, the flowers, even the grass is being pulled up by the roots, and the air is filled with them as they are hurled flying in all directions." As they had with St. Michael's, the crowd sang and danced as their target burned. Across the street from the seminary lay Joseph Corr's temperance grocery, a narrow brick building on land owned by George Cadwalader himself. Nativists suspected the store had sheltered the Irish marksmen who had defended the seminary two days prior. Now they ransacked the grocery, destroying its windows and furniture, and playfully tossing mackerels, herrings, hams, tongues, and pickled beef at one another or into the street. About twenty members of the sheriff's posse tried to intervene, but the looters fired a pistol and started chasing the posse instead.[16]

As the men of the posse ran south, they spotted safety: an advancing column of militia. Though Colonel Joseph Murray commanded the column, the most experienced officer was James Page, captain of the State Fencibles, who had served in the militia since 1814 and also bore the rank of colonel. Page suggested that Murray form a line of troops across Second

Street, giving the posse a barrier behind which to escape the mob. Then Page himself stepped forward, shouting and waving his sword to distract the rioters. The plan worked. The looters forgot their quarry and instead surrounded Page—one of the most admired men in Philadelphia—to hear what he had to say. Someone even found him something to stand on, so he could better be heard.[17]

Page scanned the crowd, seeing some old friends, but also some "brutal and desperate" men, "mad with the liquor they got from the plundered stores." "Liberty or Death," some shouted. "Fire,—fire, and be damned." If just one of them threw a brick or a punch, Page feared, he would be killed and would be followed by hundreds more as the battalion behind him avenged his death. A reporter watched in dread as "to see an armed military force proceeding in one direction, and meeting a mob, mad with desperation, ready to die." "The slightest imprudence on the part of either body," the reporter later wrote, "would have resulted in the most fatal consequences."[18]

Instead, Page calmed the crowd. His listeners, he believed, were "mad with the passion of the moment and stimulated to wrong by the wicked and vicious who are ever ready to profit by such opportunities." If he could just bore them long enough, perhaps that passion would fade. "They listened to me patiently," he recalled, "dropping away and thinning out by degrees." Though some had threatened him, none had so much as touched him. But the danger had been real. Nearly thirty years later, Page would tremble as he recorded his memories of that afternoon.[19]

Page's bravery had saved the posse, but the looters kept scouring the neighborhood for new targets. As some shouted to Page as they dispersed, "three cheers for you, Colonel—but you can't come it." Kensington families marked their homes with American flags or, if they had no flags, hastily stitched together red, white, and blue muslin to make patriotic bunting. Others displayed their copies of Kramer's *Native American*. Those who lacked even such means grabbed chalk or charcoal to scrawl on their houses the words "Native Americans" or "No Popery Here." The Natives passed over such homes and avoided torching adjoining buildings, including Corr's grocery, lest the flames spread to Native dwellings.[20]

At about 5:30, Cadwalader arrived at the head of another militia column. With him were his superior, Major General Patterson, and

Sheriff McMichael, again accompanied by a token posse to represent civil authority. Unlike Tuesday, the arrival of this combined force failed to stop the violence. The looters did not directly attack the posse or the troops; to the contrary, they continued to cheer. But when the posse tried to arrest a looter, he was rescued by his comrades. More seriously, the looters continued their work. One group headed west to the home of Alderman Hugh Clark, at the southwest corner of Fourth and Master Streets. They also attacked the neighboring tavern, belonging to Hugh's brother Patrick, which also served as the ward's polling place on election days. By six o'clock, they had gutted both buildings: spilling Patrick's liquor, smashing the windows, throwing furniture into the streets, and slashing open the beds so that feathers rained down and filled the coats of the people below. A boy sat on the steps of the tavern, beating a rhythm on an iron stove. Someone set some cotton on fire in an effort to burn down the tavern, but when Carroll Hose men protested, a man tossed the burning parcels out the window. Another group moved to the northwest and attacked Patrick Murray's grocery shop, which had served as a strongpoint for the neighborhood defenders. Here, too, they destroyed windows and furniture, looking glasses and bureaus. Even the arrival of more troops and the pointing of a brass cannon at the rioters did not stop them as it had the night before. The militia had lost its power to intimidate.[21]

Throughout the day, the mob had toyed with the soldiers, and one man got close enough to impale his hand on a bayonet. But militia officers avoided an extended clash with a crowd that outnumbered them. Though General Patterson had ordered the First Division to assemble at Second and Franklin (also the nativists' rallying point), he specified 4 P.M. as the time. From 8:00 A.M. until 4:30 P.M., only five companies of the Second and Third brigades—the Philadelphia Cadets, the Monroe Guards, the Wayne Artillery, the Lafayette Light Guards, and the Independent Rifle Corps—seem to have been on duty in Kensington. Perhaps a hundred men faced a mob of several times that size that was freely running from target to target. And while the soldier's uniforms looked splendid on parade or at a military ball, the tight coats and heavy leather caps likely slowed them down in the heat, which reached seventy-eight degrees. By 1:40 P.M., Hubbell wrote Cadwalader in frustration that he could not stop the arson, and that his men, having been on duty all day, would need relief. He had yet to see the sheriff.[22]

Moreover, the militia officers were still not sure whether they had legal authority to use their weapons. Even when nativists mocked the troops or threw dung in their faces, the officers restrained themselves. Cadwalader's artillery commander, Colonel Pleasonton, steamed at the insults. Frustration with militia service was nothing new for the West Pointer. In June 1838, he had been unable to deploy his cannon when the gun crews did not report for duty, and then he dismissed what few troops he had when they explained that they were bakers who needed to get back to their ovens before their dough spoiled. After stripping off his own uniform in disgust, Pleasonton had dressed in civilian clothes to report his failure, then "wished all citizen soldiers most heartily at the devil." Later that year, during the Buckshot War, his plan to storm the capitol had been ignored. Governor Ritner had then appointed him paymaster for the troops summoned to Harrisburg, and ever since he had been dogged by accusations that his accounts had not squared. In April 1844 Pleasonton had felt so slighted by his treatment at the hands of state officials that he had sent Cadwalader a disgusted letter of resignation. The officers of Pleasonton's regiment had begged Cadwalader not to let their commander leave, and Pleasonton was thus still in command of the First Brigade's artillery when Cadwalader summoned him to duty and gave him new reasons to be disgusted.[23]

Pleasonton had spent Tuesday night in Kensington amid dozens of burning buildings that no one was trying to save, surrounded by excited, armed men and exposed to musketry from nearby houses. Lacking orders from either the sheriff or the major general, Pleasonton did not think his troops had been authorized to fire their own weapons to disarm or disperse the mob. On Wednesday morning, a furious Pleasonton bypassed Cadwalader entirely and wrote instead to Major General Patterson, demanding a written order "to resist any attack that may be made on my command by missiles or shot of any kind from any quarter by employing my force in the most effectual prompt and decided manner without waiting for any other order from the Sheriff or any other officer." Barring that, he would not leave his parade ground. As Pleasonton later acknowledged, his going over Cadwalader in the chain of command had been "highly insubordinate." It was likely also personally insulting to Cadwalader, who had worked with Pleasonton on military affairs for nearly a decade and, when acting as the captain of the Philadelphia Grays, had loyally served in Pleasonton's regiment. But rather than sack his willful artillerist, Cadwalader gave him what he wanted: permission to kill. By the time Cadwalader's order reached him, Kensington was burning again.[24]

Along with their scant numbers and uncertain authority to use lethal force, a third reason for the militia's ineffectiveness was that no commander wanted to kill fellow Americans. As one observer explained, "Col. Murray is a most kind-hearted and amiable gentleman," not the type to fire on his countrymen if he could avoid it. So when men bared their breasts and dared Murray to fire on them, he declined. The troops apparently felt the same way. "How can we fire on our own citizens," troops asked, "who cheer us as we approach?"[25]

Some militiamen may have sympathized with the nativists. While the volunteer militia included many immigrants (including Major General Patterson and Brigadier General Augustus Roumfort, both of whom had immigrated as children), it also attracted men with nativist leanings. This was particularly true of the Monroe Guards, one of the two companies to come on duty Wednesday morning. In January 1843, the Monroes had elected as their captain Charles Jack, who at the time was helping found the American Republican Party. By May 1844, Jack was no longer in command, but some of the men who had elected him may still have served in the unit. The second company on guard duty that morning, the Philadelphia Cadets, drilled in the Kensington Odd Fellows' Hall on Queen Street in East Kensington, not far from the site of the massive Native rally on April 16. One rumor even suggested that a volunteer had joined in the sacking of Irish Catholic houses, still in his uniform. Another report noted a man in a militia jacket playing his fife from an upstairs window in Corr's grocery as the mob ransacked it below.[26]

Despite these limits, the militia did save some buildings from destruction. More importantly, it had prevented a resurgence of the open gun battles of Monday and Tuesday; the *Chronicle* estimated no more than half a dozen gunshots the whole day. Despite rumors of "armed bodies of Irishmen" marching toward Kensington, Wednesday had been a day of flame, not firearms. Moreover, the militia seemed to have contained the violence to a single ward of Kensington. As the *Spirit of the Times* assured its out-of-town readers, "Kensington has a distinct and separate government from the city of Philadelphia, has a separate police, and separate magistrates." Kensington might be near Philadelphia, the newspaper had soothed, but "we apprehend no disturbance in *the City*."[27]

"Conflagration of St. Augustine's Church."
Courtesy of the Collection of the New-York Historical Society. Photography © New-York Historical Society.

13

The Sky a Sheet of Flames

Despite the *Times*'s assurance, Kensington was not far from the city, either physically or psychologically. Patrick Aloysius Jordan, later a Catholic priest, was then a sixteen-year-old apprentice in a city dry-goods wholesale store operated by prominent Quakers. He learned of the destruction of St. Michael's from a fellow worker, a Quaker, who gloated over the news. While the managers of the firm feared the disgrace the disorder would bring to the city, in Jordan's hearing they muttered, "The Papists deserve all this and much more, and it were well if every Popish church in the world were levelled with the ground."[1]

After St. Michael's, the most obvious target was the Church of St. Augustine, founded in 1796 as the last and largest of the four Catholic churches built in the county prior to Kenrick's arrival in 1830. While not as magnificent as the new Church of St. John the Evangelist, St. Augustine's came close. About 65 feet wide and 120 deep, it housed both a main church and a basement chapel, which had recently been refurbished. Both church and chapel had their own organs, as well as gilt and silver candlesticks, paintings, and altar vessels. Soaring above the church was its bell tower, added in 1830, which housed the Stretch clock—commissioned in 1753 for use in the State House—and a 1750s bell, cast by the same London foundry that had cast the Liberty Bell. Behind the church, fronting Crown Street, lay two more church buildings: a rectory and a seminary, which hosted visiting Catholic scholars when they passed through Philadelphia. Both were crammed with books. The rectory held the pastor's personal collection, while the seminary contained as many as ten thousand books, some in a theological library on its third floor, others packed into bookcases in almost every other room. Paintings occupied whatever wall space was left over.[2]

As a large and prominent building near Kensington, the church would be easy to find. And like St. Michael's, it was a symbol of Irish pride. Its founder, Rev. Matthew Carr, had been born in Dublin, and its current pastor, Dr. Patrick Eugene Moriarty, was a prominent Irish immigrant and an advocate of Repeal. In May 1844, Moriarty was away on a fundraising tour through several southern states, leaving his church and adjoining home all the more vulnerable. Perhaps most significantly, on the morning of May 7, Levin's *Sun* reported that "more than 1000 armed persons are in St. Augustine's Church." As nativists attacked Catholics in Kensington, St. Augustine's Church had been the subject of threats, and some of its valuables had been removed for safekeeping. But there was not time to remove many of the treasures.[3]

The church's location did give it one advantage. Unlike St. Michael's in Kensington, protected by only the ward constable, the sheriff, and whatever help they could scrape up, St. Augustine's lay about fifty yards south of Vine Street, the fifty-foot-wide thoroughfare that marked the northern boundary of the City of Philadelphia. That put it under the protection of the city's mayor and police. It would not be enough.[4]

People started gathering in front of St. Augustine's at some point in the late afternoon. At first, it was just strangers talking about events in Kensington. Others were workers who had been let off early for the day, around 4:30, as anxious employers closed shop in order to get home to their families. "Before six o'clock, their usual hour for stopping work," recalled Jordan, "the most troublesome class of our citizens had already had their supper and were ready for any work of mischief." Around 6:30 P.M., the crowd grew and started muttering more menacingly. Fearing the worst, residents of houses neighboring St. Augustine's began hiring wagons to pack out their furniture and other possessions. It is not clear just who composed this new crowd. No identifiable nativist leaders, such as Levin or Kramer, or even a lesser player like Peale or Jack was identified, and in the dimming light, it was hard for police officers to get a good look at faces. Clearly not all the nativists from Kensington moved south, for throughout the evening some continued to cause mayhem in that district. But it does seem that many of those crowding around St. Augustine's had wandered south from Kensington, just a mile and a half to the north. One nativist, John McKeown, was later charged with attacking both the St. Michael's parsonage and St. Augustine's. "Go in Southwark," some cheered. "Hurrah for Kensington!"[5]

Hearing the news, Philadelphia mayor John Scott summoned some of the city police and rode on horseback to the church, where he persuaded the Catholics there—armed, according to one rumor—to entrust the church and its keys to him. Scott deployed his watchmen, their badges visible, along the curb in front of the church's Fourth Street facade, while citizen volunteers guarded its rear. William Young, captain of the night police, later guessed that he and about twenty other policemen faced a crowd of between six and eight thousand. That figure seems exaggerated, but a newspaper estimated that there could have been three thousand in the crowd, and the police certainly felt outnumbered.[6]

Climbing onto a cab, Scott begged everyone to disperse. "As you made the law and elected the officers," he pleaded, "have respect for both. Do not tarnish the honor of the city." The crowd listened sullenly. Some demanded that Scott surrender the keys to the church. Others insisted that he pledge to dismiss every Irishman from the police force. Scott refused, explaining that the law permitted naturalized citizens on the force, and he would follow the law. Mostly, the crowd merely heckled. "Blood for blood!" some cried. Officer Young arrested John Hess gathering stones and shouting, "go it, natives!" Young hauled the lad to the mayor, who spoke to him as well. Surprised by Hess's German accent, Scott asked why Hess was supporting the Natives. Hess acknowledged that he had only been in the country for about six years, but apparently his Protestant identity mattered more to him than his immigrant status.[7]

The police could expect scant help from the militia, since nearly every available volunteer had been deployed to Kensington. Still, Scott sent word to Cadwalader, and around 8 P.M. the general ordered Captain John Butler's First City Troop, then in Kensington, to ride south to the aid of the mayor. Half a dozen cavalrymen from the First State Troop joined them, but that still gave Butler only thirty-two men, including a trumpeter and a surgeon, to face a crowd of thousands. When he arrived, Butler rode into the crowd and started to speak, but Mayor Scott interrupted and asked the troops to ride two blocks west to Franklin Square and await his instructions. As Scott returned to the police, he was dismayed by the sound of a stone crashing through one of the windows of the church. But he still hesitated to order a military assault. "I then had doubt of the propriety of cavalry charging on a crowd, or of artillery or infantry firing upon them," he later explained. "I thought and still think that it was a great responsibility for any civil magistrate to order an attack upon a crowd composed of the innocent as well as the guilty." Reluctantly, though, he wrote an order asking for Butler to return.[8]

Despite the shouting, Scott's lectures kept the crowd quiet for more than an hour, and no one dared attack the mayor or his men. Then someone dared. Just one brick at first, hurled toward the watchmen. And it did not even hit, bouncing instead off the iron railing behind them. The street remained quiet enough for all to hear that echoing ring. Yet for the frustrated crowd, that one brick was enough. They cheered, and within moments started throwing whatever they could find—bricks, stones, anything—at Mayor Scott and his watch. Young lost hold of his prisoner in the crush. The gaslight behind the mayor shattered. The mayor himself was hit hard by a brickbat to the gut, and the sight of their leader, stunned and helpless, panicked his watchmen, who scattered. Another missile hit Officer John Long, leaving a gash in his cheek. Officer Alexander Jackson arrested a man waving a pistol, but other members of the crowd cried "rescue!" and pulled the suspect and his pistol away. Other missiles rained down on the defenseless watchmen, presumably hurled by unseen enemies on adjoining rooftops.[9]

As in Kensington, the violence was likely the work of what one observer estimated to be a group of about fifty people, "forty of who he could safely say were *boys*." John Hess, the immigrant whom Officer Young had collared, was eighteen or nineteen. Thomas Gansey, who would later be convicted, was nineteen or twenty. A third suspect, Joseph Daymen, was later described as "a lad." This riotous core of a few dozen drew moral support from the hundreds or thousands of less active members of the crowd, who also impeded any police response. At around 9:30, the more aggressive in the crowd started attacking the church in earnest. Men lifted boys over the iron fence, while others worked to tear it down.[10]

Then a trumpet sounded—summoned back by the mayor, Butler's cavalry was charging. Riding almost at a gallop, the thirty-two troopers chased the vandals southward down Fourth Street, then wheeled and chased others northward. But as soon as they had the street cleared, others filled in behind the horses, jeering at them. "Ride over us," shouted some boys, "if you dare!" They did not. The mayor, still reeling from the brick, watched in dismay. "The crowd opened before them just as the waves open before the prow of a boat," he later recalled, "and as they passed they closed again as the waves close behind a boat." He heard someone shout, "give them the cold steel! give them the cold steel!" but the troopers refrained.[11]

Philadelphia's finest cavalry had proven no more effective at protecting a church than had the infantry and the city watchmen. By one account, Butler spotted the mayor and begged him for permission for the horsemen to use their pistols against the stubborn crowd. Instead, Scott again ordered the troop to depart. Joseph Sill, a dry-goods merchant who witnessed the charges, was appalled. The troopers had "galloped past, without saying a word, or doing the slightest act, and then finally disappeared!" He heard whispers that the horsemen were "rather encouraging the mob than doing anything to check their progress."[12]

Beyond this humiliation was a larger problem: The men and boys in the street were merely bystanders to the main action. St. Augustine's stood on a stone platform about five feet above street level, protecting its most direct attackers from the cavalry. Even as the horsemen charged up and down the street, the men and boys on the platform kept on with their work, perhaps accelerating it lest more troops arrive before they had finished. First, they tried to batter down the front doors and then, when that proved too difficult, they smashed the front windows instead. In one account, two boys climbed through the broken windows; one lit the curtains on fire, while the second cut a gas pipe to feed the flames. In another version, a larger group climbed inside, building a bonfire of boards. In any case, the church was now alight. Half a mile to the west, Rev. Philip Mayer, a Lutheran minister, and his family were sitting in their parlor when they heard a scream from the garret. Their Irish-born servant, Mary Shails, had seen the flames, and now was "in strong hysterics." Mayer's daughter Caroline was calmer, calling the fire "a most magnificent sight—as light as day."[13]

For the first half hour, only the lower story burned, though smoke poured out of the windows. Then, suddenly, the fire spread to the steeple, conducted upward, perhaps, through the church's pipe organ. At the top of the steeple, a gilt marble cross shone from the light of the flames beneath. Below it, the clock continued to work, and the church bell struck the hour of 10 P.M. "That is the last time you will strike!" cheered the mob below. Twenty minutes later, the cross finally crashed to the street, remarkably missing any of the crowd, which applauded the fall. "Thousands of throats yelled applause," noted Isaac Mickle, "just as the Jews must have done when Jesus died upon the same emblem." Mayor Scott's sons found their injured father and pulled him away from the scene.[14]

Finally, at 10:25, the steeple itself came straight down, followed by the roof of the church. Burning cinders shot into the night sky and then cascaded down like a shower of gold onto nearby streets and buildings. The flames themselves reached nearly a hundred feet, and they were so bright that one could hardly look directly at the burning church itself. The heat blistered the doors and window frames of nearby buildings, or started them steaming. "New Street, directly opposite the church, was open to the river," remembered Jordan three decades later. "For miles around the sky was a sheet of flames, the river with its gliding bateaux containing men and women looked a stream of molten gold;—yes, it seemed a fairy scene." A Catholic sister placed her hand on his shoulder. "We know not where this may end," she warned him. "We may even be called upon to die for our religion,—God grant us strength!" A young priest sat on the curb, weeping.[15]

The flames spread to the parsonage of Dr. Moriarty, which housed his collection of more than a thousand books, many of them rare volumes. Even as the building burned, some well-wishers ran in to throw the priest's furniture and books—including some Bibles—out the windows to save them, but others in the crowd threw some of the valuables straight back into the flames, further feeding the destruction. Others built a bonfire of some of Moriarty's possessions on the pavement in front of his house. Meanwhile, the fire spread to a third building in the complex, the seminary and library. Between the destruction of the two buildings, the Augustinians lost the country's best collection of Catholic theological literature as well as their early parish records. Francis Ashe, the Irish-born, twenty-four-year-old assistant pastor left in charge in Moriarty's absence, salvaged only the record of baptisms and five other books.[16]

Though most of the firemen from the county districts were still fighting fires in Kensington, companies from the city were on hand with their engines, summoned to the fire by the ringing of the State House bell. They did not even try to save the church, which was now nothing but walls and flame. Nor did they try to douse the parsonage or the seminary. But as other buildings caught fire from sparks drifting over from the church, the firemen shot water at them, while desperate residents joined in with water and wet blankets, risking burns to save their homes. Thanks to their efforts, the fire did not spread wildly, though several houses had their roofs burned off and their shutters and doors scorched. William Newland, the church organist, lived in a house facing the church windows, and the flames shooting out of them destroyed his home. As the flames spread, the crowd quieted, watching silently as the church continued to burn or whispering to each other so as not to disturb the spectacle.[17]

With two churches destroyed, Catholics, civilian officials, and militia officers alike feared for the others. "Southwark and Moyamensing are arming," wrote one reporter, "and the Catholic churches there are marked out." People crowded into the streets in hope of seeing another spectacular church fire. "Down with the Catholic churches!" some cried, firing pistols and guns into the air. "A person was not safe hardly but I did not care," boasted one young man. "I went among the crowd hey what a time I had!"[18]

"The city is all in confusion," wrote the *New-York Tribune*'s correspondent in his 11 P.M. dispatch. "Nothing but vigorous efforts which cannot be expected from the volunteers, or the civil posse, will prevent Philadelphia from becoming a prey to the mob, and preventing a general conflagration." Another reporter doubted that would be enough, for "what can we do without arms against such infuriated mob?"[19]

Kenrick and other Catholic clergy evacuated the remaining city churches, carrying sacred vessels and vestments with them. Fearing an attack on St. John the Evangelist's Church, members of the congregation suggested that Kenrick seek shelter with Rev. Stephen Tyng. As one of the organizers of the American Protestant Association, Tyng was no friend to the Catholic cause, but perhaps that very fact might help him defend Kenrick against a mob. Kenrick considered the idea, but instead chose to find shelter with a Philadelphia Catholic family. The sisters in charge of the adjacent orphanage evacuated their charges as well, finding lodging for them in private houses. The St. Joseph's Orphan Asylum, at Seventh and Spruce, appeared to be in less immediate danger, so its girls remained in place, but the sisters, including two refugees from St. John's, stayed awake long into the night, ready to wake the girls and flee if needed. "Do pray very hard Mother," the superioress wrote to her order's leader in Maryland, "for what will become of us if the Asylum was attacked. How could we escape with 99 children, seventy of whom would not be able to assist themselves even out of the mob; and as they have sworn vengeance against all the churches and their institutions we have every reason to expect the same fate."[20]

Fortunately for the orphans, the forces of order were gaining strength. In Germantown, five miles to the northwest of the fighting, militiamen mustered to the beat of drums, their faces illuminated by the flames of the churches to the south. When these fresh troops arrived in Kensington, General Patterson could redeploy companies from that district to protect the county's surviving churches. Around 11 P.M. these troops marched south, using their bayonets to clear the nearby streets of crowds.[21]

Once they had established a perimeter around a church, the soldiers denied entry to the adjacent streets to all except their residents.

Colonel James Goodman, with four companies, covered the city's oldest churches—St. Mary's, St. Joseph's, and Holy Trinity—deploying troops and watchmen to guard the approaching streets and placing men inside the churches to block any arsonists who might sneak past. He was joined by some US Marines; it is not clear exactly who ordered their deployment, but Goodman was likely glad to have the aid. Goodman was a native-born Lutheran, but he was also a former commander of the Irish Volunteers and an advocate of Repeal, so he enjoyed the trust of the churches' congregants. Still, armed Irish Catholics took cover behind tombstones in the graveyards, ready to defend the church in case the militia failed again.[22]

Cadwalader himself, along with Pleasonton's regiment, took charge of Kenrick's finest creation, St. John the Evangelist's on Thirteenth Street. His main goal was to protect the state arsenal across the street, but Mayor Scott had asked politely if the troops guarding the arsenal could look after the church as well, since it might be in danger. As it happens, the church and arsenal were also just a few blocks from Cadwalader's own house on Chestnut Street. The militia had always pledged to defend hearth and home, but this was taking it rather literally. When Cadwalader arrived, around 1 A.M., he faced a large crowd that looked none too friendly. Riding to the front of his troops, he bellowed that he had orders to fire upon any riot or gathering, and he gave the crowd five minutes to disperse. It did, though at some point the Fairmount Engine Company tried to push through the lines. Similarly, at St. Mary's, the crowd lingered until a US Marine officer ordered his men to prepare to charge.[23]

The city remained unsettled well into the wee hours of May 9. At two o'clock, the *Daily Chronicle* went to press, telling its readers, "all is quiet," but also describing a terrifying spectacle. "The fire is still burning at St. Augustine's Church. Our city presents the appearance of being under martial law—troops are stationed at the crossings, and it is to all appearance a warlike town." At three o'clock, the *North American* warned that "mob spirit is in the ascendant, and unless an efficient body of from three to five thousand men are forthwith organized, to put down the rioters by force, scenes of bloodshed more appalling than those we have witnessed during the last three days, will be inevitable."[24]

"Ruins of St. Michael's Church, and the Priest's House."
Courtesy of the Collection of the New-York Historical Society. Photography © New-York Historical Society.

14

The Lord Seeth

The men of the First Division stayed on duty all night. Mostly, they went unchallenged, though the Germantown Volunteers, up in Kensington, noticed that someone had set fire to a stockpile of yarn that had been salvaged from a weaver's home or a factory. The troops extinguished the fire but failed to catch the arsonist. By dawn on the morning of Thursday, May 9, the men of the division were exhausted, and Major General Patterson dismissed them for a few hours' rest. The only troops remaining on duty were a single company guarding the state arsenal; if a mob seized that, it could be unstoppable.[1]

At City Hall, adjacent to Independence Hall, Philadelphia's civilian leaders debated what to do. At 1 A.M., Mayor Scott and Sheriff McMichael secured an opinion from Ovid Johnson, the state's attorney general, assuring them that they had the legal power to call out troops, and that those troops had the authority to kill rioters "in the same manner as if they were open public enemies or pirates." Still, officials feared that such a course would not be popular, and at 2 A.M. that morning, the two councils resolved to summon a public meeting. Mayor Scott accordingly advertised that citizens of the county and city should gather in Independence Square at ten o'clock "to deliberate upon the present state of the public peace." Beyond that, they had no idea how to stop the bloodshed and destruction. So they summoned Horace Binney.[2]

Binney was a former congressman and one of the most prominent lawyers in the city, as well as a client of the Cadwalader family of lawyers. Though he claimed to have retired in 1840—at the stroke of noon on his sixtieth birthday—Binney had recently represented Philadelphia in a case before the Supreme Court, defeating none other than Daniel Webster, one of the country's greatest orators. A resident of central Philadelphia, Binney had stood on his doorstep to watch St. Augustine's burn, but he assumed that suppressing the riot would be someone else's problem. Instead, after finishing his breakfast on Thursday morning and walking downstairs to his office, he found councilman Peter McCall waiting there. McCall begged Binney to come with him; the council members were stumped.[3]

Indeed, when Binney arrived at city hall, he later recalled, "I never saw a body of more unresolved men. . . . They looked as if they were excessively puzzled." They talked vaguely about possible responses until, eventually, someone mentioned the ten o'clock meeting, the first Binney had heard of it. By then, it was already 9:30, and the council still lacked a plan. So Binney took charge. He insisted on two points. First, while it might be nice to get assistance from "other quarters" (presumably militia from other parts of the state and federal troops), Philadelphians "must assist ourselves immediately." And second, they needed to be prepared to resist "a mob in the very degree, however severe and extreme, which their designs and violence made necessary." The councils agreed, and Binney hastily drafted some resolutions before walking out to Independence Square, where he faced a crowd of thousands.[4]

Binney called on his listeners to support the authorities, even if that meant more violence. "We ought to strengthen them by every means in our power," he explained, "nor should their acts be too nicely weighed by fault finders, during exigencies when time for reflection is scarcely allowed." Though Binney preferred circumlocutions like "whatever degree of force is necessary," his meaning was likely clear to all listening. The public should be prepared for posses and militiamen to start shooting into crowds.[5]

Binney was followed by General Adam Diller, the state's adjutant general, who held some nativist views. To temper Binney's vision of carnage, he suggested amending Binney's resolutions with a preamble suggesting that "a great portion of these rude assemblies is made up of young boys, who are incompetent of foreseeing the evil consequences of such illegal acts." Ending the riots might not take lethal force, just the decision by heads of families and masters "to keep their young men and boys at home during the prevailing excitement." As the meeting approved both the resolutions and the preamble, Philadelphians had essentially resolved that the riots had been the work of mostly innocent youngsters who should either be disciplined by their fathers or lawfully shot down in the street. It neatly expressed the general American ambivalence about rioting.[6]

In between these two visions of lethal force and patriarchal discipline, the meeting also endorsed Sheriff McMichael's plea that the aldermen of each ward convene citizens "to take measures to preserve the public peace." At noon, McMichael and Scott proclaimed that militia officers had the power to declare parts of the city or county to be occupied and to use "such *force of arms* as may be necessary" to keep those places clear. They emphasized that even fire and hose companies could not move freely without military permission. Broadsides with the order were posted in the streets, the words "Force of Arms" particularly visible in large, black, capital letters. About a dozen young lawyers volunteered as mounted aides to Mayor Scott, carrying his orders and messages throughout the city.[7]

Meanwhile, reinforcements were on the way. As St. Augustine's burned on Wednesday evening, William Porter, the former sheriff who had been so badly beaten in Kensington in 1843, and W. E. Whitman, a state legislator, had grabbed a midnight train to Harrisburg. On arrival the next morning, they hunted down Governor David Porter, William's father, and begged for help. The governor ordered two Harrisburg militia companies to proceed to Philadelphia, then joined his son and Whitman on an express train back to the city. During the train's stop in Lancaster, Governor Porter called out that's city's militia as well. It would take several hours, though, for the volunteer patrols to organize, for the outside reinforcements to arrive, and for the Philadelphia militia to come back on duty. Until then, the peace of the city depended on the efforts of the regular police, which from time to time shooed people away from Catholic churches.[8]

Had the nativists been determined to burn more churches, that Thursday morning would have been the time. Instead, the peace held. Perhaps the nativists were exhausted from three days of fighting. Perhaps those heads of families heeded the advice of General Diller and kept their boys at home. Or perhaps the nativists had simply achieved their objectives. By laying waste to St. Michael's, the seminary, and the Clarks' homes, they had shown the world who ruled the Third Ward of Kensington. And by losing some of their own in the fight, they had created martyrs for their own cause.

At 10 A.M., the first martyr, George Shiffler, returned to Kensington, this time as a corpse. His coffin was draped in the tattered American flag that, the nativists claimed, had been trampled by Irish Catholics during the Monday battle in which Shiffler had been killed. About three hundred people followed the body to the burial ground on Hanover Street. And yet, noted a reporter, "every thing was peaceable, quiet, and orderly; and on the conclusion of the funeral ceremonies, all who had attended peaceably adjourned to their own homes." Four more funerals—for Charles Stillwell, William Wright, Lewis Greble, and Matthew Hammitt—would be held in the afternoon, also without incident.[9]

The Third Ward remained calm. A few half-grown boys cut blocks of lead into chunks, claiming that they planned to use it as ammunition, but a reporter doubted they were serious. Most of the people wandering the streets seemed to be merely curious to see the destruction. Others were Catholics looking for shelter after losing their homes to fire. Newspapers estimated that between thirty and sixty shops and houses had been burned or gutted, not counting the St. Michael's parsonage and the female seminary. Many of the buildings had housed multiple families, so the *Ledger* estimated at least two hundred families had been displaced.[10]

"All is sadness and gloom—woe is pictured on almost every object," wrote an observer. "Business is totally at a stand—private and public houses closed, with black crape hanging from many knobs—hundreds of houses are now untenanted, their occupants having deserted them yesterday and fled with their lives, and some little property." Before leaving, the residents or their landlords posted signs telling potential vandals that the houses were owned, if not occupied, by Native Americans. Hundreds of refugees camped in the woods and fields north of Kensington, sleeping on wet grass under the trees. Some received help from nearby families, but others feared even to ask, despite not having eaten for two days. A few desperate families seized the wagons of farmers on their way to the Kensington market. Others returned to Kensington, but having lost their homes, they risked arrest as vagrants. Still others fled to New York or Baltimore.[11]

In Philadelphia City, boys picked through the ruins of St. Augustine's, looking for bits of melted brass, copper, and zinc. The fire had gutted the church, but the four stone walls remained upright. "It was an old building, strongly put together," marveled a reporter. "The noble organ, which so often had warmed the hearts of a Christian people . . . is destroyed—not an atom of it can be found, it has, every morsel of it, been devoured by the fierceness of the flames," lamented another observer. "The surrounding Church yard—the resting-place of the dead—is in sad confusion,—the graves recklessly trampled under foot—the tombstones broken and defaced, and the urn in which some pious Christian had enshrined the heart of their pastor, is cast down."[12]

Elsewhere, Catholics removed the valuables from each surviving church and scattered them to homes throughout Philadelphia County. The churches' neighbors fled, too. St. John's Orphan Asylum, near the church of that name, had already been evacuated of children. In their place, militia were barricaded inside. Amid rumors that mobs would lynch every priest in the city, Kenrick continued his flight. After two days with Catholic families in Philadelphia, he traveled to Delaware County, where he lodged with another Catholic family for two days, and finally to Baltimore, staying two more days in a seminary there. Some other priests likewise evacuated, while those who remained stayed hidden, or at least avoided wearing clerical garb in public.[13]

As more troops arrived, they reported to Major General Patterson in his headquarters at the Girard Bank, an imposing Greek Revival building on Third Street in the heart of the business district that had once housed the First Bank of the United States, when Philadelphia was still the nation's capital. Its three stories and yard provided plenty of room for men and their horses, and the towering Corinthian columns of its magnificent marble portico suggested the order that most Philadelphians desperately wanted restored. The bank also sat across the street from Levin's offices at the *Daily Sun*, allowing Levin and the generals to keep an eye on each other. Just to the east, German-born brothers William and Frederick Langenheim ran a studio devoted to the infant art of photography. One of them set a camera in the window and created a half-plate daguerreotype showing children and adults gawking at the troops. It may be the first news photograph in history.[14]

Girard Bank, at the time the latter was occupied by the military during the riots.
Courtesy of The Library Company of Philadelphia.

One of the children in the photograph could be Frederic Bird, the five-year-old son of Sheriff McMichael's friend Robert Bird and the nephew of Caroline Mayer, who had watched St. Augustine's burn. "He was perfectly delighted to see the soldiers & cannon," Mayer wrote her sister, Frederic's mother. "It looked very fine & quite warlike—a regular patrol, at Chesnut & at Market, & no one is allowed to pass, or even to hold conversation within ear shot of this guard." At the adjacent orphanage, she lifted the boy for a better look at the cannon. "But do not let his Dear Father think there is the slightest danger of his getting among the fighters," she assured her sister. "We would not, any of us, go within a mile's length of them."[15]

Back at Girard Bank, Patterson dictated his orders. Starting around two o'clock, he dispatched troops to protect the surviving Catholic churches of the city and county, while others would guard the federal Frankford Arsenal, emplacing cannon at each gate. Taking advantage of McMichael's call for citizen volunteers, Patterson authorized his brigade commanders "to organize and arm companies of citizens in undress [and] appoint suitable persons to command the new corps." By the early afternoon, hundreds of civilians assembled at ward houses, where ward leaders organized them into bands. Each volunteer was handed a white muslin badge marked "Peace Police" to be worn on the hat for most men, on the coat for captains. Most were issued muskets, taken from the state arsenal that Cadwalader had guarded on Wednesday night. Not all the Peace Police took their new role seriously; some were spotted drinking and singing, and one of the members was tossed out of a pub, his badge ripped from his hat. But most of the civilians behaved and added bulk to the uniformed forces.[16]

In the evening, Governor Porter arrived from Harrisburg, and officially the troops were transferred from local to state control. But rather than try to manage the chaos personally, Porter delegated full power to Major General Patterson. "The time has arrived for the most vigorous and energetic measures," Porter warned, "and dreadful as may be the alternative, the last and most fatal resort to means destructive even of the lives of offenders, is far better than the continuance of such disgraceful outrages." Porter did not use the term "martial law," but his meaning was clear. If Patterson were to kill, he would have the full blessing of the state's highest civilian officials. Equally important, Patterson got reinforcements from beyond his own militia division. At 9 P.M., he welcomed a contingent of about a hundred sailors and marines from the US Steam Frigate *Princeton*, who had marched from the Navy Yard. The sailors wore helmets and were armed with the pikes and cutlasses they would use if ordered to board an enemy ship. Those weapons of hand-to-hand combat seemed better suited to riot control than the muskets and bayonets of the militia.[17]

Around the same time, three militia companies from Harrisburg and Lancaster, totaling about a hundred men, arrived as well. Combined with the three Philadelphia County brigades, these reinforcements (plus a fourth company that arrived the following day) swelled the militia ranks to around 1,300 men. Along with the organization of civilian peace police, the militia now had the manpower it had so desperately lacked over the preceding three days. Rather than getting drawn away from one potential mob target while trying to save another, as happened at St. Michael's and elsewhere in Kensington, the combined forces would be large enough to guard key locations while sending detachments to patrol. The troops and the posses worked to limit movement to specified streets, thus preventing the marches and swarming of the previous three days.[18]

No one knew if this force would suffice, and throughout the day Philadelphians traded rumors of more church burnings, or perhaps a mob takeover of the federal arsenal. Returning from his Maryland farm, Sidney George Fisher noted that "Groups were at every corner, engaged in eager conversation, frightened & distressed-looking women were standing at their doors or looking anxiously from the windows, bodies of troops were marching about, sentinels were seen stationed in all directions & in the short walk up to my house I met several corps of armed citizens, acting as a police." Federal troops steamed up the Delaware River from Fort Mifflin, to the south of the city, to the Frankford Arsenal, to the northeast, to prevent a rumored attack. Except for the armed citizen's bands, Sheriff McMichael forbade people from standing or congregating on street corners, lest another mob form.[19]

By this point, Cadwalader's First Brigade was beginning to crack. Having still not gained his troops the right of self-defense to his satisfaction, Colonel Pleasonton, the seasoned veteran, refused to order them to deploy. Only so desperate a move, he feared, would "bring the Civil authorities to a proper sense of the imminent danger to life and property," and, he hoped, a declaration of martial law. Privately, he blamed Cadwalader as well, recording in his diary that "a declaration of martial Law might have been obtained if the superior military officers had desired, and had insisted upon them." Calling Pleasonton's bluff, Cadwalader relieved him of command of the First Regiment. Later, when Pleasonton read Porter's proclamation declaring something approaching martial law, he told Cadwalader he was ready to serve. After a "full and frank conversation," Cadwalader restored Pleasonton to command.[20]

As darkness fell on Thursday evening, Philadelphians anxiously anticipated another attack on the churches. At 8:30 P.M., their fears seemed confirmed when the State House bell rang an alarm and the western sky grew bright. Firemen and a large posse rushed to investigate only to find a blacksmith shop and a carpenter's shop ablaze. They suspected that arsonists had lit the fire in a vain effort to draw troops away from the Catholic churches. A "highly respectable looking man" told Cadwalader—falsely—that an officer of the First Troop had been fatally shot in Kensington. Despite such distractions, with growing numbers and the confidence of the governor's orders, the militia finally seemed in control. Troops closed most north-south streets to deter crowds from gathering. It worked. By 10 P.M., reporters found "all quiet, in every direction. Plenty of persons congregated in the neighborhood of the churches, &c., but no evidence, whatever, of an outbreak." Around 1 A.M., troops marched out from the Girard Bank to relieve units that had been on duty for nearly twelve hours.[21]

"All is now quiet," wrote the *New-York Tribune* correspondent at 6 A.M. on Friday morning, May 10. But he expected another round of fighting. Marc Antony Frenaye, Kenrick's friend and business manager, had stayed behind at St. John's, keeping the bishop informed with daily posts. That morning, he informed Kenrick that "the general opinion is that for the present all danger is over," but just in case he had "delivered the keys of the Seminary and Asylum into the hands of the Mayor. . . . If they are destroyed, the City will have to pay."[22]

From his headquarters in the Girard Bank, Patterson assigned posts to his militia officers, who would be reinforced with citizen guards from the various wards. They should be "prepared to act at a moment's notice," he ordered. "In no event are you to withdraw your force to any place not included in your command." Officers were to give crowds no more than five minutes to disperse. Then, he ordered, they should use force. "The idle, the vicious and the disorderly must be curbed, and taught to understand and respect the supremacy of the Law," warned Patterson. "If they will not take warning, on their own heads be the consequences."[23]

Remarkably, calm held. Some vandals mutilated tombstones in the graveyard of St. Michael's, while others were arrested for muttering anti-Catholic slurs. In Kensington, Captain Henry Mallory dispersed a threatening mob by ordering his Washington Artillery to a bayonet charge. Seven men with muskets were arrested. A large fire at a railroad depot in Camden, New Jersey, across the Delaware River, brought a crowd of excited Irishmen who had seen the smoke and had thought St. Mary's Church was burning. Rumors spread—that Irish refugees had stormed out of the woods beyond Kensington to kill, or that they were robbing farmers, or that a crowd had stormed the Frankford arsenal—but they were soon quashed. A few people received threatening notes. Yet already, workmen were building temporary stalls on the ruins of the Washington Market in Kensington so that farmers could again come to feed the district.[24]

In the evening, Cadwalader again deployed troops to guard key points. Pleasonton, back in command, stationed pickets in the intersections around the state arsenal on Thirteenth Street. Some men tried to ram a fire engine through the lines, while others taunted the troops by waving books they claimed to have filched from the library of St. Augustine's Church. Pleasonton ordered a few arrests but avoided serious fighting. At Thirteenth and Race, a quarter mile north of the arsenal, a posse encountered a man trying to set fire to a stable. "Shoot and be damned," he taunted them. One member of the posse did fire, apparently wounding the would-be arsonist. Around 11 P.M., the city got its first rain since the brief shower that had sent Levin and the Natives scurrying into the market house on May 6. It was "a close, nasty rain," accompanied by a drop in temperature, enough to keep troublemakers indoors.[25]

By Saturday, May 11, officials gained confidence that the peace would last. Patterson dismissed all the troops from outside Philadelphia County, praising them as "good citizens as well as good soldiers." Governor Porter himself returned to Harrisburg. But Philadelphians remained on edge. At Eleventh and Market, the appearance of a group of Irishmen carrying knives sent citizens running for the Peace Police. After explaining that they were laborers, just back from cutting willows, the Irishmen were released. Up in the Northern Liberties, "a party of mischievous rowdies" ran through the streets with one of their number on a settee, all of them shouting that he had been wounded by the militia. Several people fell for the weak joke.[26]

In Kensington, crowds continued to gather, but for a different purpose: tourism. Philadelphians came by the thousands—women and children as well as men—to view the ruins. Sunday afternoon, after church, proved a particularly popular time. "What was one week ago, a flourishing and thickly inhabited neighborhood," one visitor reported, "is now laid waste—houses levelled to the ground—and women and children cast out upon the streets, *all* the result of the three day's war. The burnt and charred walls of the brick edifices, are trembling in the air—parts fallen, and others indicating great danger; and yet we saw hundreds of persons standing on what were door threshholds, gazing about at the inner walls." Souvenir hunters made off with pieces of the seminary's ornate fence and whatever remained of Alderman Clark's official papers. One "respectably dressed man" tried to coax some boys into stealing silver from some of the ruins, but fellow tourists shamed him away. To the south, the blackened ruin of St. Augustine's also attracted visitors. Someone had nailed up boards across doorways and gateways, not so much to protect any remaining valuables—there were none—but to keep the curious away from walls that could collapse at any moment. The main attraction was a still legible and eerily appropriate inscription on the otherwise charred wall above the altar. Taken from the Douay translation of Genesis 22—the binding of Isaac—the inscription warned, "The Lord Seeth."[27]

On Thursday, May 9, following the destruction of the churches, Kenrick had suspended public worship for Catholics until "we can enjoy our constitutional right to worship God according to the dictates of our conscience." Patterson replied with a general order stating that he "believes he has sufficient force to protect all religious denominations of citizens . . . and that the closing of any Church is without his order or approbation." Privately, however, Colonel Pleasonton, whose wife was Catholic, had explained to the bishop that troops were forbidden from entering a church during services, even if someone attacked the congregation or set the building on fire. Taking the hint, Kenrick let his instructions stand, then left the city.[28]

Thus, on Sunday the twelfth, most Catholic churches remained silent, though troops and navy sailors stopped by to make sure they were safe. Only at St. Francis Xavier's—at the western edge of the city—did Father Patrick Rafferty, dressed in soutane and biretta, celebrate Mass, telling his congregants that a good place to die is near the altar. The *Pennsylvanian* registered its dismay at seeing "toleration enforced—if indeed it be toleration when thus enforced—by loaded muskets, drawn sabres, and at the cannon's mouth—charity secured through dread of 'grape and canister.'" Could this really be "a Sunday of the nineteenth century in the city of Philadelphia"?[29]

No one could be sure that the fighting would be confined to Philadelphia. In New York, Native Americans planned a rally on May 9, only to cancel it at the request of the mayor, who feared that it would become a riot. Bishop Hughes, Kenrick's protégé, had the same concern, and he called on Catholics, if attacked, to defend their homes and churches with their lives (though there is no contemporary evidence for the oft-repeated story that he threatened to turn New York into a "second Moscow" were a New York church to burn). In Boston, a group of men roamed the streets shouting, "To hell with the Pope," occasionally pausing to drink Orange toasts. The city's Catholics ignored them.[30]

Philadelphia Catholics remained wary, expecting the fighting to resume as soon as the troops withdrew. "I am hardly able to write at all," a normally composed Bishop Kenrick wrote his brother, the bishop of St. Louis, on May 15. "I am encompassed on every side with perils from the enemies of the Faith. After many calamities they still threaten us. However, just now things are quiet, and many are promising us peace and security. In the meantime help us with your prayers." The riots had not discomposed Kenrick enough to prevent his writing in his customary Latin, but rather than sending greetings as usual from the bishop of Philadelphia, he wrote as "frater in angustiis positus"—a brother in a tight spot. Along with prayers, Kenrick received help from volunteer civilians formed into improvised units. Ever the snob, Sidney Fisher wanted to avoid patrolling with "low people," but when he learned that a Catholic seminary was to be defended by a "number of young men, most of them members of the bar & all of them respectable," he joined, shouldering a musket for the first time in his life. He still was not happy about the assignment. "I have no fancy for a soldier's life," he wrote, "and consider that society is bound to protect me in person & property. Undisciplined forces for such uses are absurd."[31]

Gradually, the civil and military officers dismissed their forces. On Sunday, May 12, the marines and sailors returned to the Navy Yard. The next day, Patterson dismissed the armed civilians, though he asked them to stay organized in case they were needed again. And he told the volunteer militia to retain the ammunition they had been issued and and "hold themselves in readiness to assemble instantly at their armories on the ringing of the riot signal by the state house bell." He tried to keep these orders quiet, lest the wrong people learn that less than a full division was on duty. On Friday, May 17, two weeks after the first nativist meeting, all of the last troops were discharged except for a small force of artillerymen left to guard the arsenal, where they would remain into June.[32]

Even then, the militia had one more trial to endure: On May 18, Lieutenant John S. Dutton of the State Fencibles died of typhoid and inflamed lungs, perhaps from the smoke he had inhaled as Kensington burned. His fellow officers escorted the hearse to the cemetery, and when the militia were finally paid for their riot service, Cadwalader would donate his own pay to the support of Dutton's infant daughter. Corporal Charles Raphun of National Grays also fell ill in Kensington; he would die later in the summer. These were the only militiamen to die as a result of the May riots, though Private Michael Hartranft of the State Artillerists had been seriously wounded during the march to Kensington. An officer's pistol had dropped from his belt and fired on hitting the pavement, sending a ball upward through Hartranft's knee, fracturing his femur. Fortunately, however, the ball was small and the soldier strong, sober, and healthy, and doctors applied a hundred leeches to relieve the swelling. Though Hartranft, a carpenter, could not work for months, he would survive suffering only a "very slight limp," plus some pain when the weather changed.[33]

Some civilians were less fortunate. For two weeks after being shot in the hips on May 6, Joseph Cox lingered in "the most intense pain and anguish."

The bullet had missed his internal organs, and had it passed through his body, the hospital doctors guessed, he might have lived. But it remained in his pelvic cavity, and doctors quickly judged the case hopeless. Cox finally expired in a hospital bed on May 22, dead of peritonitis. To the end, he insisted that when he was shot, "he was standing perfectly quiet, and was taking no part in the disturbance." Nathan Ramsey, also wounded on May 6, looked like he might recover. He had been shot by a ball that had ripped through his chest, separating ribs and tearing through his lung, and the first doctor to treat him expected him to die within the week. But Ramsey was a healthy twenty-one-year-old, and his body did its best to repair the damage. By May 9, he was consuming nutritious drinks, despite the "dark and offensive" discharge from his wounds. On May 25, nearly three weeks after his wounding, his pulse, breathing, and appetite were all good. Then his luck ran out. At 3 A.M. on May 28 his lung, sliced by bone fragments, hemorrhaged, and he died two hours later.[34]

Both Cox and Ramsey were escorted to their graves by processions of Native Americans. For Cox's funeral, General Peter Sken Smith, one of the organizers of the nativist movement, led a procession that some claimed numbered two thousand, not counting a hundred of Cox's fellow members of the Globe Engine or those deterred by a hot day punctuated by storms. Ramsey's procession included, nativists claimed, nine omnibuses, thirty-one private carriages, a "large number" of mounted mourners, and three thousand people on foot, walking all or part of the fourteen miles to the Ramseys' burial plot in Montgomery County. Both coffins were draped in the flag that had covered Shiffler's. George Young, also shot through the chest, suffered terribly and seemed likely to join Ramsey and Cox. To everyone's surprise, he recovered. So did John Lusher despite an equally grim chest wound. But months later, nativists were collecting funds for "poor old Mr. Lescher of Kensington, maimed for life during that unparalleled riot."[35]

The official tally counted nine dead from gunfire: Joseph Rice and eight Protestants: Shiffler, Wright, Ramsey, Greble, Rhinedollar, Hammitt, Cox, and Stillwell. More may have perished. On the morning of Sunday, May 12, people cleaning up the ruins of a house on Cadwalader Street, two doors up from the Hibernia Hose House, found a man's body in the cellar. It had been decomposing for days, and the stench cleared the area quickly.

Another was found the following afternoon. "Many who fired from these houses were unquestionably wounded," the *Public Ledger* explained, "and in consequence were unable to leave the buildings when they were fired, and must have perished in the flames." Hannah Morton of Master Street later referred to a lady "who died of consequence of the fright," possibly a reference to a heart attack. Others suffered mental trauma. On May 14, Eliza McKeown ran screaming into the streets of Southwark, "uttering terrifying exclamations of grief and woe." Her neighbors concluded that she had "lost her reason during the late disturbances," and packed her off to the insane asylum.[36]

Perhaps we can consider seventeen-year-old Jacob Powell as the last fatality of the May riots. Late in the evening of Saturday, June 1, he and some friends were playing near St. Peter the Apostle's Church in the Northern Liberties, amusing themselves by reenacting the violence of the previous weeks. Unfortunately, while their riot was make-believe, the guns they held were real, and loaded. One of the boys shot Powell in the abdomen, and he died a day and a half later. He was buried at St. Peter's. Was this the Kensington riots in microcosm: a bunch of half-grown boys entertaining themselves with rough play, not realizing the danger of their games? Or did the riots reveal much deeper problems in Philadelphia and America as a whole? Over the next weeks, Philadelphians and observers around the world would debate that question.[37]

"Funeral of an American."
Courtesy of the author's collection.

15

Humanity Weeps

G radually, Philadelphia returned to peace, or at least to the background
levels of firemen's fights that counted as peace. On May 18, authorities
arrested John Paul, a Catholic weaver, though not an immigrant (unless
one counted New Jersey as a foreign land). Unable to explain why a load
of new rifles had arrived out at his house on May 7, and, lacking $5,000
for bail, Paul was jailed. His infant child, whom he had carried away from
danger during the riots, died while he sat in the lockup. Around the same
time, Officer William Young arrested John Hess, whom he identified as
having urged the crowd to stone St. Augustine's. But by mid-June, only

a quarter of those sought had been arrested, and not all of them were the right targets.[1]

On Sunday, May 19, Kenrick was back at St. John's, where he advised the faithful "to bear with Christian fortitude the late misfortune to their brethren." He found encouragement in the temporary chapel Kensington Catholics were raising on the ruins of the parsonage of St. Michael's, combining the paid labor of skilled bricklayers and carpenters with the contributions of volunteers who cleared what was left of the parsonage and washed the scorched bricks for reuse. Even the collapse of the front wall, which injured three workmen, did not stop the work, and the chapel was ready for worship on Sunday, June 2, the Feast of the Most Holy Trinity. Yet as late as May 29, Kenrick wrote that "things seem to be tranquil enough; but we do not feel secure; for the threats to burn the churches, and especially the Cathedral, still hold fire."[2]

As the ashes of Kensington cooled, Philadelphia, the nation, and even foreign observers struggled to learn the details, to understand the violence, and to shape others' understanding. Physically, the destruction had not been that extensive. A single steamboat explosion could kill more people; a single factory fire, if it spread, could destroy more houses. But though they lived amid such dangers, Americans could still be shocked by the deliberate targeting of neighbors and churches. They wanted to know whom to blame. For partisans in the dispute, true victory would come not with the seizure of territory or the killing of enemies, but with the acceptance of their version of the story by as many listeners as possible.[3]

Even Philadelphians, who might have been expected to be jaded by rioting, were astonished by the violence of May 7 and 8. The fight had been, Judge Joel Jones later told the grand jury, "the first time I think in our history, a regular street battle with fire-arms." That was not quite true, but the fighting had been the most violent in generations. And while Philadelphians had burned African American churches in the past, the destruction of white people's churches astonished them. "The register of the scenes of yesterday," editorialized the *Pennsylvanian* on May 9, "is such as will long give reason to blush for the name of Philadelphia."[4]

Observers elsewhere were equally shocked. The mayors of Baltimore and Pittsburgh forbade political meetings in their cities, lest the contagion of riot spread. In New York, about to inaugurate a nativist mayor, Catholics prepared for battle. Nothing happened, but, a New York Catholic newspaper boasted, "There is not a Church of the city, which was not protected with an average force of one to two thousand men—cool, collected, armed to the teeth," and ready to take "as many lives they could in defence of their property." In Montreal, some said, Irish workers on the Lachine Canal posted warnings—decorated with drawings of coffins—that their American coworkers needed to leave. In Ireland, a newspaper reported that Philadelphia Protestants had not merely knocked over tombstones but opened a grave and dragged Catholic bones through the streets.[5]

For some, the riots were nothing more than spectacle. Mixing politics, humor, and racial insight, New Hampshire Whig songwriter John Warland suggested that most remarkable thing about the violence was that unlike so many other Philadelphia riots, it had not targeted the city's African Americans. He penned a minstrel song to the effect that "de riot up in *Skensin'ton* / Beats all de darkies twelve to one." In New York, paying visitors could view a mammoth representation of St. Augustine's Church, painted on hundreds of feet of canvas and exhibited onstage alongside a smaller painting of St. Michael's. The same admission fee gained the chance to see a dwarf three inches shorter than the more famous Tom Thumb, a giantess, and a "self-playing melodeon harp," among other amusements.[6]

Other accounts offered more analysis, as editors disagreed about whether the riots constituted merely an anomaly to a basically sound civilization or something more serious. The increasingly nativist *North American* assured readers that the arsonists were "very, very few" in comparison to the city's population, and not representative of the city's character. "They must be accounted among those pestilent exceptions to the healthy growth of society," it explained, "which spring up in every dense population, peculiar to no place, characteristic of no people." By contrast, the *Spirit of the Times* saw the destruction as rooted in the broader society. "The ringleaders were not so numerous," it conceded, "but they were beset by friends ready at a moment's warning to advise, to aid or to rescue, and supported by that passive silence on the part of thousands who were lookers on." The *Pennsylvanian* feared that "a certain part of the population" had fallen in love with violence, not caring about the particular political or religious controversy that was the nominal excuse for disorder. "They engage in it as amateurs, and burn a church more for amusement than from any other cause."[7]

The despair echoed across the country. "But for the fact," commented the *Richmond Star*, "that Philadelphia is known to have civil officers (too *civil*, by half) one might suppose it is a place of barbarians and savages." In his *Evening Post*, New York editor William Cullen Bryant lamented "the stain inflicted upon the honor of the country and the pernicious effect upon its morals" and blamed overzealous Protestant clergy for "provoking hatred and opposition, and inflaming the worst passions of human nature." "As American citizens, as Protestants," wrote the editors of the Whig *Boston Atlas*, "we hang our heads in shame and humiliation." In Massachusetts, Universalist preacher Edwin Hubbell Chapin saw in the riots "a manifestation of seeds of iniquity and destruction that lie deep below." "In lack of religious principle then," he explained, "individual, spiritual morality, your riots and your disorders find fuel, and break out at the first whirlwind in angry flame."[8]

Some feared the failure of the American experiment. The *Public Ledger* pondered whether the violence had so discredited American democracy that Russian autocracy, exemplified by Czar Nicholas, would be an improvement. "Which is best," it asked, "quiet and security under despotism, or daily destruction to life and property by mobs under liberty? *We* really prefer the former; and if their majesties, the sovereign people, cannot manage liberty better than they do in our city, we advise them to give it up, and to call in Nicholas and his bayonets and his halters and his knouts and his Siberias. They are capital tamers of those wild beasts, the mob." English monarchists, including those in British North America, savored the story as evidence for the weakness of republics. "The Republicans of America are the veriest despots in the universe," sneered the *Halifax Morning Post*. "They have the will and the power, in movements of excitement, of prostrating all law and order at the feet of momentary passion, and popular impulse. Thank God for the superiority of British Freedom!" In a possibly apocryphal story, an American in Paris defended his country's lack of an army to his French hosts. "Suppose that mobs do occur with us and are less promptly subdued than with you," he conceded. That was still better than living "like you in Europe, always at the bayonet's point, and under the frowning muzzles of great guns."[9]

Protestant Philadelphians knew not whom to blame. Mary Bird, who was in Delaware during the rioting, explained the violence to her five-year-old son, Frederic, who had marveled at the soldiers and their cannon. Mary blamed the Irish: "What a dreadful, wicked set of people they are to make such horrid riots." But her sister Caroline Mayer, who was in the city taking care of Frederic, disagreed. "The Americans are ten times worse than the Irish, except the Protestant Irish," she wrote to Mary. Though a daughter of a Lutheran minister, she sympathized with the "poor Catholics." "If people persecute them much longer, and all the saintly people smile & say, 'Ah, 'tis sad, but their doctrines are so very wicked,' I shall be tempted to turn Catholic myself." Isaac Mickle, who had previously attended Levin's temperance lectures, was now disgusted by his behavior. "But for Levin and a few others on the side of the Natives, who are worse than Jesuits," he wrote in his diary, "the flame of discord would soon go out."[10]

The *Public Ledger* disparaged both sides of the conflict. It denounced Levin as a "relentless scoundrel who has erected himself and his paper into the vile organs of this detestable and fiendish spirit, cried out, even amid the more profuse carnage, for 'more blood,'" and alluded to him as "the sanguinary preacher of sedition and disorder who wants a seat in Congress." Yet the same paper began to express sympathy with a good portion the nativist cause. "The Irish," it complained, "are an ardent, excitable people, and they interfere in our politics so soon as they tread upon our shores. . . . As they are goaded by oppression beyond human endurance, they are continually in rebellion, conspiracy, riot, or some violent resistance to government; and consequently by birth and education are they turbulent and lawless." Even the *Daily Chronicle*, previously friendly to Irish Catholic causes, sounded doubts about mass immigration. "We are made to bear the burden of the pauperism of foreign countries," it lamented, "to receive and support their surplus population, and to be repaid for all this with the introduction of little else than many of the most pernicious vices and prejudices which characterize the mass of population in some of the most degraded countries called civilized."[11]

The Natives hoped to deflect any responsibility by emphasizing their martyrs, especially George Shiffler—shot dead on May 6—and the American flag that, the nativists claimed, had been "trampled under foot by the Irish Papists" on May 6 before being paraded through the streets on May 7. Rallying around martyrs was an old tactic. In 1770, Bostonians had staged an elaborate public funeral for the five men killed by British troops in Boston, helping to cement the event as "the Boston Massacre." In the 1830s and 1840s, abolitionists and Mormons had gained sympathy by documenting the persecution they had faced.[12]

Nativists had begun beatifying Shiffler almost immediately after his death on May 6. On May 7, the *Native American* described the loss in emotional terms: "The scene which exhibited itself around this dying man was too much for every one possessing the ordinary feelings of sympathy to bear without shedding a tear. . . . One grey headed old man, in the midst of his tears, raised his staff aloft, and exclaimed in the fulness of his heart— 'On, on Americans! Liberty or death.' At this thrilling cry the old man led off, and the whole crowd followed him to avenge the death of their fellow-citizen." In June, Washington Peale drew a lithograph, *The Three Days of May 1844: Columbia Mourns Her Citizens Slain*, showing the goddess-like Columbia bearing a massive American flag with one hand while placing a wreath over the misspelled name "Schiffler," inscribed on a broken column. An eagle bears a shield with the names of the wounded, including "Peale," for the lithographer's cousin, Augustus. The broken column also bore the names of the other dead: Wright, Rhinedollar, Greble, Stillwell, Hammitt, Ramsey, and Cox. Though never as prominent as Shiffler, the first to fall, they too became nativist icons, men who died, in one nativist verse, "endeavoring to save / Their Country and Flag from dishonor."[13]

The veneration of Shiffler helped portray the Irish as impossible to Americanize. The earliest accounts of his death, though detailed, made no mention of an American flag. The first such association came when Shiffler was buried on May 9, his coffin wrapped in the flag that, the nativists claimed, had been trampled by Irish Catholics during the riots, and which nativists later claimed Shiffler had been holding when shot. By May 13, the legend was complete, as the *Native American* described Shiffler as "a young man whose *only offence* was clinging to the flag of his country, that 'Star

Spangled Banner,' of which Americans have had so much cause to boast, [but] was shot through the heart, (and a noble heart it was) and died!" By claiming that the lad had been killed while holding the flag, or, better yet, that he had been killed *because* he was holding the flag, the nativists hoped to portray Irish immigrants as flag haters. The *Catholic Herald* was quick to deny the charge, stating that the flag had been soiled when the platform to which it was attached had collapsed. "The Star-Spangled Banner," it assured readers, "is a favorite and animating emblem for the naturalized as well as the native citizen; and each would freely pour out his heart's blood to maintain it unsullied."[14]

The Three Days of May 1844.
Courtesy of the Library of Congress.

While such explanations covered the native corpses, it would be harder to explain away the fires that had destroyed so much of the Third Ward. Some nativists blamed the fires on "the high excitement of the moment" or claimed that Irish houses "were used as forts from which our citizens were shot down without discrimination or mercy," and that their destruction was "justifiable, and fully required by the exigency of the occasion." *Native American* editor Samuel Kramer claimed that the attacks on Kensington's buildings had been a case of "people [rising] in their own defence, [to] drive the villains to their dens and smoke them out." Albright's improvised squad of May 7 was a "gallant band of patriots," who braved deadly gunfire until their Irish antagonists "were hunted from their dens like so many wolves." Others blamed the arson on Irish Protestants, small boys, or "the very scum of the population," of the sort that accompanied fire companies to their brawls.[15]

Certainly Natives did not want responsibility for the burning of St. Michael's and St. Augustine's on May 8. On May 9, the very day after the church burnings, a nativist meeting at Southwark resolved to help protect all churches. "Burn no churches, even if your fathers were murdered before your eyes," Levin implored his readers. "Give a more rational and effectual direction to your feelings, by making the ballot-box speak in tones of thunder against the aggravating wrongs you have endured." In denouncing the arson, nativist leaders and anti-Catholic preachers rejected any linkage between their spoken and written denunciations of Irish Catholics and the violence against those immigrants' houses of worship.[16]

Despite the efforts of Kramer and Levin to disassociate themselves from the arson, the church burnings tarnished the Native cause. Joseph Sill, the merchant who had witnessed the burning of St. Augustine himself, wrote in his diary, "people begin now to sympathize with the persecuted Irish, who were originally heated against them for their wanton attacks upon the Americans. The Smoke of this Church will arise to Heaven as a memento to the brutality of an American Mob." On receiving an invitation to join his ward's American Republican Association, one native-born Protestant replied, "Christianity shudders and humanity weeps at the recent outrages of your party, and God grant that we may have no more of the evidences of its ascendancy."[17]

Catholics, too, worked to make sense of the violence. "It is good that we are sometimes chastised," the bishop of Chicago wrote to Kenrick, "and that our Eternal Father at times permits us to feel the smart of the galling rod of affliction and persecution; otherwise we might become too lukewarm and indifferent—too forgetful [of the fact] that we are the followers of *Him* whose whole life was one uninterrupted scene of suffering, persecution, affliction." "The news of the Philadelphia riots came upon us like a sudden earthquake," the *United States Catholic Magazine* mourned. "We had thought, that under the guaranties of the American constitution, even a Catholic might worship God without being shot for it, and build a church, without danger of its being burned, because of the sacrifice at its altar." To make such a thing truly impossible, Catholics would need to tell their own story, in which they were the victims, and the nativists the villains.[18]

Like the nativists, the Catholics denied starting the violence. The *Catholic Herald* insisted on Catholics' "desire to live in friendship with their fellow-citizens." The violence, it claimed, was primarily political, and the men who attacked the rally on May 3 should be identified not as Irish or as Catholic, but as "politicians opposed to the Native American Political party," regardless of birthplace or faith. Indeed, it pointed to two Irish Protestants and John Paul, the Catholic from New Jersey, as among those arrested for allegedly shooting at nativists.[19]

Other Catholics scoffed at the notion that the fight had raged over immigration. Sister Mary Gonzaga, superioress of St. Joseph's Orphan Asylum and the Baltimore-born daughter of Protestant parents, wrote, "The truth is, it is nothing but a party of Protestants leagued against the Catholics under the name of Native Americans and the Irish." Some Irish immigrants also understood the violence as a version of Orangeism. The Philadelphia correspondent of Dublin's *Freeman's Journal*, whom the newspaper identified as "an Irishman," told his readers that the American Republican Party was "headed chiefly by the north of Ireland Orangemen," and that the May mobs had shouted "Down with Popery," "To hell with Papists," and "Burn the priests." The paper's American-born New York correspondent blamed most of the Kensington violence not on native-born Americans but on Irish Orangemen, and he deftly reversed the Natives' denunciation of

Irish Catholic immigrants as the bearers of foreign influence. While some anti-Catholicism was endemic to America, he explained, "The last dash of venom which was required to make the poisoned chalice of American bigotry run over, English Toryism and IRISH ORANGEISM have supplied." A correspondent of the *New York Freeman's Journal*, signing himself "A Catholic Native American," insisted that the May 3 meeting "was composed generally of Orangemen, and convened at a place which naturally led the Irish Catholics to believe that an assault upon their Church was designed." Their disparagement of the Catholic religion, he argued, did not justify the Catholics' attack on the platform that afternoon, but it was at least "great palliation." The *Catholic Herald* could not deny that a "political affray" had turned into an anti-Catholic raid: "the burning of the churches put this beyond all doubt."[20]

Catholics crafted their story around those burnings; St. Michael's and St. Augustine's, more than any dead or injured immigrant, would serve as the Catholic martyrs to match the Protestant Shiffler and Rhinedollar. "What have the churches done," asked the *Catholic Herald*, that they should lie in ruins?" Yet ruins could teach. One poet proposed commemorating the violence by leaving untouched the ruins of St. Augustine's, so that "their blacken'd pile" could serve as "scoffing commentary" on Independence Hall, with its promises of freedom and religious liberty.[21]

The Protestant establishment offered mixed messages. In a regretful letter to Kenrick, Governor Porter called the riots "the severest test to which republicanism has ever been subjected" and "an instance of cruelty well calculated to fill every patriotic heart with grief and indignation." But the Philadelphia County grand jury blamed the riots in part on "the efforts of a portion of the community to exclude the Bible from our Public Schools," which it linked to the attack on the Natives' meeting on May 3. It presented the Natives as "unoffending citizens" and champions of the constitutional guarantees of both freedom of religion and freedom of assembly, while their Catholic antagonists were "a band of lawless irresponsible men, some of whom had resided in our country only for a short period." "These statements are far from the truth," Kenrick wrote his brother. "But conditions are such that Catholic witnesses will hardly be believed, and they are rarely called [to testify]."[22]

Wanting to present as American an image as possible, Kenrick excluded his fellow Irish immigrants from the response, and instead summoned prominent native-born Catholics to St. John's to rebut the grand jury's interpretation. Archibald Randall, a federal judge, native born of Scottish descent, had been one of the St. Mary's trustees subdued by Kenrick back in 1831. Whatever tension remained between the two men, Randall now stood with his bishop against the Protestant supremacist threat. He was joined by such other native-born luminaries as Dr. Joseph Nancrede, a prominent physician whose father had served under Rochambeau, and Professor William Horner, the dean of the Medical School of Pennsylvania and a recent convert to Catholicism.[23]

Randall's report did not condone violence, but it suggested that the worst bloodshed in Kensington had been largely a matter of communal self-defense. "The first death occurred at the time the houses were being sacked," the report noted, "the second when the school-house was being put on fire." Had the nativists not invaded Kensington, none of this would have happened. The main thrust of the report was not to analyze the violence, but to assert the Americanness of American Catholics. These elite Catholics insisted that their allegiance to the pope "regards not the things that appertain to this world," and that as an oppressed minority, they were all the more committed to American liberty. "Unless for the shield which the Constitution gives to those who are the smaller, and therefore, the weaker party, this government would be a despotism, for the governing power would be uncontrolled," the Catholics warned. "To-day one class may be lashed by the tyrant of numbers, and to-morrow another class may feel the scourge. No man, no sect, no party, would ever be safe." They ended with resounding patriotism: "We ask for no peculiar privileges; we make no merit of the purity of our Pennsylvania descent; but WE DEMAND that the exclamation, 'I AM AN AMERICAN CITIZEN,' shall continue to protect our rights, and the guarantee of our freedom."[24]

While Philadelphians debated the cause of the riots, they also argued about their government's failure to have kept the peace. Ignoring the jurisdictional limits on his authority, Caroline Mayer wished that Mayor Scott "had had the moral & physical courage to order a cannon to be fired on Monday afternoon that would have settled the whole clash." "If a woman had been Mayor," she continued, "I'll warrant ordered [sic] would never have been infringed." A self-described "old citizen" pined for the days when a determined mayor or sheriff could subdue a mob by waving a staff and shouting, "Order! Order!"[25]

Others charged that Sheriff McMichael had been slow to act. The *Native American* reported that while Shiffler was dying on May 6, McMichael had only reluctantly left a dinner party in the city and, when he finally made it to Kensington, obeyed Hugh Clark's instructions to depart, "leaving the belligerents to fight as much as they pleased." "All parties finding it convenient to shift their own wrongdoings to somebody else, have selected me as a proper person to bear that burden," McMichael complained to a friend. "If I do not sink beneath it, it will not be because there is not weight enough to press me down." He consoled himself with the thought that "if I am to fall a victim to temporary public fury, why in good time I shall claim the martyr's crown & obtain it." Not everyone blamed McMichael. "If a mob occurs & is successful in its attempts," noted Sidney George Fisher, a fellow Whig, the sheriff "is blamed by all. If he resists by military force & life is sacrificed, he is sure of encountering the most furious persecution from the party of rioters, their friends and adherents." The result, Fisher concluded, was that "the conduct of magistrates here has always been hesitating, undecided & weak." He hoped that the law would become "a thing of teeth & claws."[26]

If the sheriff were unable to suppress a riot with his own shouts and a civil posse, Philadelphians knew, the next step was to summon soldiers, and that bore its own risks. "The sight of soldiers on duty in parts of our city, is painful," argued the *United States Gazette*. "That is the means by which anarchy is changed into tyranny." Others wished for a more forceful military response, including a greater readiness to kill. "Had Col. Murray fired one volley," claimed one letter writer, "these 'brave' rioters would have fled like hares, and there would have been no churches burned." (In fact, Murray had not arrived until after St. Michael's church and the seminary had already been torched.) Similarly, the *Spirit of the Times* lamented the militia's "shape of a military force that every one knew was to intimidate, not to act, and in whose very face the little boys could make gestures of derision, so notorious was its pitiful impotence."[27]

Cadwalader agreed that the militia had failed, and he was outraged at the way his men had been ordered into danger without being given the power to fight. Privately, he blamed McMichael, "brought into office by the votes of the Irish population," for first failing to take precautions on learning of the nativist plans and for deploying the militia for show rather than for action. Anticipating a more vigorous engagement, he unofficially suggested that the city government authorize the militia to secure hundreds of artillery rounds from federal stockpiles in Washington. Even four or five hundred rounds of solid shot, canister, and shells, he feared, "would indeed be of itself but a small supply for any real service." Colonel Pleasonton devised a more elaborate plan, by which his artillery regiment could be "considered the permanent Civic Guard of the City of Philadelphia" and held in readiness. Such "a permanent military organization" would "save the expense of innumerable posses or parties of badly armed undisciplined and inoffensive Citizens."[28]

But Philadelphia might not be ready to give the troops free rein. The *Public Ledger* cited Napoleon to suggest firing a volley of live ammunition into a crowd so that successive volleys of blanks would be properly terrifying. But such lethality would not be necessary, the editorial continued. "When the military are called out and the mob have no fire-arms, the bayonet and the sabre will answer the purposes and save life. A charge with the bayonet in flesh wounds about the legs of the rioters, or of cavalry with the sabre in cuts round their shoulders and arms, which kill nobody, will always prevail, when mere pushing or riding over them will not. In subduing the mob, the whole secret is to strike first, and threaten afterwards." Judge Anson Parsons, who asked a grand jury to investigate the conduct of city and county authorities, also offered a mixed message about the use of lethal force. He instructed the jurors:

> If a great number of persons are assembled together, armed with guns or other hurtful weapons, and their object is manifest to do great personal violence to an individual, or a certain class of individuals, or to destroy public or private property, and they refuse to submit to the law, resist the Sheriff, or his assistants when they attempt an arrest, and that with violence, when they

refuse to disperse after being commanded by that officer, and are fully bent on violence to the persons or property of others, and all the other probable means for the suppression of the outrage fail, that officer may order his posse to take the lives of the insurgents, if necessary.

That single sentence presented an eight-part test for deadly force, requiring the sheriff to consider 1) the number of rioters; 2) their weapons; 3) their object; 4) their refusal to submit to law; 5) the violence of that refusal; 6) their refusal to disperse; 7) their determination; and 8) the exhaustion of other means. While Parsons's scorn for the rioters was clear—he called them "enemies to the State" and "little better than pirates"—his instructions showed his wish that rioters be given every opportunity to survive.[29]

Even the nativists—perhaps disingenuously—suggested that authorities should have been more ready to order deadly force. "Had our Sheriff acquainted himself," they claimed, "with a fact, notorious to every well-informed citizen, that he had the power to order the military to fire on a crowd unlawfully resisting him, St. Michael's needed not to have fallen." Meanwhile, a Catholic journalist lamented "a foolish reluctance on the part of men in authority to exercise their power even to the shedding of blood in the suppression of tumult."[30]

The riots had given new importance to the militia, leading Philadelphians to ask who should belong to that body. After all, the volunteers had no special legal status, since the sheriff had the same power to order any citizens into a posse. Some proposed that men of each ward be organized into a "citizen guard," which would exist specifically to suppress disorder and riot. As one volunteer explained, these units would be composed of men "free from the prejudice that caused the late riot," and also free from compunctions about killing. "There is no longer a doubt about the right of firing on a mob," the volunteer explained. "Should this be deemed necessary, it will be done without hesitation or fear of consequences." Others argued for a professional police force, offering London's Metropolitan Police—founded fifteen years earlier—as a possible model.[31]

On July 1, Judge Joel Jones welcomed a new grand jury and called for a better system of policing the county. Lamenting not only the most recent riots in Kensington, but also the earlier violent strikes and railroad riots, he warned that traditional forms of order would no longer suffice to control "foreigners especially, used at home to a military police, taught by long oppression to regard all laws as tyranny, and all officers of the law as enemies." "With a population near three hundred thousand," he explained, "we trust the execution of the laws to the voluntary obedience of the offender or the casual support of the citizen. This is enough for our country townships," but insufficient for "a great city, with its hordes of desperate vagabonds and its hosts of foreigners."[32]

Nearly two months after the end of the Kensington riots, Philadelphians had not begun to resolve any of the questions they raised. What rights could Catholics expect in a majority Protestant country? How could immigrants become Americans? Who had the right to use force—to challenge an insult, to defend oneself from attack, to seek vengeance? How much force could authorities use in response? Who even were the proper authorities: the posse or the militia? In July, all of these questions would become more urgent.

Parade Ribbon, July 1844.

16

Won't We Give It to You on the Fourth of July?

On May 27, exactly three weeks after the first bloodshed, 1,200 Natives returned to the vacant lot at Second and Master where they had gathered before the fateful rainstorm. Fearing violence, McMichael stationed a posse nearby, and Major General Patterson ordered Brigadier General Augustus Roumfort's Second Brigade held in readiness. This time, however, the clouds did not burst, the nativists finished their speeches, and everyone made it home alive. While nativists found their voices, the Irish community movement fell silent. Immigrants canceled meetings in favor of Irish autonomy, and Kensington's manufacturers took the opportunity to reduce wages, knowing their workers could not meet to plan a march or a strike. The city remained mostly at peace, but Philadelphians spent June and early July dreading a renewal of fighting as nativists asserted a right to the streets they denied Catholic immigrants.[1]

Some of the tension was personal. On June 22, a Sister of Charity was walking along Market Street when a young man called her a "damn Papist bitch" and struck her across the face. The following week, an "American lady" was returning from Sunday services at St. Joseph's Church when a man grabbed the prayer book from her hand and threw it into the street. "You are another damned Catholic bitch," he snarled. Wesley Flavel of Kensington had been a steady employee with the mild-mannered job of clerking for a Market Street umbrella dealer. But the May fighting, which took place just blocks from his home, unhinged him. He told a Catholic neighbor, "we have not killed all the Catholics yet," and that the Catholics "will kill both you and me." He started drinking, lost his job, and, claiming he was following the sheriff's instructions, began stockpiling guns. On the afternoon of July 2, he had been drinking in a tavern when his wife fetched him to help put up a fence. He followed her, but in an ill humor. Later that afternoon he shot both his wife and his fourteen-year-old niece, mortally wounding the latter.[2]

Perhaps most alarming were the rumors that Protestants were arming. "The *Native* Americans, I perceive, are forming military companies," wrote a reporter on May 19. "There are now three, one in Spring Garden, one in Southwark, and one in West Philadelphia." On June 12, Thomas Lucas, a Protestant Irishman weaver from Kensington, tried to buy ninety-six surplus army muskets at auction. The auctioneer refused to hand them over to Lucas and his friends, some of whom appeared to be drunk. Lucas retained nativist lawyer C. J. Jack and swore "that he has entered into no combination with any man or men to form any Military Company, or to arm the Irish Protestants of Kensington or any other place—-that he never was an Orangeman, nor ever belonged to any secret order or body of men, either in Ireland or this Country—that he has no disposition to disturb the peace in any way, nor has he or any one connected with him, threatened the Catholic Irish or any others." It is not clear if Lucas eventually got the guns, but the connection between a Protestant immigrant, a leading nativist, and a supply of cheap firearms suggests the tensions of the early summer. "Judging from the temper and tone of the newspaper press and public meetings in Philadelphia," the *New York Herald* warned on June 14, "we expect one of these days a second edition of riots, murder, bloodshed, house-burning, and church conflagrations."[3]

Looking ahead to the fall election season, nativists worked to build their movement. "Day after day," Kramer's *Native American* exulted, "hundreds of our most intelligent and respectable citizens are coming forward to unite with the new party." Nativists showed their strength on the evening of June 7, when anywhere from eight thousand to fifteen thousand rallied in front of Independence Hall. Since this was too many for a single speaker, however powerful, to reach with his oratory, satellite meetings organized at the corners of Fifth and Sixth Streets. The meeting's list of dozens of vice presidents and secretaries suggests the movement's diffuse leadership; this was still a coalition of loosely affiliated ward organizations. But Peter Sken Smith and Lewis Levin, both of whom had been in Kensington on May 6, remained prominent leaders. In a speech interrupted by applause and cheers, Levin pointed to the New York City election as a sign of things to come. "That conquest of American freemen over the minions of the Pope," he bellowed, "spoke in tones of thunders, and the echo is still reverberating from hill to dale throughout the length and breadth of this broad land."[4]

Not every party rally turned out so well. On June 17, leading nativists—including Levin, Jack, Peale, and Smith—led a thousand Philadelphia nativists on an excursion to Burlington, New Jersey. As they pulled out of port, the nativists' vessel, gaudily decorated with American flags—including the famous tattered flag of Kensington—passed the packet ship *Shenandoah* and caught the eye of the hundreds of immigrants on board. The ship had departed Liverpool on May 9, so its passengers had been sailing the Atlantic as news of the Kensington riots crossed in the other direction. Unaware of the animus against them, the immigrants cheered the emblems of their new home. The nativists groaned them in response. But the nativists had their own chance to feel unwelcome when they arrived in Burlington and found no one there to greet them. After some hesitation, the Philadelphians decided that their Burlington allies "were afraid some men would make a disturbance." They gamely gave speeches to one another until it was time to go home.[5]

Despite such setbacks, the movement appeared to grow in power. After sending petitions to Congress seeking an extension of the naturalization period to twenty-one years, nativists were thrilled to find Senator William Archer of Virginia sympathetic. Philadelphia's own representatives, by contrast, were noncommittal, and the proposal faced opposition elsewhere. In Springfield, Illinois, rising politician Abraham Lincoln led his fellow Whigs to denounce the idea. "The guarantee of the rights of conscience, as found in our Constitution," wrote Lincoln, "is most sacred and inviolable, and one that belongs no less to the Catholic, than to the Protestant."[6]

The most troubling disturbance of the month combined moral debates and firemen's rivalries. In 1842, temperance members of the Weccacoe Engine Company in Southwark had insisted on "total abstinence from intoxicating drinks," leading thirstier firemen to buy a used hose carriage and 500 feet of hose to form their own company, the Weccacoe Hose, two blocks away. The two companies became bitter rivals, and they somehow decided that the summer of 1844, with Philadelphia still reeling from the Kensington riots, would be just the time to intensify the violence. On the afternoon of Sunday, May 12, a group of men ran the Weccacoe Hose apparatus through the streets of Philadelphia City, where it had no legal right to be. They charged toward a line of troops who were blockading Fifth Street, but the militiamen seized the hose carriage and one of its runners. The man they had grabbed, Levi Fort of Southwark, was more drunk than malicious, but the incident was alarming enough that General Patterson ordered the men to shoot if the assailants returned, which fortunately they did not. As matters calmed, Mayor Scott returned the apparatus to the members of the company, but the incident reminded everyone that the fire companies remained a source of chaos.[7]

The feud reemerged in late June. On the afternoon of June 24, some drunken members of the Southwark Engine (another Weccacoe Engine rival) beat up John Money, a member of the Weccacoe Engine and an employee of Levin's *Daily Sun*. On the evening of Wednesday, June 26, the

Weccacoe Hose was returning from a false alarm when they passed the Weccacoe Engine house on Queen Street. The hose men groaned the engine company, then returned an hour later, hoping to break into the house. They stopped only when someone inside the engine house fired a horse pistol into the neck of Frederic Lucas of the Weccacoe Hose. Surprisingly, Lucas survived, and the district watchmen were able to persuade a small crowd to go home, leaving a loaded musket behind.[8]

The following morning, the Weccacoe Engine formally warned Sheriff McMichael that the Southwark Engine and Weccacoe Hose were conspiring to attack its house and apparatus. The company surrendered the house and the engine to McMichael, explaining that the county would therefore be liable for any damage done to them. Not wanting to risk further violence, the Southwark authorities doubled the police force, while McMichael summoned a posse and asked for military aid. General Hubbell accordingly detailed the Wayne Artillerists to occupy the Weccacoe Engine house. On Saturday night—generally the peak of firemen's fights—McMichael's men broke up gatherings and confined a few men to the Southwark lockup. By Sunday, McMichael felt the crisis had passed. The response had been effective, and no one was hurt, but it had taken overwhelming force to keep Southwark from exploding. Would the peace last through the nation's birthday?[9]

As one of the year's few days off for workers, the Fourth of July had long been a day of "debauchery, gambling, and drunkenness," in the words of one mayor. Into the 1840s, vendors set up booths for liquor and gambling, and drunkards could be found resting on "each corner, pump, and pillar, wall and post." The *Public Ledger* wailed, "Was the American Revolution achieved for the impunity of drunkards and gamblers, and other lawbreakers?" Philadelphians of means often fled the city for cooler, calmer locales.[10]

The Fourth was also a good day to claim one's turf as an American. Political parties regularly met. African Americans and abolitionists celebrated on the fourth, or sometimes the fifth, until 1834, when they switched to August 1 in honor of the abolition of slavery in the British Empire. As citizenship remained in dispute, the Fourth could also be a chance to fight. Describing his tours in the late 1830s, British traveler Frederick Marryat claimed that "On the 4th of July there were several bodies of Americans, who were out on the look out for the Irish, after dark, and many of the latter were severely beaten, if not murdered; the Irish, however, have to thank themselves for it."[11]

And the Fourth was a chance for a parade. Like a riot—only more respectable—a parade brought hundreds or thousands of likeminded people into the streets. There, in the company of fellow believers, Americans could find their place in a changing society as members of trades, fraternal organizations, fire companies, or militias. In his days as a temperance editor, Levin had promoted a parade through the streets of Philadelphia that, he claimed, terminated with thirty thousand people packed into Independence Square to hear the speakers. In 1841, the Philadelphia Repeal Association had paraded two thousand marchers, including the Hibernia Greens militia company, and listened to an address by Dr. Moriarty of St. Augustine's. In March 1843, a massive parade of firemen attracted forty-eight companies and around four thousand firemen. And on July 4, 1843, the Pennsylvania Catholic Total Abstinence Society recruited two thousand to march in its parade.[12]

Political parties were especially eager marchers. As Andrew Jackson's followers of the 1820s coalesced into the new Democratic Party, they also developed a new visual vocabulary, often emphasizing Jackson's nickname, "Old Hickory." The marched with hickory trees, hickory poles, hickory brooms, and hickory nuts to represent the new faction. As Jackson's opponents became Whigs, they found symbols of their own, including the raccoon and the log cabin, the latter of which could be drawn through the streets by oxen to show support for William Henry Harrison. To join this party system, nativists needed parades of their own. In April 1844, New York nativists had staged an "American Republican Procession" to build support for Harper's candidacy, perhaps helping him win the mayoral race. Philadelphia's Natives looked to July 4 for their chance to stun even a city accustomed to fantastic spectacle. "It is thought this will be by far the greatest turn out that has ever occurred," predicted the *Saturday Courier*. "A larger number of citizens from other towns will visit the city on the occasion than have ever before been in Philadelphia at any one time." With luck, the parade would be less deadly than the nativist marches into the Third Ward of Kensington in May. But it would be no less assertive of their beliefs about who owned Philadelphia, and America. They would show that they belonged, and Irish Catholics did not.[13]

Nativists began readying for the procession in early June, as ward associations called for nativist ladies to help them secure banners for the march by raising funds with which to buy materials and hire professional male artists. Even this much involvement would, in the words of Alderman Peter Hay, require women "to expose themselves, even for a moment, to the public gaze, in the political arena." But, Hay assured the ladies, when the threat was great enough, such a "sacrifice of feeling" was justified. The Revolution had been one occasion when women had properly entered the arena. Now America faced another emergency: the threat of ignorant immigrants acting as "unsuspecting dupes" or, worse, the "willing instruments of political demagogues." Kramer, the editor of the *Native American*, similarly argued that while women should generally avoid "mingling in political affairs," the rules changed "when the country's cause is at stake."[14]

Some women were able to speak for themselves. Catherine Shurlock explained that the ladies of the Second Ward, Spring Garden, sought to support "our husbands, fathers, sons and brothers." But unlike the Irish Catholic women of Kensington, said to have handed guns to their menfolk, the native ladies "prefer doing our part by mild means, as most becoming our sex," offering a painted, ornamental banner depicting the Bible and George Washington. Mary Bethel, speaking for the ladies of the First Ward, Kensington, thanked the men "engaged in the struggle of freedom in protecting the land we love." "When we behold you baring your breasts to the storm, and standing between our loved homes and the battle's confusion," she told the nativist men, "we bless the God of nations that has provided us with *such* protectors."[15]

They could well bless their protectors, for everyone understood that the procession could spark renewed fighting. Two years earlier, the Lombard Street riot had started with a procession by African Americans, some of whom carried a banner depicting an emancipated slave with the rising sun behind him. Apparently, some onlookers understood this to be celebration of the Haitian Revolution and the burning of white homes, and that was enough to start a significant riot. Now, in 1844, the city had endured much worse violence, and the wrong banner could easily reignite the flames. In New York, Irish Americans heard that Philadelphia nativists "intend to have their parade as offensive as possible—displaying Orange banners, and playing Boyne Water, &c." One predicted that despite "the preparations so ostentatiously being made by the authorities to maintain order, order will not be maintained until lives are lost, and the 'Natives,' finding that it does not pay to come to blows with the Irish, wreak their vengeance by burning a few more churches." As a Catholic preacher passed two young men on Vine Street, they snarled at him: "Ah! won't we give it to you on the 4th of July?" In what might appear a grim omen, a young militiaman preparing to march in the parade brought home a musket and, while trying to clean it, shot off the top of his fourteen-year-old sister's head.[16]

"There is a dread upon our own people generally," Kenrick wrote his brother, "that as [the nativists] persist in their threats, the remaining churches, especially the Cathedral, may be burned, and that there may be a general massacre of our people." Desperate to avoid such an outcome, Kenrick counseled Philadelphia's Catholics not to plan any parades of their own. "In the present state of the public mind," he instructed his flock, "every occasion of agitation should be avoided." Likewise, a nativist editor begged the Natives to ignore any "reproaches, tumults, threats or ridicule" that might come their way, assuring the proud men that "that they are strong enough to submit to [such provocations], without any impeachment of their courage."[17]

An anxious Major General Patterson ordered that at least some trusted companies remain in town on July 4, and he asked Cadwalader to keep him informed of his whereabouts, day or night. Sheriff McMichael printed circulars, which he could distribute to every ward, warning officials that "In the present excited state of popular feeling, it is possible that some accidental cause may produce disturbance on the approaching Anniversary of our National Independence. Should such an event unhappily occur, it is to be feared, that it may lead to seriously-mischievous results, unless means can be provided for its immediate suppression." He asked each ward leader to invite "those citizens of your Ward upon whose temper, discretion and firmness you can rely" to prepare themselves to act as a posse. Yet, to avoid provoking the very violence he feared, he asked that the communication be kept confidential.[18]

By 5:30 A.M. on the Fourth of July, nativists were streaming toward their appointed places. The weather was delightful: clear, with temperatures in the sixties or low seventies. Even the regular summer dust was absent, thanks to some rain the previous day. To the parade organizers, "it seemed that Providence had resolved to smile benignantly upon the grand celebration." Natives would later boast that ten thousand people marched; more detached observers estimate no more than five thousand. Even that lower number would have made for a spectacular parade. The procession was supposed to form up at eight o'clock, but it took four hours—from 6:30 to 10:30—to get everyone ready on Arch Street. And then, with a blast from the Trumpeter of Fame at the head of the procession, it began to move.[19]

As was traditional, workmen applied the skills of their trade to civil display. Printers worked a mobile printing press, passing out copies of a commemorative ode. The carpenters of the Northern Liberties had built a Temple of Liberty—sixteen feet high, fourteen feet long, with thirteen pillars to represent the original states and a statue of Liberty on top of the dome. Parading the massive structure required fourteen gray horses, led by white and African American grooms, some dressed as American Indians or Moors. In Southwark, ship carpenters crafted a twenty-five-foot-long model ship using material donated by local lumber merchants. The "Native American Ship Washington" would be manned by a "crew of old salts" and pulled through the streets. Kensington's shipwrights outdid their Southwark rivals, making the *Native American* a foot longer and crafting it in part from the timbers of the *Constitution* and a piece of the table on which the Declaration of Independence had been signed.[20]

Other marchers bore the satin banners commissioned by the nativist ladies. While the banners depicted everything from the horn of plenty to the scales of justice, most offered variations on just five symbols: the American flag, the eagle, the goddess of Liberty, George Washington, and the Bible. These last two, especially, appeared with an exclusionary twist. In his farewell address of 1796, George Washington had written, "Against the insidious wiles of foreign influence . . . the jealousy of a free people ought to be constantly awake." As Catholics and their allies pointed out, Washington was almost certainly warning against the influence of foreign governments, not immigrants, but the nativists had adopted "beware of foreign influence" as a slogan to suggest that the father of their country would have approved their program. Accordingly, it became the most popular inscription on the ward banners.[21]

The Bible, generally depicted as lying open, made for an equally powerful nativist emblem, for it had long symbolized the Protestant—especially Presbyterian—cause in the religious wars and disputes. In 1679, Scottish Presbyterians known as Covenanters had embroidered open Bibles on the banners they carried into battle against Stuart forces, eleven years before the Battle of the Boyne. And Orangemen in both Europe and North America would at times march behind an actual open Bible. By the 1840s, the open Bible could denote a general Protestantism that embraced Quakers and Episcopalians as well as Congregationalists and Presbyterians. Thus, by mixing the open Bible with the American flag and eagle, the nativists were adapting an Orange symbol to American politics.[22]

Lest anyone miss the point that this was not merely a general celebration of the nation's anniversary, the procession featured reminders of the Kensington fights, presented as an attack on the native born. Banners depicted a torn flag, the names of the dead, or a portrait of the dying Shiffler. More striking were actual wounded veterans of the Kensington battle, riding in barouches near the front of the procession, along with the "orphans of the martyrs." Near the end of the procession, two black horses drew a pyramidal cenotaph dedicated to the memory of those slain in Kensington. And still further back, after dozens of American flags in a range of size and materials had passed, the "torn flag that was trampled on in Kensington" was borne on a car by itself. A short while behind this came William Craig, leading the Third Ward Kensington Association, whose organizing meetings in May had cost so much blood. All of this appeared designed to provoke as much as celebrate. Watching the parade as it passed the corner of Tenth and Spruce, Colonel Pleasonton judged "some of [the banners] handsome and appropriate, while others were of an opposite character, and others again inflammatory, and exciting to disturbance."[23]

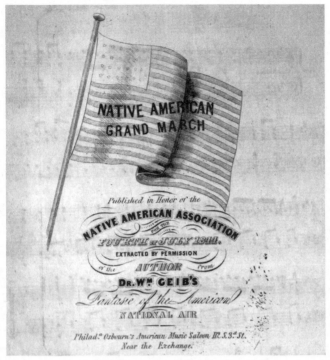

Native American Grand March.
Courtesy of the Lester S. Levy Sheet Music Collection Sheridan Libraries, Johns Hopkins University.

The parade route was unusually long; whereas the Washington Centennial procession of 1832 had totaled six miles, the 1844 march may have doubled that. Rather than confine itself to the traditional routes in central Philadelphia and adjoining suburban wards, the march was pushed all the way into Kensington, passing by the scene of the May fighting as it moved along Master Street from Third Street to Frankford Road. By choosing this route, the *Spirit of the Times* charged, Natives were "taunting the desolate heart, ridiculing the blackened hearth, and mocking at everything which the beholders may cherish as dear and holy." The organizers had included omnibuses for some elderly and infirm Natives, and instructed each ward association to designate a water carrier to refresh the walkers. Even so, and despite the mild weather, some sympathizers were deterred by the length of the march and went home. Those who did march occasionally found themselves stalled when the Temple of Liberty or one of the boats proved too tall to fit below the branches that shaded Philadelphia's streets. Pioneers moved forward to cut away the obstructions, while ladies on balconies threw wreaths to the marchers below. "Natives raise your banners high," read the note accompanying one bouquet. "For your country bleed and die."[24]

After five-and-a-half hours, the marchers reached their destination: Snyder's Woods, an open ground near the Schuylkill River. The exhausted Natives were welcomed by vendors selling refreshments from tents and booths, though, unsurprisingly, the organizers had forbidden alcohol. Spectators and people who had skipped the march entirely joined them, forming what may have been the largest public gathering in Philadelphia's history up to that point. While waiting for sunset, they were entertained by readings of the Declaration of Independence and Washington's farewell address, as well as nativist orations bemoaning "the sad music of premature widows' groans" and orphaned children's "tears shed for murdered fathers."[25]

Finally, the crowd settled down to watch a fireworks show by Samuel Jackson, the same pyrotechnist who had entertained Cadwalader's troops at Easton two years before. Jackson promised "the greatest display of Fireworks ever exhibited in this country," and emphasized that "the Boquet" would be "composed entirely of *native fires,* vieing in beauty and brilliancy with anything of foreign name." The grand finale was a fiery Temple of Liberty, fifty feet wide and thirty feet high, and featuring most of the nativists' favorite icons: an altar bearing a ballot box, "an American eagle with a medallion of Washington suspended in its mouth," and, of course, an American flag. A technician fired a rocket to set it ablaze, at which point "bright burning stars" spelled out the nativist slogan, "Beware of Foreign Influence," to the enthusiastic shouts of the crowd.[26]

To everyone's relief and surprise, the day ended without violence. "Even the rabble who always congregate about large gatherings of people . . . were uncommonly orderly and tractable," marveled the *Chronicle.* In Southwark, the captain of the watch remarked on "how uncommonly quiet everything was." "Not a single disturbance—not a man who wore the Native badge, was seen to be intoxicated," later boasted a nativist newspaper. Ladies watched the fireworks unaccompanied and unmolested, "for women need no protection where Native Americans are." That was slightly exaggerated. Some nativists camped in the woods, planning to clean up the following day. At two o'clock on the morning of the fifth, they were awoken by an attack, which they at first assumed to be an assault by their political enemies. But it turned out to be just an ordinary group of drunken rowdies who wanted nothing more than to grab pieces of ham and throw them at the ladies, then smear ham grease over their own faces. Outrageous, to be sure, but not truly dangerous. Later that morning, another group attacked the sleeping nativists of the Sixth Ward, Northern Liberties, beating some and making off with their banner and four flags. Nativists denounced the "high-handed outrage," but the incident involved just one of the dozens of wards that had marched.[27]

Pleasonton recorded the disappointment of some Natives at not having been attacked, and their effort to spin even peace as a threat. "They say," he wrote, "'the Irish would have attacked, but were restrained by their clergy, therefore the clergy of the Irish are dangerous, for if they can restrain, they can also excite,'—so they should be put down, and driven out of the country." Indeed, the peace of the day owed a great deal to Bishop Kenrick, who had silenced his flock for weeks. But a peace that depended on Irish Catholic prostration could not last. Even as Pleasonton wrote, an Irish-born priest and his brother were making a stand against Protestant domination.[28]

Church of St. Philip Neri, as it appeared about 1880.
Courtesy of the Catholic Historical Research Center of the Archdiocese of Philadelphia.

17

Are There any Guns in the Church?

On Friday, July 5, nativists disassembled the Temple of Liberty and carried it to the Chinese Museum, the city's most prominent large, indoor exhibit space. There, they placed it alongside the silk banners that had graced the previous day's march and the two miniature ships—minus their topmasts, which would not fit. On Monday, they expected, they would open the exhibition to paying visitors, with proceeds going to ease the suffering of native-born victims of the Kensington violence. Meanwhile, a mile to the southeast in Southwark, Father John Patrick Dunn, pastor of the Church of St. Philip de Neri, stared at a note from one of his Sunday school teachers. His church, she warned, would be attacked that evening. His response would provoke an even deadlier riot than the one that had rocked Kensington in May.[1]

Father Dunn's reaction to the note was rooted both in the longer history of Southwark's Irish Catholic community and in the dreadful events of 1844. By the 1830s, Southwark had become home to an increasing number of Catholics, enough for Bishop Kenrick to plan the church of St. Philip de Neri. When Kenrick appointed Father Dunn to build St. Philip's, he had already purchased a building lot on Fifth Street. But Dunn rejected it in favor of a more central location, a 79-by-117-foot lot on the south side Queen Street between Second and Third, in the heart of Southwark. The new site occupied the center of a residential block, home of cabinet makers, carpenters, carters, cordwainers, and mariners, plus the odd blacksmith, clerk, jeweler, and tobacconist. It sat near key Southwark civic buildings: the Commissioners' Hall, the library, and a public school, as well as several Protestant churches.[2]

To design the church, Kenrick hired Napoleon LeBrun, the Philadelphia-born son of French immigrants. Though he would go on to an architectural career of some renown, in 1840 LeBrun was not yet twenty years old, and the church would be one of his first commissions. Constrained by the limited budget of Southwark's Catholics and by his own inexperience, LeBrun sketched a facade with some Greek Revival elements but far less ornamentation than would normally appear with such a design. The pediment and pilasters he did deploy were awkwardly scaled and arranged, producing—in the words of a later critic—not so much a sense of monumentality but a "look of necessity." The rest of the building was a functional brick box. The building's most unusual feature might have been the disconnect between facade and interior arrangement. Although it was hard to tell from the outside, where passersby saw an enormous central door, the main church room was effectively on the second floor, twelve feet above the pavement. This left a large basement space below, "both well lighted and ventilated," to be used for a chapel or classrooms.[3]

Some of St. Philip's parishioners were likely among the Catholics who aspired to political power in Southwark's dominant Democratic Party. In the 1830s, Joseph Doran, who would gain prominence in Philadelphia's Repeal movement, was a pillar of the party, credited with saving the election for constable in 1834. In 1840, the Southwark commissioners appointed James Campbell—a Southwark-born son of Irish Catholic immigrants—as a school director, and his fellow directors in turn chose him to represent Southwark on the central board. In the 1841 county treasurer election, Hugh Clark, Kensington's Irish-born master weaver, had soundly defeated his Whig opponent among Southwark voters, 1,633 to 1,050. And in 1842, John McCoy, an Irish immigrant, easily defeated his Whig opponent to represent Southwark's First Ward on the board of commissioners.[4]

Yet Southwark also housed some committed anti-Catholics. Britton Edwards, who had organized the Orange march in 1831, was a Southwark man. He seems to have been less active in politics by the 1840s, but he took some interest in the emerging nativist party, and was willing to speak at its meetings. Just around the corner from St. Philip's, on Second Street, lay the Assembly Church, an Old School Presbyterian outpost led by Rev. William McCalla, who considered the Catholic Church to be the Antichrist and described Irish Catholics as "foreign savages." Perhaps such contempt inspired the young men who, starting in late 1843, began to hang around the street in front of St. Philip's during Sunday services, making enough trouble to annoy the worshippers inside.[5]

These toughs were part of a culture of delinquency in the district. Along with neighboring Moyamensing, Southwark was known as one of the most dangerous portions of the county, where charcoal or chalk graffiti on walls and doors named the gangs whose members lay waiting to attack any outsider who lacked sufficient escort. Knots of "disorderly boys" loitered on street corners, asking each passing man or youth, "What do you run with?" so they could attack allies of rival fire companies. "The dance-house, the brothel, the unlicensed tavern," lamented the *Daily Chronicle*, "have flourished, openly, and without disguise, under the eye, if not under the patronage, of magistrates, constables and watchmen, without a single effort for their suppression." A superintendent of police, it claimed, was fired "because he was too zealous in the discharge of duties!"[6]

By the spring of 1844, under the leadership of former Democrats Lemuel Paynter and Thomas Grover, Southwark had become an American Republican stronghold. In March, Paynter had represented his congressional district's nativists for the large gathering in Independence Square. At the same gathering, McCalla had warned that Catholics "will buy up and build up your politicians, and militia companies . . . you will have no third alternative between annihilation and self-defence. You must do or die." In late April, Lewis Levin had addressed a "tremendous gathering" in Southwark itself. Around that time, Grover made such gatherings easier, purchasing a vacant church and rededicating it as the "American Republican Hall of the Fifth Ward, Southwark." A few weeks later, the Second Ward dedicated its own Native American House. Some expected Grover to run for Congress in the fall.[7]

St. Philip's pastor, Father Dunn, refused to be intimidated. Along with Kenrick and Moriarty, he was one of the county's most prominent Irish-born priests, in part due to his role, and that of his brother William, in the Repeal movement. Described as an "eloquent and sarcastic preacher" by Aloysius Jordan, Dunn may have been the priest whose "injudicious attacks" Jordan blamed for building "a hidden but intense feeling of hatred to Catholicity and Catholics." Dunn certainly had a record of taunting Protestants, challenging readers of the *Protestant Banner* to prove that the King James Bible was the word of God.[8]

Then came May, and the Kensington riots. Several Southwark nativists marched to the battle and two, George Young and Lewis Greble, were shot, the latter fatally. As a new Catholic church in an increasingly nativist neighborhood, St. Philip de Neri was an obvious target were the violence to spread, so the Dunn brothers readied for a fight.[9]

On the evening of May 7, as news of the Kensington gun battle reached Southwark, William Dunn organized nearby Catholics into an informal watch, with squad leaders led by "captains." They armed themselves with an assortment of weapons, ranging from pistols and muskets to bayonets affixed to brush handles. The following night, May 8, St. Augustine's burned, and neighbors of St. Philip's started packing their belongings, expecting that church to be next. At about 2:30 P.M. on Thursday, May 9, the church's Protestant neighbors learned that the Dunns had stockpiled weapons and ammunition in the church. Alderman Richard Palmer seized the weapons, and Father Dunn surrendered the church and its keys as well. Of course, handing over church keys was precisely the step that had failed to save St. Michael's or St. Augustine's, and more families living near the church evacuated their homes. The church might well have burned that afternoon but for the arrival of two militia companies—the Lafayette Light Guards and the Independent Rifles. The Native Americans who surrounded the church insisted that they were merely trying to protect it.[10]

The following evening, May 10, the troops repelled some kind of disturbance near the church and discovered a trail of wood shavings, which suggested a possible plan of arson. (Later, authorities would conclude that the shavings had been accidentally dropped by some children.) Captain Thomas Florence, in charge of the militia detachment, kept sentries out in case of further trouble, and requested a cannon from the arsenal. On May 11, local residents persuaded Florence, a Southwark Democrat, to keep his men indoors. But then someone threw a couple of bricks through the windows of an Irish family living near the church, possibly as a means to see if the militia had left and it would be safe to attack the church itself. Florence's Independent Rifles chased the attackers away, but the danger was clear. "St. Philip's Church is by far the most exposed to danger of any other post," warned a reporter. "There are openings, by alleys and yards, all around it; and there are frame buildings, stables, etc.; in dangerous proximity."[11]

No attack took place, and in late May, William Dunn got back the improvised arsenal that had been confiscated by Alderman Palmer. Now he hoped for something better. When he read Major General Patterson's authorization for his brigadiers "to organize and arm companies of citizens in undress and . . . appoint suitable persons to command the new corps," Dunn asked Sheriff McMichael for weapons to defend the church. McMichael referred Dunn to Brigadier General Horatio Hubbell, whose Third Brigade comprised militia companies from the southern portions of Philadelphia County: Passyunk, Moyamensing, and Southwark.[12]

A lawyer with a home in Moyamensing and an office in the city, Hubbell was no friend of Irish Catholics. Back in 1831, he had addressed the Orangemen on their July 12 march and had later vigorously defended them in court. In 1843, as Democrats divided between the more and less nativist factions, he had joined the former. But while he was personally reluctant to arm Dunn and his fellow Catholics, as a public officer he did not want to be accused of playing favorites. "What arms do you want?" Hubbell asked. "We don't want many," Dunn explained. "We have a guard of 12 men each night through the week, which, for the entire week would make 84, and I think there would be no necessity for more than 20 muskets along with the private arms which we now have or may be able to procure." After conferring with McMichael and Major General Patterson, Hubbell endorsed Dunn's request, though perhaps without understanding Dunn's intentions. Dunn later suggested that he had been organizing a uniformed volunteer company to muster in Hubbell's own Third Brigade. But Hubbell testified that he had authorized "a mere guard to protect the church; I considered it a civil guard," organized like "any other batch of watchmen." And when Hubbell did authorize the distribution of state arms to Dunn, he specified that they were for "a volunteer company for the protection of St. Philip Neri's Church, in Queen street, in the District of Southwark, in the County of Philadelphia," not a general infantry unit. [13]

Like Hubbell, Adjutant General Adam Diller, who had his own nativist sympathies, tried to avoid issuing the weapons, but a persistent Dunn went over his head, traveling to Harrisburg to appeal directly to Governor Porter. He was persuasive, and on June 13, Porter ordered Diller to issue twenty-five stand of weapons, with the proviso that Dunn promise to return them by the end of January. Even then, Diller dragged his feet, authorizing only twenty muskets. And when Dunn actually got the weapons, they were junk, with no more than four ramrods among them, and in such poor shape that they would more likely kill the man trying to fire them than their intended target. When Hubbell warned him of the danger, Dunn returned the weapons and got twenty-five stand in somewhat better shape. He would supplement them with whatever muskets, rifles, and shotguns the St. Philip's congregation could purchase. [14]

"I merely sought to protect the church," Father Dunn later explained, "which I built with great exertions for the poor especially." He had ordered a temporary wooden fence built along the west side of the church property, planning to leave it there until after the Fourth of July. The Dunns had heard the attack might come that day—the day of the Native American parade—or on July 12, the anniversary of the Boyne. Either way, they wanted to be ready. Father Dunn's neighbor to the west, Isaiah Robbins, thought the precautions both unnecessary and dangerous, in that they could provoke the very attack that Dunn feared. "You might go in and out until you are gray-headed," he assured the priest, "without any danger of attack from the Native Americans."[15]

Despite Robbins's pledge, the Southwark nativists' behavior on July 4 was hardly reassuring. Grover served as the nativist procession's chief marshal, astride a horse sporting a new bridle ordered for the occasion: black leather with silver trim—all American-made, of course. At least 860 Southwark Natives followed him, including forty-two members of the Native American Rifle Company. Among them rolled a fifteen-foot-long boat, a twenty-six-foot-long ship, and a model ship with a Bible at its bow. Southwark's Second Ward banner had boasted a design so offensive that the *Catholic Herald* later singled it out for special mention. It depicted a "serpent . . . lying dead at the feet of Liberty, pierced with an arrow, while Fame is soaring aloft, proclaiming the extinction of Papal influence." The procession marched north along Third Street, just half a block from the church. That evening, while the nativists watched fireworks in Snyder's Woods, William Dunn drilled 150 men in his brother's church. News spread. "The Catholic churches, I was told," wrote Pleasonton in his diary that evening, "were all watched and guarded with armed men during the day and night."[16]

The spectacle of armed Catholics fed old Protestant fears. In seventeenth-century Ireland, English administrators had forbidden Catholics from bearing arms, first as a temporary measure during wartime, then, in 1695, as a permanent law. English colonists in North America shared their concerns. During the French and Indian War, five Berks County justices of the peace had warned, "it is a great Unhappiness at this Time to the other People of this Province that the Papists shou'd keep Arms in their Houses, against which the Protestants are not prepared, who, therefore, are subject to a Massacre whenever the Papists are ready." (The Pennsylvania assembly later found "very little foundation" for the charge.)[17]

Such fears persisted into 1844, with some evidence to reinforce them. In May, six Protestants had been killed and several more seriously wounded by gunfire in Kensington, much of it presumably from Catholic muskets. In the aftermath, Natives had traded rumors that Philadelphia Catholics were using their religious buildings as arsenals. Levin's *Sun* had imagined that "a large company of men, women, and children . . . well supplied with stocks of arms and munitions" had occupied St. Michael's, while "1000 armed persons [defended] St. Augustine's Church." On July 4, one nativist speaker claimed that the churches "were used as forts against Americans" to which "could have been seen the cowardly Roman Catholic retreating."[18]

Such statements could have been ex post facto justification for the destruction of the two churches and the seminary, based on nothing but hearsay. But Robbins, who lived next door to St. Philip's, could hear the sound of men drilling in the church basement, and on the morning of Friday, July 5, he went to the basement to see for himself. He found no men, but he did see several stacks of muskets. He went to alert the authorities. As if that weren't enough, a furniture cart arrived later in the day with more muskets for the church. Word spread that the Irish had stockpiled weapons not to defend the church, but to launch a midnight raid, in which they would catch Southwark's Natives asleep in their beds and murder them all.[19]

By 6 P.M. on Friday evening, a large crowd had gathered. One official estimated it to number in the hundreds; another, less probably, guessed five or six thousand. Father Dunn simply called it a "mob." Regardless, it was enough to storm, and perhaps destroy, a church. Who constituted this crowd was a subject of debate. According to one police officer, they—and the crowds that followed—were mostly the usual half-grown boys, ages seventeen to twenty-one. Whether local or not, adult or not, the members of the crowd seemed to share basic nativist suspicions of the armed Irish Catholics, and they later responded to calls for "natives" to arm themselves. "Give us the arms!" they shouted. "Give us the arms that they have got to shoot us down with!" A watchman tried to arrest a man holding a loaded shotgun, but he protested he had just been out hunting, and the mob pulled him out of the officer's reach.[20]

Against such a mob, Southwark employed only a tiny police force: one superintendent, five constables, and fifteen watchmen. As the *Public Ledger* noted, even if all of them could be brought together, this would not be enough to stop even a medium-size firemen's riot. Now, with another church burning possibly brewing, Superintendent Hugh Cassady and John Douglass, captain of the watch, tried to calm the crowd until they could get reinforcements. Alderman Charles Hortz, whose office was just down the block, saw what was happening and sent a note to Sheriff McMichael, asking him to come at once. Now, as the crowd kept asking, "Are there any guns in the church?" Cassady could respond that the sheriff was on his way. And indeed, McMichael hurried down, leaving his wife at home with their newborn son, just five days old. On the way, he stopped to meet with General Patterson, who confirmed that the Dunns had been authorized to arm the church. McMichael arrived at the church around 8 P.M.[21]

Despite two months of public calls for a better system, the sheriff was back in the predicament he had faced in May. Lacking an armed force of his own, McMichael would have to rely on whatever officials or citizens he could persuade to support his authority. He started with Hortz, the alderman who had summoned him, known as "one of the plumpest and most good natured men in the district." Hortz and McMichael had worked well together defusing the Weccacoe Engine fights the previous weekend, and, conveniently, Hortz lived across the street from the church. Feeling unwell on the fifth, he had stayed at home as the crowd gathered on Queen Street. But when McMichael asked for his aid, he rose, and soon the two were joined by Alderman James Sanders, who proved less friendly. "The arms are here by permission of the governor," McMichael explained. "Then," retorted Sanders, "let the governor protect them!"[22]

Hortz, himself a nativist, advised the sheriff that "the only way to appease the people" would be to disarm the church. So in the company of the two aldermen, McMichael knocked at the rear door. Inside, they found the Dunn brothers and the sexton. Yes, William Dunn told him, it was true: that afternoon he had brought in twelve muskets. "That was very indiscreet," muttered McMichael. Father Dunn responded by showing McMichael the note he had received warning of an impending attack. McMichael and the Dunns negotiated what they hoped would be a compromise: The Dunns would surrender the twelve muskets that had been delivered that afternoon. McMichael summoned the captain of the watch, and twelve men carried the weapons to the Commissioners' Hall amid the hoots, groans, and cheers of the crowd.[23]

But the crowd remained uneasy; now men asked, "are there any *more* arms in the church?" McMichael knew there were; the Dunns had freely told him that the twelve muskets had not been the first weapons they had acquired. This put him in a bind. Legally, he did not think he had any right to search the building, for the Dunns had committed no crime. But he faced hundreds, possibly thousands, of angry men and boys shouting in Queen Street, and they did not seem to be in the mood for a discussion of constitutional law. Following the Kensington riots, nativists had charged McMichael with inaction, claiming he had preferred to enjoy a dinner at a friend's house to taking the stern measures that would have lost him Irish votes. Could he risk further angering this crowd?[24]

To defuse the situation, McMichael suggested that trusted men be allowed into the church. He may have been thinking of events in 1834, when a delegation of African Americans had secured the mayor's permission to defend their community by stocking a meeting hall with swords, sword canes, and clubs. When the rumor spread that the hall's defenders had both guns and ammunition, however, a large mob began stoning the building. The incident could have turned violent, but High Constable Samuel Garrigues resolved it by ushering the hall's occupants out a rear exit, then searching the premises and announcing to the crowd that there were, in fact, no firearms inside. McMichael had not witnessed this episode himself, but he had served on the official committee that reported it. Perhaps, then, he hoped to emulate Garrigues's finesse. Now he turned to the Southwark aldermen. "If you can get me twenty good men, upon whom I can rely," he told them, "I will constitute them my police and we [will] go in and take possession of the church and preserve it until morning."[25]

The aldermen delegated the choice of the twenty men to Wright Ardis, a Southwark ship carpenter. Though a Whig by affiliation, Ardis had been, he claimed, "led by curiosity to visit the scene of the riots" in Kensington on May 7 and had been shot through the hips as his reward. The ball had tunneled under Ardis's skin, leaving a red streak across his back but not hitting any important bones or organs, and by the end of May he had fully recovered. Now this veteran of one riot was charged with heading off another. As he assembled his committee, he seems to have chosen nativists. Francis Longmire, a brewer, had helped carry George Young to safety after he had been shot. Thomas Roe, a shoemaker, was a member of the American Republican Party. And Alderman Nathan McKinley, who accompanied the committee, had just the day before served a prominent role in the great Native procession. The men McMichael would lead into the church were its enemies. [26]

With a few magic words, McMichael hoped to turn a potential lynch mob into a force of order. Escorting the men back into the church, he lined them up, wrote down their names and addresses, deputized them all, and explained to them their "duties and responsibilities" as his officers. When someone asked when the search would begin, McMichael replied that daytime would be better. Until then, he expected the committee to remain in the church to protect it. Some of the committee grumbled that they would not feel safe in the building if they could not search it, but McMichael was firm. [27]

The sheriff's stalling tactics might have worked, but committee member David Ford noticed that a door was slightly ajar, "as if some person was peeping from the other side." He opened the door fully, and found himself facing two Irishmen, wearing neither coats nor hats, but carrying muskets with fixed bayonets. These men had been placed by the Dunns, who thought it perfectly legitimate to defend the church with armed guards. But the appearance of these guards panicked Ardis's committee, and McMichael could no longer delay a search. [28]

After seizing the muskets from the two Irishmen, Ardis's men began their search. They likely did so with some apprehension; armed with only sticks in their hands and badges in their hats, they were hunting for men with firearms. Ford tripped over two steps, and his candle went out, but not before he had spotted the gleam of what appeared to be more weapons. He groped for them in the dark, then brought them back into the light, where they turned out to be improvised pikes fashioned from bayonets affixed to brush handles. When they found muskets, the searchers probed them with ramrods to check if they were loaded. Some were empty; others were so packed with gunpowder that the ramrods poked several inches out of the barrels, indicating a load that would have burst the guns had anyone tried to fire them. [29]

As they moved from room to room, the posse found ten more Irishmen with loaded muskets and bayonets guarding another two dozen stand of arms. The committee members later claimed to have confronted Father Dunn before the church altar. "I ask you upon your sacred word as a man and Christian," Ford growled, "have you any more men here? Have you any more arms? Have you any ammunition?" According to the committee, Dunn assured them he did not. Dunn later denied that any conversation had taken place at the altar, but he had given his word that no more armed men were in the church. The committee trusted Father Dunn no more than they had McMichael, and they continued opening cabinets and peering down into a basement sump. For his part, Dunn doubted the posse's authority, and he felt no scruple about taking as much time as he could opening doors and giving information. Still, Dunn was sure he had not lied to the posse, whereas posse members thought he had. They could agree that he had told them that a case held lemons; but had he also mentioned that another one held gunpowder? When Dunn told them that a closet contained only his personal possessions, was he pointing to the closet that in fact held only books, or the other one, full of guns and ammunition? One of the committee later claimed he "heard the priest say that with fifty men he could defend the church for five hours against any mob in Philadelphia."[30]

Father Dunn's brother, William, now took over. With two pistols in his belt, he insisted that he was a militia captain, commissioned by Governor Porter and General Hubbell, and he would store what arms he chose and drill his men as he pleased. David Ford, who had grilled Father Dunn, seems to have accepted, however reluctantly, the legitimacy of William Dunn's receipt of weapons from the governor. But that official issue in June could not, he noted, explain the additional shipment that evening.[31]

Two things were certain by the end of the search. First, the committee and the priest did not trust each other at all. And second, the church had in fact become an arsenal. The committee found thirty-nine firearms in all—single-barreled guns, double-barreled guns, pistols—as well as cartridges, gunpowder, percussion caps, and buckshot, plus two swords and the three pikes. Without determining whether the Dunns had the right to possess the weapons, McMichael ordered the committee to carry the weapons and munitions to the Southwark Commissioners' Hall—just around the corner on Second Street—and entrust them to the watch. This was an order the committee was willing to obey, and they carried the arms the short distance to the hall, satisfied that the church was no longer a fortress.[32]

A light rain had begun to fall, helping to thin the crowd in front of the church. Back in the city, rumors of planned attacks on churches had led Marc Antony Frenaye, the procurator of the diocese, to ring the bell of St. John's Cathedral to summon aid, and the priest of St. Mary's sought police protection as well. Perhaps because of the presence of police, no attack materialized there.[33]

Meanwhile, reinforcements were on the way to Southwark. After he had spoken to the crowd, announcing his plans to wait until daylight to search the church, McMichael had been tapped on the shoulder by a stranger in civilian clothes. The man offered to summon what McMichael heard to be the "civic guard." "I would be much obliged," the sheriff responded. In fact, he had been speaking with Joseph Hill, the captain of the City Guards, a militia company that had seen action in Kensington, and happened to be drilling that evening. "I obtained military aid by mere accident," McMichael later testified. "I supposed I would have a civil guard." McMichael himself regarded this as a "fortunate circumstance." But this almost accidental deployment of a single militia company would have deadly consequences.[34]

While Ardis's committee was scouring the church, Hill had mustered his men. They arrived, in uniform, about 2 A.M., much to the relief of Father Dunn, who thanked them for saving the church "from all being burned up." At McMichael's request, Hill agreed to guard the church until they were relieved. The crowd gradually diminished, and McMichael told Ardis's committee to go home. This they did somewhat reluctantly, not trusting the troops with the weapons they had so laboriously rooted out, as well as the Irishmen, whom they wanted confined. "It was our expectation before the military took possession of the inside of the church, that we were to remain until daylight, and gave up the prisoners, arms and ammunition, to the satisfaction of the Citizens," one committee member later recalled. "But we were foiled in this by the arrival of the military." This left the City Guards in the church, except for the sentries posted in the gloom of Queen Street. McMichael stayed with the troops until 3 A.M., doing what he could to make them comfortable and promising to find relief in the morning.[35]

Major General Robert Patterson and Escort, as depicted in Kensington.
Courtesy of the Library of Congress.

18

Don't You Fire!

ill's City Guards remained in the church all through Saturday morning
and into the afternoon, grumpy for want of fresh food and sweaty in
their uniforms as the temperature rose above eighty degrees. Worried
that they would leave the church undefended, county commissioner Henry
Lentz hurried off to buy them provisions and hot coffee, but by the time
he returned they were gone, having been relieved by the Second State
Fencibles.[1]

Keeping the church under guard proved a good idea, for Saturday morning's *Native American* summoned another mob. The newspaper devoted
half of its front page to a screed by "C. J." (likely Charles Jack) warning

that the tens of thousands of migrants debarking in American ports were in fact a "new-fangled army" of "foreign troops," whose arrival was part of a long-term plan by European monarchs to adulterate American constitutional government with "a little aristocracy, a little limited monarchy, a little absolute monarchy, a little despotism, and with all, a good sprinkling of Popery." The army, the author warned, had already arrived, and "the process of *arming* will be as *readily* and as *easily* be accomplished, as that of transportation has been." The essay continued onto the second page, where its rousing conclusion drew the eye to a much smaller item that seemed to confirm C. J.'s warning. Entitled "Excitement in Southwark," it described the discovery of weapons in St. Philip's on Friday. Perhaps drawn by the news, hundreds, maybe thousands, of people gathered in front of the church. Some seemed orderly enough, but others muttered threats. [2]

Again, the crowd formed a committee and conducted a second search of the church. Isaiah Robbins, who lived next door, had seen the building under construction, so he knew its layout well. He joined the new search party and, having toured the building, emerged to proclaim that the church was wholly empty of weapons. "Some seemed pacified," he later recalled, "and some seemed unsatisfied; the crowd continued." Meanwhile, General Hubbell, commander of the Third Brigade, found William Dunn at home and stripped him of his captaincy of the armed guards in St. Philip's, on the grounds that though Dunn was in the process of naturalization, he was not yet a US citizen and therefore ineligible to possess state weapons. [3]

Unsure if the peace would hold, Sheriff McMichael gathered his forces, both civilian and military. He had had a long night, not leaving the church until 3 A.M. At some point in the morning, he stopped at Major General Patterson's house, but he could not get the general out of bed. He had better luck with Cadwalader, who uncharacteristically was spending the July 4 holiday in town. At 6:30 A.M. Cadwalader ordered Colonel Murray to send a company to relieve the City Guards. Meanwhile, McMichael wrote requests for the various districts, hoping to gather a civilian posse of around five hundred men. When only about one hundred responded to his calls, McMichael again contacted Patterson, this time in writing. At first, he requested two militia companies, but then he upped the request to "such number of companies, not exceeding ten, as in your estimation you may think proper." Perhaps recalling the experience in Kensington, Patterson—awake at last—rejected the notion that even ten companies would suffice. Instead, he ordered out Cadwalader's entire First Brigade.[4]

Cadwalader acted swiftly. Having sent orders to his colonels to gather their men, he rode to Southwark to see for himself what was going on. He arrived about 2:30 P.M. and tried to persuade everyone to go home. Some people asked about the muskets in the church, and Cadwalader replied that while they had been legitimately issued by the governor, he had not known anything about it. Perhaps he hoped a tone of neutrality would calm matters, as it had when he addressed the crowd in Kensington. This time, he failed to persuade anyone, and Southwark braced for a fight. As they had in May, families living adjacent to St. Philip's vacated their homes, while the resident of a house across the street flew a small flag from his window to indicate sympathy with the Native cause.[5]

Gathering the brigade took several hours, and produced disappointing results. Since the 1820s, wealthier Philadelphians had fled the summer heat and the raucous July 4 celebrations, so it is likely that many gentleman officers were out of town. Indeed, the most elite unit—the First City Troop—could not muster at all, since all its officers had left the city. The Wayne Artillery, which had seen service in Kensington, had traveled to Wilmington, Delaware, to celebrate the holiday as guests of the Wilmington Rifles. Now, as the steamer *Balloon* returned them to Philadelphia, General Hubbell met the boat with orders that the unit remain ready to march to Southwark. Most other companies also appeared, but with greatly diminished numbers. Of the 550 men in the brigade, Cadwalader had mustered only 165 by the late afternoon; another 25 would eventually fall in.[6]

Cadwalader led what troops he had into Southwark, arriving at the church around dusk. When he had marched into Kensington two months earlier, the Natives had cheered him, perhaps seeing his troops as reinforcements for their incursion into Kensington's Catholic Third Ward. But now he was invading nativist Southwark, and the local Protestants saw him as an enemy.[7]

By the time Cadwalader's column reached the church, McMichael and his hundred-man posse had been on the ground for perhaps an hour. At first, McMichael had relied on the authority of his office. "I am the

Sheriff," he announced in front of the church. "I have come to protect this building and maintain the laws, as good citizens I call on you to disperse, and hope you will go quietly away." The more law-abiding of the crowd obeyed, leaving behind a concentrated mass of defiant, angry men. "To hell with the Sheriff!" they cried. "God damn the law!" One witness judged the crowd not to be seriously intent on violence, but rather "mischievously disposed to annoy the posse." The posse did what it could to clear and hold the stretch of Queen Street between Second and Third, and made a few arrests; McMichael bagged two men himself. But the crowd kept growing. "By 9 o'clock at night," one reporter wrote, "so dense was it that the whole of Queen street between Second and Third streets was a literal mass of human beings."[8]

The arrival of Cadwalader and his force of nearly two hundred troops did not help much. Some boys decided to head east to the wharf in search of cordwood to use as clubs, and off they marched, shouting "wood, wood, wood!" At the corner of Second and Queen, a group of slightly older youths debated what to do. They thought that the "Kensington fellows" might come and help, but that waiting for them would look cowardly. "If we rush now, the military will fire," warned one. "Some will be shot." "Let them fire," a second sneered. "They can't kill more than three or four of us before we get behind them and take their arms from them."[9]

Some threw stones, bottles, and bricks at Cadwalader. One brick hit the general's knee, another cut the jaw of an alderman, and a stone hit one of Cadwalader's staff. "Knock that man off his horse!" someone shouted. Others threw only insults, daring Cadwalader to use his sword against them. They cheered, they shouted, they hissed. "Shoot!" someone cried. "Shoot!" Cadwalader's aide used his sword to keep civilians from grabbing his horse's bridle while Cadwalader and the mob exchanged dares and vows. "Down with the minions of the Pope!" the crowd shouted. "Nine cheers for the Bible and the Native Americans, by Jesus!" Prone to swearing as he was, Cadwalader later admitted that his own language and manner on this occasion were "unusually decided."[10]

Despite the provocation, Cadwalader tried to restore order. He directed that local stores be closed, presumably to deprive the crowd of liquor, weapons, and gunpowder. One druggist refused and was promptly arrested, which persuaded the remaining merchants to shut their stores as ordered. As the crowd rushed his lines, Cadwalader pointed to individuals he wanted arrested by McMichael's posse. They caught about three dozen, confining them in the Southwark Hall lockup or the church's basement. But thousands more remained on the streets or wandered west to Moyamensing, where additional troops guarded the Catholic Church of St. Paul.[11]

Cadwalader's superior, Major General Patterson, arrived in Southwark separately, accompanied by Pleasonton and the meager force of sixty men the colonel had been able to muster, as well as two six-pounder cannon. When they reached Fifth and Queen, two blocks west of the church, they paused so that Pleasonton could order the cannon unlimbered and loaded with canister: tin cans packed with twenty-seven cast-iron balls that would spray when fired. Designed to defend artillery against a massed charge of infantry, a canister round would shred anyone standing in front or even off to the side of the cannon. With the cannon thus prepared, the force moved one more block east, where Patterson, feeling unwell, commandeered a house to serve as headquarters, then consulted with his staff, McMichael, and Pleasonton. "Well, Colonel," Patterson asked Pleasonton, "what would you advise to be done?"[12]

As he had in Harrisburg in 1838, Pleasonton proposed artillery. He suggested that Patterson send McMichael out to give the mob a three-minute warning. If that failed to disperse them, the sheriff should scurry back to Pleasonton, who would then open fire, killing and maiming as the canister ripped through the mob. A quick look at McMichael and Patterson convinced Pleasonton that they were not ready for such boldness, so, with Patterson's permission, he returned outside to his men. There he met Cadwalader, who had by now cleared Queen Street as far as Third, but could not scatter the mob off of Third Street. Cadwalader asked for one of Pleasonton's six-pounders, which the colonel was happy to supply. McMichael then asked for a company of infantrymen as an escort. Pleasonton detailed only a sergeant and two privates, with the promise that if the sheriff were attacked, Pleasonton would respond with his full force. Pleasonton himself moved to the corner of Queen and Third, along with one six-pounder and a detachment of Cadwalader Grays, commanded by Captain Robert K. Scott, a prominent lawyer in civilian life.[13]

For a moment, it seemed as though Pleasonton would finally get what he wanted: an order to fire cannon into a mob. Rather than send McMichael, Cadwalader himself rode up Third Street to warn the mob to disperse, then returned to give the orders. To Pleasonton's chagrin, the general ordered an infantry platoon to advance, thus blocking the cannon. Pleasonton at first ignored what he considered an "injudicious" order, but Cadwalader had his reasons: compared to canister, musketry would be less likely to injure innocent persons behind the mob. [14]

Pleasonton could accept that, and he readied the infantry for action. "Fire by platoon, right oblique!" he commanded. "Ready, right oblique, aim!" Captain Scott relayed the order. While the two dozen Cadwalader Grays were now pointing their muskets in the general direction of the mob, Pleasonton noticed that whether from inexperience, nerves, or mercy, they were aiming over the heads of their fellow citizens. "Lower your muskets!" Pleasonton demanded. "Lower your muskets! Lower your muskets!" Finally, the colonel was satisfied that his men were ready to kill. "Fire!" To Pleasonton's astonishment, the men did not fire, nor did Scott even repeat the command. "Fire!" Pleasonton bellowed. "Why the devil don't you fire?" Then, peering into the darkness, Pleasonton understood. [15]

Charles Naylor was the problem. Born in 1806 and orphaned and poor as a child, Naylor had risen to become a prominent Whig lawyer. In the 1830s, he twice won election to Congress, possibly with the help of ballot boxes stuffed by Peter Albright of the Northern Liberties, who would later supply weapons to the Kensington nativists. The accusations of electoral fraud led not only to a congressional investigation, but also to bad blood between Naylor and Pleasonton, who had been sent to Naylor's house to convey a challenge to a duel. Naylor threw him out, stating that he would only answer a person "who knows how to behave like a gentleman." Pleasonton had shrugged off the insult, at least publicly. "Notwithstanding the indignity attempted to be offered to me," he wrote of the affair, "I was convulsed with laughter as I walked leisurely homewards." [16]

On the morning of July 6, Naylor had happened to stop by the office of Sheriff McMichael, his boyhood friend and his fellow Whig, and McMichael asked for Naylor's help dealing with the explosive situation in Southwark. Naylor agreed to meet him at St. Philip's around nightfall.

When he arrived, he found Queen Street cleared from Second to Third, with police preventing anyone from approaching the church in the center of the block. Naylor joined the impromptu police force, and for the next two hours he stayed with McMichael, occasionally helping with an arrest. "There was no resistance," he later claimed, "no opposition, nor even a shadow of opposition, to the arrests of the Sheriff, nor to any of his movements." Just the occasional shout—"hurrah for the natives!"—but nothing truly alarming. As they patrolled, Naylor and McMichael chatted about the challenges of keeping peace with soldiers. Perhaps due to his earlier squabble with Pleasonton, Naylor thought little of the militia. When he heard that Cadwalader was coming, but needed to equip himself first, he told McMichael, "This is a good joke. . . . Rioters, with incendiary dispositions, could burn down all the churches in town, whilst a general is putting on his finery."[17]

When Cadwalader finally arrived, Naylor was appalled to see him ride up in such a rage. As he later described it, Cadwalader "rode on the footways and almost into the very doors of the houses, swore at the citizens standing at the doors of their own homes, bestowed on the people the most opprobrious epithets, declaring that he had brought two cannon on the ground and swore repeatedly with strong emphasis that he would shoot them down if they did not instantly disperse. Almost every sentence contained an oath. . . . Wherever he went, confusion, alarm, and dismay followed, and the people fled on all sides, as fast as they could."[18]

Was Cadwalader drunk? John Greaves, who had searched the church on Friday evening, thought that "he acted like a man under the influence of fear, passion, or drink." Naylor did not claim so directly, but he did report the police making such a claim. During his later service in both the Mexican War and the Civil War, Cadwalader would be suspected by fellow officers of drinking to the point of impairment. If Cadwalader was inclined to drink while commanding troops in wartime, it seems even more likely that he had been drinking at home on an apparently peaceful Saturday evening. Yet it is also possible that Cadwalader was deliberately using rage as a weapon. Just eight weeks earlier, he had saved St. John's Church without bloodshed by screaming at a crowd until it scattered. He may have been trying to repeat that success. Or he may simply have been frustrated to be taken away from his dinner and his dogs to fix a problem he thought he had taken care of months before. Drunk or not, genuinely enraged or not, Cadwalader certainly sounded incensed. "Damn you, you dare not fire!" shouted a rioter. "As there's a God in Heaven I'll fire if you don't disperse," replied Cadwalader, giving the crowd five minutes, the same warning he had given in front of St. John's Church in May. "Fire and be damned!" came the reply.[19]

It looked like he would. Expecting a blast from the cannon, those in the middle of the street began to push their way to the sides. It was at this point that Cadwalader ordered Pleasonton to prepare his infantry to fire, and that Pleasonton ordered his men to aim low. Then Charles Naylor made his move. While Cadwalader had been bellowing at the crowd, Naylor had been trying to calm everyone down, and he sought to advise McMichael to get Cadwalader away from his tormentors. Instead, he saw McMichael move north on Third Street, just where the troops would fire if Cadwalader gave the command. Hoping to save his friend, Naylor stepped forward, shouting, "No, don't fire, don't fire!"[20]

It worked. Impulsively, Cadwalader rode forward at the intruder, preventing the Cadwalader Grays from firing, lest they kill their namesake. By the time he was clear, both sides calmed down, and the mob gradually dispersed. Yet rather than thank Naylor for saving lives by risking his own, a furious Cadwalader shouted, "Who dared to countermand my order?" Naylor instantly confessed, and Cadwalader ordered him arrested. He was thinking about turning a platoon against the police or the sheriff's posse, had either body seemed inclined to follow Naylor rather than him. But the two civil forces held firm, obeying Cadwalader's orders to arrest Naylor and some other members of the crowd.[21]

Once again, Pleasonton lamented the indecision of his superior officers. "I hope, Sir," he declared, as Cadwalader approached, "when next you order an officer to fire, that you will not place yourself under his guns, and prevent the execution of your own order!" Cadwalader, no doubt surprised by this public criticism from a subordinate and friend, retorted, "you should have seen where I was, before giving the order to fire." But Pleasonton dug in. "Pardon me, General," he replied with icy courtesy. "When I receive an order, it is my duty to obey it, and promptly. I have then other things to do besides observing your motions." As the officers bickered, some of the rioters on Third Street realized that they were not going to be shot after all, and resumed throwing stones. One bounced off of General Patterson's chest and hit Pleasonton in the arm, but the colonel remained more concerned about his military honor. Turning to an army major who had witnessed the whole scene, he pleaded that he had remonstrated against the general's mistakes. "Don't be uneasy, my dear friend," the major assured him. "You are not to blame in any way."[22]

Meanwhile, the soldiers had prisoners to confine. By law, the arrested men should have been taken to the Commissioners' Hall, but there was no hope of getting them through the hostile crowd. Instead, Cadwalader turned to the most convenient structure: St. Philip's itself. At his command, policemen escorted Naylor and the other prisoners into the church's basement. They placed Naylor in a sizable-but-filthy room with no furniture except some narrow benches along the walls and a single window for some air to get in. Cadwalader had arrested Naylor impulsively, not knowing who he was except a man who had challenged his order to fire. Seeing the arrest, someone had cried out, "it is Mr. Naylor, one of our police, and the Sheriff's friend." But Cadwalader would not back down. Later, Naylor's friend Judge Robert Conrad, a leading Philadelphia political figure, tried to negotiate Naylor's release. Naylor's wife was ill, Conrad explained, and Naylor was a bit crazy. But Cadwalader's resolve was shored up by Pleasonton, perhaps still bitter from Naylor's insults four years earlier. Now Pleasonton advised that if Naylor's wife were so sick, he would not have joined the sheriff's posse. And if Naylor were so crazy, Pleasonton reasoned, "I would recommend his release on condition that his friends should confine him in the Lunatic asylum," where he could stir up no more trouble. Cadwalader decided to keep Naylor locked in the church. Clenching his fist, he explained his reasoning to a subordinate. "A man like him, who has been a representative of the people, coming here with a badge on his hat, ought to be doubly punished, or an example made of him."[23]

For some time, Cadwalader remained on the edge of firing, but by 11 P.M. he was beginning to hope he could clear the crowd without musketry. When a bottle hit his leg, leaving a painful bruise, however, he began to wonder if the mob would itself attack with firearms. Meanwhile, McMichael sent squads of posse members in response to reports that groceries or houses were being attacked. His men continued to make arrests, and he ordered them confined in the church with Naylor. Eventually, the basement became crowded with about thirty prisoners, guarded by twelve members of the Second Company of State Fencibles under the command of Lieutenant Thomas Dougherty. Outnumbered, and trying to confine angry men in a space designed for docile, religious schoolchildren, Dougherty soon felt he was losing control. While Naylor acted the gentleman, other prisoners tried to escape, to win over members of McMichael's posse, or to communicate with the outside. Eventually Dougherty asked McMichael not to imprison any more men in the church.[24]

Fortunately, the street was calming. By about 2 A.M., the situation was quiet enough that McMichael dismissed his police, and at three o'clock Major General Patterson ordered Cadwalader to withdraw his troops. Rather than escort the prisoners to a lockup in the middle of the night, Cadwalader detailed the Washington Blues, under Captain William Patterson, to stay with them in the church, promising to send fresh troops to take over during the night. Cadwalader ordered the rest of the forces to go home, but to reassemble at their parade grounds the following afternoon at three o'clock. And so the troops returned to the city. Back at home on Portico Square, an exhausted Colonel Pleasonton still found energy to write up Saturday's excitement in a detailed diary entry. It would be his last.[25]

The Montgomery Hibernia Greens.
Courtesy of the Library Company of Philadelphia.

19

By Jesus Christ
We'll Have Him Out!

As he filled St. Philip's Church with prisoners on Saturday evening, Cadwalader dispatched fresh troops to guard them. Among the companies he selected was one whose presence in Southwark was destined to make a tense situation even tenser: the Montgomery Hibernia Greens.[1]

The Greens were men of Irish descent with surnames like Donohoe and Fitzgerald, Maher and Rafferty, Murray and Murphy. As had Irishmen in other American cities, they had named their militia company named after Richard Montgomery, the Irish-born general of the Continental Army who had died an American hero's death fighting the British in 1775. While not officially a Catholic company, the Greens were associated with the Church. In 1841, for example, they had celebrated their fourth anniversary with a St. Patrick's Day festival, complete with an oration by an Irish-born priest, with proceeds to benefit a Catholic orphan asylum. [2]

Along with companies composed of men of Scottish or German descent, Irish American companies in Pennsylvania and other states occupied an ambiguous position within the volunteer militia system. On the one hand, their members displayed the American patriotism and civic responsibility that nativists claimed they wanted from Irish immigrants. Who better to defend America from British tyranny than Irishmen who knew that tyranny firsthand? But many Americans feared the sight of armed Irishmen. In 1835, a proposal to create the "O'Connell Guards" as a militia company alarmed New York City nativists. They fretted that the Guards "would soon attempt to enforce with the bayonet what too many of the misguided and ignorant of the foreign voters already boast of—the complete subjection of the Native Citizens to their dictation." The issue contributed to a nasty, two-day riot that left two men dead, and the organizers abandoned their plans for the company. [3]

During an 1837 brigade parade in Boston, six volunteer companies had marched off the field rather than appear in line with the city's Montgomery Guards. And when the Guards marched back to their armory, onlookers threw bottles, stones, and lumps of coal at them, leading the governor of Massachusetts to disband the unit to prevent further disturbances. And during Pennsylvania's Buckshot War of 1838, officers of German companies begged that that their immigrant troops not be ordered to fire the first shot against civilians, lest "a strong prejudice might be created against them." In 1842, Rev. McCalla of Southwark had complained of "volunteer companies of foreign Papists, the obedient troops of a European despot." [4]

Now ordered to Southwark, the Montgomery Hibernia Greens of Philadelphia were in a tough spot. Their riot duty the previous May had gone well; they had successfully guarded a Catholic church and the orphan asylum on Spruce Street. But here they found themselves guarding a different Catholic church in angry Southwark, painfully conspicuous in their green uniform coats trimmed with red braid, with few allies and little food or ammunition. Moreover, they were holding prisoners, seeming to verify Protestant paranoia that Catholic institutions concealed holding cells for kidnap victims. For centuries, since Martin Luther had warned that the papacy had taken the church prisoner, anti-Catholic Protestants had associated Catholicism with captivity. In the 1830s, American Protestants had devoured fabricated accounts of women held captive in Catholic convents, especially their cellars. How would Protestants react to the sight of real, armed Roman Catholics holding prisoners, including former congressman Naylor, in the actual cellar of an actual Catholic church?[5]

If Naylor were no damsel in distress, such details hardly mattered. "They have treated Mr. Naylor worse than a dog," complained one young man who brought the news to the city. "They have shut him up in the papist church!" As Naylor later explained, he himself had nothing against the Greens, who "behaved with the utmost kindness and courtesy." But the Philadelphians spreading the news of his arrest "knew that my prison was a Catholic church—the church that I had been defending. They knew that my keepers were Roman Catholic soldiery, who held me at the point of the bayonet." Worse still, they were keeping him from the bedside of his ill wife, a detail that could have been drawn from an anti-Catholic fantasy about priests' scheming to destroy a Protestant family. If Cadwalader had wanted to incite anti-Catholics to violence, he could hardly have picked a better tactic. Despite all this, Cadwalader apparently trusted the Greens to keep the situation under control. He likely knew all the captains in his brigade, and he may have had special connections to the Greens' commanding officer, Captain John Barron Colahan.[6]

Born in County Galway in 1815, Colahan had emigrated to the United States in 1834, spending some time in the District of Columbia before arriving in Philadelphia in 1841. Professionally, he was first a civil engineer, then a lawyer who used his earlier training to help clients with surveys, maps, and other technical documents. Vocationally, he was a joiner, eventually serving in Catholic charities, the Friendly Sons of St. Patrick, the Pennsylvania Catholic Total Abstinence Society, and learned societies, as well as the militia. The year before, for instance, he had shared a stage with Cadwalader and other militia officers while listening to Judge Joseph Doran—son of Irish immigrants—praise the exploits of Richard

Montgomery in the Revolutionary War. A few months later, Colahan had been chosen to read a letter from Father Theobald Mathew, the celebrated Irish temperance leader, as part of the Pennsylvania Catholic Total Abstinence Society's July 4 celebration. Yet Colahan also had connections to Protestant circles, having married Mary Dorothea Zell, daughter of a prominent Quaker merchant.[7]

Colahan also knew the Dunn brothers, having served with them in the Repeal cause. When the Repeal Association had, a year earlier, split over slavery, all three men had joined the faction that had refused to denounce O'Connell's calls for abolition. When Colahan and William Dunn helped organize a mass rally in response to the news of O'Connell's arrest, the Montgomery Hibernia Greens had attended as an honor guard. Knowing Colahan and his company as they did, the Dunns may have asked Cadwalader to appoint the Greens to guard their church.[8]

Besides the Greens, Cadwalader detached the Mechanic Rifles and the Markle Rifles. The Mechanic Rifles, only twelve of whom reported, were commanded by Lieutenant George Carroll. The Markle Rifles were not Irish, but they were green in another way, having drilled for the first time and elected their officers only on June 27. While they sported smart new uniforms—gray frock coats and pants, plus helmet caps—and knew some of the rifle drill, they lacked veterans from other companies, and the call to Southwark was their very first active duty.[9]

Before leaving around three o'clock on Sunday morning, Cadwalader asked Captain William Patterson—whose Washington Blues had been guarding the church for nearly twelve hours—to stay just one hour more. If all remained quiet, Patterson could then leave the church in the hands of the fresh troops.[10]

In that last hour of his command, Patterson made two crucial decisions. First, he gave permission to the Markles—who had arrived at the church without any ammunition for their rifles—to leave to get both ammunition and rations, provided they returned by 9 A.M. Second, he told Colahan that while he could release almost all of the prisoners to the civil authorities, he should not surrender Naylor, even to the sheriff himself. With these instructions, Patterson had both added to Colahan's burden and reduced his resources. Then Patterson departed with his command, leaving only two companies: the Mechanic Rifles and the Montgomery Hibernia Greens. These thirty hungry men, with scant ammunition, were expected to guard both the church and twenty-one prisoners. (A few prisoners had been released when McMichael arranged some hearings in the wee hours.)[11]

Colahan knew how alone he was. As McMichael prepared to leave around four o'clock on Sunday morning, Colahan appealed for ammunition and rations. McMichael told him his deputy would take care of it. William Price, the deputy, objected. It was not his job, he asserted, to supply the military. McMichael calmed him down, suggested that Colahan get food from a nearby pub, and that Price do his best to find the ammunition. The exhausted deputy still had no idea where to buy musket cartridges at dawn on a Sunday morning. He decided to take a nap instead.[12]

By 8 A.M., a crowd began to reassemble. George Roberts, who later claimed to have come to Southwark out of mere curiosity, described it as "composed of the worst class of mankind, the very dregs of the *canaille* of a large city, a great number of boys." He saw "men drunk with liquor and devilishness, boys of 16 to 21, of the most insubordinate and lawless character." These were just the sort who had burned the churches and seminary in May. Colahan set out guards and warned the crowd to disperse, but the brogue of an Irish-born officer in a green coat only antagonized his listeners. One woman, vastly overestimating the size of Colahan's force, remarked that "they have taken 72 guns designed for Irishmen out of the church, and put in 120 Irishmen with them."[13]

When someone produced an alderman's order for the release of one of the prisoners, Colahan immediately handed the man over to the custody of the Southwark watch, but he refused to release anyone else without higher authority. "In consequence of the number of prisoners that is now in the church," Colahan wrote in a hasty message to Cadwalader, "a large number of persons is collecting in the front thereof. This is calculated to create a riot." He asked permission to release his prisoners. "Would it not be better that they were legally liberated than to make the situation a further cause of tumult and especially as we have not even sufficient men (only 30) to protect the church alone?" Cadwalader replied with an authorization "to hand over to any Civil Magistrates who will take sureties for the appearance of any prisoners charged with trivial offences," which presumably excluded Naylor. "Should you apprehend any doubt as to the sufficiency of your force," Cadwalader concluded, "you will immediately give me notice of it."[14]

The men and boys in the street traded expressions of outrage at the imprisonment of Naylor and the others. "They have had Charley Naylor, one of our greatest and best men, in the church all night, without food, drink, or bed, and have refused fifteen thousand dollars good bail for him," Roberts heard a "villainous knot of men" exclaim. "By Jesus Christ we'll have him out; we'll make them smell hell if they don't let him out in half an hour!" Another group muttered about Cadwalader. "Let the damned cut throat come down here to-night, and see whether he'll get away alive!"[15]

Two Southwark aldermen—McKinley and Hortz—made their way into the church to negotiate with Colahan. With Cadwalader's permission in hand, Colahan was happy to surrender nineteen of his twenty remaining prisoners to their care, though he was dismayed that rather than set bail to make the men eventually answer charges, the two aldermen let them go without any legal formality. But Colahan had his orders not to release Naylor, and he was expecting the return of the Markle Rifles, as well as a supply of ammunition from the sheriff. He would keep the former congressman confined.[16]

By ten o'clock a large mob was clamoring for Naylor, whose continued captivity seemed to build his reputation. "This was a great Bible man!" they boasted. On the bright side, however, someone got through with food, and Colahan's men enjoyed a late breakfast, even inviting Naylor to join them. (He declined.) Outside the church, dozens of men debated what to do. Some wanted to break into the church to free Naylor, but others doubted it could be done; that church, they argued, was built like a fortress. "There's no use talking," one man advised. "Go get a cannon, and blow it to hell."[17]

Just a hundred yards east of the church flowed the Delaware River, its wharfs crowded with vessels readying for both the coastal and ocean-going trade. A gang of troublemakers—the inevitable half-grown boys, no more than eighteen years old, some as young as six—made their way to Penrose's wharf and the ship *Venice*. The *Venice*, a fairly large ship of nearly 600 tons, had arrived from Londonderry three weeks earlier carrying the usual complement of Irish immigrants. At the time, nativists had decried the arrival of "a full cargo of fellows, ready to create new Kensington riots, and shoot down Americans," and had sneeringly suggested "an impost duty on live stock." On its voyage across the Atlantic, the *Venice* probably carried no cannon, which had become rare on civilian ships crossing that ocean. But the *Venice* had, by 1844, crossed the Pacific at least twice, reaching Chile, Australia, and China, and now it was readying to sail again to Canton. Such voyages still risked confrontations with pirates, so the *Venice* now mounted two four-pounders.[18]

Wanting these weapons, the half-grown Southwark boys became pirates themselves, swarming over both sides of the ship. "What do you want?" cried the startled watchman. "None of your business!" the lads replied. When the watchman threatened to break their fingers, they explained that the Irish "had taken a Native prisoner, and they would have satisfaction." Hopelessly outnumbered, the watchman looked on as the boys rolled one cannon to the side of the ship. Using a crane, they tried to lower it to the wharf. But the boys were unskilled, and the crane collapsed, damaging the gun carriage. They fixed it up as best they could and started pulling it toward the church. The gun weighed hundreds of pounds, and on the way the carriage broke again. But someone found a pair of the small timber wheels used for moving guns short distances within shipyards, and with some ingenuity, two or three men used a rope to hoist the heavy gun onto the wheels. It still took eighteen or twenty men, hauling on the rope, to get the gun to move. But they pulled hard, and by noon, they had set up the cannon in front of the church.[19]

On seeing the gun, Colahan lost his earlier confidence. He dashed off another note to Cadwalader explaining the situation, asking his first lieutenant to deliver it "with all possible speed." Colahan promised to obey orders "at all peril" but added, in an understatement worthy of a captain addressing a general, "I would submit with all deference the removal of Mr. Naylor to some more appropriate and safer place than a Catholic Church at the present time." In his basement cell, Naylor could hear the cheers of the crowd and the scraping sound of soldiers barricading the doors with benches, and he noticed his guards getting increasingly anxious.[20]

Outside the church, a handful of Southwark officials faced a crowd that, by late morning, numbered perhaps two thousand. Theoretically, the five aldermen should have commanded five ward constables and two police superintendents, plus fifty special constables and twenty-five watchmen recruited specifically to defend the church. But that was in theory; in reality, just a few men had to jawbone the crowd as best they could. Superintendent Cassady was "short and thick" with an "iron grasp." On an ordinary disorderly Sunday, he might arrest a dozen men or more, one at a time. But even he could not arrest a crowd. "Policeman Cassiday was loudly arguing points of law and expediency, in his usual felicitous manner," recalled an observer. "Arch'y Cozzens [who had previously held Cassady's job] is said to have been bouncing about among the boys, threatening them with legal visitations, and proclaiming what he would do if he could, and what he could do if the rest of the police were worth a button."[21]

Alderman Hortz tried negotiation, pointing out that a cannon blast could kill Naylor, the very man the mob claimed to want to rescue. But the men with the cannon were insistent. "I'll be damned if we won't batter down the church" unless Naylor was released, insisted one man. When Cassady assured him that Naylor would indeed be freed, the man replied, "we'll have the church down, any how." Rather than negotiate further, Hortz managed to render the cannon temporarily useless by scooping a handful of muddy water out of the gutter and pouring it into the touchhole. While this stopped the immediate threat of a cannonade, it did not end the siege. Some men found some scaffold poles—ten or twelve feet long—and deployed them as battering rams against the church's western door, shattering some of its panels. Half-grown boys swarmed into Isaiah Robbins's yard next to the church; Robbins fretted that they would set his stable on fire in the hopes of igniting the church.[22]

Meanwhile, the crowd had maneuvered the cannon to Christian Street, to the south of the church, where they aimed it at the windows on the church's rear wall. Apparently they were able to clear out the touchhole, but they lacked real ammunition, so they loaded the gun with spikes, broken crowbars, and other small pieces of iron. Then, just after noon, they fired. The improvised projectiles only broke a couple of bricks around the church's circular window, but the blast terrified the neighborhood. To the north of St. Philip's, the congregation of Trinity Episcopalian fled their Sunday service. On Front Street, the wife of John McCoy—the Irish-born commissioner of the First Ward—frantically unhooked pictures and mirrors from her walls before they could be shaken loose by further blasts. After sponging out the gun, the boys and men reloaded with some kind of ammunition and fired again.[23]

Inside St. Philip's, Colahan did all he could to stop another church burning. He deployed every man he had to watch for rioters trying to scale the church walls or set the building ablaze. Some Greens aimed loaded muskets through the church windows and shouted for the civilians to stay back, but Colahan did not want his men to take the first life. As bricks crashed through the windows, the militiamen pulled back, out of view from outside. Colahan doubled the guard at the iron gate in front, the church's most vulnerable point. At 1:30 P.M., he was momentarily encouraged by the return of the Markle Rifle Company. The rioters were also encouraged—they gave the Markles three cheers—and Colahan soon learned why.[24]

The Markles had spent the morning in their Philadelphia armory, waiting for the ammunition they had been ordered to bring, and the company did not begin their return march toward Southwark until about noon. When they were arrived they were appalled to see "several thousand persons . . . in a very frantic wild state of mind," demanding the release of Naylor. This demand seemed reasonable enough to their commander, Captain Thomas Saunders, perhaps because of Saunders's own nativist sympathies. Indeed, the whole company may have felt that way; they were later described by nativist newspapers as a "well disciplined company of Native American citizens" and "organized on a native American foundation." Alternatively, Saunders may simply have been trying to defuse an explosive situation. He had only twenty men, none of whom were experienced. Even their rifles were best suited for long-distance engagements, since they lacked bayonets for close-quarters fighting. In all the Pennsylvania Militia, there may have been no company less inclined or prepared to face down an angry crowd of nativists.[25]

So Saunders negotiated, telling the crowd that if they would desist from destroying the church, he would do what he could to have Naylor released. Such appeasement was hardly unprecedented; it recalled other negotiations between mobs and militia officers that had been the norm for decades.

Indeed, with the exception of one lieutenant, Saunders's whole company wanted Naylor freed. Once inside the church, Saunders requested—or as Colahan reported, demanded—that Colahan release Naylor. But Colahan had a different view of the role of the militia, one based on loyalty to the chain of command rather than the will of the people. "I told [the Markle Rifles] their conduct was highly reprehensible," he later wrote, "that the first duty of a solider was to obey orders—that in doing so, at that moment, I risked my men and the destruction of the church, and that they, if necessary, should be ready to do the same." As the officer in command, Colahan ordered Saunders to defend the church, but Saunders still refused. Finally, the two captains agreed on a deal. If Cadwalader did not appear within ten minutes, Colahan would release Naylor to an alderman or justice of the peace. Only then did Saunders agree to deploy.[26]

The ten minutes came and went without any additional reinforcements, so Colahan reluctantly agreed to let Naylor go. Saunders went to the eastern gate of the church and called for an alderman, and soon Hortz arrived. He asked for Naylor's pledge to appear when summoned. Naylor objected—no one had charged him with a crime, and none of the soldiers could tell him on what charge he was being held. But when Hortz told him the alternative was that they would both be shot, Naylor relented, offering his written assurance that he would stand for any charge made against him.[27]

Naylor emerged to cheers. Standing on the church steps, he called on the crowd to disperse. "I have been fifty hours without rest," he told them. "I am so exhausted that I am scarcely able to stand." Some of the men lifted him onto their shoulders and carried him away, escorted by a large number—perhaps thousands—of the crowd. Once deposited at his Washington Square house, Naylor entered and again addressed the crowd from a window. "Merely because I charged [Cadwalader] not to fire upon my fellow citizens," he claimed, "I was dragged to a prison . . . without a chair to set upon, water to drink, or a crust to eat." Even as he slandered the Greens, who had in fact offered to share their scant rations, Naylor called for peace. "Give me your words, friends, that you will retire peaceably to your homes, and allow me to submit to the law." The crowd again cheered wildly, and some pledged to go home. But a large number hurried right back to Queen Street, where they joined with the remnant of the crowd that had remained there after Naylor's departure. These men fumed that the church was still being defended by armed Irishmen; they had merely traded Dunn for his friend Colahan. Colahan deployed the mutinous Markle Rifles at the western front door of the church—where he least expected an attack—ordering them to fire if necessary to protect the church.[28]

Disgusted with their cannon's performance, its crew had hauled it back to the wharf to reload it with something better. When they returned, they brought not only the four-pounder but a second weapon, a six-pounder, probably stolen from the Simpson & Neal shipyard on Swanson Street. Again they tried to bombard the back wall of the church. Again the improvised missiles failed to damage the wall, but they did ricochet for hundreds of yards, terrifying everyone in range. Sticks, stones, and muscle proved more effective. At about two o'clock, a few men—egged on by a larger number of more cautious onlookers—stormed the western door, guarded by the Markle Rifles. Seeing the first rioter already inside the church, Colahan shouted, "Markle Rifles, do your duty, fire!"[29]

This was the second time in two days that an officer had ordered his troops to fire on a Southwark crowd, and, like Pleasonton's order of the night before, it produced no volley. Saunders later claimed that "a voice" warned against shooting the aldermen just outside the splintered door. Despite the lack of gunfire, Colahan's order frightened the intruder away, but the Markles' disobedience demoralized Colahan and the rest of his men. Seizing his chance, Saunders stepped through the broken door of the church and begged the remaining men outside to honor their agreement. He had freed Naylor; why not go home? The men at the cannon ignored him.[30]

Thomas Grover—the Southwark commissioner and chief marshal of the nativist procession of July 4—had, by his own account, taken a remarkably passive role up to this point. He had been at St. Philip's on Friday evening, but aside from commenting that the sheriff should disarm the church, he had taken no part in events. On Saturday he saw little of the struggle, opting instead to visit the barber. One member of McMichael's posse did spot him that evening, and noted that Grover "did not commit violence, but appeared to be enjoying what was going on." On Sunday morning, the sight of a hundred men and boys hauling a cannon through the streets of

Southwark inspired Grover to do no more than ask that the muzzle not be pointed at him, and then go home for dinner. The firing of that cannon, however, was enough to get him to act. Abandoning his meal, he went in search of Lewis Levin, who lived about half a mile away in Philadelphia City's New Market Ward.[31]

Finding Levin at home, Grover persuaded the editor to return with him to Southwark. "If someone would come and speak to the people," he explained, "we could prevent mischief." "If I can do any good," Levin replied, "I will go with pleasure." As the two men walked to the church, Grover laid out his plans. There were two of them, and each must take one cannon. Pushing their way through the crowd in the rear of the church, they climbed onto the weapons, hot and sulfurous from being fired repeatedly. Then, taking turns, the two men spoke to their fellow nativists, trying to calm them. The crowd just shouted back, "Turn out the Hibernia Greens!" Others continued throwing stones at the walls and windows of the church.

Inside the church it felt like a hailstorm. The soldiers backed away from the shattering windows, expecting an attack. Captain Saunders kept pressing for negotiations, and at his urging, an exhausted Colahan agreed to meet with Levin. To Colahan—an Irish Catholic, a Repealer, and a militia officer—Levin must have appeared to be an enemy general. But perhaps it was time to negotiate terms. Colahan had already failed in his mission of confining Naylor, his post was under siege by cannon fire, he could not count on his subordinate officers to obey his commands, and his pleas to Cadwalader were as yet unanswered. And so, with a shattered church door between them, Levin and Colahan talked. Levin now told him that only the departure of the Greens would appease the mob, but that if the Greens would leave, the mob would pledge to spare both them and the church. Colahan at first refused, hoping at any minute to see the reinforcements he had requested six hours earlier. But no relief came, and Colahan's men wanted to take the deal.[32]

Finally, Colahan agreed to march the Greens away, expecting that the remaining two companies—the Mechanic Rifles and the Markle Rifles— would maintain military possession of the church. But when he ordered them to remain, they once again disobeyed, insisting that all the militia would leave the church to the mercy of the mob. "I will die on the threshold to protect the church," Levin swore, asking the crowd if they would do the same. "That we will!" came the reply. Saunders now demanded, on behalf of the crowd, that the troops open the pans of their muskets and throw out the priming, making them unready to be fired. Colahan did not object, but neither did he ensure that the weapons were emptied. At 2:30, the men all filed out. "Shoulder arms!" Colahan commanded, trying to maintain military order. "Arms at will!" The Greens—so visible in those green coats and white pantaloons—marched in the center, protected by the Mechanic Rifles on their right and the Markle Rifles on their left.[33]

Levin and Saunders had negotiated safe passage with the men immediately in front of the church, but who speaks for a mob? The troops had not made it the half block to the corner of Second Street, less than a hundred yards, before the first stone whizzed past them. Then, as the troops rounded the corner, heading north toward Philadelphia City and safety, the mob there attacked—first with groans and hoots, then with stones and brickbats. The Greens picked up the pace to a double-quick time, then broke into a run. The Markles and the Mechanics lagged behind, leaving the Greens on their own. After running the Second Street gauntlet for two blocks, Colahan led his men into German Street, "thinking by moving off smartly, to get rid of our assailants." But more rioters poured out of alleys and houses, and someone took a shot at the Greens. Colahan gave new orders: Halt! Fire! For the third time, militia had been ordered to fire into a crowd. And this time, men who had been directly attacked by a hostile crowd did not hesitate. However many Greens had ammunition and priming—perhaps only five—fired at their pursuers.[34]

The Greens had scarcely aimed their volley, and the balls went wild. Some went through the windows of a Baptist church and a grocery store, while another passed through the hat of a man standing on a cellar door. Amazingly, no one was injured. Instead, the gunshots only enraged the mob of dozens, perhaps hundreds. And it persuaded Captain Saunders, who claimed to have been nearly hit by one of the Greens, that he had done all he could, and he gave up trying to escort Colahan to safety, though two or three of the Greens did remain with the Markles all the way back to Philadelphia. Now even more desperately short of ammunition, and with no time to reload their muskets anyway, the remaining Greens fled northward. Their knapsacks, muskets, and—on this hot day—green jackets slowed them down and made them easy targets for pursuers tossing bricks and stones. They managed another volley, again missing their pursuers, but terrifying Southwark residents on their way to church, as well as a class of Sunday school students who had just made it inside before the firing began. Losing their organization, each man made a run for it, hoping to find a house where he could take shelter. Colahan himself made it all the way north to Pine Street in Philadelphia City, where a Mr. Harvey offered him refuge while a mob howled outside until the gentlemen of the ward persuaded them to abandon the chase. Colahan waited until dark, then found his way home. Other Greens were less fortunate. Stories circulated of "one strapping six-footer, who kept about thirty of the mob at bay for over an hour, but fell at last, wounded in the head with stones."[35]

Private Robert Gallagher got the worst of it. He thought he had found refuge in a house at Fifth and Small Streets in the corner of Moyamensing between Southwark and the relative safety of Philadelphia City. He made it to the garret, still grasping his musket. There, however, the mob found him. Gallagher may have fired a round at his pursuers, but they quickly overwhelmed him and dragged him downstairs and into the street, where members of the mob beat him and jumped on him. Eventually, the Moyamensing police rescued him and took the unconscious Gallagher to the lockup in the Southwark Hall. But the mob broke in there as well, and some gave Gallagher another beating, while others prepared a gallows. Finally someone got him into a cab, which took him to Pennsylvania Hospital.[36]

A twenty-five-year-old Bucks County farmer named Edward Lyon, who had helped bombard the church earlier in the day, was among the crowd that had chased Gallagher to Small Street. As others dragged Gallagher out of the house, Lyon grabbed Gallagher's musket and waved it out the window in triumph. Another member of the mob, thinking that the man waving the musket must be the soldier, fired at Lyon, who fell, severely wounded. The mob was consuming its own.[37]

St. Philip's Under Attack.
Courtesy of the Library Company of Philadelphia.

20

A Fight Must Come Off Some Time

B ack in Southwark, Levin and Grover remained on the steps of
St. Philip's, facing a crowd that one reporter estimated to exceed ten
thousand. One witness later recalled that Levin "requested them to go
home peaceably," while another insisted that "he made a violent appeal to
them." At some point they were joined by Charles Jack, whose essay in the
previous morning's *Native American* had warned of an Irish invasion. Jack
tried to make his way to the church steps, but as soon as he dismounted
from his horse, he found himself surrounded by "some very common persons" intent on setting fire to the church. When one of them, "very stout, of
brown complexion," drew a long knife from his sleeve and tried to stab Jack,

the lawyer gave up trying to get to the church itself and instead entered a neighboring house. He climbed the stairs and found a window from which he could address the crowd in relative safety.[1]

Jack was proudly expostulating to the crowd in Queen Street when someone explained to him that the real action was taking place in an alley, where rougher men in shirtsleeves were trying to break down a side wall of the church using a twelve-foot pole as a battering ram. When Jack shifted to a window overlooking that alley, the men there started throwing bricks at him. One smashed the window, showering Jack with broken glass. "I'll mark you!" Jack warned, threatening to identify them later on, presumably to the police. The men below responded with more bricks.[2]

Levin and Grover kept appealing to the crowd to remove the cannon facing the church. The crowd seemed receptive enough, but begged to fire just one more salvo at the church. John Smith, who had been among the men chosen to search the church on Friday, had helped bring the cannon, and he wanted it fired. "Mr. Grover," pleaded another man, rumored to have lost a brother in Kensington, "only let us fire this once more and we will go away." Grover refused, but he agreed to ride the cannon back to the wharf. "You may ride me any where," he joked with them, "so you do not ride me to the devil!" As it happened, the crew dragging him and the heavy gun started to take a wrong turn, but Grover directed them back to the river. Once there, he indulged their wish to fire the cannon once more, but he insisted that it be pointed toward the distant New Jersey shore. An "old gentleman" then handed Grover a nail, which he pounded into the touchhole, temporarily disabling the gun. Grover wanted to spike the second gun, the six-pounder, as well, but when he delivered it to the Simpson & Neal shipyard from where it had been taken, co-owner John Neal took charge of it and pledged to secure it as best he could.[3]

From the shipyard, Grover walked back west, stopping at the Commissioners' Hall. There he found a jumble of confused Southwark residents trying to figure out what to do next and to organize a proper meeting. Grover took the chair, and Levin improvised a speech that was partisan but also, at least on its surface, opposed to further violence. "Let our enemies tantalize us!" he bellowed. "Let them try how far they can go to disunite and disturb the American Republican party—let them set every snare they can to try us—but let us beware, let us sustain our characters as Americans and return to them good for evil!" Returning good for evil would require keeping St. Philip's intact, so Grover persuaded his neighbors to form a posse—twenty-five men from each of Southwark's five wards—to guard the church. Sending the chosen men to their wards to be issued badges, Grover went home to get symbols of even greater authority: two American flags, one for himself and one for Levin. Once again, he pushed his way to the church, unfurling the flags as he went. While Grover was gone, Levin had remained near the church, watching, he later claimed, what he expected to be the end of the affair. "Every man felt that *the crisis* had passed," he wrote. "The utmost good feeling prevailed, and the crowd began rapidly to disperse."[4]

Then men or boys came running from Second Street with terrible rumors. The Greens, they shouted, had fired into a crowd, killing one and wounding others. "The effect of such astounding news upon the minds of the people, was terrific," Levin later recalled, "and then for the first time after the withdrawal of the Greens, demonstrations of violence were made." When Joshua Mitchell—a nativist Philadelphia city alderman—arrived on horseback, Levin confided that "he might not be able to save the Church." He assented to Mitchell's suggestion that they seek aid from the sheriff. "The fighting may be said to be only commencing," wrote a *Chronicle* reporter at three o'clock. "All is dreadful excitement"[5]

Grover's flags distracted the mob long enough for Levin and Grover to make it to the front door of the church, but when they handed their flags to strangers to hold, the men promptly absconded with them. "That's no place for the Stars and Stripes," they growled. Some brought a pole, ten or twelve feet long, and began to attack the door. Dropping to his knees, Levin exclaimed, "I am pledged to defend this church, and I will do it at the peril of my life."[6]

Rather than go through Levin, the mob went around him. To the west of the church, a recently built brick wall blocked off an alley that ran along the church's side. The boys with the battering ram turned their attention to this flimsy barrier. By this time, Grover had entered the church, and he was dismayed to hear the pounding of the ram, while paving stones shattered the church's windows. "You can't get in except over my dead body!"

Grover shouted, only to fall silent as invaders smashed a hole through the wall blocking the alley, which they widened by tearing out loose bricks with their hands. With the barrier cleared, men and boys poured into the alley and through the church's side door and windows. Thomas Roe, who had helped search the church on Friday, tried fastening the shutters, but men forced them open. One doorway collapsed in a loud shower of bricks, but that did not stop the crowd pushing through.[7]

Some were drunk men, others mischievous boys, like those who had torched St. Michael's and St. Augustine's in May. Quite possibly some were themselves veterans of those church burnings; one young man was later charged both with attacking St. Augustine's in May and with taking a musket from one of the Greens in July. The *United States Gazette* reporter was sure some of the marauders in St. Philip's were Irishmen, presumably Protestants. In any case, the youths poured into the church and began to destroy it from within. "I am ruined!" Levin wailed. "I am sacrificed! And you sacrifice me!"[8]

Soon the church filled with boys and men, some trying to trash it, others hoping to preserve it. Roe first tried to guard the library and its books, but then moved to shield the altar. David Ford, another member of the Friday night search party, defended the organ. One group of boys invaded the vestry room and cut a large painting showing the flagellation of Christ from its frame. They gleefully carried it outside to great cheering, but some cooler heads scolded them and returned the painting to the church. Others climbed a ladder to set the chandeliers swinging, jumped on the confessional boxes, and pawed through Father Dunn's priestly garments. One group ran to the basement to turn over the benches in the classrooms.[9]

The cellar was full of boards and wood shavings, so it would be easy to start a blaze that could consume the church. When he saw a lad with bunches of matches trying to ignite the woodwork, Grover got angry and started hurling boys out windows. But others took their places, and Grover decided that so long as nothing was set on fire, the best thing was to let the crowd run its course, exploring the church and breaking its crosses. Robbins, the church's neighbor, told his family to watch for smoke. If the church were to burn, his house would burn with it, but he hoped for the chance to save some of his belongings.[10]

Grover tried to calm things down. John Du Solle, editor of the *Spirit of the Times*, a paper known for its sympathy with Irish immigrants, wandered into the church, where he found himself "surrounded by a mob of malignant spirits thirsting for our blood." Native leaders escorted him to safety, possibly saving his life, while denouncing the more violent men around them. "We feel bound to do them justice," Du Solle wrote of Grover and his associates, "for they seemed sincere in their efforts to restore order, and felt no doubt the full extent of the truth, that wicked spirits were perverting their cause to the worst purposes." Levin stood before the pulpit and gave a public address in the uncharacteristic venue of a Catholic church. A few people listened, but the mayhem continued. By one account, Levin asked the crowd if they would defend the church. His listeners discussed the idea, then voted no.[11]

By four o'clock, Levin was about to collapse from fatigue, and a sympathizer hustled him to the corner and hired wagoner Thomas Fisher to drive him home. On the ride north, an exhausted Levin told Fisher that in the four hours he had protected the church, he had sent three or four requests that McMichael summon troops. "If the military did not come to their assistance," Fisher later recalled Levin saying, "the church would be burnt before dark." Yet around that time, Levin's *Daily Sun* was preparing inflammatory copy, condemning Cadwalader for meddling in Southwark and repeating the false rumor that on their flight north, the Montgomery Hibernia Greens had killed "two or three persons . . . and wounded others." "The quantity of arms in the possession of the Catholics in every quarter has astonished every body," the paper reported, hardly a statement to calm matters.[12]

Eventually, around five o'clock, the crowd had had their destructive fun, and it grew easier to shoo them out. St. Philip's had been sacked: its doors and windows smashed, its west wall partially demolished, its altar desecrated. But it had not burned, and nativists later insisted that the violence would have ended there had Southwark been left alone. One resident claimed that "both above and below Queen, many women and children were sitting or standing at their doors and windows. All was quiet around the church, and good order seemed to prevail in the whole district." Another felt that matters had calmed enough for him to take a nap. Even with the State House bell ringing the alarm, Grover dispatched two men to tell the sheriff that the crowd was dispersing and there was no more danger. After enjoying a cigar outdoors, he returned to the church to keep an eye on things.[13]

Others were less optimistic. After having failed to get Colahan the ammunition he so desperately needed, Deputy Sheriff William Price had then failed to raise a posse of more than a dozen men. "I'll be damned if I'm going to fight for the Catholics," more than one citizen told him. Sunday's mob, he found, was more violent than its predecessors on Friday and Saturday. When he arrived at the church, Price was troubled to find it under the rough command of Colonel Jack. And Jack himself did not think he could maintain control. Around 5 P.M., he found a young man he could trust, and told him, "Get my horse and ride up to Gen. Cadwalader, and tell him from me to come down. I cannot preserve the church."[14]

While Captain Colahan had waited anxiously in the church, Cadwalader and the other gentlemen of the city spent Sunday morning discussing the situation with concern, but perhaps not the urgency they would have devoted had they fully understood how bad things were on Queen Street. Cadwalader was the first up. He found Major General Patterson, and the two then called on Sheriff McMichael, still in bed at 10:30 after having only gotten home some time around 5 A.M. They explained to him the peril that Colahan faced, and a similar report came in from four men from McMichael's posse of Friday night who had shared a cab from Southwark. Cadwalader planned to send troops to relieve the Greens by one o'clock, and the men of the posse returned to Southwark with the news.[15]

McMichael suggested a conference at Cadwalader's house to include Judge Anson Parsons. Cadwalader agreed, and learning that the judge had gone to church, followed him there, and the two men worshipped together. Then the general prevailed on Parsons to come to his house. Once there, Cadwalader found waiting for him one of Colahan's notes, warning that the captain doubted that he could hold the prisoners much longer, and that if not relieved the Greens would be "butchered alive." Cadwalader replied with an order giving Colahan permission to release everyone but Naylor, whose offense Cadwalader considered too grave to ignore. He persuaded Parsons to go personally to Southwark to take custody of Naylor. Before the judge could depart, however, a messenger arrived with news that it was too late: Naylor was free, and the militia had surrendered the church to a mob armed with cannon.[16]

Given the possible consequences, the choice to return to the church, in force, was not obvious. Naylor had already returned home to the city, so no invasion of Southwark would recapture him. The messages from Southwark were mixed, but some suggested that the church was safe. Even if the mob was disposed to burn the church, it would have plenty of time to do so before the arrival of more soldiers. Or it might burn the church in the presence of the troops, as mobs had burned St. Michael's and St. Augustine's. Finally, returning to Southwark was likely to leave some men dead. So why march?[17]

McMichael wanted to assert the supremacy of law. Every message he had received from Southwark, every offer to protect St. Philip's, came from men acting as private citizens; the authorities of Southwark were refusing to guarantee the safety of the church; and the men at the church were refusing to act as sheriff's officers. McMichael later explained that he and attorney general Ovid Johnson, who had joined the group, regarded these actions "as an open rebellion against the laws." Judge Parsons agreed. In his charge to the grand jury following the Kensington riots, Parsons had laid out conditions under which rioters could be considered "enemies to the State." The judge now ruled that the men in Southwark "were no longer rioters, but were in rebellion against the authorities of the County and of the Commonwealth." The militia "would be authorized to take the most favorable position they could find, and to open their fire upon them, and capture their guns, in the quickest and most summary manner, treating them as pirates, enemies of the human race."[18]

Cadwalader was ready. He had let the mob have its riot on Saturday without shooting anyone, even after Naylor interfered with his order to fire. Now Southwark was all but daring him to return. "It would have been attributed to timidity if we had not gone," he later explained.[19]

With the supremacy of the law and his own honor at stake, Cadwalader began to assemble his brigade. He found all the officers he could, telling them to muster at the state arsenal at 3 P.M. It would be "no child's play," he warned Patterson. Patterson approved, ordering Cadwalader to retake the church from the mob, then "to defend it at all hazards, and if assailed to fire upon the assailants." And if Pleasonton found "field pieces in the hands of the insurgents, about to be used against the troops," he should "open his fire upon them at once and without parley."[20]

Moreover, the generals told the company officers that, if they were detached from their superior officers, they had permission to fire. Unlike Cadwalader's order of May 8, instructing officers to defend themselves against "missiles or shot of any kind," this order was given verbally, and recalled in slightly different terms by various officers. In an unofficial statement made about eight days later, Cadwalader wrote that "I gave directions to all officers acting in command of companies which were detached for any particular service, to fire in the event of being assailed or resisted, without further orders." By contrast, two of Cadwalader's subordinate officers remembered being given permission to fire only in self-defense, rather than if merely being "resisted." But self-defense could include using musketry against the sort of stone throwing that had met troops the previous day. Pleasonton, who received the order straight from Patterson, stated that "the whole order was to maintain their post at all extremities, and if assailed with any deadly weapons, brickbats, stones or firearms, to return the fire and use their arms." Regardless of the exact wording, the senior officers were clearly contemplating the use of lethal force, even if it meant that they would fire the first shot.[21]

Despite Cadwalader's determination, ordering the brigade to assemble was easier than actually assembling it. Pleasonton got to the arsenal at two o'clock, then suffered as his troops trickled in. His regiment should have numbered at least 250, but by four o'clock he counted only 75, and only a few more came in after that. The poor showing, he noted, "was any thing but encouraging to the officers who were to command in the coming conflict." Moreover, he had been disappointed by his troops' performance the previous evening, and said so aloud. Hurt by his words, a committee of privates from the Cadwalader Grays asked for a chance to redeem themselves by taking the most dangerous post available in Southwark. "My heart filled with an emotion of joy it had never before felt," Pleasonton later recalled. But however brave his men, they were too few.[22]

Colonel Joseph Murray was scarcely more successful, gathering only a hundred men from his infantry regiment. During the weaver's strike of

January 1843, the Washington Blues alone had mustered a respectable forty-one men. Now Captain Patterson reported with a lieutenant, four noncommissioned officers, and only three privates. When Captain Saunders begged that his Markle Rifles, exhausted from their night and day in Southwark, be allowed to rest, Murray decided he could not spare them, and ordered them to the column. Cadwalader's own aide-de-camp, Captain Henry Biddle, was out of town, but a militia captain and an army lieutenant volunteered their services in his absence. The brigade's cavalry officers also remained on their holidays, and they would not be so easily replaced.[23]

In summoning the brigade, Cadwalader had reminded his officers "to report and prefer charges against any subordinate officers who may be guilty of disobedience of orders," which suggests that he was expecting some men to deliberately stay away. Some, he knew, would feel worn out from service in May, when they had been "so often called out, and as often abused and insulted by various mobs," in the words of the *Daily Chronicle*. Others may have sympathized with the men attacking the church. Lieutenant Augustus Larrantree of the Jackson Artillery, in particular, later claimed that he could not muster because he was serving with the sheriff's posse. Moreover, he claimed, the governor had not ordered out the militia, and he was disgusted by his experience in May, when the militia "had been insulted and abused in Kensington, without authority or order to protect themselves." But his commander claimed that when ordered out, Larrantree had arrived in civilian clothing and declared that he was "not going to shoot down Natives." Whichever account is true, it is certain that just three days prior to being ordered to Southwark, Larrantree had ridden in the Native American parade as an aide to the chief marshal, Thomas Grover. He was not the man to invade Southwark to suppress his fellow nativists.[24]

Other officers reacted with greater enthusiasm. On hearing the news, Captain Henry Mallory of the Washington Artillery—who had ordered a bayonet charge in Kensington in May—left his daughters and barged into a Sunday church service in Germantown to summon his troops from among the congregation. They limbered their two six-pounders and, led by a band of musicians, they marched toward the city. They were accompanied by the Germantown Blues, an infantry company. John Guyer, a leading Germantown nativist, was a sergeant in the Blues, and he is said to have wept at the thought of fighting fellow nativists in Southwark. But he marched.[25]

Disappointing as the turnout may have been, it could have been much worse. In Baltimore in 1812 and 1835, and in Cincinnati in 1842, volunteer militia had shown their sympathy with mobs by refusing to muster against them, and possibly joining the mobs themselves. Reports of fraternization between troops and rioters in Kensington in May likely gave Cadwalader reason to worry that many in his brigade would rather attack St. Philip's than defend it. Yet as troops gathered, he could see men ready to put their duty ahead of their own politics.[26]

Meanwhile, McMichael again tried to organize a posse. Fifteen or twenty men showed up at Military Hall to volunteer, but McMichael needed greater strength. Prior to the Fourth of July procession, he had circulated six hundred notices asking citizens to report to his office for posse duty if they heard the State House bell strike eight taps. Now he ordered the signal, which rang steadily for twenty-five minutes. "The State House bell is now sounding the alarm," observed a reporter at 4:15 P.M. "The firemen are out, and one general scene of tumult and confusion prevails throughout the city." But only another six or eight men showed up in response.[27]

McMichael had better luck at Independence Square, where he waded into a crowd of people who had come to gawk at the militia. He pressed several dozen into service, but few of them wanted to brave a march into Southwark with only sheriff's bludgeons in their hands. Fortunately, someone mentioned that silversmith George Childs, a captain in McMichael's posse, had fifty muskets in his Spruce Street house. Most likely the muskets were the ones that the mayor had ordered distributed to the Peace Police during the May riots, when Childs had commanded his ward's "citizen guards." That Childs still had them at home might have reminded everyone that it was not so unusual for the Dunn brothers to have stockpiled state weapons in St. Philip's, but no one remarked on the connection. Instead, McMichael instructed Childs, who had also served the previous day, to arm fifty men and report to General Patterson. McMichael would lead another detachment himself. He issued his own instructions. "Whereas, certain evil-disposed persons have unlawfully resorted to the use of fire arms, in open defiance of the public authorities," he proclaimed, "all such persons, and all others aiding, abetting, assisting, or in any way giving any encouragement or countenance to such persons, are hereby declared to be in open rebellion to the laws, and will be dealt with as traitors and insurgents."[28]

By six o'clock, Cadwalader despaired of any more troops' reporting, and he sought Pleasonton's advice. "The whole force is small, not exceeding 180 men," he confided. "If you think the men can he relied upon, we will go—but if they can't be, it will be worse than useless, as if we are beaten, there will be no force left to protect the lives and property of our citizens—and universal ruin will be the result." Pleasonton was ready and confident. He had already offered his troops "disinclined to the service" the chance to go home and retain their places in the regiment, and had felt a commander's pride when not a man took him up on the offer. "A fight must come off some time," he told Cadwalader. "It might just as well be now."[29]

Six years earlier, during the Buckshot War in Harrisburg, Pleasonton had wished for a decisive commander. "It became a matter of great moment that the officer commanding the troops, should not manifest any doubt or uncertainty either as to the extent of his authority, or any timidity or hesitation in the mode of carrying his orders into effect," he recorded in his diary. "For I knew, that if the troops should discover any indecision in their officers, at a critical moment, the most disastrous results would inevitably follow. Blood would flow, and no one could foresee where or how the affair would terminate." In Kensington in May, Cadwalader had failed to live up to Pleasonton's ideal, but now he was ready. Moreover, Cadwalader figured he just needed to hold the church until daylight. By the next morning, he hoped for a resupply of ammunition, and relief by fresh troops of the two county brigades.[30]

And so they marched. Cadwalader and his staff rode at the column's head, followed by five musicians, silent on Pleasanton's orders. Behind them came Pleasonton's artillery regiment, with its two six-pounder cannon—drawn by hired horses driven by hired men—followed by Murray's infantry. The column had only made it the short distance to Spruce Street when an officer brought word from Major General Patterson, asking Cadwalader to return for a final conference. They were joined by Cephas

Childs, the nativist editor of the *North American*, who had spent part of the afternoon defending St. Philip's from the rough men with the battering ram. Cadwalader asked if he should continue. "It is a delicate question," Childs responded, noting that he had left Southwark an hour before, and much could have changed. Patterson resolved the question by ordering Cadwalader to proceed. Cadwalader rejoined his men, and the column resumed its march into the hostile territory of Southwark.[31]

The Military Fire on the Mob.
Courtesy of the American Antiquarian Society.

21

You Bloody Sons of Bitches!

ecause of the delay required for Cadwalader to consult with Major General Patterson, it took the troops a good forty minutes to cover the mile from Walnut Street to Queen. Pleasonton later insisted that both his regimental band and Murray's had been silent, but witnesses claimed they heard marches before they saw the troops, and one even recognized the melody of "Rory O'More."[1]

As the soldiers approached, around seven o'clock, they found a crowd so thick it "appeared one dense mass of human beings." "Fellow citizens!" cried Cadwalader's aide, "let us pass on!" Instead, the crowd hissed, groaned, and shouted, "go home!" A drunken man snatched at Cadwalader's horse.

"We'll take your damned nice coat off," someone taunted a soldier. One man even seized a soldier's musket, only to release it when the soldier's comrade cocked his own gun. Pleasonton noted that many in the crowd "were much excited, while others were moody and sullen, but nearly all seemed ready for a row." He rode to the front of his regiment and ordered the crowd to disperse. He was greeted with what one reporter called "a sullen and determined silence."[2]

"Charge on them and clear the street!" an officer commanded, and the brigade began to push east from Third Street toward the church in the center of the block. "Down the street they went like a tornado," observed a member of Grover's committee. "The conduct of the soldiers . . . appeared to be ferocious and wicked." The *Sun's* reporter later charged that "some of the officers acted more like drunken men than anything else." The soldiers had their bayonets fixed, and anyone slow to move was apt to get pricked. "Don't stick me, don't stick me!" cried some civilians. "We cannot go any faster." Children wailed as they were trampled. Isaiah Robbins, who lived next to the church, watched from an alleyway until soldiers ordered him inside. "The faster the people retreated," he later recalled, "the faster military pursued them."[3]

Cadwalader ordered Colonel Murray, commanding the infantry regiment, to secure the intersection of Queen and Third. Murray in turn ordered his acting lieutenant colonel, James Page of the State Fencibles, to clear the intersection, assisted by Captain Thomas Tustin's National Guards. Page, who had so bravely waded into the crowd in Kensington on May 8, sought again to act with the same firmness, pushing back the crowd but holding his fire. "The mob retired slowly and sullenly on all sides," he later reported. And even when his troops had cleared the intersection, men and boys stood before them, "menacing by words as well as gesture." "Why in the name of God don't you stand back," grumbled a solider. "Why do you press upon us thus!" Eventually, the troops cleared the intersection and were able to position three cannon there. The Washington Artillery had brought two six-pounders, which Captain Mallory pointed west and south. The Philadelphia Artillery had brought a single twelve-pounder, which it aimed north along Third. Cadwalader ordered the cannon loaded with canister, able to hit dozens of people with a single blast.[4]

Other companies worked to clear the middle of the block. Though the Montgomery Hibernia Greens had scattered, thirty-one men of the sister company, the Hibernia Greens, marched as part of Murray's regiment. Some men in other companies had Irish accents as well. "Take away the Irish soldiers!" the crowd shouted to the senior officers. On the north side of Queen, opposite the church, the crowd taunted a sentry. "How dare you cock your musket?" they asked. "Uncock that musket—who ordered you to cock your musket?" They might have unnerved the soldier had not his commanding officer appeared at his side and confirmed the order: "Keep your piece as it is." The crowd fell back, for now. [5]

Eventually the troops had cleared a path to the middle of the block, and Cadwalader reined in his horse in front of St. Philip's, which was still occupied by nativists Grover, Jack, and some men nominally under their command. By the time the troops arrived, Grover's men believed that they had reestablished order on Queen Street, and they did what they could to keep the troops away. One lied directly to Cadwalader's face, assuring the general that "there was little or no damage done to the church," even as Cadwalader could likely see the smashed windows, doors, and walls. Whether the nativists were forces of order or a mob themselves now became a matter of perspective. For instance, Grover's men were nailing shut the shattered windows and doors of the church. Were they protecting St. Philip's from further destruction, or, as Cephas Childs believed, barricading themselves against the militia, thus becoming rioters themselves? And, with two bodies—one civilian, the other military—both claiming authority from the sheriff, who was in charge? [6]

Cadwalader apparently regarded Grover's group as more foe than friend. Matthew Berreman, who lived on Moyamensing Road, believed that he was doing the right thing by clearing the mischievous boys out of the church and helping Grover keep possession. When Cadwalader's forces arrived, he called a greeting from the church window to an artillery sergeant he knew. The sergeant, with one hand on the pull rope that would fire the cannon, only shook his head. Franklin Jones, who had also tried to protect the church, was astonished by Cadwalader's arrival. Did the general not know how unpopular he had made himself the night before? Before Jones could speak to the troops, one chased him away from the church at the point of a bayonet. [7]

Cadwalader was equally firm. He demanded that Alderman McKinley and George Nutz, who had been deputized by McMichael, unlock the gate of the iron fence in front of the church. When they hesitated, he gestured to the cannon and, as Nutz later put it, threatened to "shoot every God dam son of a bitch of you." They unlocked the gate. Then Cadwalader sent word for Grover to come out to him, but Grover twice insisted that no, the general must come into the church. Only after receiving Cadwalader's third request did Grover swallow his pride. He might not like Cadwalader after the general's performance the previous day, but "much respect was due to his office." The militia, by contrast, showed little respect in return. One soldier managed to entangle his bayonet in Grover's coat. The commissioner was unharmed, but his coat was shredded, or so Grover claimed. Another member of Grover's committee had his sleeve torn, and the arm underneath it as well.[8]

Cephas Childs was particularly eager to make peace. As a nativist who had only recently stepped down as brigade major of Cadwalader's First Brigade, he sympathized with both Grover and Cadwalader and sought to mediate an agreement. After consulting with Childs, Grover mounted a pew and explained the situation, after which the men in the church voted to to vacate the building in pairs. Grover marched them out, two by two, through the church's east door and out the Queen Street gate. "We deliver the church up into your hands," he told Cadwalader, "and are now clear of responsibility." "I hope you will be able to take as good care of the church as we have." By one account, Cadwalader—still on horseback—responded, "Mr. Grover, you deserve the commendation of every good citizen for your conduct to-day." Some of Grover's men asked the crowd to obey the soldiers.[9]

But Cadwalader would not rely on the goodwill of the crowd. Leaving Captain William Patterson's Washington Blues to take possession of the church itself, Cadwalader deployed the rest of his forces to clear a perimeter around it. He sent the Second Fencibles to take possession of a frame house. When the occupants denied him the keys to the front door, Lieutenant Thomas Dougherty drew his pistol and entered through the back. He found no arms, but he did find several men who claimed to be boarders in the house, a statement that Dougherty found suspicious, in that the house was empty of furniture.[10]

The real challenge lay at the intersection at Second and Queen, which Cadwalader entrusted to Pleasonton's artillery regiment. At Cadwalader's direction, Pleasonton's men unlimbered their two six-pounders, belonging to Cadwalader's own Philadelphia Grays, and pointed them east toward the crowd on Second Street, but even the sight of their being loaded with canister failed to overawe the crowd. One man was arrested when he threatened to whip an officer in front of his men. The posse tried to arrest another man, but his mates rescued him. Cadwalader told his officers there that they could fire if resisted, and he ordered an infantry company, R. K. Scott's Cadwalader Grays, to clear the area. Then he returned to the church, where he thanked Grover's committee and arranged for them to be escorted outside of his lines.[11]

As Cadwalader took possession of the church, Scott's twenty-four Grays were working to clear Queen Street as far as Second Street, to the east of the church. One witness recalled them shouting, "clear out, you sons of bitches!" while another testified that a soldier had coolly repeated, "stand back, gentlemen—stand back, gentlemen," even as the crowd told him to go to hell. Another witness reported that the troops started out by shoving people with the sides of their muskets, but when that proved ineffective, they resorted to prodding with bayonets.[12]

The crowd responded with brickbats. "Is this what we were brought here for?" the troops griped. "Why did you bring us here?" "By God," Sergeant Patrick Starr told Scott, "we can't maintain our position unless you give us word to fire." Scott was not yet ready for that step, but he hurried back to the church and begged for help. "General," he panted, "my company are being clubbed and stoned, and we must either have orders to fire or retreat." "Captain Scott," Cadwalader replied, "maintain your position, and I will give you the necessary orders and reinforcements."[13]

To reinforce Scott, Cadwalader chose Captain Joseph Hill's City Guards. With forty men on duty, they were the largest single company on Queen Street that evening. But they were also among the most tired, having deployed to the church on Friday and Saturday as well. Before he returned to the intersection, Scott asked where Thomas Grover was. When the commissioner was pointed out to him, Scott asked for Grover's help. "When you get down to the corner," he implored, "step in front of the companies, and ask the mob to step back, as they know you, and will probably step back sooner for you."[14]

Lacking such regard from the crowd, Captains Scott and Hill had to rely on physical intimidation. With Scott working the south side of Queen Street and Hill working the north, the two captains led their companies east, waving their swords with their right hands and occasionally shoving with their left. As one man hurried east, Scott beat him on his shoulders with every step. Behind them, troops pushed forward with fixed bayonets. "If you don't clear the road," Hill bellowed, "I will kill every God damn son of a bitch of you." "Get out of the way you damned sons of bitches," Scott echoed, "or I will cut your legs off!" The people in the street reluctantly moved away from the church. "This conduct of Capt. Scott irritated me," Moses Williams later recalled. But he obeyed.[15]

Scott and Hill had reason to shout; their two companies, totaling sixty-four men, faced between three and five hundred people. Perhaps only twenty of those were particularly aggressive, but the soldiers could not arrest them in so large a crowd. When Dougherty's Second Fencibles were done clearing the house, they formed up behind Hill's City Guards, but the troops were still outnumbered. They occupied a line across Queen Street, from the northwest to the southwest corners of the intersection. Behind them, the sun was setting, and Cadwalader's troops had been on Queen Street for half an hour, perhaps longer.[16]

Most of Grover's committee had time to march in pairs, arm in arm, through the line of troops past Second Street. Grover himself remained on the scene. As Scott had requested, he tried to help by calming down a stout man with salt-and-pepper hair who was quite agitated, and likely drunk. As they argued, Captain Hill was trying to clear space in front of his troops. Hoping to clear Queen Street as far as the eastern corners of the Second Street intersection, he stepped several paces in front of his company, still waving his sword in his right hand. "Stand back," he demanded. "Stand back!"[17]

Hill's sword had already drawn blood that summer: on May 8, in Kensington, a drunken man had attacked Hill, wounding his hand against Hill's blade. Now some other drunken fool was about to try the same trick. The stout man left Grover and grabbed the weapon, and he was joined by another man who also grabbed the sword, trying to wrest it from Hill or break it. Hill held on to the hilt and the point and tried to get it away from his antagonist, even if it would cut him. "Don't do that!" cried the crowd on Second Street. Some threw paving stones, brickbats, and bottles at the three and at the other troops, some of whom were rushing forward to assist Hill. Sergeant Starr of the Cadwalader Grays, who had earlier asked permission to fire, had two ribs broken by one stone and was knocked unconscious by another. Blood streamed from his mouth. A private in the same company went down as well.[18]

This was getting serious, and even a volley fired over the heads of the crowd would probably only invite a rush as the men reloaded. "If you fire," a Grays lieutenant cautioned the men, "fire low." As the bricks and stones rained down, the militiamen staggered back, but members of the mob grabbed their muskets to keep them from retreating, or to get hold of the weapons for themselves.[19]

Other troops made it to Captain Hill, who was still trying to keep hold of his sword. Cadwalader shouted to Hill to surrender the weapon, so that the soldiers behind him could get a clear field of fire. But Hill held on, and as his men caught up to him, Hill's assailants let go. Still furious, Hill chased his two antagonists, striking them with the flat of his sword. Then he shouted to the mob—only twenty feet away—that he would order his troops to fire. "Fire, you damned son of a bitch, and we will give you hell if you do," they replied. "You are loaded with blank cartridge!" Hill assured them that his men were loaded with ball. Then a brick smashed into the back of the captain's head, knocking him into the Second Street gutter. A man in a checked shirt—probably Enos Waters, a Southwark blacksmith and firefighter—grabbed again for the sword. "Damn you," he snarled at Hill. "You kill no one with this!"[20]

The mob outnumbered the militia, perhaps ten to one. If stripped of their weapons, the troops would be as vulnerable to injury and humiliation as the Montgomery Hibernia Greens had been hours before. If he wanted to save his brigade, and its honor, Cadwalader would need to act immediately. He drew a breath so that he could bellow the command to fire. Captain Hill beat him to it. Still sprawled in the gutter, he shouted the first word: "Ready!" Then, pausing. "Aim!" Here Cadwalader intervened, but only to order "fire by sections"; by holding their fire, some men would be able to keep up the gunfire while others reloaded. And then, finally, Hill gave the command: "Fire!"[21]

Blasts, smoke, and chaos. Hill thought the first shot came not from his men but from someone in the mob with a pistol. The ball hit James Dougherty, a fifteen-year-old Catholic, in the right temple, killing him instantly. Then the roar of twenty muskets, followed by five or six in a second volley. At least two soldiers, recalling their drill, fell back after firing so they could reload and fire a second time. Both the City Guards and Cadwalader Grays had fired, as did two or three men from Dougherty's Fencibles in the rear, though they lacked orders. Some men fired in the air, while others fired level into the crowd. The ones who did fire aimed diagonally at the intersection; had they fired directly along the axis of Second Street, even more balls would have found their targets.[22]

Bodies dropped. One witness said two persons fell. Cadwalader's aide thought he saw four killed. Waters, who had been struggling with Captain Hill, had been shot by two of Hill's men. He went down without a sound. Hill himself remained prone in the gutter, leading Cadwalader to fear that he had been shot by his own men, but then Hill regained his feet, unharmed. Isaac Freed, a sixty-one-year-old nativist from Spring Garden, had been encouraging the men around him not to run; they had as much right to be there as the troops. Now he fell dead with a hole in his chest. Ellis Lewis, twenty-five, died as well. One man tried to rise, but collapsed with a groan. James Tully was wounded in the arm, while James Lawson was hit in the heel.[23]

The soldiers had fired while members of Grover's committee were still passing through the intersection. Grover saw a man play possum, then get up and run. This may have been Nathaniel Gates, a member of Grover's committee, who had thrown himself down on hearing the soldiers cock their muskets. Gates avoided being hit with gunfire, but he later complained that his legs had been trampled as the crowd stampeded over him.[24]

Matthew Berreman, who had also helped Grover guard the church, saw a man fall three feet to his left, and felt the sting as a ball grazed his fingers. Another member of the committee, Thomas Warham, thought a musket ball grazed his knuckles, but he was more injured by being knocked down as a man next to him collapsed. Charles Jack had been scolding the militiamen nearest him for swearing at the mob rather than maintaining a soldierly silence. When the firing began, he tried to identify himself as a member of the official committee, only to have a soldier fire in his direction. The musket ball missed him, but—he claimed—he felt the powder burn his right cheek, and the blast knocked his hat into the street. Sheriff McMichael, who was just turning the corner from Second into Queen, saw a musket's flash close to his face as well.[25]

William Crozier, a thirty-six-year-old carpenter, was a relative of the captain of the Southwark watch, and he himself had been a member of the committee appointed to protect the church. Now, standing at the southwest corner of Second and Queen, he grabbed the musket of one of the Grays. His friends would later insist that Crozier begged the soldier for mercy: "I am a cripple, and will get out of the road as soon as I can." Cadwalader's aide, Colonel William Bradford, heard something quite different: "Fire and be damned!" In any case, the soldier did fire, blasting off the lower half of Crozier's face. Crozier fell into the gutter, where his body quivered for some minutes before he finally expired.[26]

Some shots flew past the crowd. Maria Lyle was visiting a friend at Queen and Front streets, one block east of the intersection. Only her left arm protruded from the door, but a musket ball ripped through the flesh above her elbow. William Manning was standing farther east, on the Queen Street wharf. A musket ball passed through his right thigh and entered his left leg, where it flattened against his femur as it cracked.[27]

"The excitement was awful," one witness later recalled. "Men rushing about hunting their relations; women in search of their children; I myself threw my children hastily into the entry, people were placing their families out to the reach of danger; dead bodies were falling around me." Samuel Rhinedollar, who had helped Grover in the church, could not believe the troops had fired into fellow Philadelphians. Surely, he thought, the cartridges were blanks, and the falling bodies were people "prostrated by fright." James Slocomb had watched from his house at the corner of Second and Queen. He too was sure the soldiers had fired blanks, "until I saw Mr. Crozier fall on my pavement with his face shot off." He turned away from the window to attend to his screaming wife and daughters.[28]

Cadwalader ordered his men to cease firing, and he called on the rioters to pick up their wounded. At least two bodies were carried away, the blood running out of them, said a witness, "like water through a seine." Neighbors mistook Freed for grocer Jacob Korndaffer and carried the body to what they thought was his Second Street house, only to be greeted by the real Korndaffer, alive and well. Such uncertainty was common. Newspapers later claimed that Jane Pennell—a widowed mother of four children—collapsed in terror and died of fright several days later, but the official coroner's report listed no women. Nor did the report include the old man, said to have had the top of his head blown off in the first fire. But no one doubted that the troops had killed. "Oh, you bloody sons of bitches!" shouted a man on Queen Street. "Oh, you bloody murderers!" "You are a set of damned cowards!" howled Andrew McClain. "We'll give you hell before morning!"[29]

Even as men dragged away the wounded, others crept into yards and fired at the troops. None hit their targets, but Cadwalader ordered his company commanders to fire back whenever possible; as he later explained, "it would not do to let the mob crowd upon us again." Meanwhile, he gained some troubling news, perhaps from sympathizers in the neighborhood. They explained the bombardment of the church earlier that day and warned that the same cannon were being readied for use against Cadwalader's brigade. Indeed, the general began to suspect that the whole affair was a trap "to pay us up for what he had done the night before." Cadwalader would match them. He ordered his own Philadelphia Grays to advance their two six-pounders to the corner of Second and Queen, "so as to show that we were ready."[30]

Within minutes, the streets were clear. "Of the dense throng that had crowded upon the soldiery," a private later remembered, "not a living soul was to be seen, from Second street to the river it was as desolate as though the angel of death had passed over the spot and blasted every breathing thing. All was silent." The soldiers stood stupefied, staring at the ground, trying to collect their wits and emotions. "God damn their souls," one remarked. "We gave it to them that time!"[31]

Perhaps Cadwalader could have withdrawn. He had made his point: The militia was willing to use deadly force to suppress disorder. But returning to the city would mean abandoning St. Philip's to the mercy of the mob, and his column would likely have endured assaults by a furious crowd of pursuers who would have the advantage of darkness. With residents cursing him and the church still in peril, Cadwalader prepared for a bad night in Southwark.

St. Philip's sat on the south side of Queen Street, just about halfway between Second Street on the east and Third on the west, with a distance of 550 feet between the two. If Cadwalader could control the two intersections, that block would become a kind of fortress, albeit one vulnerable to infiltration by men able to climb over walls or up onto rooftops. Cadwalader ordered Colonel Murray, commander of the infantry regiment, to remain on Third Street to the west, while Colonel Pleasonton, of the artillery regiment, would command the Second Street approach. Other troops guarded approaches from the north and south. [32]

Southwark residents also prepared for battle. After the first volley from the militia, some ran along Second Street, directing Natives to rally at the Wharton Market, some blocks south of the church. "Native Americans come to the meeting!" they cried. "Rescue Native Americans!" One man shouted, "Liberty or Death by God." "Get your guns," others yelled. "Get your guns!" At the market, armed men—"some noisy and some quiet"—gathered and plotted revenge. [33]

Between the church and the Wharton Market lay the Commissioners' Hall, which still held the dozens of guns that had been seized from St. Philip's on Friday evening. A wave of men rushed there from Queen Street. They tore down the railing, found the weapons, and passed muskets to eager hands. "Revenge!" they cried. "Revenge! for our murdered citizens!" Others dragged the corpses of Dougherty and Crozier—victims of the shooting on Queen Street—into the hall. Each was missing half a face. "'Good God, Colonel," a man remarked to nativist Charles Jack. "Is it not too bad, after we have saved the church, to be shot down like dogs?" [34]

Dr. Thomas Bunting, senior surgeon of Cadwalader's First Brigade, passed the hall on his way to a Second Street apothecary's shop in search of medical supplies to treat the troops wounded by stones and bricks. Seeing his blue uniform, someone shouted "Cadwalader!" and the crowd nearly lynched him. "Are you the damned son of a bitch who ordered the troops to fire?" a large man demanded. "I came to heal, not to kill," Bunting protested, but men dragged him to the Commissioners' Hall and forced him to look at the corpses. "Are you a father?" one asked, as another poked at Bunting's forehead. "Are you a brother? Look at these martyrs!" Another man grabbed Bunting's ivory-gripped sword and "flourished it about." Jack intervened. "He's a surgeon," he shouted. "Don't hurt him, he's a surgeon."[35]

Pleasonton sent Captain Heyward Drayton's Junior Artillerists to stop the raid and secure what weapons and gunpowder had not already been seized by the crowd. Drayton had only himself, a lieutenant, and twelve men, but they pushed through. At first, the rioters fled, with the exception of one man so startled by the troops that the lieutenant easily plucked a musket from his hands. Drayton found others in the cellar of the hall, where most of the weapons had been stored. Some scattered, but one man was so absorbed in picking the lock of a closet that he did not notice the troops' arrival until a sergeant clubbed him with a musket. Then he fled with the others. Drayton let him go; he had been ordered to seize weapons, not prisoners. By the time the troops had gathered the weapons, the rioters had recovered from their initial shock and, realizing they had the advantage of numbers, they surrounded the hall. Drayton's men were trapped in the cellar, their arms full of heavy muskets, with hostile men at the top of the stairs that formed the only exit. Pleasonton had promised reinforcements if needed, but how could a soldier in uniform get past the hostile crowd to deliver the request? When Drayton asked for a volunteer, not a single man stepped forward for what seemed a suicide mission.[36]

"Kill the damned rascals, we've got them now," cried the men upstairs. "Murder them—turn them out." When Alderman McKinley arrived, escorting the corpse of one of his constituents, Drayton refused him entry. "I have a right here," shouted McKinley. "I will let you know my authority is a little higher than yours—I am in authority." Drayton did not fear the alderman nor the corpse, but he did worry that if he let the body pass, the crowd would rush in behind it and overwhelm his small force. "If you do not retire, I'll fire," Drayton warned. Then, to make the threat credible, he issued the preliminary orders. "Fire by file!" he shouted. "Ready!" McKinley paused, then relented. After demanding Drayton's name, he took the corpse back upstairs. "You have murdered citizens enough already," cried the mob. One man with black whiskers pointed a musket toward Drayton's men in the cellar, "swearing he would shoot each soldier as he came out—every son of a bitch of them."[37]

John Douglass, captain of the Southwark watch, hid himself in one of the lockup's cells until the worst of the storm had passed, then went in search of help. Dressed in civilian clothes, he could pass through the crowd in Second Street more easily than one of Drayton's men, but he risked the opposite danger of approaching the militia position while *not* in uniform. As he approached the mouth of a militia cannon, he tipped his hat to the soldiers to show himself to be friendly, then explained the dire situation at the hall. Pleasonton sent the Cadwalader Grays, who were able to scare off the men inside the hall and rescue Drayton's troops. With the Grays as escort, the fourteen Junior Artillerists shouldered the forty muskets and hauled them back to Cadwalader's command post. Dr. Bunting took the opportunity to escape his tormentors. As the troops hustled him to safety, the surgeon warned the men remaining in the hall, "if I am sacrificed by this crowd, my death will be revenged by the military in less than six hours."[38]

The muskets in the hall were hardly the only arms and ammunition in Southwark. One group returned to the riverfront and seized a cannon, possibly one of the two that had been fired at the church that morning. They pulled it to the Front Street home and store of John McCoy, the Irish-born Southwark commissioner. Forewarned, McCoy had fled with his family, but Thomas Byrnes, a member of the First Ward posse, tried to defend the premises. "Bring out the powder and shot!" the mob demanded, threatening to batter down the door if not satisfied. Byrnes handed them a keg of gunpowder and two bags of shot. "That's all there is," he explained. "Liar!" someone shouted. But when Byrnes threw open the doors and invited them to search, the mob simply cheered and moved on.[39]

Another raiding party broke into the yard of the Merrick & Town Steam Engine Foundry on the west side of Third Street, which stored scrap iron and slugs due to be melted down for government projects. Now those scraps could become cannon ammunition. More scraps, a witness claimed, were donated by a Swanson Street dealer in secondhand iron. At Wharton Market, one or two hundred men gathered. About half were armed, and more weapons arrived, apparently donated by Southwark residents. The men had a cannon or two, probably taken from the *Venice*. "Damn the military," men muttered as they loaded the muskets. "They shall never see day light!" They especially hoped to get Cadwalader. One man tied a handkerchief around his head and vowed revenge for his "brothers that were murdered."[40]

Back on Queen Street, McMichael, Alderman McKinley, and some members of Grover's committee stood in front of the church, where at least they were out of immediate danger. Challenged by a soldier, committee member John Greaves fished in his pocket for his muslin badge, which served to prove his bona fides. Two police brought in a prisoner, apparently thinking that the church could again be used as a jail, as it had been for Naylor. But they were interrupted by Cadwalader, still on horseback. When McKinley asked, "What shall be done with the prisoners?" Cadwalader replied—or so one nativist would claim—"Shoot them all." Even one of Cadwalader's officers testified that Cadwalader had ordered his troops to kill anyone they saw trying to fight the military, rather than to seek prisoners. But no one claimed that his men killed anyone who had surrendered. Instead, they released their prisoner after about ten minutes. The troops then searched the houses and shops along Queen Street and expelled anyone they found. From Second to Third, they owned one block of Southwark.[41]

After the initial shooting and the scuffle at the Commissioners' Hall, the blocks around the church calmed. Cadwalader had told the Southwark watchmen not to light the lamps, leaving the scene "intensely dark," and, Page later recalled, "the quiet of the grave prevailed." Pleasonton permitted his exhausted troops, on their feet for hours, to rest. Infantrymen sat on the curbstones, their weapons still in their hands, while artillery crews leaned on their guns' carriages. A few militiamen seized the chance to slip away in the dark. At least some of the civilians who had been guarding the church took this opportunity as well. Jack found his horse at the Commissioners' Hall and rode home, assuring everyone he met that the law would punish the guilty.[42]

"The Battle of Southwark."
Courtesy of the Library of Congress.

22

Secret, Covert, Murderous

Despite the quiet, Colonel Pleasonton was uneasy. A US Navy officer had spotted the rioters with ship cannon—likely the *Venice*'s four-pounders—but did not know where they were. Pleasonton asked some police to slip off their badges and go scout, but they could find nothing. For perhaps an hour, the troops waited anxiously, as the sky grew even darker. Then, around 9 P.M., Lieutenant Dougherty spotted a light to the east. It seemed to be coming closer. He pointed it out to Pleasonton, who assured him it was stationary. "It is moving!" Dougherty insisted, and a few minutes later he and Pleasonton heard the rumble of an approaching cannon. Now persuaded, Pleasonton ordered his men to their own guns, but to stay as close to the houses as possible.[1]

To the east, men were rolling the stolen cannon into position on wheels muffled by blankets supplied by neighborhood women. When they reached Front and Queen, they presented it to John Cook, a thirty-year-old oysterman associated with the Weccacoe Hose Company. Cook was a seasoned rioter, having survived a major scrap in 1842, even rescuing some comrades from the police. Lacking cannonballs or other standard ammunition, he and his comrades loaded the cannon with whatever metal they could find. And lacking a slow match, Cook resorted to a lit cigar to fire the gun at Pleasonton's men. But the men had nothing like a proper gun carriage that could compensate for the upward slope of the street, so their cannon fired high. One militia officer looked up to see "a regular hardware shop, every imaginable piece of iron that one could think of" fly over over his head. The eaves of Queen Street houses took most of the damage.[2]

Now the battle began in earnest, with what Dougherty remembered as "almost constant discharge of cannon and musketry all night." In the darkness, muzzle flashes worked both ways. By ordering his two cannon to fire back, Pleasonton revealed his own position to the rioters, who returned fire. Cook stayed at the touchhole, ready to fire the cannon again as soon as it was reloaded. "By God," exclaimed a comrade, Bill Wood. "You'll be shot!" "I'll be damned if I will," Cook replied. "I fired three shots with this segar, and I'm damned if I don't fire this. I know I'll be buried and wrapped up in the American flag." Wood was right; as Cook blew on his cigar stump to keep it lit, Pleasonton's men fired at the light. As Cook fled, two balls—either musket balls or grapeshot—slammed into his back and exited his groin. He was dead.[3]

Pleasonton was himself hit in the groin, but he kept his feet and continued directing cannon fire for ten minutes, until the pain grew too great. Transferring command to his deputy, he staggered off to the vacant house on Queen Street a few doors west of the church that surgeons had designated their field hospital. There, a surgeon examined Pleasonton and found a musket ball that had penetrated all of Pleasonton's clothing but had been stopped and flattened by a purse of silver half-dollars, which had saved the wealthy officer's life. Even so, the shot had left a six-by-ten-inch contusion, spreading outward from a spot exactly the size of a half-dollar. Captain Scott was also carried in, with a gunshot wound in his back. Other soldiers were wounded less seriously, or had their uniforms torn by flying metal. Back on at the corner, Pleasonton's artillerists fought on until they exhausted their ammunition. Under the cover of musketry, they pulled their cannon back to the church at the center of the block. The crowd, beating a tin kettle and shouting "Go it, Natives!" seized the intersection.[4]

To the west, at Third and Queen Streets, Colonel Murray and his regiment had yet to see action. The southern position, commanded by Colonel Page, stretched across Third Street. The State Fencibles deployed from the western sidewalk to the center of the street, where Captain Mallory's Washington Artillery positioned its brass six-pounder, pointing south. A second infantry company, the Germantown Blues, covered the rest of the distance to the nearest building on the east. They remained there peacefully for some time, with little to do but loan ammunition to Pleasonton's cannoneers as they ran out. Lieutenant Edmund Bockius of the Blues heard a whispered voice from the south—"keep quiet"—but thought he had orders not to fire first, so he did nothing. That was a mistake. The voices had come from Third and Christian, just one hundred yards south of Murray's position, where the crowd had stealthily set up a cannon, likely an iron six-pounder. Page had no idea he was about to be attacked until he was blinded by the flash of the cannon and equally startled by its boom.[5]

The first blast was devastating. Like the men attacking the Second Street position, these rioters had loaded their gun with the scraps of metal from the foundry scrap heap, along with chisels, knives, files, glass bottles, and fragments of bricks. The flying junk missed the Fencibles on the western side of the position but tore into the Washington Artillery and Germantown Blues. A projectile—maybe a glass bottle, maybe a drill bit, maybe a piece of chain—tore off the top of the head of twenty-eight-year-old Sergeant John Guyer of the Blues, splashing his brains into the street and onto the faces of the men around him. Other fragments seriously wounded Corporal Henry Troutman in the groin and artilleryman James Crawford in the arm. Several other militiamen were wounded and two more had bits of metal shot through their hats. John Ashworth of the Blues was startled when his musket "shivered to pieces" as it absorbed a ball, but he himself was unhurt. John Waterhouse, also of the Blues, was hit in the back of his neck, but the ball had passed through his knapsack, which absorbed most of the momentum.[6]

Captain Mallory himself had narrowly survived; one of the bits of metal had blown the pompon off his cap. One of his gunners, Crawford, was disabled, and others, spattered with bits of Sergeant Guyer, fled, taking with them the slow-burning match rope needed to fire the gun. But Mallory, who had served twenty-three years in the US Army, stayed at his post. He was joined by fellow army veteran Andrew Maxwell of the Germantown Blues, who had seen combat against the Seminoles in Florida. Maxwell stepped into Crawford's place, Captain Jonas Fairlamb lent four members of the Wayne Artillery, and Mallory himself fired the cannon with a lit cigar in lieu of the slow-match. To keep the weapon ready, he ordered Private John Crout to chain-smoke cigars over the course of the night. After his twenty-seventh, Crout moaned that he could take no more. "Smoke away, my brave fellow, for God's sake smoke," Mallory told him, "and if you die smoking for your country, your death will be as glorious as if you had been shot in its service." While Crout took over at the cannon, Mallory borrowed muskets and cartridges from some of his men and shot hopefully into the darkness.[7]

Fortunately for the militia, they were not facing well-drilled, well-supplied artillery like Cadwalader's Philadelphia Grays. Rather, their opponents were the same boisterous young men of the sort who had caused so much trouble in Kensington and in many a fireman's riot and street brawl. Thanks in part to the suppressing fire from the infantry, it took the rioters on Third Street roughly an hour to fire a second time. This time, the militia were kneeling in anticipation of a second blast, and the rioters fired high—hitting second-story windows. Moreover, the rioters appear to have overloaded their gun, reducing muzzle velocity to the point that some of the projectiles bruised rather than seriously wounded the men they hit. The rioters had better luck attacking Murray's westernmost position, managing to wound some of Fairlamb's Wayne Artillery.[8]

As bleeding men staggered into the temporary hospital a few doors west of the church, military surgeons did what little they could. The building they had chosen—perhaps the one seized by Dougherty early in the evening—was empty, lacking even furniture. Since it was exposed to enemy gunmen in and on the roofs of nearby houses, Pleasonton ordered all the windows shuttered, which protected him and the other men inside but made the building "insufferably hot." Worse still, the water was barely drinkable. Cut off from the city, they would have to wait out the night. Troutman, wounded on Third Street and bleeding dangerously from his femoral artery, remained conscious; an officer later claimed that Troutman "expressed his satisfaction in suffering in the uniform of the American citizen soldier."[9]

The remaining militiamen rallied, firing muskets and cannon at whatever rioters they could glimpse in the dark. With Pleasonton incapacitated, Cadwalader spent most of his time near Second Street, trusting Murray, Page, and their officers to cover the Third Street corner. The general remained a conspicuous target, and one newspaper reported that ten musket balls passed through his coat without hitting flesh. The cannon fire at Queen and Second was so intense that the concussions shattered every window in the house on one corner. St. Philip's itself remained a target, and since the church lay in a hollow, the snipers attacking it had the advantage of high ground. The afternoon mob had splintered much of the woodwork but had failed to deface most of the church's paintings. These now succumbed to gunfire, as did windows and curtains. From inside, the nine Washington Blues fired back, but they had little hope of hitting their adversaries. At ten o'clock, the *Pittsburgh Chronicle*'s correspondent reported "a continual roar of cannon, muskets, rifles and pistols," and believed a rumor that a hundred people had already perished.[10]

What the rioters lacked in weapons, ammunition, or training, they made up for in stealth and mobility. While the militia attempted to maintain the formations they had learned in their drills and encampments, the rioters resorted to what one newspaper called "Indian warfare." They had attached long ropes to each of their three cannon so that after they fired, they could be dragged to a new position before the militia could return fire. While they did so, others beat tin kettles to drown out the sound of the muffled wheels. One witness later condemned the rioters' tactics as "secret, covert, murderous, ungoverned by any of the rules of civilized warfare." Under the conditions, it was also extremely effective. After their first attacks up Third Street, the rioters rolled the cannon west and north to fire down Queen, hitting some of the Wayne Artillery before moving the cannon yet again. One observer, sitting in safety five blocks to the north, counted a total of nineteen artillery discharges before he went home at 11:30 P.M.[11]

Cadwalader desperately missed his cavalry; without them, he could not pursue the rioters as they pulled the cannon through Southwark's small streets and alleys. He hastily penciled a message to Major General Patterson, asking for all available horse. By this point, Captain Butler of the First City Troop had returned to town and learned of the crisis in Southwark, and, with seventeen fellow horsemen, reported for duty at the Girard Bank headquarters, eager to reprise their role from May, when they had charged the crowd in front of St. Augustine's. But Butler did not know that Cadwalader's regular aide-de-camp was absent, so when a stranger in army uniform passed him, Butler had no idea that it was Lieutenant Palmer acting as Cadwalader's aide, and possibly bearing Cadwalader's plea for cavalry. Lacking clear communication, the First Troop remained at the bank, useless.[12]

Fortunately for Cadwalader, Sheriff McMichael had also arrived with news of the battle, and Patterson had already called for his Second and Third Brigades—composed of troops from Philadelphia County's outlying regions—to reinforce Cadwalader's First. As they reported for duty, Patterson threw them into the fight, to the point that he had committed almost his entire division, and needed to rely on armed civilians to guard the state arsenal and the city's Catholic churches. He initially ordered Horatio Hubbell, commander of the Third Brigade, to protect St. Paul's Catholic church in Moyamensing, but as the fighting in Southwark intensified, Patterson redirected him to join Cadwalader there.[13]

Patterson also threw in the Second Brigade, commanded by Brigadier General Augustus Roumfort, who marched south at about 10 P.M. with a much larger force than Hubbell's. His column consisted of 178 men, around as many as Cadwalader had brought himself. Most crucially, it included the Washington Cavalry and the First State Troop, the horsemen that Cadwalader so desperately lacked. Moving south on Fifth Street, they arrived at Queen Street about 11 P.M. The previous year, Roumfort and Cadwalader had squabbled about precedence; they were both brigadiers, but one would have to be senior to the other, and they disagreed about which rules of seniority should apply. Patterson apparently knew about this unresolved matter, for he told Roumfort not to raise the question of rank; he had given Cadwalader a mission, and Roumfort's duty was to "assist and sustain" Cadwalader. Despite these instructions, and the gravity of deadly combat, neither brigadier seems to have taken orders from the other, and Cadwalader later accused Roumfort of acting "without any instructions from me." Indeed, it is not clear that they even spoke to each other as their men crouched under enemy musketry.[14]

Whichever brigadier was truly in charge now that Roumfort had brought some cavalry, the tactics were straightforward enough. The horsemen should wait for the flash of an enemy cannon, then charge to chase away the gunners. Infantrymen would follow at a run and spike the cannon, making it useless to the enemy. Not long after Cadwalader explained the plan, another blast revealed the enemy cannon at Second and Queen. Roumfort's men knew what to do. Rather than ride into the cannon's mouth, they rode north on Third, then east on Catharine, and then down Second to capture the gun, an iron six-pounder. They not only disabled the cannon but also bore it back to their lines. At least this part of the battle resembled the kind of warfare described in military training manuals. Eventually, Butler's First City Troop found its way into the battle, and it too captured a cannon. Unfortunately, that cannon belonged to the Washington Artillery, part of Murray's Third Street command. After hearing the artillerymen swear in German, the cavalrymen realized their mistake and returned the gun undamaged, with laughs all around.[15]

In addition to the cannon, the rioters had the muskets and other small arms, including some initially collected by the Dunns at St. Philip's, that they had seized from the Commissioners' Hall, as well as some muskets they had stolen from the retreating Montgomery Hibernia Greens. Rather than fight as regular infantry formations, which would have made an easy target, they acted as individual guerrillas, extinguishing whatever streetlamps had been lit, and in the darkness firing at the troops from alleys, windows, and housetops. They could then dash away before the troops could respond. A few crept through lanes and alleys to approach St. Philip's itself but fell back after the soldiers inside spotted them and fired.[16]

The troops spent most of the night fighting defensively, maintaining a perimeter around the church. At times, infantry companies pushed forward to scout out the enemy, but they were elusive in the dark night. Horsemen had an easier time scouting the mob's position, but they were targeted with bricks and gunshots. To the west of the church, the rioters had assembled a full Parisian-style barricade, apparently built of materials hauled from a wheelwright's shop. At midnight, Cadwalader ordered Fairlamb's Wayne Artillery to creep forward to dismantle it, allowing the cavalry to charge an enemy cannon.[17]

Some of the troops likely believed they were not fighting foes at all. Whether from fear or sympathy with their opponents, some militiamen deserted their units. Ironically, the deadliest nativist fire hit troops from Germantown, the site of early nativist feeling. Both Lieutenant Edmund Bockius of the Germantown Blues and Lieutenant John Bringhurst of the Washington Artillery had been among the founders of the Native American Association there in 1837, and in June 1844, Bringhurst had helped revive the group. Minutes before he was decapitated by nativist artillery, Sergeant John Guyer, a member of Bockius's command, had expressed "his regret at the service, and jokingly remarked that if ordered to fire he would elevate his piece so as not to injure." Bockius himself was grazed by a musket ball that passed through his cap.[18]

Distinguishing friend, foe, and onlooker was no easy matter. One reporter witnessed "wives screaming for their husbands, children for their fathers, and all alarmed and terrified in the extreme. Mangled and dead bodies ever and anon borne along, reports of friends or relatives killed, rushes of the crowd from some false or real ground of apprehension—all bore witness to a frightful drama that was in progress." As their houses shook from the concussion of the cannon, and their windows shattered from gunfire, terrified Southwark residents fled the battle, lifting old women and children over alley fences rather than expose them to the streets. Others fled to their cellars, as rifle balls slammed into the plaster walls of the rooms upstairs. As Roumfort's cavalry scoured the district, an officer called to a woman watching from her second-story window. "Where are the rioters?" he asked. "All the rioters are on horseback," she answered. "You are the rioters!"[19]

Sometime after 10 P.M., a full hour into the hottest part of the battle, a lieutenant was confronted by Alderman McKinley, who wanted to know why he was firing up Queen Street, wounding citizens. "I'll be damned if this must not be stopped!" The soldier pointed out that he was returning fire from a cannon and sent the alderman away, muttering to himself. What the alderman believed to be a residential neighborhood was, to the soldier, an open battlefield. At Queen and Fourth, one man staggered as a stray round bounced off his silk neckcloth and smashed into his chest; another man went down when a ball hit his calf. At Third and Christian, around 1:30 A.M., a girl watched part of the battle from her window and heard a musket ball whistle past her head, knock off a piece of woodwork from her house, and lodge in a neighbor's shutter. One cavalry sergeant had enough faith in the kindness of strangers to ride through the streets of Southwark, seeking a doctor to help an injured comrade. Each time he rang the doorbell at what appeared to be a doctor's office, rioters shot at him from alleys. After five tries, he gave up.[20]

According to one account, in the midst of the fighting, a woman appeared at the corner of Second and Queen, begging that her son—a militia volunteer but also the only support of his widowed mother—be allowed to depart. She was allowed to take him to safety, having first blurted out the position of an enemy cannon, information more valuable than the services of any one volunteer. But civilians could also be scouts for the enemy. Men with badges, claiming to be police, crossed through Cadwalader's lines to speak with him. Once they had departed, the rioters' accuracy increased, leading the general to distrust all badge wearers as potential spies. When one man got too near Captain Mallory's position, Mallory leveled a musket at him and commanded "Come here, you damned rascal, or I'll fix your head to the doorpost!" When the man surrendered, Mallory forced him to sit by a cannon, where he was exposed to rioters' gunfire until he begged Mallory to lend him a musket so that he could shoot back.[21]

Not all the armed locals considered all the militia to be the enemy. One group intercepted a gray-coated private, hurrying to Southwark some time after the first firing. "Are you not one of the damned Cadwalader Grays who fired upon and shot Americans down like dogs?" they demanded. When he explained that he was in the National Grays, commanded by nativist

Peter Fritz, they put down the rope with which they were preparing to lynch him and let him proceed. Brigadier General Hubbell had a similar experience. As he approached Queen Street, at about nine o'clock, a group of men aimed their muskets toward him, but an "old gentleman" recognized him and persuaded his comrades not to shoot. The gentleman saw Hubbell not as an anonymous soldier, but rather a familiar resident of Moyamensing who lived less than a mile away. And perhaps he saw an ally, knowing Hubbell's 1831 support for the Southwark Orangemen. Having survived this encounter with the rioters, Hubbell was then almost shot by the militia. Captain Fairlamb had spotted a shadowy figure approaching, and he gave his commands: *ready*, and *aim*. But before he could shout *fire*, Hubbell passed the only remaining streetlamp on the block, which illuminated the gold braid of his uniform. For the rioters, the night was equally chaotic. Some likely fired on one another, killing at least one man.[22]

By 12:30 A.M., the most intense combat was over, and the big guns had fallen silent, but the troops still searched for enemy artillery. Roumfort's cavalry had cleared out positions to the east and west of the church. Rioters still held the Wharton Market, a few blocks south of the church. There they erected a gallows for Cadwalader and muttered about re-arming and reorganizing. At two o'clock a reporter recorded the scene: "The rioters have generally been driven to a distance, where they are rallying round their guns, and preparing, it is said, for something dreadful with which to begin the morning. Even at this hour there are crowds of people in the streets. . . . All is in confusion. Families are weeping and mourning in great distress." The Commissioners' Hall became both a temporary hospital and a morgue. Other wounded men made it to the Pennsylvania hospital, only to suffer restless twitching and an agonizing thirst as they succumbed to their wounds.[23]

The rioters still had some fight in them. Expecting to be charged by cavalry, Bill Wood and some other men stretched a rope across Third Street, tying the ends to tree boxes on opposite sides. Then, after an hour and a half, during which the cannon had been silent, they fired their gun up Third at the militia and waited for the horsemen to charge. Charge they did. The Washington Cavalry, from Holmesburg, in the northeastern part of the county, had already captured a cannon at Front and Queen, to the east of the church. Now they rode south, toward Christian. As they approached rioters peppered them with musketry. Bleeding heavily from a gunshot wound in his arm, Lieutenant Richard Wagner turned his horse to ride back. A musket ball through his hand, plus two spent balls that bounced off his jacket, persuaded him that greater safely lay in numbers, so he rejoined the troop. A private was also hit in the hand, and Wagner's horse endured sixteen wounds from various missiles. Then the horses hit the rope, throwing their riders, including General Roumfort himself.[24]

As the cavalrymen regained their mounts, the rioters reloaded their cannon, hoping to fire point blank into the massed formation. But the gun misfired, giving the troopers time to seize it, along with some prisoners, while the remaining rioters fled. As dismounted cavalrymen vainly sought their enemies in a nearby lumberyard, a furious, swearing Roumfort ordered others to search the nearby houses, where they barged into bedrooms and poked sabers into closets in the hopes of finding the enemy responsible for the rope. Eventually, they arrested four residents, whom they hauled back to militia lines at Third and Queen and thrust in front of Colonel Page, a lawyer. "These are exciting times," Page told them, in perhaps an indirect criticism of their doubtful arrest. "People are apt to go to extremes." Whatever the legal niceties, Roumfort had scattered most of the remaining resistance.[25]

At this point, the rioters had one cannon left, but in pulling it over a curbstone, they broke the dray they were using as a gun carriage. While some men remounted it, others entered a tavern, drank two dozen bottles of ale, and broke the necks off the glass bottles to serve as ammunition for the cannon, along with some chains and pins taken off the broken dray. They managed to keep the last cannon away from Cadwalader's patrols, but the battle was winding down. The insurgents had made good use of the darkness, but they were fighting on one of the shortest nights of the year. As the sky lightened around 4 A.M., the militia's cavalry could see well enough to disperse any knots of rioters before they became a threat, without tripping over ropes in the process. Cadwalader found a welcoming sofa in the Third Street home of the bookkeeper for the *United States Gazette*. Perhaps he even got a little sleep.[26]

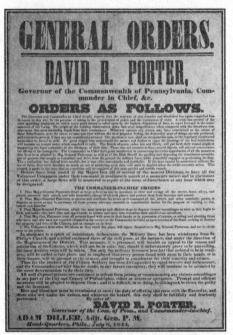

David R. Porter, General Orders, July 8, 1844.
Courtesy of the Library Company of Philadelphia.

23

The Mob Is Now Supreme

At 4:40 A.M. on Monday, July 8, the sun finally rose over the Delaware River, illuminating the ruins of Queen Street. It had not been gutted by fire the way that Kensington had, but the blasts of the cannon had broken trees, shattered windows, cut downspouts, and chipped bricks. One house bore the marks of thirteen grapeshot. "Window shutters, doors, fronts of houses, trees, tree boxes, awning posts, lamp posts, pumps, watch-boxes, signs, are all pierced with balls and shot," wrote a shocked reporter, "and the pavements, gutters, streets, steps and door-jams stained with blood. In some places it flowed down the gutters—this was mostly the blood of the military, drawn by the fire of the Natives." "Some of the balls passed through and through even the iron fire-plugs," noted another, "and many houses look like the top of a pepper-box."[1]

Most of the militia force remained on Queen Street, in the positions where Cadwalader had posted them the evening before. Exhausted and hungry, the men stopped a passing baker to buy up all his bread. But when they asked Southwark residents for water to drink, they got buckets of it dumped on their heads instead. "The women were the worst," Cadwalader later recalled. Colonel Page—who later claimed to have gone twenty-four hours without sitting—could sense "a deep seated feeling of hostility . . . in the breasts of the citizens of Southwark," and he feared a renewal of combat. A man taunted the troops: "If we had got the cannon turned in Fifth street in time enough," he boasted, "we would have knocked thunder out of you." When Colonel John Jones ventured outside the military's lines to purchase a coffin for Sergeant Guyer, a man threatened him so convincingly that Jones hurried back to his men as quickly as he could.[2]

Back in the city, Major General Patterson did what he could, gathering food and all the ammunition cartridges then ready in the arsenal, promising to have more prepared. But he had no more troops to send, having committed every available man in his division the previous night. Lacking even enough to guard the supplies he was sending to Southwark, Patterson organized an escort of civilian police, commanded by former city mayor John Swift. "I am engaged every minute trying to rally & form the Citizens," he wrote Cadwalader, and explained that express trains were heading to Harrisburg and Washington in the hopes of reinforcement. For the time being, however, all he could offer was praise, telling Cadwalader that "your conduct is approved of so far as I hear by the friends of order."[3]

Cadwalader transferred four prisoners to Swift's police and sent his wounded troops, escorted by cavalry, to the city hospital, a mile northwest of St. Philip's. They arrived around 6 A.M. Guyer was the only militiaman to have died in the fighting itself, but another twenty-four militiamen had been wounded, seven of them severely. Several of the worst wounds had been the result of the same surprise blast that had decapitated Guyer. Two militia horses had also perished in the battle. Cadwalader's aide William Bradford had escaped injury, but when he returned to the city to deliver a message to Patterson, he collapsed with exhaustion. A doctor diagnosed fever and dysentery.[4]

Casualties among civilians were less certain, since wounded rioters, and the families of the dead, had reason to hide their participation. Levin's *Sun* published an extra with an imaginative account of the battle, claiming that the troops had repeatedly fled from one position to another while scarcely harming their armed antagonists, called "citizens" by the paper. Conversely, nativists could exaggerate the suffering of innocents. The *Native American*, for instance, reported that Maria Lyle had been "shot dead whilst standing in her own door with a child in her arms." She had, in fact, been wounded, but she had been at a friend's house, was holding no child, and would live another thirty years. Still, the magnitude of the suffering is suggested by one list that included eight killed, four mortally wounded, and eighteen with trauma ranging from gunshot wounds through both legs to the bayonet tear in Thomas Grover's coat, the result of his rough handling before the troops' first fire. Most of those listed were men who might well have been fighting the troops, but two women were wounded, and an elderly man was killed, as was a German journeyman leather dresser who had the bad judgment to stick his head out of his garret window to see what was happening. A musket ball or round shot from a cannon spattered his blood and brains onto his employer's roof.[5]

At the hospital, Dr. Norris, who had amputated Augustus Peale's arm in May, was again ready with his saw. Versed in the latest findings of European military surgery, Norris and his colleagues knew they could not save the arm of Private James Crawford of the Washington Artillery, so they amputated it at the shoulder. When they came to nineteen-year-old William Manning, however, they hesitated. In its first volley, the militia had shot Manning through both thighs, the musket ball fracturing his left femur. Surgical experience dictated amputation, but noting Manning's "youth, temperate habits, and good constitution," they took the risk of trying to save the leg. In this case, the gamble paid off, for Manning retained both life and limb. Thomas Street, age forty-five, also kept his leg, despite having been shot through the knee during the same first volley that wounded Manning. Doctors would give him opium for the pain, and eventually he would walk again. James Barr, John Huested, and James Tully were easier cases. All had been shot in their arms, but they had suffered mere flesh wounds, and all would recover.[6]

Others fared less well. Militiaman Henry Troutman and civilian James Linsenbigler had both been wounded in the groin. Though they both made it to the hospital alive, they each would die that Monday. Two more civilians—thirty-two-year-old Elijah Jester and twenty-five-year-old Edward Lyon—found their way to the hospital. Lyon had been shot Sunday afternoon while showing off the musket he had seized from Private Gallagher of the Montgomery Hibernia Greens. The ball had entered the front of his arm and traveled all the way to his shoulder. Jester had been wounded Sunday evening, hit in the throat by a spent ball, fired by either the militia or the rioters. Neither would survive. Reporting Lyon's death, the *Catholic Herald* detected evidence of "a superintending and just Providence." The *Daily Chronicle* spoke just as ill of Jester, whom it named as the lad who had torched Vauxhall Garden a quarter century before. A correspondent of the *Ledger* insisted that Jester had been hit with an irregularly shaped slug, the kind of ammunition used by mobs, not militia.[7]

At the State House, not far from the hospital, Mayor Scott convened the usual Philadelphia gentlemen—Sheriff McMichael, William Meredith of the select council, and the like—to deliberate on what to do. With Patterson having sent all available troops into battle the previous evening, they had few fresh forces to command. McMichael, his deputy, and Scott had all tried to recruit a force of civilian volunteers, but, unsurprisingly, they had failed to find many men willing to face cannon with nothing more than bludgeons and the sheriff's best wishes. And few militiamen not already on duty were reporting. The group dispatched a messenger to Washington to ask that the president order the US Army's Flying Artillery—commanded by Cadwalader's cousin, Samuel Ringgold—to Philadelphia. While the messenger waited in Baltimore for crews to fire up a special locomotive to take him to the capital, someone had the bright idea to transmit the gist of his request using a new invention: nativist Samuel F. B. Morse's magnetic telegraph. The Washington-Baltimore telegraph line, the first in the country, had been installed just weeks before, and now it performed perfectly, getting the news to Washington faster than any locomotive. As it turned out, President John Tyler denied the request for army troops, judging it inappropriate for city officials to request federal aid; only the governor could do that. Nevertheless, observers agreed that the new invention was a marvel, and that a fuller network could allow troops to reach future trouble spots even faster.[8]

It was easier to get federal help through personal connections. McMichael begged Captain George Ramsay of the US Army's Philadelphia arsenal for five hundred stand of arms, as well as a thousand rounds of cannon ammunition and ten thousand musket cartridges. "An armed mob is gathering on all sides," he warned, "& we are without the means of defense unless we can get aid from you." Ramsay seems not to have issued any weapons, but he did supply McMichael with 6,460 musket cartridges, 231 cannon cartridges, and 5,000 musket flints, all of which were later deducted from Pennsylvania's annual quota of militia supplies authorized by Congress.[9]

At this point, Charles Jack appeared, as he always seemed to in times of nativist trouble. Jack suggested that rather than reinforce the troops, the civil authorities should withdraw them. Southwark was so angry, he argued, "that their removal was indispensable to peace and the preservation of the church." As before, McMichael was reluctant to listen to the representative of a self-appointed committee. Likewise, judges Joel Jones and Edward King insisted that "self constituted committees from the Wharton market, or mob meetings, were in no way regarded by the Court as fit persons to treat with," and they ordered Jack out of their courtroom. But Jack was both a trusted nativist leader and had served as a member of McMichael's posse, so perhaps he was the best person to make peace. Eventually the Philadelphia authorities agreed to negotiate.[10]

On Scott's request, Jack found a cab and traveled to the Southwark Commissioners' Hall, where he found "an immense meeting of the citizens." Angry residents had been gathering since nine o'clock, and tempers rose with the temperature, on its way to eighty-two degrees. Flags flew at half mast or shrouded in crape. Weccacoe Hose men collected money to bury their comrade John Cook, as well as another body they could not identify. "I know I'll be buried and wrapped up in the American flag," Cook had boasted the night before. That morning, he was.[11]

Others prepared to fight on. Rumor had it that while the militia had seized two cannon, their enemies now had seventeen. The *Sun* ran an extra claiming that "Many thousand citizens are arming themselves with plenty of ammunition, guns, cannons & c., with a determination to resist until the military be withdrawn." George Roberts, back in Southwark after counting cannon flashes the night before, doubted that the cannon were more than tall tales "passed from one to another, to enable them to keep their cowardly courage up," but he could not be sure. The nativists had, in fact, retained at least one cannon, which a group wheeled about on a dray cart to keep it out of the hands of the troops. One of the men pulling it was Lemuel Paynter Jr., who had been reported dead. "Lem, you're not killed after all," exclaimed a friend. "Oh the murderers," Paynter replied. "We'll give them hell to eat before tonight." Such boasts were common. At a nearby grog shop, Nativists had erected a tall flagstaff with a banner reading, "Native American Head Quarters." Inside, Roberts observed, a "room was filled with men drunk, uttering curses, blasphemy and vulgarity in every imaginable form of words." Some were trying to recruit an army: "Who will be one of five hundred to go and attack the bloody murderers!" At the Wharton Market, men boasted that they could shoot as well as any man in uniform, but they hated the idea of fighting fellow Americans. "Now the Irish can sit down and laugh at natives shooting each other down," one lamented. "Damn the sons of bitches, let's us kill every mother's son of them!" "Yes," others responded, "let's kill the damned Catholics!"[12]

Discussions in the Commissioners' Hall were only slightly more temperate. Some speakers counseled calm, but they were followed by angry shouters. The commissioners themselves formally resolved that "the continuing of the military force now in this District has a tendency to keep in existence the present excitement, and that if the troops now occupying the public streets of Southwark, are not withdrawn, there will be probably an additional shedding of blood." Jack buttonholed two Southwark aldermen and then got the crowd to agree to a deal: the troops would pull out if the civil authorities would take possession of the church and protect it from further harm.[13]

Eventually, the Southwark meetings resolved to send twenty-five men to Cadwalader's headquarters next to St. Philip's. Cadwalader refused to negotiate, telling them they would have to find Major General Patterson, his superior officer. Another delegation, led by prominent nativists Peter

Sken Smith and Lemuel Paynter Sr., found Patterson at his headquarters, in the city's Girard Bank. They warned of "terrible consequences" were the troops to remain in Southwark. Patterson initially refused to yield any ground. He had reinforcements coming in from other counties, he warned, "and no menaces could induce him to withdraw the troops." Then he softened, perhaps at McMichael's urging. Patterson allowed that his objective was to "preserve peace, and not to retain possession of any church or dwelling" that civil authorities could protect, and Southwark's aldermen in return pledged a posse of five hundred Southwark men to protect the church. With that assurance, Patterson ordered his troops to withdraw from Southwark. While a messenger brought Patterson's orders to Cadwalader, Charles Jack announced the settlement to "thunders of applause" at the Commissioners' Hall.[14]

At 2:30 P.M., on this hot July afternoon, Cadwalader led his exhausted men north. One soldier was so fatigued that he collapsed and had to be sent home in a cab. But the others proceeded to the state arsenal, where Cadwalader could stash not only his own artillery, but also the cannon captured during the night. A furniture wagon carried the small arms seized first from the church by Ardis's committee, and then from the Commissioners' Hall by troops determined to keep them away from the mob.[15]

Philadelphia City, at least, was secure. Throughout the afternoon, troops from other parts of Pennsylvania arrived, reporting for duty to Major General Patterson. As he had in May, Governor Porter himself hurried from Harrisburg to provide whatever political and legal authority the general might need. Into the evening, horse and foot patrols clattered through the city. The city's theaters closed, and residents instead entertained themselves with talk of the battle to the south. A messenger arrived in Germantown to report the deaths of Guyer and Troutman; the suddenly widowed Mrs. Troutman fainted at the news. Southwark's fate remained uncertain. Despite the negotiations, Cadwalader had left the church before Southwark's aldermen arrived to take charge of it. Fortunately, other Southwark notables stepped in, and what was left of St. Philip's was again placed in the hands of more or less the same men who had held it before Cadwalader's arrival the previous evening. Thomas Grover again intervened. To deter further vandalism of the church, he pledged to pay personally for any damages to it.[16]

Perhaps Cadwalader had made a point, but he had not secured any territory. And the peace—or "armistice," as one newspaper called it—was uneasy. In the adjacent district of Moyamensing, an alderman persuaded a crowd of men and boys to stop wheeling a cannon toward the Catholic church, though he had more trouble getting them to stop throwing stones. The *New York Daily Herald*'s correspondent gaped at the dead and wounded in the Southwark Commissioners' Hall and listened to men swear revenge against Cadwalader and his officers. He reported—mistakenly—that Captain Scott had died—as well as the rumor that 1,200 Kensington Natives were marching down the Jersey shore to the lower ferry to stage an amphibious invasion of Southwark. At the Wharton Market, a reporter listened as men "openly avowed their determination to burn St. Philip de Neri." "They were," he reported, "of the riotous class."[17]

Even before the troops' departure, Southwark nativists were looting Irish stores and beating Irishmen they found on the street. Around 8 A.M., a mob of about 150 men approached the Southwark home of Mordecai Cullen, an Irish Catholic immigrant. Cullen was somewhat relieved to see a neighbor, with whom he was on good terms, among the three men who came to his door, but another man, a stranger, was less friendly. He demanded Cullen's guns and, after Cullen had handed over his double-barreled shotgun, insisted on searching the house, turning over mattresses and sheets. When Cullen's wife produced the parts of an old gun that had been left in the attic, the stranger accused Cullen of bursting the gun while "firing at the Natives last night." The mob confiscated both the shotgun and the wreck, leaving Cullen and his family shaking in the kitchen. James McCann fared worse; also suspected of having a gun in his house, he was pulled outside and beaten by a mob. Another Irishman, James O'Neil, had the courage or foolishness to appear at St. Philip's itself. The mob knocked him down and kicked him in the mouth, breaking his jaw in two places. The old, consumptive sexton of St. Philip's was beaten as well. On the corners, groups of women shouted encouragement to the mob.[18]

Some expected another battle against the troops. Panicked Philadelphians fled to Baltimore where they spread rumors that the mob had seized the city, that Cadwalader had fled, and that Patterson was mortally wounded. The *United States Gazette* speculated that had Cadwalader not withdrawn, he would have been attacked by a force of three thousand armed men commanding six cannon and every round of ammunition in Southwark. Natives claimed to have officers and well-drilled troops. The *Sun* imagined a citizenry armed with "a large number of chains, pieces of pig lead, about a cart load of grape shot, and canisters of musket balls, besides 900 muskets and more than a dozen heavy field pieces." The *Spirit of the Times* claimed that Southwark blacksmiths were cutting iron into slugs for the cannon, and casting bullets. According to one rumor, a nativist schooner lay at anchor in the Delaware, ready to land cannon in Southwark to repel another militia invasion. More elaborately, some claimed they had plans to float nine kegs of gunpowder on batteaux down the sewer to a spot beneath the troops, so they could have "blown the soldiers to hell." William Springer suggested firing sulfur at the troops to suffocate them. One reporter likened the relative repose to that of a beast of prey that has fed and grown "temporarily averse to violent exertion." Militia officers were equally ready for renewed battle. Officially, Patterson ordered his men to return their ammunition to Captain Mallory, the chief of ordnance, but he quietly told some trusted officers to take ammunition home with them, in case another riot should break out.[19]

And yet the peace held. David Ford, who had searched the church on Friday and witnessed the shooting on Sunday, returned to the scene on Monday and saw only "knots of people standing about, talking of what had been done." Alderman McKinley confiscated the one cannon that the cavalry had failed to find; later he returned it to the *Venice*. If it was fired at all on Monday, it was likely in salute to John Cook's funeral procession. By evening, a few hundred people remained on Queen Street, a few engaged in "somewhat belligerent conversation," but most gawking at the scars left by musket and cannon fire. The church itself was guarded by men whose authority took the form of white printed badges pinned to their coats. That sufficed.[20]

On Tuesday, July 9, Philadelphians began to grapple with the greatest violence their city had seen since the Revolution. Troops continued to arrive from several other counties. By July 10, at least 1,200 soldiers occupied Philadelphia, about half of them from the city and districts and the other half from Philadelphia County and elsewhere. Newspapers inflated the number to six thousand. "Our city and suburbs are now a garrison," noted the *Public Ledger*. "Military companies are continually arriving from distant counties, to relieve those of our own and the adjoining counties; and we exhibit to a stranger almost every appearance of a town besieged, or threatened with an attack from an invading army."[21]

Once again, the Girard Bank became military headquarters. Hecklers gathered to denounce Governor Porter for authorizing the Dunn brothers to requisition muskets for St. Philip's church, "one of the most monstrous deeds that was ever committed by any man having pretentions to sanity." In response, sentries ordered passersby off the sidewalk at the point of bayonet, and city police broke up groups of more than two. Patterson ordered his troops not to discuss religion or politics with any civilians. "The soldier knows no sect or party," he reminded them, "it being his duty, simply to assist in maintaining the laws supporting the government." While some Philadelphians mocked the troops who marched or rode through the city for "playing soldiers all day," a more sympathetic observer noted that it was no easy duty to stay in the saddle for hours in what he exaggerated as 110-degree heat. Each evening, Cadwalader drilled his brigade in the State House Yard. The city councils offered other parks as parade grounds.[22]

But no soldiers patrolled Southwark. On July 9, a nativist boasted that the troops dared not return. "There is scarcely a house in the immediate vicinity of the battle-ground occupied by Native citizens, but is well prepared for defence," he warned, "and from which destruction would be poured into the ranks of the military." Not only were the native-born residents of Southwark "maddened to an extent you can little imagine," he also claimed they were extremely well armed, with twenty cannon, four thousand muskets, and plenty of ammunition. "Even the women are armed, urging bitter retaliation against the military for the wanton and unnecessary destruction of life." When a lone member of the City Guards wandered into the district, a group of men chased him out, threatening to kill him. Even soldiers' families had to evacuate the district. A correspondent of the *Liberator*, presumably an abolitionist with some experience of mob violence, lamented that "The mob is now supreme, and Southwark and her citizens have virtually declared themselves independent of the State of Pennsylvania." The *Spirit of the Times* agreed that "the Rioters have triumphed and that the Law, abandoned by the people, has confessed its weakness, and surrendered the victory to its antagonists! We are now, in plain words, living under mob rule." It suggested that Governor Porter order a reoccupation of Southwark to seize arms, arrest rioters, and end "the rebellion."[23]

Far from planning another invasion of Southwark, Major General Patterson fretted about maintaining the fragile peace with the forces he had. Cadwalader's First Brigade was crumbling. One colonel—Pleasonton—was seriously wounded, while the other—Murray—lay "extremely ill." Other brigade officers were ill, had resigned their commissions, or were facing charges for neglect of duty. The Montgomery Hibernia Greens had been effectively obliterated. The company's members had survived their retreat from Southwark, and Colahan tried to muster them again. "Whether they are so much injured from wounds and bruises, or feared to be killed before they could assemble en masse," he despairingly reported, "none came."[24]

Southwark had separated the true fighters from the tin soldiers, but it would take time to rebuild the brigade. In the meantime, Patterson feared an attack on any of three federal institutions: the Navy Yard, the Frankford Arsenal, or the Schuylkill Arsenal. Lightly guarded and rich in munitions, any of these could have been the target of a successful raid. No one tried, but someone threaded twelve feet of rope, saturated in saltpeter, among the timbers of the main railroad bridge over the Schuylkill River. Had the enormous slow match been lit, it could have disrupted the arrival of troops from western Pennsylvania. But it was discovered and given to Governor Porter, who showed it off to the press. Another potential target was the Moyamensing Prison, where men charged with the Southwark rioting were confined. Fearing a prison break, the militia told the guards there to fire rockets if they needed assistance. On the evening of Saturday, July 13, two rockets shot into the sky. Cavalrymen galloped through the streets, their spurs rattling, while infantrymen hurriedly donned their uniforms and loaded their muskets. When the troops arrived, they found the prison sedate; the rockets had been set off by Southwark pranksters who had learned of the signal.[25]

Even the smallest provocation could set people on edge. Hearing hoofbeats, a reporter expected cavalry, then was relieved to see a group of ladies and gentlemen returning from an evening ride. A sailor, getting drunk in a tavern, bragged to his brother that he would challenge a soldier to a fight; if he whipped the soldier, then all troops would have to depart the city. In ordinary times, a boast like that would be overlooked, or at worst earn the braggart a fine. But these were not ordinary times, and the two brothers were imprisoned for weeks, until a ship captain offered the sailor a place on his brig, which was ready to sail that day. When an explosion rang out in Independence Hall, a woman collapsed, and people ran to her aid, thinking she had been shot. They were about to seize her apparent assailant when she realized she had only been hit by the cork of a ginger-pop bottle that opened with an unusually loud bang.[26]

In fact, the people of Southwark were done with large-scale fighting. When reporters walked through the district on the evening of Tuesday the ninth, they found no large meetings of insurgents, only amused residents sitting at doors and windows to escape the heat. A posse occupied St. Philip's throughout Monday the eighth and Tuesday the ninth, but on Wednesday the tenth, authorities warned members of the congregation that they would not protect it past four o'clock that afternoon. After consulting with Bishop Kenrick, the congregation agreed to retake custody of the church, managing the transfer without incident. The district authorities dismissed their five hundred volunteer police, leaving one watchman to guard the church during the day, and a second at night. Workmen hurried to repair the worst of the damage.[27]

Father Dunn was gone. During the riots, he had taken shelter in the home of Protestant couple who lived not far from the church. The husband, Paul Field, was a close friend of Dunn's, and though he was serving in McMichael's posse during the riot, his wife insisted that Dunn hide with them until the danger passed. Then, with the fighting over, Kenrick advised him to leave town, possibly to go as far as St. Louis, where Kenrick's brother Peter presided as bishop. Kenrick himself remained in Philadelphia, not without some apprehensions for his own safety. On Sunday, July 14, just a week after the battle, the assistant pastor of St. Philip's celebrated Mass in a packed church. The *Catholic Herald* suggested a prayer: "Father, forgive them—for they know what they do!"[28]

In addition to attracting worshipers, the church, like the scenes of fighting in Kensington before, became a draw for tourists. They could marvel at the bullet scars in the trees, doors, and windows of Queen Street. Of course, Southwark remained Southwark, and "three respectable young looking men" were chased away from the church by "a number of rowdies" who took them to be members of a rival fire company. Riot tourism was safer in Philadelphia City. Nativists—including smiling ladies—could visit the Chinese Museum for a close look at the Temple of Liberty, the miniature ships, and other objects from the July 4 parade, enhanced in the evening by band music, gaslight, and exceptional ice cream. For devout nativists, the most sacred object was "the torn flag" that Shiffler had allegedly clutched as he died. As they took their turns fingering it, a mother admonished her daughter, "Now, Margaret, remember you have touched the flag which was defended by the life's blood of a poor young man, whose only offence was carrying that flag at a peaceable meeting of his countrymen." (Catholics and their allies responded with their own flag libel, trading rumors that the Southwark rioters had seized American flags and used them as wadding for their cannon.)[29]

At the hospital, doctors continued to treat the wounded. Two nineteen-year-old boys—Thomas Saunders and David Kithcart—had made it to the hospital after being wounded during their fight against the militia on July 7. Saunders had been shot through the chest, the ball likely ripping through his left lung. He died on the ninth. Kithcart's abdomen had been split open by a large musket ball, allowing his intestines to spill out. Doctors cleaned him up as best they could and reinserted the guts, but Kithcart developed peritonitis and died on the tenth. Elijah Jester, shot in the throat on Sunday, died on Friday the twelfth. This brought the official total death toll to thirteen: two soldiers and eleven civilians. Perhaps the true toll was higher. The *Spirit of the Times* accused the rioters of having "concealed most of their killed and wounded." Conversely, the two dead militiamen—Guyer and Troutman—were buried quite publicly on July 10, in what may have been the best-attended funerals to date in Germantown. Their comrades in the Germantown Blues escorted each to the grave. As the *Telegraph* noted, the entire First Division would likely have attended as well, had most of its units not still been needed to patrol Philadelphia.[30]

Other victims of the fighting recuperated. On the advice of a military surgeon, Colonel Pleasonton sought "quietude and repose" in Baltimore, as well as treatment by the prominent surgeon Charles Bell Gibson, who prescribed poultices and bed rest. "I have suffered and am still suffering a good deal of pain," the colonel wrote Cadwalader, but he felt "very proud of the noble bearing of my regiment" during its fight against adversaries he had the grace, through his pain, to call "our misguided fellow citizens." He was harsher in his letter to his regiment, charging the enemy with "seeking every shelter in alleys, blind passages, on the roofs of houses, and in the cross streets, from your fire, [while they] discharged their cannon with slow matches retreating from the explosion into darkness and obscurity; and fired their muskets from their concealments." He praised his men for standing by their guns and quietly closing ranks as men around them fell. Outnumbered and on unfamiliar ground, they had, he assured them, "defended that post with a gallantry, that will carry far into future time, the fame of the Citizen Soldier." Pleasonton gradually recovered, though he appears not to have resumed his diary. Despite a musket ball still lodged in his back, Captain Scott was, by the twenty-first, able to take a few steps out of bed. He retreated to his parents' home in Bristol, Pennsylvania, for what would prove a long convalescence.[31]

On July 11, his seventy-seventh birthday, former president and current congressman John Quincy Adams passed through on his way from Washington, to his Massachusetts home. Judging Philadelphia to be "yet in an amphibious state between mob and martial law," the statesman caught the first train to New York. As the city's financial markets all but shut down, a panicked *United States Gazette* assured its out-of-town readers that the riot had taken place not in Philadelphia proper, but in Southwark, a separate jurisdiction. "The shipping, the counting houses, and the stores, are far away from the scene of disturbance," it explained on July 11, "and those in the city who do not choose to have part in the matter, may he as exempt from any care or trouble, as if the riot had taken place in Baltimore." The *Daily Chronicle* promised that "business men and others need not . . . hesitate a moment to give us an opportunity to welcome them among us." Prospective visitors were not convinced. Father Theobald Mathew, the Irish Catholic temperance leader whom Levin had once praised, cancelled his planned visit. "Recent calamitous occurrences in Philadelphia have blighted all my hopes," he explained to an American correspondent. "Since I heard the fearful details ... I can speak or write or think of nothing but churches in flames and streets flowing with blood."[32]

Troops, on the other hand, continued to arrive, parading smartly through the streets. "Many people wonder what the military are on duty for, when all is quiet," noted the *Chronicle*. "We think they should be continued where they are, as long as it is possible. They can do no harm, and may do much good." The force peaked at 1,780 men on July 15, and by July 17, the adjutant general was telling troops from other counties not to come; he had all the men he needed. At the Girard Bank, hecklers were replaced by peaceful citizens eager to hear the impromptu choral concerts by German troops in the courtyard. Other troops took advantage of the free entrance offered them by the city's museums. If soldiers were spending their days singing and sightseeing, perhaps it was time for them to go home, and over the next few days, Major General Patterson dismissed them by the hundreds. On July 22, more than two weeks after the riot, Patterson officially informed the governor of "a cessation of disorder within the bounds of the City and County of Philadelphia." Patterson himself felt confident enough to leave the city for a week at Cape May, though he took care to authorize Cadwalader to act without further orders during his absence, just in case. Philadelphia returned to its ordinary levels of mayhem. Rival fire companies still fired pistols in the street. A member of the Mechanic Rifles brought his loaded weapon home, intending to remove the ball. Before he could find the right tool, his sixteen-year-old cousin started playing with the gun and, thinking it unloaded, fatally shot another cousin, a twenty-three-year-old blacksmith.[33]

If the nativists had any fight left in them, they might have been expected to show it on July 12, the anniversary of the Battle of the Boyne and the most important day in the Orange calendar. As it turned out, the worst violence took place far to the north, in Montreal, where—reports had it—a brawl between Orangemen and Catholics knocked over some scaffolding, injuring several. Philadelphia avoided such rows. Most remarkably, at the end of July, Kensington hosted a truly peaceable meeting of nativists, as the Native American Association of Third Ward, Kensington, gathered at the very same vacant lot at the corner of Second and Master where it had battled immigrants during those terrible days in May. Once again, William

Craig had organized the event, and once again, he had persuaded leading nativists—a John Wise of Lancaster as well as Rev. John Perry—to offer uncompromising defenses of the Native platform and jabs at the pope. Even Peter Albright, one of the May combatants, was given a chance to speak.[34]

The nativists were as offensive as ever. "Catholicism," shouted Wise, "defies all law and order, making by its tenets obligatory on the members of that church to uproot protestantism as heretical, by any and every means in their power, not stopping even at that of murder." Albright boasted that he could speak "without the fear of the murderous rifle of a concealed foe." "They dare not show themselves," he said to cheers, for if they did, "the Natives would rise *en masse*, in their majesty, and assert their rights!" For a moment it looked like there might be trouble. As one nativist newspaper reported, "there were several riotous demonstrations manifested by a number of *flat skulls*, who had mixed in with the orderly disposed persons. The Natives kept their temper, requested them to be quiet or leave the ground. There was much loud talking but no blows were struck." At the end of the meeting, the Natives went quietly home. Back in the city, the band stopped at the building housing the *Daily Sun* and the *American Advocate*—just launched as the city's third nativist daily newspaper—to play "The Star-Spangled Banner."[35]

A month after the fighting on Queen Street, Philadelphia was, on the surface, peaceful again. "The glittering bayonet, the tramp of soldiery, and the display of gay, dashing uniforms have given place to the staff of the Policeman, the hurried gait of the man of business, and the plain unassuming garb of the citizen," noted the *Home Journal and Citizen Soldier*, almost regretfully. "The rumbling of artillery carriages has been substituted by rattling dray and the noisy cart, with the product of the farmer, manufacturer, and mechanic."[36]

Cartoon for George Cadwalader, 1844.
Courtesy of the Historical Society of Pennsylvania.

24

Saviors of the Homestead and Hearthstone

ighting "rebels," George Cadwalader later complained, offered "nothing to arouse those feelings of interest which are felt in an engagement with an honorable foe." But most Philadelphians were intensely interested. Within a week of the Southwark fighting, an entrepreneur had commissioned a painting by artist George Heilge, who had painted one of the ward banners for the July 4 parade. For a 12.5-cent admission fee, visitors could see "the Military charging and firing upon the mob, and the mob resisting with desperation, returning the fire from the narrow alleys, from windows and tops of houses, women running through the streets, and spectators fleeing from the scene in every direction," alongside equally dramatic battle scenes of the Revolution and the War of 1812. Beyond such spectacle, Philadelphians and other Americans pondered the broader implications of the Southwark riot. Pessimists saw evidence of the collapse of the American republic, while optimists hoped that the militia's firm stand might at last put a limit to American mobbing.[1]

Some saw only cause for despair. "We have had mobs and riots before, but none so formidable in its character as this," wrote Sidney George Fisher, using his pen name, "Cecil." He argued that Southwark was the predictable consequence of Philadelphia's tolerance of mobs, dating back at least to the 1838 destruction of Pennsylvania Hall. "The worst tyranny in the world is that of a mob," he warned, "and if the choice must be made between the despotism which provides peace, security and degradation, and the despotism which offers tumult, alarm, violence, and greater degradation, the former will be preferred." Others shared his sense of doom. The *Baptist Advocate* feared that some Philadelphians had come to believe that a majority could assemble and overturn any laws they did not like. Such notions would turn America into "a nation of rioters." Boston's *Law Reporter* warned that "a new principle of government has been practically advanced in America. . . . Its upholders declare at the mouth of the cannon and by the light of the incendiary torch that the ancient and established modes of political action have become obsolete." While the author hoped that "early training of the schoolroom" could teach Americans to govern themselves, he feared that "a people accustomed to the unrestrained freedom of the United States" would have to learn to live with a strong police force, like that already in place in London.[2]

The renewed violence was, of course, deeply embarrassing to Philadelphia's boosters, for it tarnished the city's reputation around the world. The *Liberator*, written by abolitionists who knew well the dangers of mob violence, described in detail what it termed "the Civil War in Philadelphia." The *Practical Christian* mourned that "Philadelphia, the city of brotherly love, founded in equity, charity and peace," was "now the habitation of dragons, a broken cage of wild beasts, a battle field of incarnate demons!" "English burghees and matrons," wrote the *New York Republic*, "if they do not laugh outright, they will be surely tempted to think that free institutions are a farce, or that their spirit and administration are singularly misunderstood and abused." Indeed, the *Illustrated London News* delighted in Americans' disgrace. "How fast are they proving that their Constitution is a deception!" it crowed. "It announces religious freedom to all—but burns the churches and chapels of those who hold a different faith!"[3]

Yet some who feared the mob found hope in the firm, if bloody, response by the troops during their terrible ordeal in Queen Street. Though horrified by the assault on St. Philip's, Catholics could take some comfort in the fact that a majority-Protestant militia had fought and died to defend a Catholic church. The *Freeman's Journal*'s New York correspondent, an American-born Catholic, considered Philadelphia unusually degenerate, and he would not have been shocked had it collapsed into vice. But the outcome of the July riot, especially the conduct of Cadwalader's troops, restored his faith in "the great conservative principle of our government—the moral force of public opinion," which had persuaded most Philadelphians to support the law, rather than fanatical hatred. "Although the cause at issue was that of public order against a lawless mob," an admiring Kenrick wrote Cadwalader, he praised the general's "determined action" for saving the cathedral in May, and acknowledged that Cadwalader had "exposed your valuable life for the protection of the Church of St. Philip . . . I trust and pray that your life may be long preserved, and that your example will be effectual for the maintenance of order, and the support of the national institutions." Cadwalader replied without mentioning either church, stressing instead his troops' having "protected rights guaranteed by our constitution, and by our laws."[4]

Following the Southwark battle, a few men resigned from volunteer companies out of nativist sympathies, from a wish to get home to help with the harvest, or from the realization that militia service could require deadly combat as well as parades and balls. But these "sunshine soldiers," as militia enthusiasts called them, were easily replaced as others joined. The new recruits might lack the polish of the seasoned troops they were replacing, but at least they knew what they had signed up for. So would the people of Philadelphia. "Hereafter, as they march along our streets, with banner and plume," wrote the *Daily Chronicle*, "they will be watched by bright eyes, not as holiday heroes, but as the saviours of the homestead and hearthstone." A few days later, it published a poem that insisted that Guyer and Troutman had died in a cause every bit as glorious as defeating a foreign invader. "Fell they not in an unhallowed deed," the poet explained. "They died defending liberty and laws / Religion, freedom, wept above their sod, / And bore their spirits to the throne of God!"[5]

The Spring Garden Board of Commissioners praised the troops "for the courage exhibited in standing and firing against a concealed and skulking mob of ruffians," while the Philadelphia City Council formally thanked the militia and offered condolence "to the families and the relatives of those who were slain in their praiseworthy exertions in quelling an attempt to overcome the civil authorities and prostrate the laws of our land." A volunteer committee of relief organized to collect money for a permanent fund for the wounded and for the families of the dead. Some members set up shop in Independence Hall, to accept contributions as donors came in, while others walked down Market Street, collecting cash from their fellow merchants, whose property the militia had effectively protected.[6]

Philadelphians also collected funds to honor individual militiamen who had played conspicuous parts in the fighting. In October, Captain Mallory received a sword and a set of silver pitchers, along with a speech crediting him with saving the battle by remaining at his gun after his men scattered. In December, a body of gentlemen presented a gold-mounted sword to Captain Scott, whose Cadwalader Grays had joined Hill's City Guards in the first volley of July 7, and who had been shot in the subsequent fighting. Scott, one speaker argued, had not merely saved St. Philip's; he had saved Philadelphia. Privates and noncommissioned officers got less attention, but eventually veterans of Southwark were authorized to wear red chevrons on their uniform sleeves for "having displayed exceeding good conduct and gallantry under the most disheartening circumstances." A former Pennsylvania militia officer, now residing in New York, ordered medals for wounded cavalrymen. Country troops, despite having arrived in Philadelphia too late for combat, returned home to cheers and banquets.[7]

Cadwalader himself declined, for the time being, a sword or other memento. Whatever satisfaction he might have taken in his victory was soon tempered by the sudden death of his younger brother Henry on July 27,

1844, just five months after the death of Tom, the brother between George and Henry in age. George's own Philadelphia Grays escorted the funeral.[8]

Other officers boasted of their own valor, or impugned that of their brothers in arms. One officer—rumor had it—accidentally broke his scabbard while sitting on it. Seeing an opportunity, he let it be known that the scabbard had been hit by a rioter's bullet. The bitterest dispute involved Captain Saunders of the Markle Rifles, who had failed to obey Colahan's orders in St. Philip's. Somehow, Saunders and Colahan managed to reconcile, with the latter crediting the Markles for trying to escort his men out of the church, however poorly they had defended it. But the bitterness between the Markles and the Wayne Artillery remained. The two companies had shared a position at the west side of the intersection of Third and Queen during the battle of July 7–8; one company could fire while the other reloaded. Apparently the coordination failed to meet parade-ground standards, for the experience left them sworn enemies.[9]

On July 19, in the presence of General Hubbell, the Waynes' Captain Fairlamb taunted Saunders: "You are a damned liar and your company a set of cowards!" Saunders replied with a fist to Fairlamb's nose, only to be separated from his antagonist before they could develop the fight. Eventually both men were arrested and held to $1,000 bail to keep the peace. Even then, they continued to insult each other in court testimony and in print. Fairlamb testified that as the rioters fired cannon, Saunders had left his men exposed but "had sheltered himself in a doorway to protect himself from the shot." Saunders in turn swore the Fairlamb had spent most of the battle safely indoors, emerging only to hand out cigars to his men, which had the effect of endangering everyone with their light.[10]

Some militiamen faced courts-martial for their conduct, which in several cases may have resulted from nativist troops' reluctance to fight fellow nativists. Three members of the Monroe Guards—Charles Jack's old unit—faced charges of desertion and cowardice for their behavior in Southwark, but someone recalled that the regimental court-martial assembled to try them lacked the power to adjudicate those capital offenses. Lieutenant John Bringhurst—who had helped found the Germantown Native American Association in 1837—was charged, but acquitted, of "secreting himself in a neighboring cellar" during the Southwark fight. Perhaps the most serious penalty to stick was that laid on Second Lieutenant Augustus Larrantree of the Jackson Artillery, who had paraded with the Natives on July 4 and then refused duty in Southwark. Convicted by a court-martial, he was suspended from holding a state commission for seven years. Other courts-martial were less clearly political. The *Public Ledger* noted that desertion under fire carried the death penalty. But since "the war is over now," it advised that "such heroes ought to be shot with blank cartridges, or muskets charged with sausages."[11]

Even civilians quarreled about their conduct during the fight. On August 2, Charles Jack published a graphic report of his experience of July 7, climaxing with Jack courageously exposing himself to gunfire until Judge Robert Conrad pulled him out of danger with the exclamation, "My God! Colonel, you will be killed." Conrad responded with the public announcements that his own recollections did not accord with those of Jack, who in turn wrote that he was "not at all surprised . . . that Judge Conrad should not recollect in the morning what passed between us at night." This statement—perhaps an insinuation that Conrad had been drunk—was enough for Conrad to dispatch a friend with a challenge to a duel. When Jack declined, Conrad himself appeared at Jack's door with a cowhide, with which he lashed Jack—"a small weak man" in the words of his friends—until Jack's daughter seized his arm and begged him to stop. Given that the affair began with conflicting memories of violence, it was perhaps appropriate that someone later claimed that Jack had seized the cowhide and flogged Conrad.[12]

As they had after the violence of May, Philadelphia gentlemen turned to Horace Binney to express their thoughts about public order. In an address to Governor Porter, Binney again insisted on obedience to the law and support of the troops. "They have been acting under the civil authority, in obedience to its commands," he wrote. "They were *citizens*, and only *citizens*, using the lawful force which unlawful force made necessary." Eventually around two thousand Philadelphians signed on.[13]

"Every good citizen who desires to see the laws faithfully enforced," insisted the *Home Journal and Citizen Soldier*, "must step forward at this crisis, and support the military." Civilian papers agreed. The *Public Ledger* defended the troops, praising "the citizen soldiery . . . the hard-working mechanics . . . the honest yeomanry, who had left their firesides, their wives and their little ones, and come forward in defence of their country, their liberty, and their laws." "How many soldiers must have their ribs broken," it asked, "how many have their arms wrested from them, how many commanders be knocked down and stabbed by their own swords, before they must fire on the mob?" Nor did the troops' involvement represent any departure from civil government. "Every soldier was a special constable," it explained, "with a staff of iron instead of wood; for the law, not being able to strike hard enough with the wood, was compelled to strike with the iron." The *North American* and the *Philadelphia Gazette*, despite their nativist leanings, also approved the militia's conduct as the only alternative to mob rule.[14]

In these accounts, Cadwalader was the hero of the day. "It is easy to censure an officer who takes the responsibility of ordering troops to fire on a mob," noted the *New-York Tribune*, "but somebody *must* take it at last, if Law is to be upheld." The author of a long account published in the *Pennsylvanian* lauded the general "whose eye never flinched and whose heart never failed during two sleepless days of conflict, but who was ever at his post to direct the efforts of his soldiers, and to mitigate their sufferings," despite the gunfire aimed at him. If he were now insulted rather than honored, the writer warned, "farewell to the hopes of this young and great republic." At a Brooklyn gathering of militia officers from Massachusetts, New York, and New Jersey, a colonel proposed a toast to "Brig. Gen. Cadwalader, the *first* militia Gen[eral] who *dared* to fire on a Riotous Mob." The party exploded with agreement. "Three times three!" the officers yelled in response. Then, "one more!"[15]

Some observers were especially impressed by the militiamen's willingness to fight fellow Philadelphians. While a New Orleans newspaper feared that "the volunteers and militia of the city are not to be relied upon, on account either of sympathy with the rioters or aversion to fire upon a crowd in which are mingled probably their relatives, associates and friends," the *Boston Times* praised the "moral courage" of the men who had obeyed "the most painful duty that ever fell to the lot of a citizen soldiery . . . by shooting down their own fellow citizens."[16]

The good news, some hoped, was that mobs would no longer think they could act with impunity. "We now know where we are," the *Ledger* assured its readers. In 1831, G. N. Steuart, a Maryland militia general, had been ordered to suppress a railroad strike. He himself had managed to arrest dozens of angry men without violence, but he did not think that would always be possible. "It is most humane to fire as soon as circumstances justify it," he now advised. "The postponement of the 'only remedy' even for an unlucky moment, *does harm*, by encouraging the rioters to *greater* excesses, which after all, have to be stopped with perhaps a greater shedding of blood than was requisite at first."[17]

Not everyone believed that the militia's fire had been necessary. James Morrow, a medical student who attended some of the wounded at the hospital, condemned the "demagogue adventurers" who had stirred up trouble in Southwark. Yet he also faulted Cadwalader, believing that the crowd on Queen Street could not possibly have dispersed in the time between his warnings and the first fire; the people closest to the troops would have been hemmed in by those farther away, who had not heard the order. He lamented the deaths of "curious & silly spectators."[18]

Some nativists sought to present the Southwark violence not as a riot but rather as an act of "the people" asserting their will in the tradition of republican self-government. The *American Advocate* wrote of the "battle of Queen Street" and the "Battle of Southwark," conferring military dignity on both sides of the struggle. If others wanted to say that the men who fought the militia were rioters and rebels, the paper suggested they were the rightful heirs of the "rioters" of the Boston Tea Party and the "rebels" of Lexington and Concord. Such analogies, of course, turned Cadwalader's troops into redcoats. The *Advocate* attacked the militia as the kind of "standing army" about which Anglo-American philosophers had been warning since the seventeenth century.[19]

Nativists mocked the honors offered to militia commanders. "Our citizens," wrote the *American Advocate*, "have found time and money to present gingerbread heroes with gold-hilted swords, for valor which displayed itself in nothing more than a soldierly strut and fearless 'Oh, damme!'" The nativist ladies of Southwark crafted a slier riposte, ordering a gorgeously bound Bible for Charles Naylor, in recognition of his "timely interference" with the militia on July 6. On behalf of the "immense mass of females" present, Lewis Levin presented the Bible to Naylor at Third and Queen

Streets, where Guyer and Troutman had fallen to Nativist cannon fire. "What a contrast there is between this present and the presentation of a sword," remarked the *American Advocate*. A Bible "contains a balm for the wounded spirit," while the sword "is made to draw blood."[20]

"I have no fault to find with the conduct of the privates," wrote one Southwark nativist, who had been briefly arrested. "They merely obeyed orders." Rather, he disparaged their commander, the French-born Brigadier General Roumfort, for both a false arrest and the use of language "of most vulgar and blasphemous character." The nativist *American Woman* mocked Captain Scott's speech upon accepting a sword in recognition of his service in Southwark as a combination of "braggadocio, tasteless bluster, and gnat-like malignancy."[21]

Along with the highest praise, Cadwalader attracted the greatest scorn. Nativists argued that Cadwalader should never have marched to Southwark, since it was his arrival that sparked the worst violence. Thomas Grover claimed—improbably—that had the military not fired on July 7, he could have cleared the streets around the church in fifteen minutes. John Dutton, a member of the posse that searched the church, complained of "the haughty, overbearing manner of the military," which, he believed, inflamed the crowd on Sunday evening. A Lancaster newspaper accused the general of "insulting unarmed citizens in the public streets and ordering them to be shot down like dogs," and ordering the killing of prisoners. Best of all, an anonymous critic, who signed himself "Lieut. Col. James Gruff Charcoal, Colonel Commandant of the Night-Hawk Indian Flying Artillery," sent Cadwalader a crude cartoon, showing the general, alone and on horseback, behind a cannon belching fire. The drawing was "Dedicated to Brigadier General George Cadwalader for his Chivalrous Valor, and Military Glory, Achieved by Him, in the Firm, Courageous, and Dignified Method of Suppressing an Unarmed Body of American Citizens by Firing Upon Them on The Afternoon of Sunday July the Seventh A.D. 1844." Cadwalader carefully preserved it in his files.[22]

Militiamen reacted angrily to the nativists' attacks. Soon after the fighting, the *Home Journal and Citizen Soldier* had insisted that "a man sitting calmly and quietly down in his workshop or his parlor" should not pass judgment unless he could "place himself in imagination in the heat of the battle, he must live for the time being amid the din and confusion of the scene, the thunder of artillery and the rattling of musketry, he must listen to the shouts of an infuriated mob, the shrieking of the wounded, the groans of the dying, the whistling of bullets and missiles of every description, and see his own comrades falling around him." The volunteers, they argued, "are the people—the farmer, mechanic, merchant, laborer, property holder and tax payer." Far from taking sides in a domestic conflict, they constituted "the only organized body of men in our country that has never been united for the purpose of defeating some political party or for their own advancement." "We should much like to know whether the Natives are for us or against us."[23]

For us. Perhaps realizing that it would be self-defeating to continue to attack so popular an institution, Natives instead made peace with the militia. Only days after warning the militia from reentering Southwark, the *Native American* claimed that "not a word was uttered against the military as a body," most of whom had "behaved like men and nobly." One nativist ward association praised "the military for the courageous and noble manner in which they performed their duties upon that unexampled and trying occasion," while condemning "the recent riotous and murderous proceedings of a lawless mob" which, it insisted, had no connection to the Native American Party. Another writer argued that the officers should have given more warning before opening fire. Yet he praised the troops for their "intentions and their sacrifices," their "firmness and moral courage."[24]

While the Southwark clash created some bad blood between volunteers and Natives, considerable mutual attraction remained. By late July, the *Sun* and the *American Advocate* were boasting that many militiamen were viewing nativist relics at the Chinese Museum, and perhaps considering becoming American Republicans themselves. Not long after that, the *Advocate* claimed that two-thirds of militiamen "are strong Natives." It might continue to criticize Cadwalader and other commanders, but, it promised, "we are not opposed to the *rank and file*; most of them are good natives, and some of the officers, too." Indeed, Peter Fritz—who had run against Cadwalader for brigadier general in 1842—had been speaking at Nativist meetings since at least June, and continued to do so into the fall.[25]

Even before the July fighting, Southwark men had established a nascent Native American Rifle Company. At the time of the July 4 parade, they had not yet gotten their full uniforms, so they marched in civilian suits and "half bell" caps "with pompoons four inches high, tipped with red, white and blue." They did not, however, turn out to take part in the July fighting—perhaps just as well for all involved. By September, though, thirty-six Southwark men paraded as the Native American Rifle Corps, this time fully equipped. Marching in gray uniforms with yellow trimmings and those tricolor pompons on their caps, "they appeared exceedingly well drilled" to the *Public Ledger*. Philadelphia's militia now had both Irish and Native companies.[26]

The most explicit debate over the proper role of the militia concerned a proposal to maintain a force specifically for suppressing disorder. As one of Cadwalader's officers observed, the battle had demonstrated the value of the volunteers to those who had previously mocked them as "mere popinjay soldiers." But it had also shown the fragility of existing arrangements: "the whole disposable force of the city and county, that could be collected, were centered upon, and together were scarcely able to defend, the single post in Southwark." And, he could have added, that force had only been able to hold that single post for about twenty hours, after which it had ceded the ground for want of reinforcements.[27]

Some of the leading gentlemen of the city—Horace Binney and his peers—warned that Philadelphia could no longer depend on its volunteer troops, however gallant. In May, they reminded the councils, "a natural reliance upon good feeling and good sense" had restrained the "strong arm" of the militia, leading to "wanton destruction of property." In July, the militia had been willing to kill, but it had been unable to deter violence from the start. The gentlemen suggested "a full regiment of infantry, a full battalion of artillery, and one or more full troops of cavalry" to be ready to act anywhere in Philadelphia County at the orders of the mayor or sheriff. On July 11, just days after the Southwark fighting, the councils put the plan in place, promising $20 in public funds to equip each volunteer enrolled in these units, and to purchase ammunition and stores for the use of the militia when called into service by the mayor or sheriff.[28]

Cadwalader liked the plan. He was furious at the rioters, but he was almost as furious at his official superiors. He believed that he had been promised that "in case of an assault the whole city would have assembled *en masse*" and marched to his relief, armed with 1,500 muskets provided by the governor. "Had they done so," he later testified. "you never would have heard of another riot in the city or suburbs." Instead, a mere two hundred men had faced a mob of thousands. He saw in the ordinance assurance that in the future, he or his successors would command sufficient numbers.

Not all officers agreed. Flat on his back in a Baltimore hotel, Pleasonton was outraged to read the suggestion of including only one battalion of artillery. Whether the councils intended to reduce his artillery regiment to a battalion or accept only half of the regiment into service, the ever-prickly Pleasonton took the measure as an insult to him and to his men. Here he was, recovering from a painful wound suffered "in defense of order and society against riot and rebellion," and his reward was to be a reduced command. Eventually Cadwalader was able to include almost all of Pleasonton's regiment—560 men—in the new force, and by late September the colonel was well enough to return to duty.[29]

The infantry posed a thornier problem, one that touched on the militia's identity as a volunteer force. The $20 allowance for "the purchase of accoutrements, and to the necessary arming, outfit and equipment" came with a catch: Companies accepting the funds would have to wear blue uniforms resembling those of their counterparts in the regular army, replacing the profusion of colors and styles that had long distinguished the militia. Army uniforms offered several advantages over the tradition of allowing each company to design its own. Companies would no longer compete to be the most smartly dressed, allowing them to discard showy uniforms that were tight, uncomfortable, and costly to purchase and repair. After their service in Southwark and at the Girard Bank, militiamen fretted at the expense of repairing coats pierced by buckshot or scuffed by hard service. An army jacket would have held up better, or could have been replaced for a few dollars. Cadwalader hoped that a regiment or brigade dressed more or less alike would look and act more like a unified, powerful force than a collection of fraternal orders. If all companies dressed in blue, it would be harder for rioters to identify whom they were up against and to seek revenge later. Cadwalader's main concern may have been to avoid a repeat of the afternoon of July 7, when the people of Southwark chased the green-coated Montgomery Hibernia Greens through the streets. In the future, Cadwalader argued, "the Red and the Green uniforms . . . would create a riot wherever they appeared in times of excitement."[30]

Despite the advantages of a blue coat, many volunteers were proud of their distinctive uniforms and would rather decline the city money than give them up. As if to spite Cadwalader's demand, the National Grays—commanded by Cadwalader's rival, the nativist Peter Fritz—ordered new gray uniforms. James Page's State Fencibles went even further, going through with their plan, already in place before the riots, for "an elegant crimson coat with fancy epaulettes, and in summer time white pantaloons, which will be superseded in winter time by blue pantaloons," and to top it off, a large bearskin cap. They might look like British redcoats, but at least they would not be mistaken for American regulars. Disputes about fashion signified larger debates about the place of the militia in the political structure. A gaudy uniform, however ridiculous, showed that volunteers were making decisions for themselves, including—potentially—decisions about whom to fight, and when to kill. Dress the same men all in blue, and they could be mistaken for a standing army, or a civilian police force.[31]

Nativists mocked the new uniforms, hiring boys to shout "city harness!" when they saw a blue-coated company on parade, or even blue-coated actors portraying soldiers on stage. In September, an anonymous pamphleteer argued that the militia were already too soldierly for safety. Armed only with the most lethal weapons, and incapable of tolerating insults lest their precious honor lose its shine, even good men would become trigger-happy soldiers. For their part, the volunteers fretted that the ordinance was the first step toward downgrading them into common policemen. A Cadwalader Gray feared that the city would supply the brigade "not [with] bayonets and muskets, but maces and loaded canes," and then mobilize on the slightest pretense. "The 'Blue-light-Brigade,'" he warned, "will be called forth armed and accoutred with its bruising utensils, the Brigadier offici-ating as a High Constable, and the Colonels and their officers as Captains and Lieutenants of Police. . . . The peace-loving Sheriff and Mayor may in a fit of panic look upon a spree between two dogs as an 'emergency' calling for the interference of a Corporal's guard." He cannot have been reassured when the *Public Ledger* blurred the distinction between soldier and police officer: "Whether the weapon be a musket or a mace," the paper claimed, "whether the coat be police or soldier-like, it is all a civil force."[32]

Ignoring critics from within and without the ranks, Cadwalader pushed through. On September 16, an "astonishing pleasant" fall day, he paraded his men. "The companies on parade" noted the *Daily Chronicle*, "mustered very strong, looked exceedingly well, and marched with great precision," crediting the council ordinance for the militia's new strength. On September 26, Cadwalader reported to the councils that the new force was ready, a mix of old and new companies totaling 1,350 men, eight times as many as he had mustered for the march into Southwark on July 7. They included officers and companies that had proven themselves in Southwark: Pleasonton as commander of the artillery regiment, Drayton and his Junior Artillerists, Scott and his Cadwalader Grays, Hill and his City Guards. Even if a good number of them could not be found at a moment of crisis, Cadwalader could still hope to organize a force large enough to deal with an emergency. Lest anyone doubt it, Cadwalader requested a massive supply of ammunition, including 1,500 rounds of canister shot and 100,000 small-arms cartridges.[33]

As for uniforms, Cadwalader led the way, ordering his own Philadelphia Grays outfitted in the US blue, however poorly it matched their name. Other companies followed. When, at Cadwalader's suggestion, Colahan's Montgomery Hibernia Greens abandoned their Irish name to become the Washington Guards, they also replaced their green coats with the blue uniform of the US infantry. At their inspection in November, they hosted several veterans of the Battle of Queen Street: Cadwalader, Pleasonton, Scott, and Hill. When Cadwalader paraded his brigade to celebrate Washington's birthday in February 1845, sixteen of the twenty-one companies wore army blue. "Aye, these men look like soldiers," nodded veterans of the War of 1812. "These uniforms were made for service, not for holiday show."[34]

CIRCULAR

OF THE

NATIVE AMERICANS OF PHILADELPHIA

TO THE VOTERS OF THE CITY.

FELLOW CITIZENS:

The time has arrived when it becomes the important duty of the freemen of the City and County of Philadelphia, to select suitable persons to fill the different Municipal, County and State Offices.

The candidates whose names are submitted to the voters of the City, and for whom the Native American Party ask your sufferance, are from the ranks of the people, and we apprehend are such persons as are entitled to the confidence of their fellow citizens.

We do not deem it necessary to enter into an elaborate exposition of our principles; they have been proclaimed through the press, and reiterated from the rostrum, until all classes of our citizens have had an opportunity to become familiar with them; but we may be permitted briefly to present the following:

We maintain the freedom of the press and of opinion within the pale of law.

Uncompromising opposition to all union of sectarianism with politics.

We maintain that none but American Citizens by birth should hold political office in the United States.

The just equality between the Native and Adopted Citizens, in relation to the right of suffrage, requiring hereafter a residence of twenty-one years in this Country before a foreigner can become a naturalized Citizen.

The expediency of education at the public expense, and hence we oppose all efforts to diminish the opportunities now afforded our children of obtaining such education, believing that the perpetuity of our institutions depends upon a well regulated system of public instruction.

We oppose with equal unanimity the attempts of any and of every sect to interfere with the course of studies in our public schools, established by our laws, and subjected to the care and guardianship of the Citizens of this Commonwealth, through agents of their own selection.

We protest against, and will endeavor if placed in power, to reform the gross abuses of the ruling powers in relation to appropriations of the public funds. In a word, our motto is, a judicious and economical expenditure of the Public moneys.

Maintaining these principles, and determined in all things to follow the dictates of their reason and their consciences, our candidates are presented for your suffrage.

They have been chosen not at their own suggestion, but on the deliberate judgment of the people of our political faith.

We, therefore, present you with the accompanying ticket, and ask of every man who loves his country more than the mere selfish struggle of contending factions, led onward by vague party watch words, to abandon his former predilections, and give our Entire Ticket a hearty support.

Do your duty as American Citizens.

Vote for AMERICAN MEN... vote for AMERICAN MEASURES—And VOTE EARLY!

☞ By a decision of the Judges of the Court, no vote can be received after 10 o'clock, P. M.

Circular of the Native Americans of Philadelphia to the Voters of the City.
Courtesy of the Library Company of Philadelphia.

25

Congress or the Penitentiary

Even as troops patrolled the city in mid-July, some Philadelphians were looking ahead to what they hoped would be the more peaceful contests of the fall: the state and national elections. Both Democrats and Whigs sought out militia heroes of Southwark. The Democrats nominated Captain Robert Scott, who had been shot in the back, for a city post, while the Whigs of the county nominated Captain Henry Mallory of the artillery for a state senate seat. Nativists called Mallory "a bitter and inveterate enemy to the Native American party [who] never can receive the votes of American freemen," but his supporters insisted that Mallory had fought "not for Protestantism or Catholicism, not for this or that political party, but for the *only true Native Americanism, in defence of order and law.*"[1]

Some Whigs and Democrats hoped that the Southwark riots would discredit the Native American movement, leaving not even a "grease spot." "The 'Native' party is destined to a very brief existence," the *Spirit of the Times* assured its Democratic readers, "and when it *does* die, and the Coroner is permitted to sit upon its defunct remains, we have no doubt but that the verdict of the inquest will be 'died of the Pope.'" Others were less confident. At the end of July, a native-born Catholic warned readers in Ireland that Philadelphia nativism "seems to have a hold too firm to be shaken on by any misconduct," and that "a depraved public opinion evidently regards the persecution of foreigners and Catholics as of more importance than the maintenance of peace and law, and the preservation of the social system from anarchy."[2]

In fact, many Philadelphians saw no reason to choose between maintaining order and restricting immigration and immigrants' political power. The *Daily Chronicle*, for instance, denounced both the "discord and strife which disgraced Christianity in the old world" and "the ignorant pauper population, who swarm to our shores by thousands, every season, bringing with them no money, no arts, and very little civilization, but a superabundance of discord and mischief." Sidney George Fisher detested mobs, but he did not blame them on the Native Americans, whose principles he thought sound. Calling Irish immigrants "the refuse population of Europe," he admired the Natives and hoped they would merge with the Whigs. Merchant Thomas Cope had prospered from the fares immigrants and their families paid to his line of Liverpool packets, yet now he worried about the consequences. "Thirteen thousand persons within the City & districts have been naturalized by our courts within a few days to prepare themselves for voting at the approaching elections," he fretted in his diary. "This influx of foreigners & their speedy admission to the rights of citizenship inflicts a serious injury on our country."[3]

Hoping to court gentlemen like Fisher and Cope, nativists insisted that their goal was a change in naturalization laws, not armed rebellion. Unlike Henry David Thoreau—who some years later would spend a night in jail rather than obey what he considered an unjust law—the nativists did not admit to law-breaking, nor did they openly defy the law. To the contrary, they presented themselves as the agents of municipal reform. Russell Jarvis, a former writer for the *Public Ledger*, explained to his old officemates that while the New York Native Americans included some "self-seeking demagogues" who hoped to rile up hatred for the pope, "the great body of the party" was more concerned with replacing "the corrupt practices of our own political traders and political priests." They wanted, he claimed, "an honest and efficient municipal government," not "a Protestant ascendancy." The strategy worked. "Our Associations increase in numbers at all their meetings, aye, even since the Southwark riots," boasted Samuel Kramer's *Native American*. "All that is now wanting to ensure success is a good Ticket."[4]

After balloting in early September, Lewis Levin was chosen, almost unanimously, as the American Republican Party's nominee for the US House of Representatives from Pennsylvania's First District, which comprised the districts of Southwark, Moyamensing, Passyunk, and the two southernmost wards of the city of Philadelphia: Cedar Ward and New Market Ward, where Levin lived. The nomination made some sense. Levin was one of the best-known nativists in the county, and by 1844, dozens of editors and publishers had served in Congress. Following the July riots, he repeatedly returned to Southwark to speak at party rallies, boosting his recognition there.[5]

On the other hand, given nativists' obsession with one's place of birth and familiarity with local institutions, it was a bit odd for them to seek to be represented by the son of immigrants to the United States who himself had arrived in Pennsylvania less than five years before. And Levin had antagonized the Philadelphia establishment. On July 9, just one day after the withdrawal of the troops, his *Sun* argued that "the dreadful slaughter of human life . . . was not the work of a mob of citizens, but of the military." The editorial concluded that "the entire proceedings of the military from first to last were illegal, unnecessary and wanton. . . . The military on such occasions, only exasperate—and become themselves the very mob they are sent to quell." Reversing the categories favored by Philadelphia's establishment, Levin presented the soldiers as "rioters" and their opponents as "citizens."[6]

The authorities were not amused. On the morning of July 11, court officers arrested both Levin and Samuel Kramer of the *Native American* on charges of incitement to riot and treason for the criticism of the troops they had published in the preceding days. Officers also arrested former sheriff John Watmough, brought up on the same charge for telling a militia officer that, in the officer's words, "he would not have pitied us if we had all been shot down—that the military shot them down in cold blood." Watmough and Kramer disowned their words, but Levin remained defiant. In court, his lawyer briefly feinted at denying that Levin had written the offending editorials—could the Commonwealth prove that he was the editor of the *Sun?*—before shifting to a defense based on freedom of the press. "What a man may speak of the conduct of public officers," the lawyer argued, "he may publish. This is an attempt to fetter the press, and neither law nor public sentiment will sustain it it." When the recorder set bail at $4,000 (considerably more than that imposed on Kramer and Watmough), one of Levin's business partners quickly came up with the sum, and soon Levin was back at the *Sun* office, addressing a crowd of supporters. "Do not create mobs," he told them, slyly. "Leave that to the military." Some nativists began walking the streets in muzzles they crafted of tin and wire, symbols of the death of free speech. Into the fall, Levin remained under indictment for treason. By nominating him, the Natives were thumbing their noses at Philadelphia's elites.[7]

In addition to his recent conduct, Levin also bore his older reputation as a violent, bankrupt drunkard. Careful not to name Levin (perhaps for fear of a libel suit), the *Daily Chronicle* warned that "if there be among the candidates now in nomination for Congress, in the county of Philadelphia, a man whose life has been that of an abandoned debauchee, who has lost his fortune at the gambling table—who has been distinguished for murderous broils and affrays—who has drawn a knife, with deadly intent, upon a fellow being—who has run the round of riot and drunkenness—we care not what may be the *present* character of that man, *he cannot be trusted. His election would be a lasting disgrace to a moral and enlightened community.*" The blunter *Spirit of the Times* attacked Levin as "a Reformed Drunkard—a blasphemous Bible-libeller—an apostate Jew-christian—an inciter of Treason—an encourager and defender of mobs." (Lest anyone miss the swipe at Levin's ancestry, the paper followed up a few days later by calling Levin's arguments "absurd and in-*jew*-dicious.") "Calculating and observing men" gave the Natives better odds in the Third and Fourth Congressional Districts than in Levin's First.[8]

Levin did have the advantage of running in a three-man race. Rather than win an outright majority, he just needed to outrun E. Joy Morris, the Whig incumbent, and Democrat George Lehman, a physician. To do so, Levin tried to broaden his party's appeal beyond anti-Catholicism. On September 13, he equated nativism with honest toil. "Go into our factories, of any description," he advised, "and see who plies the tools of labor, of ingenuity, or invention, with most skill and surprising effect, and you will find them, not Irish Catholics, but American workingmen." In fact, the Native American leadership was scarcely different in its occupational structure than the Whigs and Democrats. In the city, professionals and merchants led. In the county, a more varied group, including skilled workers and manufacturers, represented each party. The Natives did distinguish themselves by giving women a greater role. In September, one nativist, Harriet Probasco, even launched a weekly newspaper, the *American Woman*, to advance the cause.[9]

Both before and after his nomination, Levin maintained a busy speaking schedule, sometimes addressing rallies in two parts of the county on the same day. As the featured speaker at a mass meeting of Southwark ladies who sought to aid the poor "and the fatherless children of those who were slain during the Kensington Massacre," Levin did not disappoint. Much of the speech was devoted to self-pity, as if he, not Shiffler, Ramsey, or the Torn Flag, were the greatest martyr of the cause. "My enemies are ready at work hatching all the foul machinations against my private character," he whined. "Let them drive the hot iron of tyranny and make an impression into my inmost soul, I shall not swerve one moment from the truth." If he were imprisoned, he asked the women of Southwark to bring him "pure cold water," not brandy. And, he continued, "if Lewis C. Levin falls by the assassin's dagger, hundreds of better men than he will rise and take his place—and he knows the people of Southwark would not let his family suffer."[10]

In between such pleas, Levin disparaged the sheriff, the generals, and the gentlemen of the city as incompetents or, worse, unknowing stooges of the pope. "I would not be surprised if each of these gentlemen get a

Cardinal's cap before the year's out," he sneered. "The Jesuits have been driven out of Europe, and now they flock to this land, and are secretly plotting together, such schemes as will carry out their own ends. . . . If the Native American ticket be defeated, it will be a Roman Catholic triumph and none other." And yet, he insisted in another speech, Nativists were not "sectarians, bigots, fanatics and church burners—an association got up expressly to wage war against a particular religious sect." They were merely Americans who sought to preserve the right to "meet peaceably together to discuss measures relative to their own government."[11]

No one could be sure that the campaign, or the election, would proceed so peaceably. Nativists traded rumors that Cadwalader had stockpiled artillery ammunition in preparation for election day. Fortunately, what incidents did occur remained relatively minor. At a Native meeting in Southwark, not far from St. Philip's, an Irishman heckled the crowd: "Shut your mouth or I'll pull you down." They chased him away. Later in September, two men in a buggy whipped their horse through the crowd at a Native rally in the Northern Liberties, injuring several people. And on September 16, someone severely wounded Thomas Logue with an axe, possibly the result of a tavern quarrel about nativism between Logue and an Irishman.[12]

For the most part, Philadelphians expressed their animosity in print and lawsuits. Justus Moore, a freethinking dentist, described Levin as "a renegade Jew, a drunken, rioting vagabond. . . . A man in whose countenance are strongly depicted the cut-throat propensities of a Marat, with something of the low, cowardly chicanery of a would-be Robespierre." The *Spirit of the Times* wondered if Levin was destined "for Congress or the penitentiary" and relentlessly mocked him for having once been both a Jew and a drunkard. Levin responded with a libel suit, but he would have to wait in line. Jonas Fairlamb sued four members of his former command, the Wayne Artillery, while Hugh Clark was suing the *American Advocate*.[13]

The Native American campaign climaxed on September 30. That afternoon, nativist Mayor Harper of New York arrived by boat, to the cheers of thousands of eager Philadelphia nativists who escorted him to his hotel. In the evening, rivers of nativists poured into Independence Square, which had been lit by limelight and lanterns. "The steady tramp of the thousands arriving," Levin later boasted, "was like the sound of seas!" The

Daily Chronicle guessed that at least twenty thousand people eventually crowded in; the *American Advocate* estimated fifty thousand. Certainly it was too many to be satisfied with a single set of orators, so men declaimed simultaneously from six platforms scattered around the square, while rival groups of musicians played "Hail, Columbia," "Yankee Doodle," and "The Star-Spangled Banner." The *Advocate* warned immigrants against using forged documents to vote, lest they risk prosecution. Yet nativists may have engaged in their own fraud; the night before the election, someone distributed placards falsely claiming that E. Joy Morris, the Whig congressman whom Levin hoped to unseat, had withdrawn from the race.[14]

Finally, on Tuesday, October 8, Philadelphians cast their votes. The day was nearly cloudless and a bit cool, the temperature rising only to sixty degrees, but still mild enough that voters could endure long lines at the polls, especially if refreshed by the vendors of apples and pies. Early in the morning, loyalists of each party arranged their flags and banners and sent messages back and forth. Bands played on furniture wagons and omnibuses; handbills warned that rival parties would sink the republic. Those who could crowded the polls, and even invalids arranged carriages to take them to the ballot box for this important election. Despite the excitement, the day passed mostly without violence, though the *Chronicle* noted "some few of the little amateur skirmishes which are unavoidable upon such occasions." Sidney George Fisher judged that "the general expectation of a tumult probably prevented it. I think also the firing of the troops in the July riots had a salutary effect. It settled a great question—viz—whether a mob should be fired on."[15]

The returns showed that the American Republican Party, which had scarcely existed a year before, had triumphed. In the heaviest turnout in Philadelphia's history, several Natives who had been involved in rioting won key races. Thomas Grover, who had claimed that the militia's presence in Southwark had been unnecessary, won as county commissioner. Augustus Peale, who had lost an arm in the Kensington fighting, won as county auditor. Enough nativists won election to the county board that militia officers rushed to seek payment for their men before the old board adjourned. The new board, they feared, might veto payments to the troops "owing to their well known participation in feeling with a certain party."

Nativists did equally well in races for the state legislature. Oliver Cornman, the painter who had organized the first American Republican ward meeting back in December 1843, won the county's seat in the state senate, defeating a Democratic incumbent and Whig candidate Henry Mallory of the Germantown Blues. And while the City of Philadelphia sent five Whigs to the state house of representatives, the surrounding county sent a solid slate of eight Native Americans, including William Hollingshead, who had called for the State House crowd to march into Kensington on May 7.[16]

Even in the Whig-dominated city, the Natives made an impressive showing. In the mayoral race, Whig Peter McCall (who had helped organize the town meeting on May 9) defeated his Native rival, Elhanan Keyser, by only 441 votes out of 14,610 cast, leaving the Democratic candidate in third place. Nativists also did well in contests for the US House of Representatives. Though the party's candidate narrowly lost in the Fourth Congressional District, Native American John Campbell won a congressional seat in the Third District in the north of the county.[17]

And Lewis C. Levin, the man perhaps most responsible for the hatred and carnage, a man with treason charges weighing against him, won election to Congress, thanks primarily to Southwark voters. "We have quietly avenged the murdered martyrs of liberty, who fell beneath the rifles of the assassins of Kensington," Levin gloated. "From this point *we start* in a career of political triumph without any precedent in history. Three years hence, we must elect a Governor, and four years hence, a President of the United States; men who will openly acknowledge the precious value of the Bible, and publicly espouse the naturalization law of 21 years." Nativist giddiness was tempered when, on the Saturday after the election, a cannon cartridge exploded prematurely, tearing a forearm off of each of two nativists who had been firing salutes. One died the following day.[18]

The Natives' success came largely at the expense of the Democrats. Writing to her staunchly Whig husband, Mary Bird opined that "it was scandalous to put in such men as C. Ingersoll & that Levin—But good comes from evil sometimes, and they say this Native American party is the first thing that ever broke the [Democratic] ranks, and they have done wonders that way." The *Ledger* suggested that the Natives and the Whigs had formed a "coalition," dividing offices between them rather than competing in every race. But that did not make the Native Americans into Whigs, and the results showed that a great many Philadelphians remained sympathetic to the Nativist cause, and perhaps suspicious of the militia's new power. Anti-Catholics cheered the evidence that the Catholic vote was now a liability, not an asset. Conversely, Catholics and their sympathizers were understandably appalled by Levin's victory. "It appears that the church burners have been too many for you," wrote Bishop Hughes from New York to his old friend Father Donaghoe, "and you will perceive that they have elected their chief to Congress, a result for which I am not the least sorry. It is fit that such a city should place its leading infamy on a pinnacle."[19]

The Native Americans would face a greater challenge in November's presidential election, which pitted the Democratic ticket of James K. Polk and George Dallas against the Whigs Henry Clay and Theodore Frelinghuysen. Whatever resentments they might still hold about the way the Democrats had treated Hugh Clark, these nominations steered Irish Catholics toward the Democratic Party. Dallas was reasonably friendly to Irish Catholics, having represented them in court after the riots of both 1831 and 1844. (At one point, the trial of a Kensington Catholic—charged with the May 7 death of Matthew Hammit—was interrupted by a Democratic parade that marched to the courthouse and demanded that Dallas step outside the courtroom to address them.) By contrast, Clay was rumored to hold nativist views, and Frelinghuysen was more openly nativist. In 1841, he had accepted the inevitability of mass immigration, but warned of its dangers. "We must enlighten, reform and purify these masses of men, that are crowding upon us from abroad," he had argued. "They know nothing of the nature or spirit of our institutions—many among them are unfriendly to those forms of religion established here and dear to our hearts." In any year, such statements would have alienated immigrant voters, and in 1844 the dangers of nativism were particularly clear. Following the Southwark riots, New York editor Mordecai Noah predicted that "Not a single adopted citizen—Irish, German, or French, we think, will vote the Whig ticket any where as a body."[20]

He was right. In November, Clay carried both the city and the county of Philadelphia, but only narrowly, allowing the state of Pennsylvania to go for Polk. And Clay met a more serious defeat in New York. There, "Bible

Politics" connoted not fights over school curricula, but the moral fervor behind the antislavery Liberty Party, which may have pried enough votes from the Whigs to deliver the state, and the presidency, to the Democrats. Although the second-largest state in the Union, Pennsylvania lacked the electoral votes to have swung the election on its own. But perhaps, as Noah had predicted, the Philadelphia riots had helped mobilize New York Irish for the Democrats. Nativists later grumbled that "Henry Clay was elected President by 300,000 majority of his *American-born* countrymen, but was defeated by the 470,000 foreign balance-power-vote thrown for Mr. Polk." More sober Whigs realized that by concurring with some nativist demands and by nominating Frelinghuysen, the party had all but forced naturalized citizens to vote Democratic. By stirring up trouble, Levin may have conjured the very "foreign-dominated election" that he feared.[21]

"Cadwalader's Silver Vase."
Courtesy of the Philadelphia Museum of Art: Gift of John Cadwalader, Jr., 1998, 1998-157-1a,b.

Epilogue

"I hesitate between hope and fear."
Kenrick and American Catholicism

The ruined walls of St. Augustine's survived into the summer of 1845, serving, one Catholic noted, as "a frowning monument of religious intolerance and persecution for conscience sake." Unable to worship there, the congregation opened a chapel—piously named Our Lady of Consolation—on the site of Dr. Patrick Moriarty's destroyed parsonage. To deter further attacks, this new building was "built with an unusual eye to strength," with windows protected by wire netting and iron bars. One observer found that it had "more the appearance of a prison than a church." "Large sums of money have been collected, and distributed amongst the rioters who marched to Kensington armed, and determined to burn the Irish Catholics in their houses," wrote Moriarty. "But not the slightest relief has been afforded, nor compassion exhibited, to those who were marked out to be the victims of arson and murder months before the 6th of May, 1844." Eventually, however, juries found the county liable for its failure to protect Catholic property, and awarded significant funds that helped their trustees to rebuild.[1]

Bishop Kenrick had been shaken by the riots, which left him worried that any act of Catholic assertion would be met with violence. "I hesitate," he wrote his brother in 1845, "between hope and fear." As late as December 1846, he fretted that opening a second church in Southwark could provoke renewed violence. Gradually, though, Kenrick took courage from each sign that the riots had been an aberration from the American tradition of liberty. In July 1845, he had written with pride of returning from a trip to Europe to get "home at the close of the festival of our National independence," and he looked forward to a fellow bishop's arrival on "these free shores." "There is no likelihood of the renewal of the scenes of last year," he wrote the following month. "The firemen have had riots among themselves without reference to religious differences."[2]

By that time, Philadelphia Catholics were already rebuilding, hoping to make St. Augustine's as "the most magnificent public edifice in the city," aided by contributions from Protestants as well as Catholics. In August 1846, Kenrick laid the cornerstone for a new St. Michael's church in Kensington, accompanied by twelve priests, and two drunken hecklers who started singing "an indecent song" just as Kenrick laid the stone. Work progressed steadily until October, by which point workers had completed the walls and had begun placing rafters for the roof. Then disaster struck again, this time in the form of the Great Havana Hurricane, which wrecked buildings from the Caribbean to New England. The eastern end of the church collapsed, along with all the joists and rafters. By February 1847, however, workers had gotten the building, though still unfinished, complete enough to be dedicated. By the tenth anniversary of the Southwark riot, Kenrick had laid cornerstones for another fourteen churches in and around Philadelphia. Most ambitiously of all, Kenrick planned a full-size cathedral for the city, to be designed by architect Napoleon LeBrun, who had cut his teeth on St. Philip de Neri's and was already at work designing the replacement church of St. Augustine's. LeBrun specified that the light come from above to "impart a solemn and religious effect," but later lore claimed that he had omitted side windows to protect the cathedral in case of future riots.[3]

Philadelphia would need these churches, for it was about to receive a great many new Catholic immigrants. In September 1844, the same newspapers that announced the verdicts in the Kensington riot cases reported on "a disease hitherto unknown among our farmers," affecting the potato crop. The disease spread from New England into New York and Pennsylvania, where observers saw "acres of land on which they had been planted, looking as black as though the vines had been assailed by fire." By September 1845 the blight had reached Ireland, whose people ate more potatoes per capita than almost anyone in Europe, and it came back even more powerfully in 1846. Evicted from their farms, Irish families packed into workhouses, begged in the streets, and died outdoors, their funerals poorly attended, if they were even given the dignity of a burial. As many as a million Irish starved or died of famine-related disease. But an even larger number left: 600,000 to England and other parts of the empire, and as many as 1.5 million to the United States.[4]

While New York City received the highest number of famine refugees, Philadelphia took in a good share. Between 1845 and 1850, around thirty-five thousand Irish—the vast majority of them Catholic—arrived in Philadelphia, doubling the city's Irish-born population. Protestants made a faint effort to convert the newcomers, and nativists continued to try to delay their citizenship and keep them from holding office. In 1848, some Southwark residents petitioned for the establishment of a special police force, or the summoning of a citizen posse, to repel the landing of immigrants at Southwark wharves. Ultimately, neither Catholic welcome nor nativist hostility mattered to families desperate to escape starvation, and immigrants kept coming.[5]

In 1851, Kenrick was named archbishop of Baltimore, the senior Catholic post in all the United States, and in that position he continued his revision and annotation of the Douay Bible. When he died in 1863, he had published a complete New Testament, and much of the Old, though not the entire Bible. Kenrick made some bold choices—particularly using "repent" in place of the older translation, "do penance." In 1866, the Second Plenary Council of Baltimore considered adopting the Kenrick Bible as the official English version for the United States, but the proposal was rejected, in part due to the opposition of his own brother, Archbishop Peter Kenrick.[6]

Nor would Kenrick's Douay Bible be read in Philadelphia's public schools, which continued to rely on the King James. As the fall term of 1844 began in Kensington, teachers resumed the practices that had caused such confusion: allowing Catholic students to excuse themselves before reading from the Protestant translation of the Bible. Catholics "leave the school room en masse when the Bible is being read," complained the *Native American*, "and in consequence many complaints are made by Protestants whose children are annoyed and disturbed, and the schools put into a state of disorder and confusion." Elsewhere, teachers would occasionally read a chapter, but so infrequently as to make the book's use, Protestants complained, "more nominal than real." Still, they had kept the Bible in Pennsylvania schools, and Catholics remained wary of sending their children there.[7]

Long before the riots, Kenrick had hoped to create Catholic schools for all the Catholic schoolchildren who wished to attend, and successors gradually expanded the number of Catholic schools in the city. By the end of the nineteenth century, Catholic schools educated about 11 percent of all schoolchildren in Philadelphia, but most Catholic students continued to attend public schools, ignoring the King James Bible as best they could.[8]

Germantown, Pennsylvania, home of Pennsylvania's first nativist association, became part of a consolidated Philadelphia in 1854. A century later, its schools were rotating their holy books—sometimes using the King James, sometimes the Douay, sometimes the Revised Standard Version, and sometimes a Jewish translation of the Old Testament. But the Schempp family, who were Unitarians, did not want the school to promote *any* religious doctrine, nor did they want their children to be ostracized for standing in the hallway outside their homerooms as the Bible was read. In 1963, the US Supreme Court ruled in their favor. Bible readings and prayers at the start of the school day, the court held, "are religious exercises, required by the States in violation of the command of the First Amendment that the Government maintain strict neutrality, neither aiding nor opposing religion." At the time of the decision, the president of the United States was John F. Kennedy, a

Catholic American of Irish descent. At his inauguration in 1961, he had taken the oath of office with his hand resting on a Douay Bible.[9]

"This people are henceforth to be united." McMichael and the Consolidation of Philadelphia

Compared to May and July 1844, the remainder of Morton McMichael's tenure as sheriff was uneventful. As his three-year term wound down in 1846, he was praised by both Democrats and Whigs for "his endeavor to be just as well as merciful, at a time when justice and mercy were both badly abused in the public mind." Forbidden by law from seeking immediate reelection, McMichael returned to private life. He and his deputy, William Price, advertised their services as lawyers, but McMichael's main interest was in resuming his first career: journalism. In late 1846, he invested in the *North American*, becoming its coeditor alongside George Graham.[10]

Even before McMichael joined the paper, Graham had moved the *North American* away from the nativism of its previous editor, Cephas Childs. In early 1847, with McMichael on the masthead, the paper condemned Levin for opposing federal aid to the victims of the famine in Ireland, and for his "embittered hostility against the Irish." By the end of the decade, however, McMichael seemed willing to accept nativism as part of a Whig coalition. In 1850, he endorsed Levin for reelection, noting that "on all important questions of public policy he has invariably voted with the Whigs," and tarring Levin's opponent, Thomas Florence, as the ally of Southwark's gangs.[11]

The riots of 1844 had pointed to the problem of political fragmentation and the consequent lack of a police force that could cross borders from the city into its adjoining districts. Accordingly, in February 1845, Pennsylvania legislators proposed a countywide board of police, the position of chief marshal, and a force of up to one marshal's deputy for every hundred taxable inhabitants. Unlike the existing forces in the city and each district, the new force would have jurisdiction throughout Philadelphia County. And if a riot proved too much for them, the chief marshal could inform the sheriff, who in turn could notify the major general, who would order out as many troops as needed.[12]

That first effort proved ineffective. In October 1849, a Moyamensing gang attacked the California House, a tavern owned by a mixed-race couple and popular with African Americans. Since the tavern lay just within the boundaries of the city of Philadelphia, the city police responded, but they were repelled by the mob, which threw bricks and fired warning shots from pistols and muskets. Braving the bricks thrown by the African American defenders, the mob got into the tavern, tore open its gas lines, and started a fire. When fire companies responded, the mob attacked them as well. For the first time since 1844, the militia was called to riot duty, but it arrived too late to stop the worst destruction. When the troops briefly withdrew, the rioting resumed, requiring the militia to return and hold their ground for two days. The riot left three men dead, including Edward Lelar, who had been assisting his brother, nativist Sheriff Henry Lelar, McMichael's successor.[13]

Rather than taking this as a cue for a greater militia role, the state legislature created a new "Marshall's Police" with jurisdiction over the entire metropolitan area. Like the New York Municipal Police, established in 1845, this new force was distinct from the militia. Armed with pistols and maces rather than muskets and cannon, they might be able to find a happy medium between the posse's ineffectiveness in Kensington and the militia's slaughter in Southwark. These police were loyal to the political parties that appointed them, as well as occasionally drunk, lazy, and corrupt. Yet they managed to prevent major riots, in part by arresting troublemakers at the first sign of disorder.[14]

McMichael and other boosters wanted more. Consolidating the entire 129-square-mile county under a single government, they believed, would encourage investment and produce untold riches for the private and public good. In 1854, state legislators concurred, passing the necessary law. In recognition of his achievement, McMichael was honored with the chairmanship of a massive celebratory banquet, attended by Cadwalader among other grandees. There, McMichael praised the erasure of the "absurd geographical lines" that had divided a people "homogeneous in their pursuits and interests and affections." "This people," he crowed, "are henceforth to be united; to become one and indivisible."[15]

In June 1854, voters elected Robert Conrad, the *North American*'s political editor, as the first mayor of the consolidated city. Conrad—who had cowhided Charles Jack back in 1844—ran as a Whig but also picked up the nominations of the Temperance Party and the resurgent Native American Party. Whether to pay his debt to the nativists or from sincere conviction, Conrad pledged in his inaugural address that the city police would be "constituted of men known as born in this country." But in a rematch election in 1856, Conrad was defeated by Democrat Richard Vaux, who reversed Conrad's policy and hired some Irish-born police.[16]

This force, after New York City the second professional, London-style police force in the United States, eventually became an effective instrument of riot control. With up to a thousand men, able to concentrate their numbers thanks to a new telegraph system, the new force finally reduced the city's levels of public violence. The 1844 riots had shown the value of a force that would be—leaders hoped—both quicker to mobilize and more measured in its actions than a militia armed and trained for open warfare. Today's city police forces, in Philadelphia and elsewhere, thus owe their existence at least in part to the bloodshed of 1844. To be sure, the volunteer militia—increasingly known after the Civil War as the National Guard—continued to intervene in riots too big for the police to handle. Periodically they fired into crowds, from Astor Place in New York City in 1849 to Kent State University in Ohio in 1970, and each time Americans reacted with the mix of horror and praise that had greeted Cadwalader's troops in 1844. But increasingly it would be not militia but city police who had to balance the public's right to protest with their own duty to maintain order and their need for self-defense, especially when confronted with mostly peaceful crowds surrounding a few half-grown boys hurling bricks.[17]

Following Philadelphia's consolidation, McMichael turned his attention to state and national affairs. The national Whig Party, to which he had been so loyal since 1840, had largely disintegrated by 1854, and the nativist American Party was not doing much better. In 1858, McMichael joined the effort to unite these and other factions—basically, anyone opposed to the Democratic Party—into a "People's Party," Pennsylvania's version of the new Republican Party. That required McMichael to ally with some nativists, and he served on a committee that endorsed some nativist positions, including "the purity of the ballot box to be preserved at all hazards, and frauds on the naturalization laws prevented by proper legislation." Yet McMichael's heart lay not with nativism or antislavery, but with the Republican support for high tariffs, which he hoped would aid Pennsylvania industry.[18]

McMichael served a term as the mayor of Philadelphia, using his 1866 inaugural speech to downplay Philadelphia's internal divisions in favor of a rousing call for the city to outdo its rivals in manufacturing, commerce, and the provision of clean water, transportation, outdoor recreation, and effective law enforcement. His main achievement as mayor was to help create Fairmount Park along the Schuylkill, absorbing, among other lands, the Snyder's Woods where the nativists had watched fireworks on the evening of July 4, 1844. Three years after his death in 1879, his admirers chose the park as the site of a memorial statue. The bronze McMichael is not the young sheriff, frantically running from one brawl to the next, knocking on armory doors in the hopes of finding a militia company at drill. Rather, it is the mature, relaxed editor, peacefully seated in an armchair, his left hand clutching his eyeglasses, his right hand raised, palm up, as if to invite a comment. Perhaps he is ready to consider a proposal to make Philadelphia all the greater. Perhaps he just wants to make a friend.[19]

McMichael's career shows the ambiguity of that hope. At times a Democrat, a Whig, and a Republican, he had gained power with Irish votes, served as quartermaster in Cadwalader's militia, and befriended Charles Naylor, as well as defended Philadelphia's African American and abolitionist communities, with the help of the city's violent firemen. Try as he might to be everyone's ally, his actions—and inactions—earned him disdain as well as praise. Yet he would not abandon his optimism or treat a Philadelphian as an enemy. If he underestimated his fellow Americans' capacity for selfishness and hatred, perhaps there are worse crimes.

"But no! I could not be heard." Levin and Nativism

Levin won his 1844 election to Congress with the July charge of treason still hanging over his head, and on October 12, just four days after his electoral victory, he was indicted. "We are glad of it," Levin claimed, presenting the indictment as further proof of a Catholic conspiracy. "We only desire that the people may understand the reason why their *Representative elect to Congress*, is dragged before the Jury of a Criminal Court, to answer the charge of a *Roman Catholic King*, FOR BEING AN AMERICAN! *That* is our offence." By the time the charges went to trial in February 1845, tempers had cooled, and the prosecuting attorney declined to press the case. Levin crowed that he had "driven the last nail in the coffin" of "a Popish Plot, to destroy Native Americans," and reiterated his claim that the people of Southwark had been "wantonly slaughtered by their armed invaders."[20]

In the spring of 1845, Levin could glory in his party's triumph in local elections in Philadelphia City, Southwark, and the Northern Liberties. These triumphs, more than fear of the militia, may explain the calming of nativist mobs. Why fight, when they had already achieved victory? By the fall of 1845, however, Philadelphia nativism was already fading. Natives remained strong in Kensington (except for the Third Ward), Southwark, and Spring Garden, but the Whigs dominated the city, and the Democrats gained a plurality in the county as a whole. Nowhere else in Pennsylvania did the Natives gain significant support, and they failed to elect a single member to the state legislature. And since policies on voting or naturaliza- tion were decided on the state and national levels, the Philadelphia Natives had no chance of effecting the central planks of their platform. At best, they were able to replace some Irish-born police officials with natives, and to control local liquor licenses.[21]

In December 1845, following this discouraging result in Pennsylvania, it was finally time for Levin to journey to Washington, where he became one of only six Native Americans among 217 Whigs and Democrats in the House of Representatives in the Twenty-Ninth Congress. Predict- ably, Levin made naturalization law a top priority, starting just two weeks into the new term. In an eight-thousand-word speech in support of the tightening of naturalization laws, Levin told the story of the Kensington violence as an attack on American democracy. "Drilled bands of armed foreigners rushed with impetuous fury upon native-born Americans, who carried no weapons but what equal rights had given them." Levin concluded with a passage so graceful that it would later be reprinted in anthologies of American rhetoric. "The love of our native land is an innate, holy, and ineradicable passion. . . . It is nature's most holy decree, nor is it in human power to repeal the law which is passed on the mother's breast and confirmed by the father's voice. The best policy of the wise statesman is to model his laws on the holy ordinances of nature."[22]

Despite the quality of his prose, Levin was assailed by Democrats and Whigs alike. Jefferson Davis, in his maiden speech to Congress, ridiculed Native proposals to require a twenty-one-year naturalization period. That would, Davis warned, "create enemies of our Government, and fill our country with discontented men." Stephen Douglas denounced "the Native American creed, with all its narrowness and bigotry and selfishness and injustice." James Dixon of Connecticut, a Whig, claimed that St. Augustine's had been torched by "a Democratic mob from the Democratic precinct of the Northern Liberties!" After members of both major parties had been given the chance to distance themselves from Levin, the petitions, in the words of a Catholic newspaperman, "were delivered to the hangman, the Judiciary Committee, and there they hung, strangled, lifeless and dishonored."[23]

Thus, by the end of his first month as an active congressman, Levin had tried and failed to advance the only issue he cared about. In subsequent years, he continued to disparage immigrants and warn about Catholic influence. In 1846, when Congress proposed a regiment of mounted riflemen to protect the Oregon Trail, Levin demanded that "that the officers and soldiers of said regiment shall be Americans at birth." This proposal was met with laughter. In 1847, Levin opposed federal aid to victims of the Irish potato famine on the grounds that the money would be better spent on the "thousands of American poor who are excluded from the benefit of American alms-houses and poorhouses because of the influx of foreign paupers and criminals who now fill them to overflowing." When, in March 1848, Congress debated the establishment of diplomatic relations with the Papal States, Levin called the proposal "a stroke of policy to conciliate the *foreign* Catholic vote."[24]

Mostly, Levin proved an erratic and ineffective legislator. One newspaper charged him with entering the House of Representatives only four times during one of his years in office. As a member of a tiny party, he had little power to get patronage appointments, except for a few friends. He also extended his reputation for violence. When, in a crowded hotel, he called second assistant postmaster general Fitz Henry Warren "a damned scoundrel," Warren beat Levin with his fists. Though Levin tried to defend himself with a small cane, he "came off second best."[25]

In 1846, Levin won reelection by only a narrow margin to become the only Native American in the Thirtieth Congress, where he sat directly in front of a freshman Whig named Abraham Lincoln. By 1848, Levin was a joke. A political satirist reported "Mr. Levin's Great Speech on the Pope of Rome" as a series of boasts by Levin about his actions in July 1844. "I mounted the cannon barefoot—Mr. Grover following after and holding my hat," he had Levin tell Congress. "I applied my ten toes to the touchholes of ten cannon, as they were about to fire; and blowing right into the church, I blew the Jesuits into the middle of the week. I and Mr. Grover then put the whole of the ten forty-two pounders in our breeches pockets. Yes—we carried off the guns; and our pockets were big with the fate of Rome." To retain his seat and that of another Native candidate, Native Americans had to endorse Whig candidates for every other seat. Even then, some Whigs shuddered at the thought of voting for Levin and nominated two rivals, but Levin prevailed. Levin's luck finally ran out in 1850. He continued to command Southwark and the southern wards of Philadelphia City, but Moyamensing went heavily for Democrat Thomas Florence, who in May 1844 had commanded the Independent Rifles in defense of the Church of St. Philip de Neri. Levin's allies alleged that Florence was associated with criminal Irish gangs, but they could not substantiate their charges of election fraud.[26]

By 1853, Levin was loitering in Washington hotels, seeking fees from inventors who thought a former member of Congress might help them secure or extend their patents. In 1855, he expressed interest in a US Senate seat and collected tens of thousands of dollars that he claimed were to bring his supporters to Harrisburg—where the Pennsylvania legislature would choose a senator—or perhaps to pay off old debts, discharged in bankruptcy in 1842 but nevertheless lingering on his conscience. Others suspected that Levin had collected the funds to buy legislators' votes.[27]

Meanwhile, Levin was losing ground to nativists more interested in secretive rituals than in traditional party forms. Since 1845, some nativists had been forming fraternal orders, such as the Order of United Americans and the Junior Order of United American Mechanics. Like the Orange Order in Canada, their lodges offered companionship, ceremony, funeral benefits, and the chance to do business with members of one's own ethnicity. At first, these orders emphasized friendship and trade with native-born workers and shops. By the early 1850s, however the orders were becoming more political. On May 6, 1851, the anniversary of the Kensington riots, for example, while Levin spoke in Spring Garden, the United Sons of America held a rival event in central Philadelphia, strutting on the stage of the Chestnut Street Theatre in their red, white, and blue uniforms. In 1853, the most secretive of these groups, New York's Order of the Star-Spangled Banner, gained prominence with the nickname "Know-Nothings," which would eventually come to signify the entire nativist political movement.[28]

To a degree, the Know-Nothings regarded themselves as upholding the nativist traditions of the 1840s. In 1856, for instance, the *Daily American Organ*, a Know-Nothing newspaper in Washington, reprinted documents from Philadelphia in 1844 in an apparent effort to reignite anger against the dangerous Irish Catholics. "The Know-Nothings of 1855 are a copy of the Native Americans of 1844," observed one Catholic writer. "Like the latter they are impelled by Free Masonry, and Irish Orangeism in crossing the Atlantic has lost neither its nature nor its principles." In a particularly terrifying echo of the Philadelphia riots, Know-Nothings in Louisville, Kentucky, seized the polls on election day, August 6, 1855. The result was fighting between immigrants (both Irish and German) and nativists, complete with the threatened burning of a Catholic church rumored to have weapons and ammunition stored inside. By the end of the fighting, more than a dozen were dead. The resurgence of nativism under this new name alarmed Irish Catholics, including Archbishop Francis Patrick Kenrick. "For a year past," he wrote in the aftermath of the Louisville riot, "I have felt that we ought to be prepared for martyrdom."[29]

One distinction, however, is that the Know-Nothings had little use for Lewis C. Levin. The fraternities gradually pushed him out of the party, even denying him the nomination for his old seat in Congress. Levin's final public act took place during the bitter presidential election of 1856, as the country entered its last agonies before civil war. The Democrats nominated James Buchanan, the new Republican Party nominated John Fremont, and former president Millard Fillmore ran as a Know-Nothing candidate. Levin supported Fillmore but opposed efforts to create a "union ticket" of electors who would be ready to vote either for Fillmore or Fremont in the Electoral College, depending on who seemed better poised to defeat Buchanan. On September 16, Levin organized a meeting to denounce the union and ordered placards reading, "Come up, boys of '44, you are about to build up your glorious party!" But the hall filled with union supporters, who turned the event into what the *Ledger* judged "one of the most disorderly meetings that ever assembled in Philadelphia." Union men hooted Levin off stage and physically shoved him out of the building, then approved a resolution denouncing him "as the mere tool of corrupt political tricksters." As he was chased out, Levin kept up a brave face, waving his hat and cheering for Fillmore. The next day, he decried his treatment. "I asked them not to plunge the knife into my heart until I was found guilty! But no! I could not be heard. The Black Republicans have denied me the right of public speech in our city, now disgraced!"[30]

Twelve years earlier, in the Washington Street Market, Levin had been denied his right to speak, and he had leveraged that silencing into a career in national politics. His 1856 silencing, however, marked the end of that career. Less than two weeks later, a policeman escorted Levin to the Pennsylvania Hospital for the Insane, an imposing structure on the west bank of the Schuylkill. His embarrassed supporters blamed mental illness for his odd behavior in the previous weeks, and hoped that "he may soon be restored to his family and to usefulness as a citizen." Others insisted that "Mr. Levin is merely laboring under partial religious and political excitement of recent development," and needed only temporary removal "from contact with any peculiar subject of irritation."[31]

Levin spent most of the last four years of his life in the Hospital for the Insane, where he would have found himself in the company of hundreds of English, Germans, and, of course, Irish. He died among them at 1 A.M. on March 14, 1860. "He was at one time the leader of the Native American party in Philadelphia," noted the *Pittsburgh Daily Post*, "but of late years, lost all his popularity, and has been regarded, even by his best friends, with pity and regret as a man of brilliant gifts, misapplied and prostituted."[32]

By the time of Levin's death, the American Party had been absorbed by the rising Republican Party, and some even claimed that the new party's name was inspired by American Republicans of the 1840s. Nativists were only one faction of the Republicans, who also included such antinativist leaders as William Seward and Abraham Lincoln. But as Republicans, nativists achieved some federal immigration restriction in the 1880s, and they narrowly failed to gain congressional approval of a constitutional amendment forbidding the use of tax money in support of parochial education. Over the decades, nativism's main targets shifted from Irish Catholics to radicals and Chinese, and then Mexicans and Muslims, but they continued to charge immigrants with pauperism, criminal proclivities, incompatible religious beliefs, and foreign allegiances. Into the twenty-first century, American nativists would echo the warnings that Lewis Levin had once voiced.[33]

"You can distinctly hear the blow & the bones crack." Cadwalader and the Citizen Soldier.

Criticism of George Cadwalader's actions in Southwark continued strong enough that, a year after the battle, Fanny Cadwalader told her husband she wished for another riot, so that "all parties might be compelled to acknowledge the necessity of the course you pursued last year." Instead, in 1846, American soldiers sought larger targets, as Congress declared war on Mexico. Philadelphia sent veterans of the fights in Kensington and Southwark, as well as nativists. The First Regiment of Pennsylvania Volunteers included the City Guards and the Cadwalader Grays, commanded by Captains Hill and Scott, who had ordered the first fire in Southwark. It also included Surgeon Thomas Bunting, who had been mobbed at the Southwark Commissioners' Hall and, curiously, Lieutenant Augustus Larrantree, despite his seven-year suspension from holding a state commission—a punishment for refusing to march into Southwark. Charles Naylor, who had put his body in front of the Cadwalader Grays' muskets on July 6, 1844, organized a new company: the National Rangers. Perhaps it is just as well that the Grays and the Rangers served in separate regiments.[34]

Both regiments caused their share of trouble while deployed. One of Naylor's acquaintances later related that his company "was known as the Killers and Bouncers and was composed of the roughest element of the Quaker City." While in Pittsburgh, en route to Mexico, the men broke out of their barracks, until Naylor subdued them by slashing one of his own men in the face with a sword. Isaac Hare, who had been pardoned for his role in Kensington, served as a lieutenant in Naylor's company and eventually got into the most trouble. On April 5, 1848, he was one of three officers in a group of soldiers who broke into a Mexico City gambling hall and, when the owner appeared, shot him in the head, killing him. Found guilty of burglary and murder, Hare was sentenced "to be hanged by the neck until he is dead, dead, dead." But, as in 1844, he avoided the gallows, and he steamed home to the United States.[35]

Captain Joseph Hill of the City Guards, who had ordered the first fire on Queen Street, faced trouble with his own troops. As his regiment camped outside of New Orleans en route to Mexico, some men snuck out to enjoy the pleasures of the city. Hill tracked them down to a ballroom, where a police officer tried to arrest him for entering the room armed. "I will show you that an officer in the United States army is above a police officer," Hill snarled, and with superior force arrested the policeman. Ordered to pay damages of $400, which he lacked, Hill remained stuck in Louisiana while his regiment sailed for Mexico. He sorted things out in time to lead his company at the Battle of Cerro Gordo in April 1847. "He is not the man to back out," one of the City Guards boasted, "or catch the bomb fever, when the shells and shot are flying among us."[36]

In spring 1847, George Cadwalader was commissioned a brigadier general in the US forces and sent to reinforce General Winfield Scott, who had landed at Vera Cruz in March. In his first engagement, the Battle of National Bridge, Cadwalader displayed the same boldness that had earned him both praise and scorn at home. Determined to rescue an ambushed American column, he ordered his troops forward at night, which exposed his men to friendly fire as well as enemy attack. Writing in his diary, an army surgeon claimed that most of Cadwalader's officers considered his actions wrongheaded, and that Cadwalader himself was a "pompous, overbearing . . . ignorant . . . conceited . . . ass." Cadwalader's superiors clearly thought differently, entrusting him with the command of three regiments, about two thousand men.[37]

Cadwalader won his greatest renown on September 13, 1847, after his commander, Major General Gideon Pillow, was wounded and unable to continue, leaving Cadwalader in command of the Third Division, along with a few stray marines who had gotten separated from their comrades. Braving gunfire that killed an officer at his side, Cadwalader led his troops as they stormed the fortress of Chapultepec, then received the enemy commander's sword and the fortress's flag as trophies. In recognition of his "gallant and meritorious conduct," Cadwalader's superiors brevetted him major general and assigned him one of the plushest dwellings in Mexico City for his quarters, perhaps even exceeding the standards of his Chestnut Street mansion. He later told Sidney George Fisher how much he had enjoyed the war. "When cannon shot struck a company of men," Cadwalader told him, "you can distinctly hear the blow & the bones crack."[38]

When he returned home in May 1848, sporting a suntan and a huge moustache, the citizens of Philadelphia welcomed him with cheers and bouquets as he rode through the streets. They commissioned a medal composed of blue enamel, sixteen diamonds, and a large ruby. And, nearly four years after the Southwark riots, they finally pressed him to accept a symbol of their gratitude for his actions in 1844: an ornate silver vase, thirty inches high, crafted by silversmith George Childs, who as a captain of McMichael's posse had served under Cadwalader in Southwark on July 6. The inscription praised Cadwalader's "distinguished ability, intrepidity & prudence manifested by him in Suppressing the riots of May & July 1844" and expressed Philadelphia's "profound respect for him as A Citizen, a Soldier, & a man." Cadwalader, in turn, expressed no ill will toward the rioters, judging their "misconduct" to have been "the result of ignorance of the laws in a greater degree than of a desire to violate them."[39]

At the beginning of the Civil War in April 1861, Philadelphia crowds swarmed the houses of anyone they suspected of Southern sympathies, including both Major General Patterson, who owned Louisiana plantations, and Cadwalader, who owned land in Maryland. Patterson lost some windows in his home and greenhouse before he assured the men of his loyalty by offering to lead them against the South. Cadwalader simply displayed the American flag he had fought under in Mexico, earning nine cheers from the crowd. Appointed major general of state volunteers by the governor of Pennsylvania, Cadwalader was placed in command of Union forces in Baltimore, then full of true Confederate sympathizers. In that role, he gained a lasting place in American legal history by imprisoning John Merryman, a Maryland militia officer, and defying a writ of habeas corpus from Chief Justice Roger Taney. The Catholic chief justice found he had something in common with the Southwark nativists who had decried the imprisonment of Naylor: the sense that Cadwalader locked people up unfairly. Even Francis Patrick Kenrick, now archbishop of Baltimore, had mixed feelings about Cadwalader, who "imprisoned those whom he mistrusts with no regard for constitutional rights." Eventually, Merryman was released and the charges dropped. Cadwalader moved on to divisional command in Maryland, Virginia, and very briefly in Mississippi, before being summoned to Washington, where he served on various boards, commissions, and courts.[40]

With Cadwalader away, the defense of Philadelphia from possible Confederate attack fell to his old subordinate: Augustus Pleasonton. Citing "Domestic Considerations," Pleasonton had resigned his militia commission in June 1845. But at the outbreak of the Civil War in April 1861, the City of Philadelphia commissioned him as brigadier general and placed him in command of the Home Guard, a force of up to ten thousand men designed both to repel rebel invasion and suppress any "popular tumults and commotions" inspired by the rebellion. In the summer of 1863, those threats became particularly realistic as Confederate forces marched into Pennsylvania. Pleasonton spent late June and early July mustering volunteer companies, including one commanded by Captain John B. Colahan, formerly of the Montgomery Hibernia Greens. But mostly Pleasonton squabbled with Pennsylvania politicians and Union Army major generals, who refused him an army commission and, he felt, treated him and his men with gross indignity. "The State lay without any preparation for defence," he later complained, "like an immense whale on the ocean, awaiting its death blow from its enemy." Fortunately for Philadelphia, Union victory at Gettysburg prevented the Confederates from harpooning the whale.[41]

Following that battle, the main threat was less a second Confederate invasion than an outburst of draft riots of the sort that raged in New York City from July 13 through 16, leaving more than one hundred dead. Nothing of the scale took place in Pennsylvania, but by July 18, mobs had interfered with draft agents in several eastern Pennsylvania counties and murdered one enroller. Fearing a much larger disturbance in Philadelphia, the army sent Cadwalader to command all Union forces in and around the city. "He is admirably fitted for the position," commented McMichael's *North American*, "and in case of need will undoubtedly act with the same courage and decision which characterized his movements on a former occasion." In July 1865, following the Confederate surrender, Cadwalader resigned his commission as a major general, finally ready to hang up his sword after thirty-nine years of military service.[42]

On February 3, 1879, Cadwalader collapsed on the floor, felled by a stroke. Three days later, amid wretched weather, Cadwalader's remains were escorted to the Christ Church burying ground by the First Brigade of the Pennsylvania National Guard. Members of Cadwalader's old company, the Philadelphia Grays, and veterans of the First Brigade of Pennsylvania Militia marched in a place of honor behind the hearse. Morton McMichael, who could have penned the most eloquent eulogy, had died just weeks before, but Cadwalader's death still brought tributes. "For nearly half a century George Cadwalader has been a prominent citizen," noted one obituary, "prominent for his public spirit in times of emergency in his city, State and country." It quoted the silver vase he had been given in 1848: "The Defence of the Laws is the Hero's Highest Glory."[43]

One imagines Cadwalader disagreed. He complained in 1844 about the absence of "an honorable foe," and his refusal of a ceremonial sword that year may have reflected the disdain he felt for riot duty. Even in 1848, when he accepted the silver vase, he may have preferred its panels showing Chapultepec Castle, where he had found an enemy worthy of his courage and a more traditional source of military glory. Yet the citizens who honored Cadwalader's service in Kensington and Southwark understood the value of his distasteful duty at home. By leading his brigade in defense of St. Philip's, Cadwalader had protected the rights of a minority against the tyranny of the majority. If nothing else, the riots reminded Americans that all deliberative politics and law ultimately depend on the control of violence. Democracy walks a narrow path between military oppression and mob rule.

ACKNOWLEDGMENTS

God bless the archivists and librarians! Perhaps all historians' acknowledgments should begin that way, but having worked through so many pages of brittle paper, and encountered so many crucial documents that barely survived, as well as references to those that did not, this project made me all the more appreciative of their work.

I am especially grateful to George Oberle of George Mason University, as well as the interlibrary loan staff there; to Brianne Barrett, Nathan Fiske, Vincent Golden, and Kimberly Toney Pelkey at the American Antiquarian Society; Patrick Shank at the Catholic Historical Research Center of the Archdiocese of Philadelphia; David Haugaard, Sarah Heim, and Steve Smith at the Historical Society of Pennsylvania; Cornelia King, Emily Smith, and Sarah Weatherwax at the Library Company of Philadelphia; Arlene Balkansky and Bruce Kirby at the Library of Congress; Eleanor Gillers and Mariam Touba at the New-York Historical Society; Megan Rentschler and Michael Sherbon at the Pennsylvania State Archives; David Baugh at the Philadelphia City Archives; and Iren Slavely at the State Library of Pennsylvania.

Thanks also to Jennifer Barr, Edward Blessing, Nell Carlson, Mitch Fraas, Sarah Horowitz, Andrew Isidoro, Scott Keefer, McKenzie Lemhouse, Shane MacDonald, Tim Murphy, Charlene Peacock, Stacey Peeples, John Pollack, and John Shepherd, all of whom helped me find pieces of the puzzle.

George Mason University's Department of History and Art History remains a wonderful intellectual home, and I am especially grateful to colleagues Joan Bristol, Alison Landsberg, Abby Mullen, Lincoln Mullen,

Jennifer Ritterhouse, Randolph Scully, Suzanne Smith, John Turner, and Rosemarie Zagarri for their comments on drafts. Brian Platt and Matthew Karush provided steady leadership, and Sue Woods expert administration. The department also provided funding for some image reproductions and, thanks to the generosity of the Alan and Gwen Nelson Fund for Faculty Research, for my travel to the American Antiquarian Society. I also benefited from a research leave from Mason's College of Humanities and Social Sciences, and from the insights of my students, especially members of my graduate seminars on protest and disorder.

Scott Berg of Mason's English Department served as both teaching partner and writing coach as I explored the craft of narrative history. Over several years he generously shared his time and wisdom, gave the book its fiery title, and, I hope, made me a better storyteller. Christopher Capozzola, Geoff Rodkey, and Dan Sharfstein also served as guides, and their writings as models. Matthew Gilmore generously read a full draft manuscript and tightened up the prose.

Early in this project, I spent a delightful half-year at the Library of Congress as a Kluge Fellow. I am especially grateful to Johanna Bockman, Carolyn Brown, Marcy Dinius, JoAnne Kitching, Mary Lou Reker, and Srividhya Swaminathan for making my time there so productive. Later, I was able to refine my thinking as part of a National Endowment for the Humanities summer seminar on the works of Alexis de Tocqueville, led by Arthur Goldhammer and Olivier Zunz, and I thank all members of that group for their insights. Howard Gillette and Matthew Fishbane kindly published early findings from my research.

Beyond these specifics, I am indebted to the wider community of scholars of cities, immigration, and urban violence, especially Rit Aggarwala, Tyler Anbinder, Erik Chaput, Russ DeSimone, Bruce Dorsey, Alex Elkins, Glenn Gordinier, Owen Gutfreund, Andrew Heath, Dallett Hemphill, Hidetaka Hirota, Clifton Hood, Dan Horner, Marilynn Johnson, Timothy Lombardo, Sara Mayeux, Tim Meagher, Angela Murphy, Margot Sheehan, Eric Schneider, Ian Watson, and Tim Winkle. All my work reflects the superb training I received from my teachers, including Sue Ikenberry, Helen Kimmelfield, John Stilgoe, Alan Brinkley, Howard Gillette, Ron Grele, Owen Gutfreund, Kenneth Jackson, and Herbert Sloan. I am especially indebted to the late Judith Vichniac, under whose supervision I first wrote about rioting, and to Elizabeth Blackmar, who introduced me to the fascinations of the antebellum city.

For hospitality during my research travels, I am grateful to Will Bachman, Jessica Bennett, Stephanie Burt, Chia Chu, Tony Lee, Margarita Soto, and, most especially, Michael Kulikowski and Ellen Stroud.

Special thanks to David Cohen for strengthening my back so I could bend over newspapers and ledgers for hours, and to Keith Blount for creating Scrivener.

This project moved from manuscript to book thanks to the expert care and enthusiasm of Giles Anderson of Anderson Literary Agency and Jessica Case of Pegasus Books. Charles Brock designed the gripping cover, Maria Fernandez designed the striking interior, Michael Siegel crafted the exquisite maps, copy editor Peter Kranitz and proofreader Meredith Clark improved the text throughout, and Julie Grady created the index.

I depend on the patience and support of my family: Will Adler, Elizabeth Alexander, Judy Bickart, Thomas Emberg, Bob Fenichel, Lisa Lerman, Sam Lerman, Shoshana Lerman, David Schrag, Eleanor Schrag, Kristina Schrag, Philip Schrag, Sarah Schrag, Eve Tushnet, Mark Tushnet, and Erin Walter-Lerman. Rebecca Tushnet is my inspiration and my strength. She is also my most careful reader.

During the years I worked on this book, Leonard Schrag and Nora Schrag grew from toddlerhood to adolescence without ever losing their appreciation of a good story. I hope they like this one.

NOTE ON SOURCES

n May 1844, the *Saturday Courier* reported that in the wee hours of May 5, the Neptune Hose Company had been attacked by men they believed to belong to two rival fire companies. When those two companies denied having attacked the Neptune, and vouched for each other, the *Courier* sarcastically concluded, "Nobody did it!" The same could be said for the nativist riots, as well as most other riots in history. Unlike battles between organized armies, in which even defeated soldiers may be proud to have participated, riots are criminal acts, and few participants are willing to publicly acknowledge taking part. If we were to take all eyewitness testimony at face value, we would have to conclude of much of the violence that nobody did it. As a historian, however, I am inclined to think that somebody did it, and I offer my best guess who it was.[1]

In the aftermath of the events described here, Philadelphians disagreed so strongly with one another's understandings of what happened that they disparaged one another in print, sued one another for libel, and on at least one occasion, cowhided a lawyer when he declined to fight a duel to resolve the dispute. In some cases, I have included multiple accounts. Perhaps William Crozier's last words were "have mercy on me—I am a cripple, and will get out of the road as soon as I can." Or perhaps they were "Fire, and be damned!" Since both versions tell us how different groups of Philadelphians understood Crozier's death, I have included them both. In most cases, however, presenting parallel narratives would produce a tedious book, so I have offered what I consider the most plausible version. Like all histories, this story is a work of inference based on the best available evidence, and I can only claim to have made reasonable, not definitive, judgments.

Even basic chronology is hard to determine. Most of the witnesses to the riots likely did not possess watches, and even if they did, they did not take careful note of the time as they scrambled for cover amid flying bullets and burning buildings. Months later, they would recall events to the nearest hour, and even these vague ranges are impossible to reconcile. This makes it difficult, for example, to determine the order in which various figures were wounded or killed. Even a single witness's sense of sequence can be hard to make out if they described events in the order in which the lawyers posed the questions, not in chronological order. (Witnesses were no better a century later. Historian Cornelius Ryan complained, "I never found one man who landed on Omaha Beach who could tell me the exact time when some incident occurred.")[2]

A good example of the confusion concerns the cavalry's actions on May 8, 1844. The *North American* told readers that Mayor Scott dismissed the cavalry at a moment of calm, *before* any attack on St. Augustine's Church. By contrast, *United States Gazette* provided a vivid description of charging horsemen failing to stop the destruction *after* it had commenced. In this case, a third source, an 1875 history of the First City Troop, explains that the mayor dismissed the horsemen, summoned them back, and then dismissed them again, perhaps reconciling the apparently contradictory newspaper accounts. But even this third account, which claims that the troops succeeded in "completely clearing the streets" cannot square with the *Gazette*'s account of a failed cavalry charge.[3]

Similarly, it is impossible to construct a timeline of the events of the afternoon of July 7, 1844, that agrees with all eyewitness accounts. Some witnesses swore that Charles Naylor had been freed before the first cannon was fired at the Church of St. Philip de Neri; but more testified that the cannon had been fired around noon, and Naylor was not released until some time after 1:30 P.M. Even in calmer circumstances, reporters for rival newspapers, sitting in the same courtroom, could disagree on the names of the witnesses and details of their testimonies. Sometimes a single newspaper struggled to settle on one version of events. "Respecting the origin of the tragic scenes which followed," lamented the *Inquirer*, "we have really heard so many conflicting accounts that it is utterly impossible for us to give the details with confidence."[4]

Whom to trust? When many witnesses reported one thing, and another witness was clearly an outlier, I tend to trust the many. An exception is when there appears to have been a concerted campaign to spin the story, as with the nativist accounts that appeared in the *American Advocate* in February and March 1845. Accounts by participants with clear personal agendas strike me as less trustworthy than those from more neutral observers. Accounts with telling details also seem more credible. Lawyer C. B. F. O'Neill could give exact distances between points in Kensington. And I was hesitant to believe that Cadwalader's brigade had marched behind music until Thomas Warham told me the tune they were playing. In general, I had trouble taking any nativist story at face value, given their persistent political lies, such as their claim not to bear any animus against Catholics. Throughout, I have tried to narrate events in ways that fit with most of the available evidence without interrupting the story to note each uncertainty. Yet I recognize that another historian, given the same pool of evidence, could tell a different story.

In May 1844, when editors sought to assemble accounts of the Kensington riots from "the entire Philadelphia press," they ended up with clippings from eighteen newspapers. Some of these have vanished entirely in the years since the riot, but I have read as many of them as I could locate. In addition to those eighteen, I consulted the *American Advocate* (which first appeared only in July 1844) as well as newspapers from New York and Baltimore, which printed accounts from their own correspondents, along with occasional accounts from more distant newspapers, including those in Great Britain and Ireland. The result has been a range of perspectives, since various publications catered to Democratic, Whig, Native American, Catholic, and military readers, while others claimed independence in hopes of gaining subscribers across party lines. The emergence of searchable databases of scanned microfilm has, of course, made the task of gathering newspaper accounts greatly easier than it would have been a generation ago, as has the invention of the digital camera and of optical character recognition software, which made it possible for me to photograph hundreds of pages of newspapers that have never been microfilmed, and to create searchable files of key articles.[5]

With so many editors trying to fill their pages, the newspapers of the 1840s less resemble the dailies of the mid-twentieth century, with their large professional staffs, than the social media of the early twenty-first century. Philadelphians of high position, and even ones of relatively modest rank, could make themselves heard through letters to the editors or "cards" addressed to the general public. Men and women of lower rank appear as the organizers of meetings, in speeches printed verbatim to the best of the reporter's ability, and, eventually, in transcripts of testimony before petty and grand juries. As with the social media of a later century, Philadelphians commented on one another's writings, occasionally in the spirit of the honest exchange of ideas, more often with provocative insults and denunciation. In some cases, the conversations spilled over into pamphlets. This rich print culture allows me to tell the story of the riots from multiple perspectives.

Beyond printed sources, I have benefited from key manuscripts. Only a handful of letters by Lewis Levin and Morton McMichael survive, but we have a good number from two other key figures: George Cadwalader and Francis Patrick Kenrick. Kenrick wrote his diary and most of his correspondence in Latin, and I have relied on translations. Augustus Pleasonton's diary, written with superb penmanship and biting sarcasm, is a treasure. Sidney George Fisher, mostly an onlooker, was one of the most thorough diarists of the century.

Some accounts of the riots were produced decades later. James Page of the State Fencibles seems reliable. I am less confident of the reminiscences of Father P. Aloysius Jordan, who witnessed the riots as a sixteen-year-old employee of a dry-goods store and thirty years later set down his memories in the *Woodstock Letters*, a journal of the Jesuit order. His stories are wonderfully colorful but erroneous in dates and largely unconfirmed by other sources. Aside from the events he claimed to have witnessed himself—the mutterings in the store and the burning of St. Augustine's—I have chosen not to rely on his account.

Most of the dialogue in the text appears as it was recorded at the time, but, as indicated in the notes, I have reconstructed some dialogue from paraphrases in the original sources. For instance, the *Public Ledger* reported that Mary Mallon testified that the men who broke into her house "asked me if I would die for my religion." I have rendered that as their saying, "Would you die for your religion?" I have also spelled out expletives in dialogue that 1840s texts delicately rendered with dashes, such as "Fire, you d—d son of a b—h, and we will give you h—l if you do."[6]

The visual depictions of the violence of 1844 often appear to owe more to the artists' imagination than their familiarity with places and events. But even images created by artists unfamiliar with the scenes they depicted offer a sense of how people dressed, how they were armed, and, perhaps most importantly, of the emotional impact of the riots. Images created at calmer times, such as the watercolor painting of the Hibernia Hose House, appear to match written descriptions more closely.

I have walked the streets of Kensington, Southwark, and central Philadelphia, but little of the landscape of the 1840s remains. Independence Hall and the Girard Bank (preserved as the First Bank of the United States) still stand. The churches that were targeted in 1844 burned then (arson) or in later decades (accident), though their rebuilt versions give some idea of their appearance in 1844. Such buildings as George Cadwalader's house, the state arsenal, and the building housing Levin's *Sun* were cleared for development. The Locust Street mansion of Major General Robert Patterson, commander of the First Division of the Pennsylvania Militia, was one of the casualties. In the early twentieth century, it was demolished to make room for a fireproof building to store the collections of the Historical Society of Pennsylvania, so many of which I have used in my research. Paper covers rock.

ABBREVIATIONS

Archives and Libraries

AAS   American Antiquarian Society, Worcester, MA.

HSP   Historical Society of Pennsylvania, Philadelphia, PA.

LC   Library of Congress, Washington, DC.

LCP   Library Company of Philadelphia, Philadelphia, PA

PCA   Philadelphia City Archives, Philadelphia, PA

PSA   Pennsylvania State Archives, Harrisburg, PA.

SLP   State Library of Pennsylvania, Harrisburg, PA.

UP   Kislak Center for Special Collections, Rare Books and Manuscripts, University of Pennsylvania, Philadelphia, PA.

Manuscript Collections

ACHS   American Catholic Historical Society collection, Digital Library, Villanova University, https://digital.library.villanova.edu/Item/vudl:208284.

AJP   A. J. Pleasonton, diary, HSP.

GC   Cadwalader Family papers, collection 1454, series 7, General George Cadwalader papers, HSP.

Books

The following two books reproduce key documents, which are cited individually as appropriate.

OB   [John Reinhard Goodman], *The Olive Branch, or, an Earnest Appeal in Behalf of Religion, the Supremacy of Law, and Social Order* (Philadelphia: M. Fithian, 1844).

K-F   Francis Patrick Kenrick and Marc Antony Frenaye, *The Kenrick-Frenaye Correspondence: Letters Chiefly of Francis Patrick Kenrick and Marc Antony Frenaye, Selected from the Cathedral Archives*, trans. and ed. Francis Edward Tourscher (Philadelphia: Wickersham, 1920).

Philadelphia Newspapers

Except where noted below, these titles are available on microfilm or in digital form. In addition to these, I consulted original paper editions of the *Christian Observer* at the Presbyterian Historical Society, the *Dollar Newspaper* at the American Antiquarian Society, the *Philadelphia Gazette* at the Historical Society of Pennsylvania, the *Protestant Banner* at the New York Public Library, the *Saturday Courier* at the Library of Congress, and the *Sentinel* at the State Library of Pennsylvania.

AA   *American Advocate*, LC. Citations to depositions from February and March 1845 are to clippings in GC, box 432, folder 5.

DC   *Daily Chronicle*, AAS.

CH   *Catholic Herald*

DS   *Daily Sun*, AAS (missing May–July 1844) and HSP (scattered issues, June and July 1844).

HJCS *Home Journal and Citizen Soldier*, HSP.

NatAm *Native American*, AAS.

NG   *National Gazette*

NorAm *North American*

PI   *Pennsylvania Inquirer*. After 1860, the *Philadelphia Inquirer*.

PL   *Public Ledger*

ST   *Spirit of the Times*, AAS, HSP, SLP, and LC.

TALR *Temperance Advocate and Literary Repository*, New-York Historical Society.

USG   *United States Gazette*

WS   *Weekly Sun*. HSP has May 11, 1844, issue.

ENDNOTES

A NOTE ON TERMINOLOGY
1   *NatAm*, November 14, 1844.

CHAPTER 1: HURRAH FOR THE NATIVES, AND KILL THE DAMNED IRISH!
1   *DS*, January 11, 1844.
2   *DS*, November 29, 1843.
3   *NatAm*, May 4, 1844.
4   *DC*, *PL*, and *ST*, all May 7, 1844; *NatAm*, May 6, 1844.
5   *PL*, May 7, 1844.
6   William Rankins testimony, *PL*, September 19, 1844.
7   *NatAm*, April 11, 1844.
8   *PL*, May 7, 1844; *NatAm*, May 23, 1844, June 1, 1844; William Rankins, John McManus, J. J. Gumper, and David McGinnis testimony, *PL*, September 19, 1844.
9   *PL*, May 3, 1844; *NatAm*, May 2, 1844; *PL*, January 1, 1838; *NatAm*, May 3, 1844; *DS*, January 24, 1845.
10 *PL*, May 7, 1844.
11 Peter Albright testimony, *PL*, October 17, 1844; *PL*, September 13, 1844; William Small and Joanna Maloy testimony, *PL*, September 14, 1844.
12 *Saturday Courier*, May 18, 1844; *A Full and Complete Account of the Late Awful Riots in Philadelphia: Embellished with Ten Engravings* (Philadelphia: John B. Perry, 1844), 59; *PL*, June 30, 1841; *PL*, May 11, 1844; *PL*, January 13, 1843.
13 David Fields testimony, *PL*, September 20, 1844; *PL*, January 13, 1843; John Donnell testimony, *PL*, September 13, 1844; *DC*, May 7, 1844.
14 Elizabeth Brown testimony, *PL*, September 16, 1844; *DC*, May 7, 1844; "The Philadelphia Riots," *New Englander* 2 (July 1844): 476.
15 *USG*, May 7, 1844; Fields testimony, *PL*, September 20, 1844; *DC*, May 7, 1844; Small and Alfred Clark testimony, *PL*, September 14, 1844.
16 Gumper testimony, *PL*, September 19, 1844. William Friheller and John Donnell testimony, *PL*, September 13, 1844; Augustus Peale and Joseph Wood testimony, *PL*, September 14, 1844; *DC*, May 31, 1844; *PL*, February 1, 1845; *DC*, May 7, 1844.
17 *PL*, February 9, 1844; *PL*, September 20, 1844.

18 *PL*, November 9, 1843; *DC*, November 28, 1843; Alfred Clark and Joseph Wood testimony, *PL*, September 14, 1844; Samuel Palmer testimony, *PL*, February 1, 1845. Some contemporary sources identify Fisher as Protestant, but Joseph Wood, a reporter, testified that Fisher was Catholic, and a Patrick Fisher of about the right age was buried in St. Michael's Roman Catholic Cemetery in 1854.

19 Alfred Clark and Joseph Wood testimony, *PL*, September 14, 1844; Ted Gurr, "Psychological Factors in Civil Violence," *World Politics* 20 (1968): 274.

20 Sidney George Fisher, *A Philadelphia Perspective: The Diary of Sidney George Fisher Covering the Years 1834–1871* (Philadelphia: Historical Society of Pennsylvania, 1967), 169.

21 Kerby A. Miller, *Emigrants and Exiles: Ireland and the Irish Exodus to North America* (New York: Oxford University Press, 1988), 178; James Matthew Gallman, *Receiving Erin's Children: Philadelphia, Liverpool, and the Irish Famine Migration, 1845–1855* (Chapel Hill: University of North Carolina Press, 2000), 32. The 1840 census did not record nativity. By 1850, the Irish comprised 27 percent of Philadelphia County's population, but that was only after the Famine migration. Bruce Laurie, "'Nothing on Compulsion': Life Styles of Philadelphia Artisans, 1820-1850," *Labor History* 15 (1974): 338.

CHAPTER 2: BRILLIANT AND UNSCRUPULOUS

1 Isaac Markens, *The Hebrews in America: A Series of Historical and Biographical Sketches* (New York: 1888), 176; James William Hagy, *This Happy Land: The Jews of Colonial and Antebellum Charleston* (Tuscaloosa: University of Alabama Press, 1993), 15; *Catalogue of the Euphradian Society of the South Carolina College* (Columbia, SC: 1842), 16; Edwin L. Green, *A History of the University of South Carolina* (Columbia, SC: State, 1916), 272; *Columbia Telescope, and South Carolina State Journal*, January 13, 1826; *South Carolina State Gazette* (Columbia), June 9, 1827, December 5, 1827; *Roll of Students of South Carolina College, 1805–1905* (Columbia, SC, 1905), 12; *The Cincinnati Directory for the Year 1829* (Cincinnati: Robinson and Fairbank, 1829), 76. "The Genealogy of Lewis C. Levin," Zachary M. Schrag, https://zacharyschrag.com/riots/the-genealogy-of-lewis-c-levin/.

2 *Cincinnati Chronicle and Literary Gazette*, May 23, 1829; *Woodville Republican*, May 29, 1830, June 19, 1830.

3 "Woodville Academy," *Mississippi Democrat*, April 23, 1831, July 9, 1831; Henry Stuart Foote, *Casket of Reminiscences* (Washington, DC: Chronicle Publishing, 1874), 66; *Woodville Republican*, December 4, 1830; Markens, *Hebrews in America*, 176; *Biographical and Historical Memoirs of Mississippi* (Chicago: Goodspeed, 1891), 2:309.

4 John W. Forney, *Anecdotes of Public Men* (New York: Harper & Brothers, 1873), 135; Foote, *Casket of Reminiscences*, 66; Sidney Smith, *The Principles of Phrenology* (W. Tait, 1838), 211; Madeleine Vinton Dahlgren, *A Washington Winter* (J. R. Osgood, 1883), 188; Alexander Kelly McLure, *Old Time Notes of Pennsylvania* (Philadelphia: John C. Winston, 1905), 89.

5 Foote, *Casket of Reminiscences*, 66–67; *Boston Pilot*, January 16, 1847; *Baltimore Sun*, March 16, 1860; Jonathan D. Sarna, "Intermarriage in America: The Jewish Experience in Historical Context," in *Ambivalent Jew: Charles Liebman in Memoriam*, ed. Stuart Cohen and Bernard Susser (New York: Jewish Theological Seminary of America, 2007), 128–129; Charles Reznikoff and Uriah Zevi Engelman, *The Jews of Charleston: A History of an American Jewish Community* (Philadelphia: Jewish Publication Society of America, 1950),

118; James Patrick, *Architecture in Tennessee, 1768–1897* (Knoxville: University of Tennessee Press, 1990), 109; James Knox Polk, Herbert Weaver, and Wayne Cutler, *Correspondence of James K. Polk: 1833–1834* (Knoxville: University of Tennessee Press, 1972), 225n5.

6   Foote, *Casket of Reminiscences*, 67; Jean Muir Dorsey and Maxwell Jay Dorsey, *Christopher Gist of Maryland and Some of His Descendants, 1679–1957* (Chicago: J. S. Swift Co., 1969), 136–161; Thomasina Hammond Gist in Maryland, Births and Christenings Index, 1662–1911, available at Ancestry.com. The 1850 census lists Julia as forty years old. All individual census listings cited here are available at Ancestry.com.

7   Loren Schweninger, *Petitions to Southern County Courts, 1775–1867* (Champaign: University of Illinois Press, 2008), 165; Julia A. M. Gist, *Maryland, Compiled Marriages, 1655–1850,* available at Ancestry.com; *Baltimore Gazette and Daily Advertiser,* December 4, 1834.

8   *National Banner and Nashville Whig* (Tennessee), January 6, 1834; *Baltimore Sun,* March 16, 1860; Alexander Kelly McLure, *Old Time Notes of Pennsylvania* (Philadelphia: John C. Winston, 1905), 89; *ST,* October 4, 1844; *Weekly Raleigh Register* (North Carolina), June 28, 1836; *ST,* September 25, 1844; *TALR,* January 14, 1843; *AA,* September 12, 1844; *Richmond Enquirer,* November 27, 1849.

9   *Baltimore Patriot,* November 28, 1836; *Matchett's Baltimore Directory* (Baltimore: R. J. Matchett, 1837–1838), 204; Reverdy Johnson and Hugh Davey Evans to Theodoric Bland, Chancellor of Maryland, October 23, 1846, in Louis [*sic*] C. Levin and Julia A. M. Levin, wife, vs. John H. Iglehart, Baltimore City, 1846, 17,898-9350, Chancery Court, Chancery Papers, Maryland State Archives, 512-11-9350.

10   The 1850 census states that Louisa was born in Maryland in January 1840. Levin was admitted to the Pennsylvania bar "about 1840." John Hill Martin, *Martin's Bench and Bar of Philadelphia* (Philadelphia: Rees Welsh, 1883), 287; William S. Hastings, "Philadelphia Microcosm," *Pennsylvania Magazine of History and Biography* 91 (April 1967): 166, 173; Domenic Vitiello and George E. Thomas, *The Philadelphia Stock Exchange and the City It Made* (Philadelphia: University of Pennsylvania Press, 2010), 69; Thomas Hamilton, *Men and Manners in America* (Edinburgh: W. Blackwood, 1833), 1:337; George Rogers Taylor, "'Philadelphia in Slices' by George G. Foster," *Pennsylvania Magazine of History and Biography* 93, no. 1 (January 1969): 29, 71.

11   *ST,* September 30, 1848; *DS,* November 20, 1844.

12   Joanne B. Freeman, *The Field of Blood: Violence in Congress and the Road to Civil War* (New York: Farrar, Straus and Giroux, 2018); Foote, *Casket of Reminiscences,* 67.

13   Ian R. Tyrrell, *Sobering Up: From Temperance to Prohibition in Antebellum America, 1800–1860* (Westport, CT: Greenwood Press, 1979), 25–26; Marcia Carlisle, "Disorderly City, Disorderly Women: Prostitution in Ante-Bellum Philadelphia." *Pennsylvania Magazine of History and Biography* 110, no. 4 (October 1986): 552; *PL,* September 26, 1843; Ric Northrup Caric, "'To Drown the Ills That Discompose the Mind': Care, Leisure, and Identity Among Philadelphia Artisans and Workers, 1785–1840," *Pennsylvania History* 64, no. 4 (October 1997): 483–484; Matthew Warner Osborn, "A Detestable Shrine: Alcohol Abuse in Antebellum Philadelphia," *Journal of the Early Republic* 29, no. 1 (2009): 101–32; *PL,* September 25, 1844; Bruce Dorsey, *Reforming Men and Women: Gender in the Antebellum City* (Cornell University Press, 2002), chap. 3.

14   Foote, *Casket of Reminiscences,* 69; *ST,* September 28, 1844; *TALR,* February 25, 1843; *PL,* February 1, 1842; Tyrrell, *Sobering Up,* 164; *Daily Pennsylvanian* (Philadelphia),

March 30, 1841. Levin is listed as insolvent on April 15, 1841. List of Insolvents, March 1841, Commencing Wednesday, April 14, 1841, Insolvent Docket, April 1836–August 1842, PCA.

15 Tyrrell, *Sobering Up*, 165–170; James R. Rohrer, "The Origins of the Temperance Movement: A Reinterpretation," *Journal of American Studies* 24 (1990): 228–35; *Vermont Watchman and State Journal* (Montpelier), January 23, 1832; *PI*, March 18, 1841; *TALR*, February 25, 1843.

16 *TALR*, December 4, 1841; *TALR*, February 25, 1843; *DS*, October 23, 1843; William Elliot Griffis, *John Chambers: Servant of Christ and Master of Hearts and His Ministry in Philadelphia* (Ithaca, NY: Andrus & Church, 1903); John Edmands, "The Early History of the Ninth Presbyterian Church and the Chambers Independent Church," *Journal of Presbyterian History* 5 (December 1910), 376–377; James E. P. Boulden, *The Presbyterians of Baltimore:* (W. J. Boyle & Son, 1875), 125–127; John Thomas Scharf and Thompson Westcott, *History of Philadelphia, 1609–1884* (Philadelphia: L. H. Everts, 1884), 2:1293; *Baltimore Gazette and Daily Advertiser*, December 4, 1834.

17 Griffis, *John Chambers*, 49–51; *DC*, June 29, 1843.

18 *ST*, September 3, 1844; Statement of Peter Hay, appended to Hugh Davey Evans and Reverdy Johnson to Theodoric Bland, Chancellor of Maryland, April 13, 1844, Louis C. Levin and Julia A. M. Levin vs. John H. Iglehart, Samuel J. Donaldson, and Hugh Davey Evans, Anne Arundel Co., 1844, Chancery Court, Chancery Papers, Maryland State Archives, 512-11-9214; *TALR*, June 18, 1842; *TALR*, September 10, 1842; "Temperance and Religion," *Journal of the American Temperance Union*, June 1, 1842; *DS*, November 25, 1843; *PL*, February 24, 1845; *DS*, April 1, 1844; *DS*, September 12, 1844.

19 July 4, 1838, AJP, 168; *ST*, August 22, 1845; *TALR*, December 4, 1841; "Progress of Temperance," *Advocate of Moral Reform* 7 (November 15, 1841).

20 *ST*, September 5, 1844; *TALR*, September 25, 1841; *TALR*, October 5, 1842.

21 *TALR*, June 4, 1842, January 14, 1843.

22 *DS*, October 24, 1843; *DC*, December 13, 1842; William Fearing Gill, *The Life of Edgar Allan Poe* (New York: W. J. Widdleton, 1880), 125; *TALR*, December 4, 1841; "Excursion to Philadelphia," *Journal of the American Temperance Union*, February 1, 1843, 25; *TALR*, January 29, 1842.

23 *TALR*, August 14 and 28, 1841; Nicholas B. Wainwright and Samuel Breck, "The Diary of Samuel Breck, 1839–1840," *Pennsylvania Magazine of History and Biography* 103 (1979): 504; Alexis de Tocqueville, *Democracy in America*, trans. Arthur Goldhammer (New York: Library of America, 2012), 211.

24 *PL*, February 1, 1842.

25 Edward J. Balleisen, chap. 4 in *Navigating Failure: Bankruptcy and Commercial Society in Antebellum America* (Chapel Hill: University of North Carolina Press, 2001), 120; Francis Wyse, *America, Its Realities and Resource* (London: T. C. Newby, 1846), 1:146; Sarmiento is identified as a tailor in *McElroy's Philadelphia City Directory, 1842*, 233; Levin to the Honorable Judge of the District Court for the Eastern District of Pennsylvania, April 6, 1842, Louis [*sic*] C. Levin and Julia A. M. Levin, wife, vs. John H. Iglehart, Baltimore City, 1846, 17,898-9350, Chancery Court, Chancery Papers, Maryland State Archives, 512-11-9350.

26   *TALR*, January 14, 1843, January 28, 1843; *PL*, November 28, 1842; *TALR*, December 3,
     1842; *Baltimore Sun*, February 23, 1843; *Baltimore Saturday Visiter*, August 12, 1843.
27   *TALR*, February 25, 1843, March 11, 1843, May 20, 1843; *Pennsylvanian*, February 25,
     1843; *New-York Tribune*, September 1, 1843.

CHAPTER 3: THE BEST AMATEUR OFFICER IN THE UNITED STATES

1   I. Pemberton Hutchinson to Cadwalader, September 16, 1831, box 403, folder 3, GC; Edward
     Pessen, *Riches, Class, and Power Before the Civil War* (Lexington, MA: D. C. Heath, 1973),
     40–54; Sven Beckert, *The Monied Metropolis: New York City and the Consolidation of the American
     Bourgeoisie, 1850–1896* (New York: Cambridge University Press, 2003), 19; A Merchant of
     Philadelphia, *Memoirs and Auto-Biography of Some of the Wealthy Citizens of Philadelphia*,
     (Philadelphia: The Booksellers, 1846). The 1850 census lists Cadwalader's wealth as $250,000,
     which could have placed him among the city's wealthiest forty.
2   Thomas Allen Glenn, *Merion in the Welsh Tract* (Norristown, 1896), 257; Sandra L.
     Cadwalader, *The Cadwaladers, 1677–1879: Five Generations of a Philadelphia Family*
     (Wawa, PA.: S. L. Cadwalader, 1996), 12–13, 71; Henry Simpson, *The Lives of Eminent
     Philadelphians, Now Deceased* (Philadelphia: William Brotherhead, 1859), 167–69.
3   Cadwalader, *Cadwaladers*, 103; Nicholas B. Wainwright, "The Penn Collection,"
     Pennsylvania Magazine of History and Biography 87, no. 4 (October 1963): 419; George
     Cadwalader to Gabriel Shaw, October 29, 1841, vol. 187, George Cadwalader Letterbook,
     1841–1848, GC; Henry R. Stills (?) to George Cadwalader, February 20, 1828, 403, 1, GC;
     George Cadwalader to Horace Binney, March 15, 1834, box 403, folder 5, GC.
4   J. S. Buckingham, *America: Historical, Statistic, and Descriptive* (New York: Harper, 1841),
     1:362; John C. Cruger to George Cadwalader, November 6, 1829, box 403, folder 1, GC;
     John Sartain, *Brigadier General George Cadwalader*, mezzotint, ca. 1842, Library of
     Congress; Charles J. Peterson, *The Military Heroes of the War with Mexico*, 3rd ed.
     (Philadelphia: William A. Leary, 1849), 274; D. Corcoran, *Pickings from the Portfolio of the
     Reporter of the New Orleans "Picayune"* (Philadelphia: T. B. Peterson, 1846), 160.
5   James Mease, *The Picture of Philadelphia* (Philadelphia: Kite, 1811); Malcolm Bell Jr., *Major
     Butler's Legacy: Five Generations of a Slaveholding Family* (Athens: University of Georgia
     Press, 2004).
6   John C. Cruger to George Cadwalader, November 6, 1829, box 403, folder 1, GC; Fanny
     Cadwalader to George Cadwalader, July 20, 1842, box 404, folder 3, GC; Fanny Cadwalader
     to George Cadwalader, July 15, 1845, box 404, folder 7, GC; Cadwalader, *Cadwaladers*, 115;
     Beckert, *Monied Metropolis*, 33; Pessen, *Riches, Class, and Power*, 214; George Cadwalader to
     Richard Penn, October 29, 1841, vol. 187. George Cadwalader Letterbook, 1841–1848, GC.
7   Horace Wemyss Smith, *Life and Correspondence of the Rev. William Smith* (S. A. George,
     1880), 551; Brewster, Lawrence, & Co. to George Cadwalader, May 10, 1831, box 403, folder 3,
     GC; George Cadwalader to Messrs. Welles & Co., Paris, April 1, 1836, box 403, folder 6, GC;
     Sidney George Fisher, *A Philadelphia Perspective: The Diary of Sidney George Fisher Covering
     the Years 1834–1871* (Philadelphia: Historical Society of Pennsylvania, 1967), 44, 76, 97;
     Jack L. Lindsey, "The Cadwalader Family during the Early Nineteenth Century,"
     Philadelphia Museum of Art Bulletin 91, no. 384/385 (October 1996): 41; William S.
     Hastings, "Philadelphia Microcosm," *Pennsylvania Magazine of History and Biography* 91

(April 1967): 170; William Newnham Blane, *Travels through the United States and Canada* (London: Baldwin, 1828), 24.

8   Charles Fletcher (?) to George Cadwalader, September 1835, box 403, folder 5, GC; Fisher, *Philadelphia Perspective*, 105; Middle Ward Assessment for 1841, 155, PCA; Edward G. Leffingwell, "'A Fine Animal': Portraits of General George Cadwalader of Philadelphia" (master's thesis, University of Cincinnati, 1985), 72; Pessen, *Riches, Class, and Power*, 28n14; *The Philadelphia Club, 1834–1934* (Philadelphia, 1934), 14, 36–42.

9   Fisher, *Philadelphia Perspective*, 81; Fanny Cadwalader to George Cadwalader, July 20, 1842, box 404, folder 3, GC.

10   *Times* (Philadelphia), February 4, 1879.

11   Lawrence Delbert Cress, *Citizens in Arms: The Army and the Militia in American Society to the War of 1812* (Chapel Hill: University of North Carolina Press, 1982), chap. 2; Edmund S. Morgan, *Inventing the People: The Rise of Popular Sovereignty in England and America* (New York: W. W. Norton, 1988), 156–157.

12   Joseph J. Holmes, "The Decline of the Pennsylvania Militia: 1815–1870," *Western Pennsylvania History* 57 (April 1974): 202; Jessica Choppin Roney, "Government without Arms; Arms without Government The Case of Pennsylvania," in *Between Sovereignty and Anarchy: The Politics of Violence in the American Revolutionary Era*, ed. Patrick Griffin et al. (Charlottesville: University of Virginia Press, 2015), 85; Cress, *Citizens in Arms*, 48–49, 55; David Ammerman, *In the Common Cause: American Response to the Coercive Acts of 1774* (Charlottesville: University Press of Virginia, 1974), 141; Morgan, *Inventing the People*, 172.

13   David P. Szatmary, *Shays' Rebellion: The Making of an Agrarian Insurrection* (Amherst: University of Massachusetts Press, 1980), 129–130; US Const., art. I, § 8; "Republican Government: Brutus, no. 1," in *The Complete Anti-Federalist*, ed. Herbert J. Storing, vol. 1, chap. 4, doc. 14, The Founders' Constitution, University of Chicago Press and the Liberty Fund, http://press-pubs.uchicago.edu/founders/documents/v1ch4s14.html; Noah Shutserman, *Armed Citizens: The Road from Ancient Rome to the Second Amendment* (Charlottesville: University of Virginia Press, 2020), 198–214.

14   Susan G. Davis, *Parades and Power: Street Theatre in Nineteenth-Century Philadelphia* (Philadelphia: Temple University Press, 1986), 55, 78–81; Gary B. Nash, *First City: Philadelphia and the Forging of Historical Memory* (Philadelphia: University of Pennsylvania Press, 2006), 163; Kenneth McCreedy, "Palladium of Liberty: The American Militia System, 1815–1861" (PhD diss., University of California Berkeley, 1991), 44–47; David Tatham, "David Claypoole Johnston's 'Militia Muster,'" *American Art Journal* 19 (Spring 1987), 8; *NorAm*, June 29, 1839; A. V. Parsons, Circular, September 3, 1842, Militia Letter Book, 1839–1861, series 26.22, PSA; "The Militia," *New York Military Magazine* 1 (December 11, 1841), 409, quoting *NorAm*; *DC*, November 7, 1843.

15   Mark David Luccioni, "'Fire and Be Damned': Philadelphia Volunteers and the Use of Force in the Riots of 1844" (PhD diss., Temple University, 1996), 18–21.

16   *PL*, September 23, 1844; Stewart Lewis Gates, "Disorder and Social Organization: The Militia in Connecticut Public Life, 1660–1860" (PhD diss., University of Connecticut, 1975), 164–65; "The Present Militia System," *Portsmouth Journal of Literature and Politics*, October 5, 1833. Some independent companies had been formed in the colonial era; see Lyle D. Brundage, "The Organization, Administration, and Training of the United States

Ordinary and Volunteer Militia, 1792–1861" (PhD diss., University of Michigan, 1959), 10; Joseph J. Holmes, "National Guard of Pennsylvania: Policeman of Industry, 1865–1905" (PhD diss., University of Connecticut, 1970), 42; *American State Papers: Military Affairs* (Washington, DC: Gales & Seaton, 1860), 3:430; Senate Committee on the Militia, *Memorial of Militia Officers of Baltimore, Maryland*, 29th Cong., 1st sess., 1846, 4.

17 "War," *New York Military Magazine*, September 4, 1841; McCreedy, "Palladium of Liberty," 345–346; Adam Diller to Brigade Inspectors, March 30, 1840, box 1, General Correspondence, 1839–41, General Correspondence, Office of the Adjutant General, series 19.29, PSA; *NG*, March 7, 1835; Russell F. Weigley, *History of the United States Army* (New York: Macmillan, 1967), 162–163; Editorial, *New York Military Magazine*, June 26, 1841, 41; Hector Tyndale et al. to George Cadwalader, November 15, 1842, box 404, folder 3, GC; Augustus Pleasonton to Thomas Burrowes, November 23, 1837, box 2, folder 1837–1839, Militia Returns, 1st Div-1st Brig, 1800–1849, RG 26, PSA; John Titcomb Sprague, *The Origin, Progress, and Conclusion of the Florida War* (New York: D. Appleton, 1848), 102.

18 Gates, "Disorder And Social Organization," 174; "To the Soldiers of Uniform Corps," *New York Military Magazine*, July 3, 1841, 59; "Mohican Riflemen," *New York Military Magazine*, June 19, 1841, 30; Robert A. Margo, *Wages and Labor Markets in the United States, 1820–1860* (Chicago: University of Chicago Press, 2000), Table 3A.6; Holmes, "National Guard of Pennsylvania," 41; *New York Military Magazine*, October 16, 1841; McCreedy, "Palladium of Liberty," 101; Luccioni, "'Fire and Be Damned,'" 55; Ricardo A. Herrera, "Self-Governance and the American Citizen as Soldier, 1775–1861," *Journal of Military History* 65 (January 2001): 26.

19 Brundage, "Organization, Administration, and Training," 92; Jerry M. Cooper, *The Rise of the National Guard: The Evolution of the American Militia, 1865–1920* (Lincoln: University of Nebraska Press, 1997), 13–15; Luccioni, "'Fire and Be Damned,'" 48–49; *Dollar Newspaper*, February 28, 1844.

20 *American State Papers: Military Affairs*, 3:421; "Annual Report of the Adjutant General," in *Reports of the Heads of Departments to the Governor of Pennsylvania, in Pursuance of the Law for the Fiscal Year Ending 30th November 1843* (Harrisburg: Isaac G. M'Kinley, 1844), 3; *Lives of David R. Porter and Joseph Ritner, the Two Candidates for the Office of Governor of Pennsylvania* (n.p., 1838), 14; Francis Wyse, *America, Its Realities and Resource* (London: T. C. Newby, 1846), 107; "Union Guards, Captain Stillwell," *New York Military Magazine*, September 4, 1841, 221. *PL*, October 4, 1838; "Disgraceful," *New York Military Magazine*, November 6, 1841, 351.

21 *History of the First Troop Philadelphia City Cavalry* (Philadelphia, 1875), 168, 185; Charles Penrose Keith, *The Provincial Councillors of Pennsylvania*. (W. S. Sharp, 1883), 382; "Philadelphia Grays," *Military Magazine and Record of the Volunteers of the City and County of Philadelphia* I, no. 4 (June 1839); James Abbott testimony, 1st Brig., 1st Div., Pennsylvania Militia, testimony concerning 1835 militia election, box 429, folder 6, GC; Arms, Military Stores and Armories, 1st Brig., 1st Div. PM, Requisition & Army Record Books, vol. 1, 1840–1844, p. 1, series 19.68, PSA.

22 "Cost of Equipment Company. D.," n.d., box 430, folder 8, GC; John Thomas Scharf and Thompson Westcott, *History of Philadelphia, 1609–1884* (Philadelphia: L. H. Everts, 1884), 2:1018; *New York Herald* (?), November 1843, box 429, folder 12, GC; *DC*, November 7,

1843; Dinger to George Cadwalader, November 13, 1843, box 430, folder 8, GC; Charles J. Peterson, *The Military Heroes of the War with Mexico*, 3rd ed. (Philadelphia: William A. Leary, 1849), 270; George Cadwalader to James Reeside, May 21, 1833 [copy], box 403, folder 4, GC.

23 Circular, First Brigade, First Division, PM, January 13, 1834, box 429, folder 1, GC; List of Names for whom Commissions are required, December 24, 1835, box 2, folder: 1835–1836, Militia Returns, 1st Div-1st Brig, 1800–1849, RG 26, PSA; Terry M. Mays and Spencer C. Tucker, "Samuel Ringgold," in *U.S. Leadership in Wartime: Clashes, Controversy, and Compromise*, ed. Spencer Tucker (Santa Barbara, CA: ABC-CLIO, 2009), 243–244; Kenderton Smith, et al., "Military Encampment," October 26, 1841, box 430, folder 2, GC.

24 George Cadwalader to Henry Allen Johnson, July 10, 1841, vol. 186, George Cadwalader Letterbook (Jan–Aug 1841), GC; Multiple letters, October 29, 1841, vol. 187, George Cadwalader Letterbook, 1841–1848, GC.

25 *Saturday Courier*, April 16, 1842, April 23, 1842; William Jackson et al. to George Cadwalader, April 18, 1842, box 430, folder 3, GC.

26 Major General R. Patterson, October 20, 1835, box 429, folder 10, GC; *NorAm*, June 6, 1842, June 7, 1842; William Jackson et al. to George Cadwalader, April 18, 1842, box 430, folder 3, GC; *PI*, June 18, 1835, June 8, 1842; Wyse, *America*, 2:112.

27 H. D. Maxwell to George Cadwalader, June 25, 1842; *Whig and Journal* (Easton, PA), undated clipping and September 7, 1842; *Democrat and Argus* (Easton, PA), September 8, 184; *Whig and Journal* (Easton, PA), all in box 430, folder 4, GC.

28 *Whig and Journal* (Easton, PA), September 7, 1842, and *Democrat and Argus* (Easton, PA), September 8, 1842, box 430, folder 4, GC; George Cadwalader to Mary Cadwalader, September 5, 1842, box 404, folder 3, GC.

29 Hector Tyndale et al. to George Cadwalader, November 15, 1842, box 404, folder 3, GC; Leffingwell, "Fine Animal," 9–10, 87; *DC*, June 7, 1843; Sartain, *Brigadier General George Cadwalader*; Waldron & Ackerman to George Cadwalader, July 27, 1842, box 404, folder 3, GC.

CHAPTER 4: AMERICAN-BORN CITIZENS

1 Kenneth Silverman, *Lightning Man: The Accursed Life of Samuel F.B. Morse* (New York: Alfred A. Knopf, 2003), 236.

2 Samuel Finley Breese Morse, *Foreign Conspiracy Against the Liberties of the United States*, 2nd ed. (New York: Leavitt, Lord, 1835), xxvi, 9; Charles Brecher, "Mayoralty," in *The Encyclopedia of New York City*, Kenneth T. Jackson, ed. (New Haven: Yale University Press, 1995), 735.

3 Abednego Seller, *The History of Passive Obedience Since the Reformation* (Amsterdam: T. Johnson, 1689), 2; Linda Colley, *Britons: Forging the Nation 1707–1837* (New Haven: Yale University Press, 2005), 18; Tony Claydon and Ian McBride, "The Trials of the Chosen Peoples: Recent Interpretations of Protestantism and National Identity in Britain and Ireland," in *Protestantism and National Identity: Britain and Ireland, c. 1650–c. 1850*, ed. Tony Claydon and Ian McBride (New York: Cambridge University Press, 1998), 3–30.

4 Jason K. Duncan, *Citizens or Papists?: The Politics of Anti-Catholicism in New York, 1685–1821* (New York: Fordham University Press, 2005), 23; Maura Jane Farrelly, *Papist Patriots: The Making of an American Catholic Identity*, chap. 5 (New York: Oxford University Press, 2012);

Rodger M. Payne, "Nativism and Religion in America," in *Oxford Research Encyclopedia of Religion*, ed. John Barton (New York: Oxford University Press, 2017).

5   Sister Blanche Marie, "The Catholic Church in Colonial Pennsylvania," *Pennsylvania History: A Journal of Mid-Atlantic Studies* 3, no. 4 (1936), 241; Joseph J. Casino, "Anti-Popery in Colonial Pennsylvania," *Pennsylvania Magazine of History and Biography* 105 (July 1981), 289; Thomas Hughes, *History of the Society of Jesus in North America: Colonial and Federal. 1605-1838* (Burrows Brothers, 1917), 500; Joseph Louis J. Kirlin, *Catholicity in Philadelphia* (Philadelphia: J. J. McVey, 1909), 83.

6   Thomas S. Kidd, *God of Liberty: A Religious History of the American Revolution* (New York: Basic Books, 2010), 58; "Remarks on the Quebec Bill: Part One, [June 15, 1775]," Founders Online, National Archives, last modified June 13, 2018, http://founders.archives.gov/ documents/Hamilton/01-01-02-0058 (Original source: *The Papers of Alexander Hamilton, vol. 1, 1768–1778*, ed. Harold C. Syrett [New York: Columbia University Press, 1961], 165–169); Owen Stanwood, "Catholics, Protestants, and the Clash of Civilizations in Early America," in *The First Prejudice: Religious Tolerance and Intolerance in Early America*, ed. Chris Beneke and Christopher S. Grenda (Philadelphia: University of Pennsylvania Press, 2011), 239–240; *The Papers of George Washington Digital Edition*, ed. Theodore J. Crackel (Charlottesville: University of Virginia Press, Rotunda, 2008).

7   Updegraph v. Commonwealth, 11 Serg. & Rawle 394 Pa. 1824, The Founders' Constitution, University of Chicago Press and the Liberty Fund, http://press-pubs.uchicago.edu/ founders/; Joel Jones, "Protestantism," *Biblical Repertory and Princeton Review*, January 1837, 25; Joseph Story, *Commentaries on the Constitution of the United States* (Boston: Hilliard, Gray, 1833), 3:725.

8   *AA*, November 9, 1844; Ira M. Leonard, "The Rise and Fall of the American Republican Party in New York City, 1843–1845," *New-York Historical Society Quarterly* 50 (April 1966): 159–162; Leonard Tabachnik, "Origins of the Know-Nothing Party: A Study of the Native American Party in Philadelphia, 1844–1852" (PhD diss., Columbia University, 1973), 118.

9   "The Philadelphia Riots," *Freeman's Journal* (Dublin, Ireland), May 31, 1844. See also "The New Clay-Whig Native-American Party," *ST*, April 23, 1844; *Native American* (Washington, DC), March 17, 1838; *Indiana State Sentinel*, July 23, 1846.

10   Kerby A. Miller, *Emigrants and Exiles: Ireland and the Irish Exodus to North America* (New York: Oxford University Press, 1988), 169, 178–198, 219–221, 252–259; Emma Jones Lapsansky, "South Street Philadelphia, 1762-1854: 'A Haven for Those Low in the World.'" (PhD diss., University of Pennsylvania, 1975), 5; Richard L. Forstall, ed., *Population of States and Counties of the United States: 1790 to 1990* (Washington, DC: Bureau of the Census, 1996); Campbell Gibson, *Population of the Largest 100 Cities and Other Urban Places in the United States: 1790 to 1990* (Washington, DC: Bureau of the Census, 1998); Malcolm Campbell, *Ireland's New Worlds: Immigrants, Politics, and Society in the United States and Australia, 1815–1922* (Madison: University of Wisconsin Press, 2008), 7; Hugh J. Nolan, *The Most Reverend Francis Patrick Kenrick* (Philadelphia: American Catholic Historical Society, 1948), 180 (title hereafter shortened to *Kenrick*); *DC*, July 31, 1843; John Belchem, *Irish, Catholic and Scouse: The History of the Liverpool-Irish, 1800–1939* (Liverpool: Liverpool University Press, 2007), 5; Pennsylvania Secretary of Internal Affairs, *Annual Report, Part III: Industrial Statistics* (Harrisburg, PA: Edwin K. Meyers, 1891), 29:16C; *PL*, June 1, 1844.

11   *DC*, April 29, 1843.

12   *Long-Island Star*, July 20, 1835, October 26, 1835; Leo Hershkowitz, "The Native American
      Democratic Association in New York City, 1835–1836," *New-York Historical Society Quarterly*
      46 (1962): 51–53, 58; *Weekly Standard* (Raleigh, NC), November 19, 1835; Louis Dow
      Scisco, *Political Nativism in New York State* (New York: Columbia University Press, 1901),
      30; *New York Herald*, March 14, 1837; *Evening Post* (New York), June 25, 1835.

13   William W. Warner, *At Peace with All Their Neighbors: Catholics and Catholicism in the
      National Capital, 1787–1860* (Washington, DC: Georgetown University Press, 1994),
      206–212; *Germantown Telegraph*, September 13, 1837, June 12, 1844; *PI*, September 26,
      1837; *Address of the Louisiana Native American Association, to the Citizens of Louisiana and the
      Inhabitants of the United States* (New Orleans, 1839), 7. After 1837, the next reference I could
      find to a Germantown nativist association in the *Germantown Telegraph* is in June 1844. It is
      described as "the first Native American Meeting in this place," suggesting that the *Telegraph*
      editors were unaware of any extant group.

14   Tabachnik, "Origins of the Know-Nothing Party," 9.

15   Charles Ellet Jr., *A Map of the County of Philadelphia from Actual Survey*, 1843; William S.
      Hastings, "Philadelphia Microcosm," *Pennsylvania Magazine of History and Biography* 91 (April
      1967): 168; Tax Assessor's Ledger: Southwark, 1841, State Tax Assessment, RG 1.8, PCA;
      William Heighton, *The Principles of Aristocratic Legislation* (Philadelphia: J. Coates, 1828), 6;
      Ronald Schultz, *Republic of Labor: Philadelphia Artisans and the Politics of Class, 1720–1830* (New
      York: Oxford University Press, 1993), 232; Louis H. Arky, "The Mechanics' Union of Trade
      Associations and the Formation of the Philadelphia Workingmen's Movement," *Pennsylvania
      Magazine of History and Biography* 76 (1952): 142–176; *Pennsylvanian*, April 7, 1836.

16   Thomas D. Grover, *The Will of the Late Thomas D. Grover, Esq.* (Southwark, PA: H. B. Pierson,
      1849), 5-6; George McLeod and James Stuart, To the Board of Commissioners of the District of
      Southwark, *PI*, August 31, 1833, June 28, 1844; John Thomas Scharf and Thompson Westcott,
      History of Philadelphia, 1609–1884 (Philadelphia: L. H. Everts, 1884), 3:1775; *PL*, March 31,
      1838; *NG*, October 18, 1836, April 11, 1839, April 23, 1840; *Pennsylvanian*, November 29,
      1834, April 17, 1835, April 12, 1836; *ST*, October 8, 1845; *Poulson's American Daily Advertiser*,
      September 30, 1823; *NorAm*, September 3, 1840.

17   *Pennsylvanian*, April 7, 1836, September 27, 1837, April 15, 1840, March 31, 1841, March
      15, 1842; Donald B. Cole, *Martin van Buren and the American Political System* (1984; repr.,
      Princeton, NJ: Princeton University Press, 2014), 308–309, 331–332; *PI*, July 30, 1836; *PL*,
      March 18, 1842, March 19, 1842; *NorAm*, May 18, 1842; Scharf and Westcott, *History of
      Philadelphia*, 3:1727.

18   "Paynter, Lemuel," *Biographical Directory of the United States Congress*, https://bioguide.
      congress.gov/search/bio/P000155; Thomas Lynch Montgomery, ed., *Pennsylvania
      Archives, Sixth Series* (Harrisburg, PA: Harrisburg Publishing, 1907), 7:42; *Pennsylvanian*,
      July 24, 1834; November 28, 1834; *PI*, February 12, 1833; *The Philadelphia Directory and
      Stranger's Guide* (Philadelphia: Thomas Wilson, 1825), 108; *The Philadelphia Directory and
      Register for 1819* (Philadelphia: John Adams Paxton, 1819), page "PEA"; *NG*, May 5, 1825;
      "Southwark," *Register of Pennsylvania* 1 (May 10, 1828): 304; "Proceedings of the Meeting
      of the Democratic Members of the Legislature of Pennsylvania," *Washington Review and
      Examiner* (Washington, PA), April 5, 1834.

19   *PI*, July 4, 1833, August 22, 1836, September 23, 1836; John Hugh Campbell, *History of the Friendly Sons of St. Patrick and of the Hibernian Society for the Relief of Emigrants from Ireland* (Philadelphia: Hibernian Society, 1892), 441; *Pennsylvanian*, September 17, 1834, January 20, 1835, January 30, 1836, June 4, 1836; John W. Jordan, *Colonial and Revolutionary Families of Pennsylvania* (Baltimore: Genealogical Publishing, 2004), 255; *PL*, June 26, 1844; John McCoy, Philadelphia, PA, Death Certificates Index, 1803–1915, available at Ancestry.com.

20   *PI*, August 23, 1836, September 21, 1836; *Star and Banner* (Gettysburg, PA), September 19, 1836; *Pennsylvanian*, August 24, 1836, September 24, 1836, October 7, 1836.

21   *PL*, January 4, 1842; Alexander Kelly McLure, *Old Time Notes of Pennsylvania* (Philadelphia: John C. Winston, 1905), 69; Thomas McCully testimony, *AA*, July 16, 1844; *PI*, June 28, 1844; *PL*, October 7, 1843; *New-York Tribune*, July 12, 1843, August 2, 1843, September 26, 1843.

22   *PL*, August 8, 1843, October 5, 1843, October 21, 1843; *New-York Tribune*, July 12, 1843; *DC*, October 7, 1843; *Brooklyn Eagle*, October 12, 1843.

23   Leonard, "The Rise and Fall of the American Republican Party in New York City, 1843–1845," 162.

24   Leonard, "The Rise and Fall of the American Republican Party in New York City, 1843–1845," 162–164; *New York Herald*, November 8, 1843.

25   *PI*, December 6, 1843; "The Kensington Massacre, Philadelphia," *Republic: A Magazine for the Defence of Civil and Religious Liberty* 1 (August 1845): 8; *DS*, December 13, 1843, December 21, 1843, January 11, 1844; *PL*, January 26, 1844, January 30, 1844; *NatAm*, April 22, 1844; *ST*, July 26, 1844.

26   Bruce Laurie, *Working People of Philadelphia, 1800–1850* (Philadelphia: Temple University Press, 1983), 169; *DC*, October 8, 1844; *NatAm*, May 14, 1844, June 10, 1844; Amy Bridges, *A City in the Republic: Antebellum New York and the Origins of Machine Politics* (New York: Cambridge University Press, 1984), 93–98; Michael Feldberg, *The Philadelphia Riots of 1844: A Study of Ethnic Conflict* (Westport, CT: Greenwood Press, 1975), 51–58.

27   "Obituary," *Potter's American Monthly* 4 (1875): 160; *Commercial Advertiser* (New York), March 23, 1827, October 19, 1832; David Nolan, *Fifty Feet in Paradise: The Booming of Florida* (San Diego: Harcourt, 1984), 42–43.

28   Nolan, *Fifty Feet in Paradise*, 46, 54; *Florida Herald and Southern Democrat* (St. Augustine), July 5, 1839; Arthur W. Thompson, *Jacksonian Democracy on the Florida Frontier* (Gainesville: University of Florida Press, 1961), 12; William D. Kelley, "For the Spirit of the Times," *ST*, September 5, 1844.

29   *Gettysburg Compiler*, May 2, 1827, December 19, 1827; Fourth Regiment, volume 5 (1821–1827), 28, Military Commission Books, 1800–1944, RG 26.65, PSA; *Star and Banner* (Gettysburg, PA), July 24, 1832; *Pittsburgh Weekly Gazette*, October 30, 1832; *PL*, March 28, 1837, July 27, 1837, December 11, 1837, October 28, 1839; *Saturday Courier*, April 23, 1842; *DC*, January 12, 1843.

30   *NG*, May 21, 1829; Charles James Jack, *A Political Lecture upon the Influence of Slavery on the Constitution and Union* (Brooklyn: E. B. Spooner, 1860), 13; Charles James Jack, family Bible inscription, 1821–1834, from typescript prepared in 1921, copy sent to author by Mr. Grant Taylor.

31   John F. Quinn, *Father Mathew's Crusade: Temperance in Nineteenth-Century Ireland and Irish America* (Amherst: University of Massachusetts Press, 2002), 22–23; *DS*, November 9, 1843, November 24, 1843.

32 *DC*, February 3, 1844, February 6, 1844.

33 *DS*, February 10, 1844, February 13, 1844, February 15, 1844.

34 *DS*, November 12, 1843, January 11, 1844.

35 "Lewis Levin," in *Biographies of Philadelphians*, Thompson Westcott, HSP; Charles Nordhoff, *Sailor Life on Man of War and Merchant Vessel* (New York: Dodd, Mead, 1883), 26.

36 "Grand Temperance Celebration of Washington's Birthday," *Journal of the American Temperance Union* 8 (March 1844): 34.

37 *DS*, February 26, 1844.

CHAPTER 5: THE MOB SHALL RULE

1 John Hugh Campbell, *History of the Friendly Sons of St. Patrick and of the Hibernian Society for the Relief of Emigrants from Ireland* (Philadelphia: Hibernian Society, 1892), 487; "Current Memoranda," *Potter's American Monthly* 12 (February 1879): 151; *DC*, December 24, 1842; "Morton McMichael," in *Biographies of Philadelphians*, Thompson Westcott, HSP (profile from the *Sunday Dispatch*, ca. 1860); Albert Mordell, ed., *In re Morton McMichael, Including Unpublished Letters* (Philadelphia: Charles McMichael, 1921), 12.

2 "Morton McMichael," in *Biographies of Philadelphians*; Hon. Morton McMichael, ca. 1848, daguerreotype, 1/2 plate, Library Company of Philadelphia.

3 *NG*, January 26, 1831, January 9, 1833; *Daily Pennsylvanian*, October 4, 1832, March 20, 1837; *Poulson's American Daily Advertiser* (Philadelphia), October 11, 1832; *Proceedings and Debates of the Convention of the Commonwealth of Pennsylvania: To Propose Amendments to the Constitution, Commenced and Held at Harrisburg, on the Second Day of May, 1837* (Packer, Barrett, and Parke, 1837), 477; *PI*, May 8, 1833, August 1, 1836.

4 "Town Meeting—Riots," *Hazard's Register of Pennsylvania* 14 (September 1834): 201–202.

5 Carl E. Prince, "The Great 'Riot Year': Jacksonian Democracy and Patterns of Violence in 1834," *Journal of the Early Republic* 5 (Spring 1985): 8; David Grimsted, *American Mobbing, 1828–1861: Toward Civil War* (New York: Oxford University Press, 1998), 4, 7; Ted Gurr, "Psychological Factors in Civil Violence," *World Politics* 20 (1968): 271; *Niles' Weekly Register*, August 8, 1835; Abraham Lincoln, "Address to the Young Men's Lyceum of Springfield, Illinois," January 27, 1838, Papers of Abraham Lincoln Digital Library, papersofabrahamlincoln.org.

6 *DC*, August 23, 1843; *PI*, May 21, 1838.

7 Ric N. Caric, "From Ordered Buckets to Honored Felons: Fire Companies and Cultural Transformation in Philadelphia, 1785–1850," *Pennsylvania History* 72 (2005): 135; "Ballads of the Philadelphia Firemen," *Literary World* 12 (February 26, 1853): 174.

8 Grimsted, *American Mobbing*, 182–183; Richard Franklin Bensel, *The American Ballot Box in the Mid-Nineteenth Century: Law, Identity and the Polling Place* (New York: Cambridge University Press, 2004), 9–21.

9 Grimsted, *American Mobbing*, 199, 204; "Inquest of the Grand Jury," *Hazard's Register of Pennsylvania* 14 (October 1834): 253; "Pennsylvania Elections," *Niles' Weekly Register* 47 (October 18, 1834): 104–105.

10 Sean Farrell, *Rituals and Riots: Sectarian Violence and Political Culture in Ulster, 1784–1886* (Lexington: University Press of Kentucky, 2000); *A Full and Accurate Report of the Trial for Riot Before the Mayor's Court of Philadelphia, on the 13th of October, 1831* (Philadelphia: Jesper Harding,

1831); Francis W. Hoeber, "Drama in the Courtroom, Theater in the Streets: Philadelphia's Irish Riot of 1831," *Pennsylvania Magazine of History and Biography* 125 (2001): 191–232.

11 Cassandra L. Yacovazzi, *Escaped Nuns: True Womanhood and the Campaign Against Convents in Antebellum America*, chap, 2 (New York: Oxford University Press, 2018); Jack Tager, *Boston Riots: Three Centuries of Social Violence* (Boston: Northeastern University Press, 2001), 111; Daniel A. Cohen, "Passing the Torch: Boston Firemen, 'Tea Party' Patriots, and the Burning of the Charlestown Convent," *Journal of the Early Republic* 24 (Winter 2004): 566, 579; Joseph G. Mannard, "The 1839 Baltimore Nunnery Riot: An Episode in Jacksonian Nativism and Social Violence," *Maryland Historian* 11 (June 1980): 13–23.

12 Grimsted, *American Mobbing*, 12; Angela G. Ray, "Learning Leadership: Lincoln at the Lyceum, 1838," *Rhetoric & Public Affairs* 13, no. 3 (2010): 354; John Runcie, "'Hunting the Nigs' in Philadelphia: The Race Riot of August 1834," *Pennsylvania History* 39, no. 2 (April 1972): 190; "Riots—Monday Night," *Hazard's Register of Pennsylvania* 16 (July 1835); "Scenes of Tuesday Night," *Hazard's Register of Pennsylvania* 16 (July 1835).

13 Pennsylvania Hall Association, *History of Pennsylvania Hall* (Philadelphia: Merrihew and Gunn, 1838), 5, 76; Beverly C. Tomek, *Pennsylvania Hall: A "Legal Lynching" in the Shadow of the Liberty Bell* (New York: Oxford University Press, 2013), 99–116, 130–132.

14 *Newark Daily Advertiser*, May 22, 1838, reprinting *USG*; *PI*, May 19, 1838.

15 *PI*, October 9, 1843; "More Riots in Philadelphia," *Columbian Centinel* (Boston), May 23, 1838; *NG*, August 3, 1837; *PL*, September 11, 1838; *Wyoming Republican and Farmer's Herald* (Kingston, PA), May 30, 1838, reprinted from *DC*; *Emporium & True American* (Trenton), May 25, 1838, reprinting *Daily Pennsylvanian*; Morton McMichael, "A Card," *PI*, May 21, 1838; *Newark Daily Advertiser*, May 22, 1838, reprinting *USG*.

16 Riots in the United States, 1828–1844, Outline, box 4, folder 1, David Maydole Matteson Papers, LC; H. R. Robinson, *A View of the City of Brotherly Love*, lithograph, New York 1843. The print is sometimes dated to 1842, but the 1843 date is established by *DC*, August 31, 1843.

17 "Constitution of the Commonwealth of Pennsylvania—1790," PA Constitution, Duquesne University School of Law, https://www.paconstitution.org/texts-of-the-constitution/1790-2/; "Constitution of the Commonwealth of Pennsylvania—1838," PA Constitution, Duquesne University School of Law, https://www.paconstitution.org/texts-of-the-constitution/1838-2/; *NatAm*, August 26, 1844; *PL*, September 1, 1842, November 6, 1844; *DC*, June 14, 1844; J. E. Parsons, *Henry Deringer's Pocket Pistol* (New York: William Morrow, 1952), 17–26.

18 Perry K. Blatz, "Boundaries of Responsibility: Philadelphia, Pittsburgh, and the Pennsylvania Riot Damage Law, 1834–1880," *Pennsylvania History* 78 (2011): 396–398; Elizabeth M. Geffen, "Violence in Philadelphia in the 1840's and 1850's," *Pennsylvania History* 36 (1969): 390; *PL*, August 3, 1842; *AA*, December 27, 1844; John Charles Schneider, "Mob Violence and Public Order in the American City, 1830–1865" (PhD diss., University of Minnesota, 1971), 99; Grimsted, *American Mobbing*, 191.

19 *AA*, December 27, 1844; *DC*, January 12, 1844; *American Sentinel* (Philadelphia), February 22, 1840; *PL*, July 18, 1838.

20 John Hill Martin, *Martin's Bench and Bar of Philadelphia* (Philadelphia: Rees Welsh, 1883), 99–101; "Town Meeting—Riots," *Hazard's Register of Pennsylvania* 14 (September 1834): 201; *DC*, January 20, 1843.

21   Joel Schwartz, "'To Every Mans Door': Railroads and Use of the Streets in Jacksonian Philadelphia," *Pennsylvania Magazine of History and Biography* 128 (January 2004): 57; *NG*, July 28, 1840; *Baltimore Sun*, July 29, 1840; *PL*, August 3, 1840; *Saturday Courier*, July 29, 1843.

22   *DC*, November 9, 1842, November 10, 1842, November 16, 1842, January 11, 1843, January 12, 1843, January 13, 1843.

23   *DC*, December 2, 1842, January 11, 1843.

24   *DC*, January 12, 1843, January 13, 1843; *PL*, January 13, 1843; William Porter to George Cadwalader, January 12, 1843, box 430, folder 7, GC.

25   Muster rolls, box 430, folder 6, GC; *PL*, January 13, 1843; John St. George Joyce, *Story of Philadelphia* (Philadelphia: Rex, 1919), 228–229; *DC*, January 14, 1843.

26   Allen Steinberg, *The Transformation of Criminal Justice, Philadelphia, 1800–1880* (Chapel Hill: University of North Carolina Press, 1989), 105; *Daily Pennsylvanian*, October 4, 1832; *NG*, September 21, 1840, October 16, 1840, November 27, 1840; 1st Division appointment of Division Staff Officers, October 24, 1842, box 2, folder: 1840–1849, Militia Returns, 1st Div-1st Brig, 1800–1849, RG 26, PSA.

27   *New-York Tribune*, October 13, 1843; *DC*, July 10, 1843.

28   *DC*, July 29, 1843, September 16, 1843, September 28, 1843, September 30, 1843, October 7, 1843, October 9, 1843.

29   Campbell, *History of the Friendly Sons of St. Patrick*, 487; *DC*, October 4, 1843, October 7, 1843, October 9, 1843; David Montgomery, "The Shuttle and the Cross: Weavers and Artisans in the Kensington Riots of 1844," *Journal of Social History* 5 (Summer 1972): 427.

30   *PL*, October 12, 1843; *New York Herald*, October 27, 1843; *NatAm*, May 6, 1844; *Alton Telegraph* (Illinois), August 3, 1844, reprinting the *Whig Standard*.

31   Preamble and Resolutions offered by Th. T. Firth, November 27, 1843, Raymond F. Schmandt, "A Selection of Sources Dealing with the Nativist Riots of 1844," *Records of the American Catholic Historical Society* 80 (June and September 1969): 70–72; *DC*, November 28, 1843.

32   *PI*, May 29, 1844.

CHAPTER 6: BAYONETS AND BALL CARTRIDGES

1   *New-York Commercial Advertiser*, April 11, 1834; *The Report of and Testimony Taken Before the Joint Committee of the Senate and House of Delegates of Maryland, to Which Was Referred the Memorials of John B. Morris, Reverdy Johnson and Others, Praying Indemnity for Losses Sustained by Reason of the Riots in Baltimore, in the Month of August, Eighteen Hundred and Thirty-Five* (Annapolis, MD: W. McNeir, 1836), 11, 53–54.

2   Peter Way, *Common Labour: Workers and the Digging of North American Canals, 1760–1860* (New York: Cambridge University Press, 1993), 286, table 16; David R. Porter to Lt. Col. G. Talcott, January 18, 1844, Militia Letter Book, 1839–1861, series 26.22, PSA; Samuel Cooper, *A Concise System of Instructions and Regulations for the Militia and Volunteers of the United States* (Philadelphia: Robert P. Desilver, 1844); AJP, May 14, 1838, 99; *New York Military Magazine*, published throughout 1841.

3   Kenderton Smith et al., "Military Encampment," October 26, 1841, box 430, folder 2, GC.

4   Emmons Clark, *History of the Seventh Regiment of New York, 1806–1889* (New York: The Seventh Regiment, 1890), 222; *Salem Gazette*, July 15, 1834; *Recollections of the Early Days*

of the National Guard (New York: J. M. Bradstreet & Son, 1868), 149–157; Aaron Clark, Report, January 28, 1839, Doc. 29, *Documents of the Board of Aldermen of the City of New York* (New York: Common Council, 1839), V:305; Mark David Luccioni, "'Fire and Be Damned': Philadelphia Volunteers and the Use of Force in the Riots of 1844" (PhD diss., Temple University, 1996), 69.

5   *New-York American for the Country*, July 8, 1831; *Niles' Weekly Register*, June 21, 1834; John M. Werner, *Reaping the Bloody Harvest: Race Riots in the United States During the Age of Jackson, 1824–1849* (New York: Garland, 1986), 34; Jay M. Perry, "The Irish Wars: Laborer Feuds on Indiana's Canals and Railroads in the 1830s," *Indiana Magazine of History* 109 (2013): 245.

6   *History of the Providence Riots from Sept. 21 to Sept. 24, 1831* (Providence: H. H. Brown, 1831), 17.

7   Charles Morris, *Men of the Century* (Philadelphia: I. R. Hamersly, 1896), 300; George Washington Cullum, *Register of the Officers and Graduates of the U.S. Military Academy, at West Point, N.Y., from March 16, 1802, to January 1, 1850* (New York: J. F. Trow, 1850); *NG*, June 11, 1835; John Neagle, *Colonel Augustus James Pleasonton*, 1846, oil on canvas, 91.8 x 74.2 cm (36 1/8 x 29 3/16 in.), National Gallery of Art, Washington.

8   "How the Declaration Was Saved," *Scribner's Monthly* 10 (1875): 633; AJP, June 23, 1838, 159; AJP, July 9, 1838, 172.

9   AJP, June 8, 1838, 143; AJP, June 10, 1838, 144; AJP, April 17, 1841, 303.

10   Frank Otto Gatell, "Roger B. Taney, the Bank of Maryland Rioters, and a Whiff of Grapeshot," *Maryland Historical Magazine* 59 (1964): 263; Napoleon, *Memoirs of the History of France During the Reign of Napoleon* (London: Henry Colburn, 1823), 3:79; *New-York Spectator*, June 6, 1836; *Cincinnati Enquirer*, January 13, 1842.

11   *Cincinnati Enquirer*, January 13, 1842; Joshua D. Rothman, "The Hazards of the Flush Times: Gambling, Mob Violence, and the Anxieties of America's Market Revolution," *Journal of American History* 95 (December 2008): 660, 669; Jack Tager, *Boston Riots: Three Centuries of Social Violence* (Boston: Northeastern University Press, 2001), 122–124; Stephen C. LeSueur, *The 1838 Mormon War in Missouri* (Columbia: University of Missouri Press, 1987), 113–116; Thomas Ford, *A History of Illinois, from Its Commencement as a State in 1818 to 1847* (Chicago: S. C. Griggs, 1854), 249.

12   William Henry Egle, "'The Buckshot War,'" *Pennsylvania Magazine of History and Biography* 23 (1899): 142–146, 156; AJP, December 11, 1838, 271.

13   Egle, "Buckshot War," 145–149; *Madisonian* (Washington, DC), December 11, 1838; AJP, December 7, 1838, 258; AJP, December 8, 1838, 261; AJP, December 11, 1838, 273; Report of the 3rd Regiment, 128th of the Line, PM, Harrisburgh [sic], December 11, 1838, box 429, folder 8, GC.

14   General Robert Patterson, Division Order no. 3, December 9, 1838, Pennsylvania House Committee on Disturbances at Seat of Government, *Report of the Committee Appointed to Enquire into the Causes of the Disturbances at the Seat of Government, in December, 1838* (Harrisburg: Boas & Coplan, 1839), 154; William Henry Egle, ed., *Notes and Queries: Historical, Biographical and Genealogical, Relating Chiefly to Interior Pennsylvania* (Harrisburg, PA: Harrisburg Publishing, 1894), 1:187; AJP, December 11, 1838, 267–270.

15   AJP, December 11, 1838, 271–272.

16   Egle, ed., *Notes and Queries*, 1:187; AJP, December 11, 1838, 273; Egle, "Buckshot War" 153–154; Robert Patterson to Joseph Ritner, December 14, 1838, *Report of the Committee Appointed to Enquire*, 142.

17   John Thomas Scharf and Thompson Westcott, *History of Philadelphia, 1609–1884* (Philadelphia: L. H. Everts, 1884), 1:638, 2:1539; John Charles Schneider, "Mob Violence and Public Order in the American City, 1830–1865" (PhD diss., University of Minnesota, 1971), 100–101, 109; *PL*, May 18, 1838.

18   *PL*, August 3, 1842; company count from *Journal of the Select Council of the City of Philadelphia for 1841–1842* (Philadelphia: J. Crissy, 1842), 117.

CHAPTER 7: THE GOSPEL OF THE DEVIL

1   Hugh J. Nolan, *The Most Reverend Francis Patrick Kenrick* (Philadelphia: American Catholic Historical Society, 1948), 3–5, 23–28, 32–48; *DC*, July 31, 1843.

2   James F. Connelly, *The History of the Archdiocese of Philadelphia* (Philadelphia: The Archdiocese, 1976), 130; Jennifer Schaaf, "'With a Pure Intention of Pleasing and Honouring God': How the Philadelphia Laity Created American Catholicism, 1785– 1850," (PhD diss., University of Pennsylvania, 2013), chaps. 2 and 4; Dale Light, "The Reformation of Philadelphia Catholicism, 1830–1860," *Pennsylvania Magazine of History & Biography* 112 (July 1998): 375–405; Joseph Louis J. Kirlin, *Catholicity in Philadelphia* (Philadelphia: J. J. McVey, 1909), 219, 264.

3   Nolan, *Kenrick*, 52, 92, 150; Francis Patrick Kenrick to John Purcell, May 7, 1830, 32.09, and Francis Patrick Kenrick to Fenwick, August 29, 1830, Right Reverend Kenrick Correspondence, MC 72, Catholic Historical Research Center of the Archdiocese of Philadelphia.

4   Nolan, *Kenrick*, 129, 133; Light, "Reformation of Philadelphia Catholicism," 387.

5   Kirlin, *Catholicity in Philadelphia*, 189, 273–274; Patrick Carey, "Arguments for Lay Participation in Philadelphia Catholicism, 1820–1829," *Records of the American Catholic Historical Society of Philadelphia* 92 (1981): 45–46; Francis Patrick Kenrick to Bishop Fenwick, May 17, 1831, Right Reverend Kenrick Correspondence, MC 72; Light, "Reformation of Philadelphia Catholicism," 387, 392–393.

6   *Catholic Telegraph*, April 28, 1832; Martin I. J. Griffin, "History of the Church of Saint John the Evangelist, Philadelphia," *Records of the American Catholic Historical Society of Philadelphia* 20 (1909): 350–405; Samuel John Klingensmith, "The Architecture of Napoleon LeBrun: The Philadelphia Churches" (master's thesis, University of Virginia, 1976), 24–26, 41.

7   "Thomas H. Burrowes, and the School System of Pennsylvania," *American Journal of Education* 6 (March 1859): 111–112; *DC*, January 28, 1843, March 21, 1843, May 29, 1843; John Robert Godley, *Letters from America* (London: John Murray, 1844), 2:153.

8   Michael Meranze, *Laboratories of Virtue: Punishment, Revolution, and Authority in Philadelphia, 1760–1835* (Chapel Hill: University of North Carolina Press, 1996); Tracy Fessenden, *Culture and Redemption: Religion, the Secular, and American Literature* (Princeton, NJ: Princeton University Press, 2008), 66.

9   Alec Ryrie, "'Protestantism' as a Historical Category," *Transactions of the Royal Historical Society* 26 (December 2016): 72.

10   F. L. Cross and E. A. Livingstone, "Douai–Reims Bible," in *The Oxford Dictionary of the Christian Church*, ed. F. L. Cross and E. A. Livingstone (New York: Oxford University

Press, 2009); Ellie Gebarowski-Shafer, "The Transatlantic Reach of the Catholic 'False Translation' Argument in the School 'Bible Wars,'" *US Catholic Historian* 31 (2013): 54–55.

11 *The Holy Bible, Translated from the Latin Vulgate* (New York: Edward Dunigan, 1844), 864; *The Holy Bible: Containing the Old and New Testaments* (Boston, 1834), 123; *CH*, March 7, 1844, March 21, 1844; "Penance," *Protestant Banner* (Philadelphia), July 15, 1842; Gebarowski-Shafer, "Transatlantic Reach," 54–55, 68–71; *DC*, September 7, 1843; John Fea, *The Bible Cause: A History of the American Bible Society* (New York: Oxford University Press, 2016), 66; Gerald P. Fogarty, "American Catholic Translations of the Bible," in *The Bible and Bibles in America*, ed. Ernest S. Frerichs (Atlanta: Scholars Press, 1988), 120. Emphasis added to quotations.

12 Fea, *Bible Cause*, 13–17, 63; *DC*, May 13, 1843, September 13, 1844.

13 Gebarowski-Shafer, "Transatlantic Reach," 66; Pope Leo XII, *The Encyclical Letter of Pope Leo the XII* (London: Keating and Brown, 1824), 16; Fea, *Bible Cause*, 66–68; *New York Observer and Chronicle*, September 20, 1834. Dialogue reconstructed from paraphrase.

14 William Nevins, *Thoughts on Popery* (New York: John S. Taylor, 1836), 29; *New York Observer and Chronicle*, September 20, 1834; *CH*, July 27, 1843.

15 Speech of Richard B. Warren, Society for Promoting the Education of the Poor of Ireland, *Report of the Proceedings at a Meeting of the Society (8th Annual Meeting)* (Dublin, Ireland: Christopher Bentham, 1820), 7–8; Irene Whelan, *The Bible War in Ireland: The "Second Reformation" and the Polarization of Protestant-Catholic Relations, 1800–1840* (Madison: University of Wisconsin Press, 2005), 135.

16 Society for Promoting the Education of the Poor of Ireland, *Report of the Proceedings*, 9; William Thomas Latimer, *A History of the Irish Presbyterians* (Belfast, United Kingdom: J. Cleeland, 1902), 449–454; T. Ó Raifeartaigh, "Mixed Education and the Synod of Ulster, 1831–40," *Irish Historical Studies* 9, no. 35 (1955): 281–299; Donald H. Akenson, *The Irish Education Experiment; the National System of Education in the Nineteenth Century* (London: Routledge & K. Paul, 1970), 180–181; *CH*, October 19, 1843, March 28, 1844.

17 Thomas Brainerd, *Our Country Safe from Romanism* (Philadelphia: L. R. Bailey, 1843), 19; Nicholas Murray, *Romanism at Home: Letters to the Hon. Roger B. Taney, by Kirwan* (New York: Harper, 1852), 250; *Baptist Advocate* (New York), quoted in *CH*, November 2, 1843; Pastoral Letter of 1840, Peter Guilday, ed., *The National Pastorals of the American Hierarchy, 1792–1919* (Westminster, MD: Newman Press, 1954), 133–134.

18 William Oland Bourne, *History of the Public School Society of the City of New York*, (New York: W. Wood, 1870), 160–163; Petition of the Trustees of the several Roman Catholic Churches in the City of New York, February 17, 1840, New York Board of Aldermen, *Journal and Documents of the Board of Assistants* (New York: The Board, 1840), 15:356; John W. Pratt, "Governor Seward and the New York City School Controversy, 1840–1842: A Milestone in the Advance of Nonsectarian Public Education," *New York History* 42 (1961): 355; Vincent P. Lannie, *Public Money and Parochial Education: Bishop Hughes, Governor Seward, and the New York School Controversy* (Cleveland: Press of Case Western Reserve University, 1968), 211; *Speech of the Right Rev. Dr. Hughes, Delivered on the 16th, 17th and 21st Days' of June, 1841* (New York: Freeman's Journal, 1841), 21.

19 Pratt, "Governor Seward," 360–361; Lannie, *Public Money and Parochial Education*, 178, 232, 251.

20 Lannie, *Public Money and Parochial Education*, 241–242; *New York Herald*, April 14, 1842.

21 Vincent P. Lannie and Bernard C. Diethorn, "For the Honor and Glory of God: The Philadelphia Bible Riots of 1844," *History of Education Quarterly* 8 (Spring 1968): 96n9, 97n10; *CH*, March 14, 1844.

22 *CH*, April 18, 1844; Resolutions passed December 9, 1834, *Twenty-Sixth Annual Report of the Controllers of the Public Schools of the City and County of Philadelphia* (1844): 6–7; Thomas H. Burrowes, *Fourth Annual Report on the Common Schools, Academies, and Colleges of the Commonwealth of Pennsylvania* (Harrisburg, PA: Packer, Barrett, and Parke, 1838), 13.

23 *Tralee Mercury*, June 15, 1839; *CH*, December 30, 1841, January 20, 1842, April 14, 1842.

24 *CH*, April 14, 1842, May 5, 1842, May 12, 1842, May 19, 1842.

25 *Tralee Mercury*, June 15, 1839; Mary Ann Meyers, "The Children's Crusade: Philadelphia Catholics and the Public Schools, 1840–1844," *Records of the American Catholic Historical Society of Philadelphia* 75 (January 1964): 106–107; Nolan, *Kenrick*, 385–391; *CH*, March 21, 1839; George W. Biddle to F. S. Eckard, Joseph Donath, John Keating, Robert Ewing, June 18, 1844, *PL*, January 7, 1842, June 22, 1844.

26 *Fifteenth Annual Report of the Board of Commissioners of Public Schools of Baltimore* (Baltimore: John Cox, 1879), xii; "Diocess of Philadelphia," *United States Catholic Magazine* 2 (1843): 126.

27 *Christian Observer* (Philadelphia), November 25, 1842, December 9, 1842, January 27, 1843; *Christian Secretary* (Hartford, CT), January 29, 1841; *Address of the Board of Managers of the American Protestant Association* (Philadelphia, 1843), 18.

28 *PL*, January 14, 1843; *CH*, March 7, 1844; *The Truth Unveiled*, (Baltimore: Metropolitan Tract Society, 1844), 27; Francis Patrick Kenrick, *Substance of a Sermon on Charity towards Enemies* (Philadelphia: T. B. Town, 1843), 13; Kenrick to Paul Cullen, March 28, 1843, "Papers Relating to the Church in America. from the Portfolios of the Irish College at Rome, First Series," *Records of the American Catholic Historical Society of Philadelphia* 7 (1896): 309.

29 *Address of the Board of Managers of the American Protestant Association*, 17; *DS*, November 16, 1843; *CH*, November 30, 1843, December 7, 1843, April 11, 1844; *AA*, September 12, 1844.

CHAPTER 8: AROUSE, NATIVE BORNS!

1 AJP, January 27 and 29, 1844, 371; Walter Colton, "The Bible in Public Schools," *Quarterly Review of the American Protestant Association*, January 1844, 21.

2 *PL*, January 30, 1844, February 27, 1844; *DS*, February 8, 1844; *NatAm*, May 29, 1844.

3 Miss Gibbon's testimony, in *The Truth Unveiled* (Philadelphia: M. Fithian, 1844), 31–32; *Twenty-Sixth Annual Report of the Controllers of the Public Schools of the City and County of Philadelphia* (1844), 41; *PL*, March 1, 1844.

4 "Manufactures," *Hazard's Register of Pennsylvania* 1 (January 1828): 28; Seventy-Ninth Regiment, vol. 5 (1821–1827), 32, Military Commission Books, 1800–1944, RG 26.65, PSA; John Hugh Campbell, *History of the Friendly Sons of St. Patrick and of the Hibernian Society for the Relief of Emigrants from Ireland* (Philadelphia: Hibernian Society, 1892), 379; John Hill Martin, *Martin's Bench and Bar of Philadelphia* (Philadelphia: Rees Welsh, 1883), 93; *NorAm*, January 7, 1841; *PI*, July 19, 1843.

5 John Binns, *Recollections of the Life of John Binns* (Philadelphia, 1854), 326–380; *PL*, September 10, 1841, September 14, 1841; *PI*, October 14, 1841, August 30, 1843; "Speech of Mr. James Dixon," *Appendix to the Congressional Globe*, December 30, 1845, 68; *NorAm*, October 15, 1841, August 29, 1843.

6   Statement of Alderman Clark, in *Truth Unveiled*, 30. Dialogue reconstructed from paraphrase.

7   Hugh Clark and Louisa Bedford statements, in *Truth Unveiled*, 30-31; *PL*, March 1, 1844; *DS*, March 21, 1844.

8   *PL*, January 14, 1843

9   *DS*, February 28, 1844; *PL*, March 1, 1844; *Christian Observer*, May 17, 1844, OB, 29; W. (Chauncey Webster), "The Crisis," *Protestant Banner* (Philadelphia), March 7, 1844.

10 *DS*, February 10, 1844, February 23, 1844, March 12, 1844.

11 *DS*, February 28, 1844; *PL*, February 28, 1844, February 29, 1844; Pennsylvania Hospital Historic Collections, Meteorological Records, March 4, 1844.

12 *A Guide to the Lions of Philadelphia* (Philadelphia: T. T. Ash, 1837), 33; *NorAm*, March 12, 1844; *DS*, March 11, 1844; *AA*, July 13, 1844.

13 *CH*, March 21, 1844; *PL*, Francis Patrick Kenrick, "A Card—To the Citizens of Philadelphia, and the Public Generally," *PL*, March 13, 1844; *NorAm*, March 16, 1844.

14 *PL*, February 29, 1844; March 14, 1844; *Twenty-Sixth Annual Report*, 4; Statements (Miss Bedford and Gibbon, March 16, 1844?), ACHS; B. (Joseph Berg), "A White Feather," *Protestant Banner* (Philadelphia), March 21, 1844.

15 *DC*, March 16, 1844; *DS*, March 15, 1844

16 *DC*, March 16, 1844; *PL*, March 18, 1844; *NorAm*, March 18, 1844.

17 *Brooklyn Evening Star*, March 11, 1844; Ira M. Leonard, "The Rise and Fall of the American Republican Party in New York City, 1843–1845," *New-York Historical Society Quarterly* 50 (April 1966): 167, 172; Leonard Tabachnik, "Origins of the Know-Nothing Party: A Study of the Native American Party in Philadelphia, 1844–1852" (PhD diss., Columbia University, 1973), 120.

18 *Evening Post* (New York), April 4, 1844; *DS*, April 8, 1844; *New York Herald*, April 5, 1844, April 6, 1844, April 9, 1844.

19 John Rose Greene Hassard, *Life of the Most Reverend John Hughes* (New York: D. Appleton, 1866), 274–275; Leonard, "The Rise and Fall of the American Republican Party in New York City," 170; *New York Republic*, reprinted in *NorAm*, April 11, 1844.

20 *DC*, April 12, 1844; *DS*, April 11, 1844.

21 *NatAm*, April 11, 1844, May 1, 1844 (misprinted as May 30, 1844), May 28, 1844, July 26, 1844; *DS*, October 9, 1843; *TALR*, November 5, 1842.

22 *NatAm*, April 30, 1844, May 9, 1844, May 11, 1844, June 7, 1844, June 10, 1844, August 7, 1844.

23 *Commercial Advertiser* (New York), August 8, 1845; *NatAm*, April 11, 1844, April 19, 1844.

24 *NatAm*, May 4, 1844; Dale T. Knobel, *"America for the Americans": The Nativist Movement in the United States* (New York: Twayne, 1996), 64–65; *DS*, April 16, 1844.

25 *NatAm*, April 15, 1844, April 16, 1844, April 18, 1844; *USG*, April 16, 1844, April 18, 1844; *NorAm*, April 16, 1844, April 17, 1844; *PL*, April 10, 1844; *New York Herald*, April 18, 1844.

26 *DC*, April 24, 1844; *Saturday Courier*, April 20, 1844; Hugh Davey Evans and Reverdy Johnson to Theodoric Bland, Chancellor of Maryland, April 13, 1844, Louis [sic] C. Levin and Julia A. M. Levin vs. John H. Iglehart, Samuel J. Donaldson, and Hugh Davey Evans, Anne Arundel Co., 1844, Chancery Court, Chancery Papers, Maryland State Archives, 512-11-9214; *NatAm*, April 25, 1844, April 29, 1844.

27 John Thomas Scharf and Thompson Westcott, *History of Philadelphia, 1609–1884* (Philadelphia: L. H. Everts, 1884), 1:623. In 1850, 80 percent of the ward's residents were foreign born, of whom 55 percent came from Ireland, and 83 percent of handloom weavers in the Third Ward were Irish born. The figures may not reflect the demographics of 1844, since the Great Irish Famine spurred increase migration in the late 1840s. Tabachnik, "Origins of the Know-Nothing Party," 30; *NatAm*, April 30, 1844; *DC*, April 30, 1844; *New-York Tribune*, April 30, 1844.

28 *DC*, May 8, 1844; George Lippard, *The Nazarene: Or, The Last of the Washingtons* (Philadelphia: T. B. Peterson, 1854), 168; John Steele testimony, *PL*, September 14, 1844; Nicholas B. Wainwright and Samuel Breck, "The Diary of Samuel Breck, 1839–1840," *Pennsylvania Magazine of History and Biography* 103 (1979): 503; *PL*, May 11, 1844; John McKee testimony, *PL*, September 13, 1844; Michael Keenan testimony, *PL*, September 14, 1844; Ellen O'Donnell testimony, *PL*, September 20, 1844; Jane Develin testimony, *PL*, October 15, 1844; William Buckley testimony, *PL*, November 8, 1844; George Roberts testimony, *PL*, November 9, 1844; John Fagan and unnamed witness testimony, *PL*, January 31, 1845. Some of these courts, though with different names, appear on Ernest Hexamer, *Map of the Whole Incorporated City of Philadelphia*, Plate 5: North, West Phila. (Rufus L. Barnes, 1867).

29 Craig's age was between twenty and thirty years, based on the 1840 census; Roll of Members of the First Presbyterian Church of Kensington, Pennsylvania and New Jersey, Church and Town Records, 1708–1985, available at Ancestry.com; *PL*, August 21, 1843; *McElroy's Philadelphia Directory for 1844*, 9; *NatAm*, April 18, 1844; William Craig testimony, *DS*, September 13, 1844; Catharine Storm testimony, *PL*, October 17, 1844; David McGinnis testimony, *AA*, October 17, 1844.

30 *NatAm*, April 26, 1844; John Hancock Lee, *The Origin and Progress of the American Party in Politics* (Philadelphia: Elliott & Gihon, 1855), 44.

31 Gee as rope manufacturer in brick house, Kensington 3d., Tax Assessor's Ledger: Kensington 1, 2, & 3 Ward, 1841, p. 56, PCA; William Craig testimony, *AA*, October 18, 1844; John Gee testimony, *PL*, October 17, 1844; *NatAm*, May 2, 1844, June 1, 1844; William Craig and Christopher Steele testimony, *PL*, September 13, 1844; Joanna Maloy and C. B. F. O'Neill testimony, *PL*, September 14, 1844.

32 Joanna Maloy testimony, *PL*, September 14, 1844; David McGinnes and Patrick Wall testimony, *PL*, September 20, 1844; *AA*, December 19, 1844; *NatAm*, April 11, 1844; *Nazarene and Universalist Family Companion* 4 (October 13, 1843); Abel Thomas, *A Century of Universalism in Philadelphia and New York* (Philadelphia: Collins, 1872), 119; *PL*, May 4, 1844. Perry is not to be confused with John B. Perry, bookbinder. That the two Perrys were different people is established by the 1850 census, which lists John Perry as a forty-year-old printer in Moyamensing, while John B. Perry is a forty-seven-year-old bookbinder in the Northern Liberties.

33 "Charge of Judge King on the Trial of John Daley for Murder," in Francis Wharton, *A Treatise on the Law of Homicide in the United States* (Philadelphia: Kay & Brother, 1855), 470; William Craig testimony, *PL*, September 13, 1844; Joanna Maloy and Samuel Kramer testimony, *PL*, September 14, 1844; David Fields testimony, *PL*, September 20, 1844.

34 Joanna Maloy testimony, *PL*, September 14, 1844; John Mayer and Thomas McWilliams testimony, *PL*, September 20, 1844; *PL*, May 4, 1844; *NatAm*, May 4, 1844; "Fox Hall

location: An Act to Apportion the District of Kensington, and to Regulate the Board of Commissioners," *Laws of the Commonwealth of Pennsylvania* (Harrisburg: J. M. G. Lescure, 1846), 49; *NatAm*, May 4, 1844.

35   David Grimsted, *American Mobbing, 1828–1861: Toward Civil War* (New York: Oxford University Press, 1998), 184, 199.

36   *NatAm*, May 4, 1844.

37   *NatAm*, May 6, 1844.

38   *NatAm*, May 4, 1844; May 6, 1844; Eliza Choate testimony, *AA*, October 17, 1844.

39   Alfred M. Clark testimony, *PL*, September 14, 1844.

CHAPTER 9: A BAND OF ARMED RUFFIANS

1   William Craig testimony, *DS*, September 13, 1844. William Buck testimony, *PL*, September 14, 1844; Daniel Maginnis testimony, *PL*, October 17, 1844. Hare's age is established by St. John's Street Methodist Episcopal Church, Pennsylvania and New Jersey, Church and Town Records, 1708-1985, available at Ancestry.com.

2   *DC*, May 4, 1844, May 7, 1844, May 8, 1844; John Thomas Scharf and Thompson Westcott, *History of Philadelphia, 1609–1884* (Philadelphia: L. H. Everts, 1884), 3:1912; Shiffler's age taken from J. L. Magee, *Death of George Shifler in Kensington. Born Jan 24 1825. Murdered May 6 1844*, ca. 1844, lithograph, 46 x 30 cm; M. D. Lichliter, *History of the Junior Order United American Mechanics of the United States of North America* (Philadelphia: J. B. Lippincott, 1909), 9; *NatAm*, May 7, 1844; *Daily Atlas* (Boston), September 6, 1852; Daniel A. Cohen, "Passing the Torch: Boston Firemen, 'Tea Party' Patriots, and the Burning of the Charlestown Convent," *Journal of the Early Republic* 24 (Winter 2004): 570; Amy S. Greenberg, *Cause for Alarm: The Volunteer Fire Department in the Nineteenth-Century City* (Princeton, NJ: Princeton University Press, 1998), 89; Maginnis testimony, *PL*, October 17, 1844.

3   *PL*, July 9, 1841, December 28, 1841; *PL*, September 9, 1842, September 25, 1843, January 29, 1844; *DC*, December 18, 1843.

4   *DC*, May 6, 1844.

5   Patrick Wall, John Donegan, and James Murray testimony, *PL*, October 15, 1844; William Buck testimony, *PL*, October 16, 1844; Patrick Wall testimony, *AA*, October 16, 1844; William H. Hartnett testimony, *PL*, October 18, 1844.

6   Mary McAdam testimony, *PL*, April 30, 1845; Saunders Gavit testimony, *PL*, November 8, 1844; *CH*, May 30, 1844.

7   *DC*, May 7, 1844; George Friheller testimony, *PL*, September 13, 1844; James McAdams testimony, *PL*, September 21, 1844; Joseph Cox, Philadelphia, Pennsylvania, Death Certificates Index, 1803–1915, available at Ancestry.com; *PL*, August 7, 1841, September 9, 1842, May 23, 1844; *NatAm*, May 23, 1844; *Daily Atlas* (Boston), September 6, 1852; "Stated Meeting, November 5, 1844," in *Summary of the Transactions of the College of Physicians of Philadelphia. Volume I. From November, 1841, to August, 1846, Inclusive*, 252–253 (hereafter cited as *College of Physicians of Philadelphia*); *WS*, May 11, 1844. Of the eight Protestants killed in May 1844, six were between the ages of nineteen and twenty-four. *NatAm*, July 11, 1844; David T. Courtwright, *Violent Land: Single Men and Social Disorder from the Frontier to the Inner City* (Cambridge, MA: Harvard University Press, 1996); Cohen, "Passing the Torch," 555.

8   *DC*, May 7, 1844; Elizabeth Brown testimony, *PL*, September 16, 1844; *WS*, May 11, 1844.

9   Eliza Choate testimony, *PL*, October 17, 1844; *PL*, July 2, 1844; William F. Small testimony, *PL*, September 14, 1844.

10 *A Full and Complete Account of the Late Awful Riots in Philadelphia: Embellished with Ten Engravings* (Philadelphia: John B. Perry, 1844), 19; *ST*, July 4, 1845; "Commissioners of Kensington versus County of Philadelphia," in *Pennsylvania State Reports* 13, ed. George W. Harris (Philadelphia: George T. Bisel, 1873), 78; John Blair testimony, *PL*, September 20, 1844; William Rankin testimony, *PL*, October 17, 1844; Saunders Gavit testimony, *PL*, November 8, 1844.

11 *Saturday Courier*, November 4, 1843; Rankin testimony, *PL*, October 17, 1844; *DC*, May 9, 1844.

12 Cadwalader to C. H. Turner, March 21, 1844, vol. 187, George Cadwalader Letterbook, 1841–1848, GC; *NatAm*, May 7, 1844.

13 Edward King and G. M. Dallas to Gen. A. M. Prevost, August 16, 1834, box 432, folder 1: Suppression of Riots, GC; *USG*, May 7, 1844; *PL*, May 8, 1844.

14 *USG*, May 7, 1844; *PL*, May 7, 1844; Rankin testimony, *PL*, October 17, 1844; *NatAm*, June 4, 1844.

15 John Daly and Allen Weinberg, *Genealogy of Philadelphia County Subdivisions*, 2nd ed. (Philadelphia, 1966), 29; C. B. F. O'Neill and William Buck testimony, *PL*, September 14, 1844; Henry M. Phillips speech, *PL*, September 17, 1844; *USG*, May 7, 1844.

16 *USG*, May 7, 1844; C. B. F. O'Neill testimony, *PL*, September 14, 1844. On O'Neill's Catholicism, see the 1835 internment of his infant child at St. Michael's burying ground. Pennsylvania, Historical Society, Historic Pennsylvania Church and Town Records, reel 961, available at Ancestry.com. For O'Neill's first name, see 1835 Enumerations, Kensington 1st, PCA.

17 Sisters of Charity of the Blessed Virgin Mary, *In the Early Days: Pages from the Annals of the Sisters of Charity of the Blessed Virgin Mary* (St. Louis: B. Herder, 1925), 36, 83, 101; M. Jane Coogan, "A Study of the John Hughes–Terence Donaghoe Friendship," *Records of the American Catholic Historical Society of Philadelphia* 93 (1982): 49–54; Ann M. Harrington, "Sisters of Charity of the Blessed Virgin Mary: The Philadelphia Connection 1833–1843," *U.S. Catholic Historian* 27 (2009): 17–30.

18 Sisters of Charity of the Blessed Virgin Mary, *In the Early Days*, 101; Mary Baker testimony, *PL*, September 14, 1844.

19 *DC*, May 8, 1844; Dr. Duffie testimony, *DS*, October 18, 1844, May 7, 1844; *NatAm*, May 30, 1844; O'Neill testimony, *PL*, September 14, 1844; *PL*, May 7, 1844, October 28, 1844; *USG*, May 7, 1844.

CHAPTER 10: I HAVE GOT MY MAN!

1   *DC*, May 8, 1844; George Roberts testimony, *PL*, November 9, 1844.

2   *NatAm*, May 8, 1844, June 4, 1844; *DC*, May 8, 1844; *USG*, May 8, 1844; *PL*, May 9, 1844.

3   *USG*, May 8, 1844; *DC*, May 8, 1844; *PL*, May 7, 1844.

4   Lillian B. Miller, "The Peale Family: A Lively Mixture of Art and Science," *Smithsonian*, April 1979, 74; Charles Coleman Sellers, *Charles Willson Peale* (New York: Charles Scribner's Sons, 1969), 422–423; Augustin R. Peale, Ronaldson Cemetery, Pennsylvania and New Jersey, Church and Town Records, 1708–1985, 322, available at Ancestry.com; Augustin's

birth date of November 19, 1819 is given in Algernon Peale, Application for Membership, Sons of the American Revolution, January 3, 1910, Sons of the American Revolution Membership Applications, 1889–1970, available at Ancestry.com.

5   *PL*, December 28, 1837. The 1840 census shows Ralph Brown living with a woman in her twenties and a boy under the age of five, so perhaps Mrs. Brown recovered. Augustin Runyon Peale to Titian R. Peale, March 23, 1843, VIIIA/8D14-E3, *The Collected Papers of Charles Willson Peale and his Family, 1735–1885* (microform); *DC*, May 8, 1844.

6   Augustus Peale and Samuel Kramer testimony, *PL*, September 14, 1844; *NatAm*, June 4, 1844.

7   *CH*, May 9, 1844; *DC*, May 8, 1844; William McDonough and Catharine Lukins testimony, *PL*, November 8, 1844; *PL*, November 8, 1844. Paul later claimed not to have ordered the rifles, and their origin remains unknown. *NatAm*, May 20, 1844.

8   *PL*, May 8, 1844; *DC*, May 8, 1844, May 9, 1844; John Hugh Campbell, *History of the Friendly Sons of St. Patrick and of the Hibernian Society for the Relief of Emigrants from Ireland* (Philadelphia: Hibernian Society, 1892), 354; Francis Brady testimony, *PL*, September 16, 1844.

9   *DC*, May 8, 1844; *PL*, May 8, 1844; Morton McMichael to George Cadwalader, May 7, 1844, and Brigade Order no. 13, May 7, 1844, both in box 432, folder 1: Suppression of Riots, GC; AJP, December 7, 1838, 255–259.

10 *DC*, May 8, 1844; Joanna Maloy testimony, *PL*, September 14, 1844; *New-York Tribune*, May 21, 1844; Sidney George Fisher, "The Diary of Sidney George Fisher, 1844," *Pennsylvania Magazine of History and Biography* 79 (1955): 502.

11 Jacob Loudenslager testimony, *PL*, September 14, 1844; "Meeting of the Native Americans," *WS*, May 11, 1844.

12 *WS*, May 11, 1844; *NatAm*, May 8, 1844.

13 *WS*, May 11, 1844; *PL*, May 8, 1844.

14 *PL*, May 8, 1844; George Young and William Rankin testimony, *PL*, September 13, 1844; John Matheys and Lewis Snell testimony, *PL*, September 14, 1844; Joseph Hagany testimony, *PL*, September 16, 1844; William Buck testimony, *AA*, October 16, 1844.

15 C. B. F. O'Neill, Hannah Morton, and William Buck testimony, *PL*, September 14, 1844; Elizabeth Brown testimony, *PL*, September 16, 1844; *PL*, November 20, 1844; Francis Brady testimony, *PL*, October 25, 1844.

16 Stephen Winslow testimony, *PL*, September 13, 1844; Hannah Morton, Joanna Maloy, and John W. Keen testimony, *PL*, September 14, 1844; William Stevens testimony, *PL*, October 17, 1844.

17 Augustus Peale testimony, *PL*, September 14, 1844.

18 C. J. Jack, letter, *USG*, May 10, 1844; Thomas S. Harris testimony, *PL*, September 13, 1844, September 14, 1844.

19 John Matheys and George H. Martin testimony, *PL*, September 14, 1844; James S. Funk testimony, *PL*, October 17, 1844; George Roberts testimony, *PL*, November 9, 1844.

20 *Saturday Courier*, November 18, 1843; Thomas S. Harris testimony, *PL*, September 14; 1844; Edward Sherridan testimony, *PL*, September 16, 1844.

21 *DC*, May 8, 1844; Thomas S. Harris and John Matheys testimony, *PL*, September 14, 1844; George Roberts testimony, *PL*, November 9, 1844.

22 *WS*, May 11, 1844; William Rankin testimony, *PL*, September 13, 1844; John Matheys, John Craig, C. B. F. O'Neill, Alexander Brown, R. J. Fougeray, William Headman, John W.

Keen, Thomas S. Harris, and Augustus Peale testimony, *PL*, September 14, 1844; Joseph Sharpe testimony, *PL*, September 16, 1844; George Roberts testimony, *PL*, November 9, 1844.

23 *Saturday Courier*, May 11, 1844; George Young testimony, *PL*, September 13 1844, September 21, 1844; Isabella McDermot and Nancy Brown testimony, *PL*, April 30, 1845.

24 *PL*, February 28, 1842; *PL*, March 15, 1842; *NatAm*, May 9, 1844; Alexander Brown testimony, *PL*, September 14, 1844; Francis Weiss testimony, *PL*, October 16, 1844; John Stevens testimony, *AA*, October 17, 1844; James S. Funk testimony, *PL*, October 17, 1844; Lyman Ackley, Frederick Crowley, and Frederick Williams testimony, *PL*, April 30, 1845; *PL*, May 1, 1845.

25 *New-York Tribune*, May 9, 1844; Augustus Peale testimony, *PL*, September 14, 1844.

26 *DC*, May 8, 1844; *A Full and Complete Account of the Late Awful Riots in Philadelphia: Embellished with Ten Engravings* (Philadelphia: John B. Perry, 1844), 39; *PL*, July 23, 1839, September 30, 1839; Stillwell age from Pennsylvania, Philadelphia City Death Certificates, 1803–1915, available at Ancestry.com; John A. Beck and Peter Albright testimony, *PL*, October 17, 1844; Dr. Duffie testimony, *DS*, October 18, 1844.

27 *WS*, May 11, 1844; Thomas S. Harris testimony, *PL*, September 14, 1844; William Fife and James Riddle testimony, *PL*, October 25, 1844; Catharine McCrea testimony, *PL*, April 30, 1845.

28 *DC*, May 8, 1844; *NatAm*, June 6, 1844; Alderman Isaac Boileau and James Riddle testimony, *PL*, October 25, 1844.

CHAPTER 11: A RUSH OF THE SOLDIERS

1 Rudolph Harley, Pennsylvania General Assembly, House of Representatives, Committee on Disturbances at Seat of Government, *Report of the Minority of the Committee Appointed to Enquire Into the Causes of the Disturbances at the Seat of Government, in December, 1838* (Harrisburg: Boas & Coplan, 1839), 119.

2 Frederick Albright, Pennsylvania, Church Marriages, 1682–1976, Family Search, familysearch.org; "Registers of St. Augustine's Church. Philadelphia," *Records of the American Catholic Historical Society of Philadelphia* 1 (1884): 362; Henry De Courcy, *The Catholic Church in the United States*, trans. John Gilmary Shea (New York: Edward Dunigan and Brother, 1856), 257; Louis A. Rongione, "Sister to the Liberty Bell," *Records of the American Catholic Historical Society of Philadelphia* 87 (1976): 23; "Northern Liberties," *Daily Pennsylvanian*, November 4, 1834; *Pennsylvanian*, September 16, 1834, December 14, 1835, June 26, 1837; US House of Representatives, *Contested Election—Naylor and Ingersoll*, 26th Cong., 1st sess., H.R. Rept. 588, 1840, 427–428; *New-York Tribune*, October 19, 1844. In 1856, Catholic historian Henry De Courcy claimed that Albright "led the mob at St. Michael's and exulted that the record of his baptism was destroyed at St. Augustine's." By 1976, historian Louis Rongione reported an embellished version of what he called an "unconfirmed legend" that Albright himself set the fire in St. Augustine's. Neither story appears supported by contemporary evidence.

3 *PL*, August 27, 1841; Peter Albright testimony, *PL*, October 17, 1844; Susan G. Davis, *Parades and Power: Street Theatre in Nineteenth-Century Philadelphia* (Philadelphia: Temple University Press, 1986), 93–95; *Pennsylvanian*, May 30, 1835; *PI*, May 24, 1833; C. B. F. O'Neill and unnamed witness, *PL*, January 31, 1845.

4   Peter Albright testimony, *PL*, October 17, 1844; *Pennsylvanian*, May 8, 1844.

5   Peter Albright testimony, *PL*, October 17, 1844; Joseph Wood testimony, *PL*, January 31, 1845.

6   *ST*, May 8, 1844; *DC*, May 8, 1844; *New-York Tribune*, May 9, 1844, May 11, 1844; *College of Physicians of Philadelphia*, 254; John McKee testimony, *PL*, September 13, 1844; R. J. Fougeray, John Matheys, and William F. Small testimony, *PL*, September 14, 1844; *A Full and Complete Account of the Late Awful Riots in Philadelphia: Embellished with Ten Engravings* (Philadelphia: John B. Perry, 1844), 23.

7   *DC*, May 8, 1844; *ST*, May 8, 1844; *Saturday Courier*, May 11, 1844; Sanders Gavit and Thomas Goldsmith testimony, *PL*, October 15, 1844; John Fagan testimony, *PL*, October 16, 1844; Peter Albright testimony, *PL*, October 17, 1844; William B. Mann testimony, *PL*, January 31, 1845.

8   *NatAm*, May 10, 1844; Edwin Greble testimony, *PL*, September 13, 1844; On Edwin's relation to Lewis, see *DC*, May 8, 1844; Charles Orte and Elizabeth Brewer testimony, *PL*, November 6, 1844; Peter Albright testimony, *PL*, November 8, 1844.

9   *PL*, May 9, 1844; William Friheller testimony, *PL*, September 13, 1844; Sarah Dillon testimony, *PL*, September 14, 1844; John Kohn testimony, *PL*, September 21, 1844; Mason James and George Trefts testimony, *PL*, November 5, 1844.

10   William Shields and William Friheller testimony, *PL*, September 13, 1844; Joanna Maloy, Alexander Brown, and C. B. F. O'Neill testimony, *PL*, September 14, 1844; Thomas Goldsmith testimony, *PL*, October 15, 1844; Peter Albright and Mary Wetham testimony, *PL*, November 8, 1844; Mary Haughey testimony, *PL*, November 21, 1844.

11   *DC*, May 8, 1844; *The Full Particulars of the Late Riots* (Philadelphia, 1844), 12; William Shields, Dr. J. W. Duffee, Daniel H. Brown, John Daley, John M'Leary, and George Friheller testimony, *PL*, September 13, 1844; William Shales testimony, *DS*, September 13, 1844 (Shales is the same witness as Shields; in this as in several cases, reporters for different newspapers disagreed about the spelling of a witness's name); Peter Albright testimony, *PL*, October 17, 1844; Hammitt's age: Mathew Hammett (Matthew Hammitt), Philadelphia, Pennsylvania, Death Certificates Index, 1803–1915, available at Ancestry.com; "Charge of Judge King on the Trial of John Daley for Murder," in *A Treatise on the Law of Homicide in the United States*, ed. Francis Wharton (Philadelphia: Kay & Brother, 1855), 468.

12   *PL*, May 13, 1844; Martha Longshore testimony, *PL*, September 13, 1844; Dr. Thomas Oliver Goldsmith testimony, *AA*, October 16, 1844.

13   William Friheller, John Steele, and C. B. F. O'Neill testimony, *PL*, September 14, 1844; Francis E. Brady testimony, *PL*, September 16, 1844; Edward Wood testimony, *PL*, November 9, 1844; Elizabeth McDermott testimony, *PL*, November 20, 1844.

14   John Gorman and John Fagan testimony, *PL*, October 16, 1844; Mary Mallon testimony, *PL*, September 16, 1844. Dialogue reconstructed from paraphrase; Mallon's age from 1850 census; *PL*, February 8, 1845.

15   *USG*, May 8, 1844; *DC*, May 8, 1844; *ST*, May 8, 1844; *Saturday Courier*, May 11, 1844; *American* (South Port, WI), May 25, 1844.

16   Bridget Rice, John Shaffer, Sanders Gavit, Jane Develin, and C. B. F. O'Neill testimony, *PL*, October 15, 1844; John McKee testimony, *PL*, October 16, 1844; Washington J. Duffy testimony, *PL*, October 18, 1844; *DC*, October 19, 1844.

17   *PL*, May 9, 1844; *PL*, May 11, 1844; *Saturday Courier*, May 11, 1844; Jane Develin, testimony, *PL*, October 15, 1844; C. B. F. O'Neill testimony, *PL*, October 18, 1844; *PL*, February 8, 1845.

18   *USG*, May 8, 1844; *DC*, May 8, 1844; *WS*, May 11, 1844; *PL*, May 13, 1844.

19   Peter Albright testimony, *PL*, October 17, 1844; *DC*, May 8, 1844.

20   Along with four staff officers, Cadwalader led twenty-seven men of the First Troop Philadelphia City Cavalry and 223 men of Pleasonton's First Regiment of Artillery. Some portion of Murray's infantry regiment marched as well, but since Murray did not report the figures by day, it is not clear how many marched into Kensington that first day. Return of the Officers, Non-Commissioned Officers, Musicians and Privates of the First Brigade, box 431, folder 4, GC; *DC*, May 8, 1844; *PL*, August 5, 1844; C. B. F. O'Neill testimony, *PL*, October 18, 1844.

21   *DC*, May 8, 1844; *USG*, May 8, 1844; *WS*, May 11, 1844; George H. Martin testimony, *PL*, September 14, 1844; Philip English Mackey, ed., *A Gentleman of Much Promise: The Diary of Isaac Mickle, 1837–1845* (Philadelphia: University of Pennsylvania Press, 1977), 444 (hereafter cited as *Diary of Isaac Mickle*).

22   *CH*, May 30, 1844; *DC*, May 8, 1844; *Saturday Courier*, May 11, 1844.

23   *American* (South Port, WI), May 25, 1844; *ST*, May 8, 1844.

24   *ST*, May 8, 1844; *Diary of Isaac Mickle*, 444; *DC*, May 8, 1844.

25   *PL*, May 8, 1844; *College of Physicians of Philadelphia*, 256–7; *New-York Tribune*, May 9, 1844; *NatAm*, May 20, 1844.

26   *DC*, May 8, 1844, May 9, 1844; *Freeman's Journal* (Dublin, Ireland), May 30, 1844.

CHAPTER 12: HOW CAN WE FIRE ON OUR OWN CITIZENS?

1   *DC*, May 9, 1844; *ST*, May 17, 184; *WS*, May 11, 1844; *PL*, May 11, 1844.

2   *PL*, May 9, 1844.

3   *PL*, May 9, 1844; *DC*, May 9, 1844.

4   *PL*, May 9, 1844; Francis Brelsford testimony, *PL*, October 15, 1844; *AA*, July 16, 1844.

5   *DC*, May 9, 1844; *ST*, May 17, 1844; *NorAm*, May 9, 1844; *WS*, May 11, 1844.

6   *NorAm*, May 9, 1844; *DC*, May 9, 1844; *PL*, May 9, 1844, January 3, 1845.

7   John Gilmary Shea, *The Catholic Churches of New York City* (New York: L. G. Goulding, 1878), 486; *Evening Post* (New York), April 13, 1842, August 15, 1834; William Augustine Leahy, "Archdiocese of Boston," in *History of the Catholic Church in the New England States*, ed. William Byrne (Boston: Hurd & Everts, 1899), 144; *Freeman's Journal* (Dublin, Ireland), May 9, 1842; *New York Herald*, April 5, 1844.

8   Francis W. Hoeber, "Drama in the Courtroom, Theater in the Streets: Philadelphia's Irish Riot of 1831," *Pennsylvania Magazine of History and Biography* 125 (2001): 200; *A Full and Accurate Report of the Trial for Riot Before the Mayor's Court of Philadelphia, on the 13th of October, 1831* (Philadelphia: Jesper Harding, 1831), 31; *Liberator*, August 23, 1834; Samuel Otter, *Philadelphia Stories: America's Literature of Race and Freedom* (New York: Oxford University Press, 2013), 136.

9   Joseph Louis J. Kirlin, *Catholicity in Philadelphia* (Philadelphia: J. J. McVey, 1909), 283; Mary Mallon testimony, *PL*, September 16, 1844; "Trustees of St. Michael's Church v. The County of Philadelphia," in *Pennsylvania Law Journal Reports*, ed. John A. Clark (Philadelphia: John Campbell & Son, 1872), 182; *WS*, May 11, 1844; *ST*, May 17, 1844.

10   Jane Coogan, "A Study of the John Hughes–Terence Donaghoe Friendship," *Records of the American Catholic Historical Society of Philadelphia* 93 (1982): 54–56; "Donoghue v. The County," Robert M. *Barr Pennsylvania State Reports* 2 (1845): 230; Joanna Maloy testimony, *PL*, September 14, 1844; Francis Patrick Kenrick, *Diary and Visitation Record of the Rt. Rev. Francis Patrick Kenrick: Administrator and Bishop of Philadelphia, 1830–1851, Later, Archbishop of Baltimore* (Lancaster, PA: Wickersham, 1916), 225; *DS*, November 26, 1844.

11   Elizabeth Fagan, testimony, *PL*, September 21, 1844; *ST*, May 17, 1844; Francis Patrick Kenrick to Peter Kenrick, May 29, 1844, in K-F, 191; *USG*, May 10, 1844; Hubbell wrote that Fairlamb had forty men; Horatio Hubbell, "For the United States Gazette," *USG*, May 10, 1844.

12   *DC*, May 9, 1844; *ST*, May 17, 1844; Hubbell, "For the United States Gazette."

13   *DC*, May 9, 1844; Hubbell, "For the United States Gazette"; *PL*, May 9, 1844; *ST*, May 17, 1844.

14   *ST*, May 17, 1844; Thomas Rakestraw, Philip Banks, and Alexander Blackburn testimony, *PL*, November 7, 1844.

15   *DC*, May 9, 1844; *ST*, May 17, 1844; Hubbell, "For the United States Gazette."

16   *DC*, May 9, 1844; *ST*, May 17, 1844; Kensington 3rd., Tax Assessor's Ledger: Kensington 1, 2, & 3 Ward, 1841, 35, PCA.

17   Thomas South Lanard, *One Hundred Years with the State Fencibles* (Philadelphia: Nields, 1913), xxxv, 68.

18   Lanard, *One Hundred Years with the State Fencibles*, 68; *DC*, May 9, 1844.

19   Lanard, *One Hundred Years with the State Fencibles*, 68–69; *DC*, May 9, 1844.

20   *DC*, May 9, 1844; *PL*, May 9, 1844; *ST*, May 17, 1844; *NatAm*, May 9, 1844.

21   *NorAm*, May 9, 1844; *ST*, May 17, 1844; John Hugh Campbell, *History of the Friendly Sons of St. Patrick and of the Hibernian Society for the Relief of Emigrants from Ireland* (Philadelphia: Hibernian Society, 1892), 379; *DC*, May 9, 1844; *PL*, May 9, 1844, September 18, 1844; *DS*, November 12, 1844.

22   *DC*, May 9, 1844; 1st Division, Pennsylvania Militia, Division order no. 1, May 8, 1844, box 431, folder 2, GC; *PL*, May 9, 1844; *HJCS*, July 2, 1845; Pennsylvania Hospital Historic Collections, Meteorological Records, May 8, 1844; Horatio Hubbell to George Cadwalader, May 8, 1844, box 431, folder 4, GC.

23   *American* (South Port, WI), May 25, 1844; "The Philadelphia Riots," *New Englander* 2 (July 1844), 478; AJP, June 10, 1838, 146; Augustus Pleasonton to George Cadwalader, April 26, 1844, box 431, folder 1, GC; George Cadwalader to Augustus Pleasonton, May 16, 1844, box 431, folder 3, GC.

24   Augustus Pleasonton to Robert Patterson, May 8, 1844, box 431, folder 2, GC; Augustus Pleasonton to George Cadwalader, May 20, 1844, box 431, folder 3, GC; *NG*, March 7, 1835; *Germantown Telegraph*, August 16, 1843; Augustus Pleasonton testimony, *PL*, November 16, 1844.

25   P. A. B., "To the People of the City and County of Philadelphia," *PL*, May 14, 1844; *ST*, May 17, 1844.

26   *Saturday Courier*, January 21, 1843; *PL*, April 13, 1842; *NG*, May 7, 1833; *DC*, May 9, 1844.

27   *DC*, May 9, 1844; *PL*, May 9, 1844; *ST*, May 17, 1844.

CHAPTER 13: THE SKY A SHEET OF FLAMES

1   P. Aloysius Jordan, "St. Joseph's Church, Philadelphia," *Woodstock Letters* 3 (1874): 184.

2 Robert Edward Quigley, "Catholic Beginnings in the Delaware Valley," in *The History of the Archdiocese of Philadelphia*, ed. James F. Connelly (Philadelphia: The Archdiocese, 1976), 54; Louis A. Rongione, "Sister to the Liberty Bell," *Records of the American Catholic Historical Society of Philadelphia* 87 (1976): 6, 15; *USG*, May 9, 1844; *ST*, November 17, 1847, November 25, 1847.

3 *PL*, July 1, 1842; May 27, 1844; *DC*, May 8 1843, May 10, 1843; Joseph George Jr., "Very Rev. Dr. Patrick E. Moriarty, O.S.A., Philadelphia's Fenian Spokesman," *Pennsylvania History* 48 (1981): 222; *Baltimore Sun*, May 22, 1844; *WS*, May 11, 1844; *ST*, May 17, 1844.

4 Mary Yee, "Vine Street Expressway," Encyclopedia of Greater Philadelphia, http:// philadelphiaencyclopedia.org/archive/vine-street-expressway/.

5 *DC*, May 9, 1844; *PL*, May 9, 1844; Jordan, "St. Joseph's Church," 184–187; Alexander Johnson testimony, *PL*, September 10, 1844; *DS*, September 4, 1844; "In Re Riots of 1844," 2 Pa. L. J. Rep. 275 1842–1852; McKeown: *PL*, June 11, 1844, March 15, 1845.

6 *PL*, May 9, 1844; *USG*, May 9, 1844, May13, 1844; *NorAm*, May 9, 1844; William Young testimony, *PL*, September 10, 1844; Sidney George Fisher, *A Philadelphia Perspective: The Diary of Sidney George Fisher Covering the Years 1834–1871* (Philadelphia: Historical Society of Pennsylvania, 1967), 165.

7 Dialogue reconstructed from *NorAm*, May 9, 1844. *ST*, May 10, 1844; *DC*, May 9, 1844; William Young and Mary Hess testimony, *PL*, September 10, 1844; *Philadelphia Gazette*, September 9, 1844. Hess's brother, Frederick, was described as "a German boy." Hess told Young he had been in the country for about six years. *PL*, February 6, 1845. A cigar maker named John Hess was listed as having been born in Switzerland about 1825. Historical Society of Pennsylvania, Historic Pennsylvania Church and Town Records, available at Ancestry.com. Since John Hess the defendant was also a cigar maker, this seems to have been the same person.

8 John Scott testimony, *ST*, November 29, 1847; *History of the First Troop Philadelphia City Cavalry* (Philadelphia, 1875), 55; Report of the daily Strength of First Troop Philadelphia City Cavalry during their late Special duty, May 18, 1844, box 431, folder 3, GC.

9 *USG*, May 9, 1844; *ST*, May 10, 1844; *CH*, May 16, 1844; *DC*, May 9, 1844; William Young testimony, *PL*, September 10, 1844. Long and Jackson's first names are given in *PL*, March 11, 1844.

10 *DC*, May 9, 1844; *USG*, May 9, 1844; *Dollar Newspaper*, May 15, 1844; *PL*, May 29, 1844, September 5, 1844; John Shea testimony, *PL*, September 10, 1844.

11 *History of the First Troop*, 55l; *USG*, May 9, 1844; P. A. B., "To the People of the City and County of Philadelphia," *PL*, May 14, 1844; John Scott testimony, *ST*, November 29, 1847.

12 Fisher, *Philadelphia Perspective*, 165; *ST*, November 29, 1847; Joseph Sill, diary extracts, in Raymond F. Schmandt, "A Selection of Sources Dealing with the Nativist Riots of 1844," *Records of the American Catholic Historical Society* 80 (June and September 1969): 84.

13 *USG*, May 9, 1844; *ST*, May 10, 1844; Caroline Mayer to Mary E. Bird, May 10, 1844, Robert Montgomery Bird family correspondence, Ms. Coll. 1074, UP. Details on family from 1850 census.

14 *DC*, May 9, 1844; *PL*, May 9, 1844; *CH*, May 16, 1844; Caroline Mayer to Mary E. Bird; *Diary of Isaac Mickle*, 445; John Scott testimony, *ST*, November 29, 1847.

15 *NorAm*, May 9, 1844; *PL*, May 9, 1844; *USG*, May 9, 1844; Jordan, "St. Joseph's Church," 187–189.

16   *CH*, May 16, 1844; *USG*, May 9, 1844; *PL*, May 24, 1844, September 5, 1844; Samuel John Klingensmith, "The Architecture of Napoleon LeBrun: The Philadelphia Churches" (master's thesis, University of Virginia, 1976), 75; Rongione, "Sister to the Liberty Bell," 25.

17   *DC*, May 9, 1844, May 10, 1844; *PL*, May 9, 1844; *USG*, May 9, 1844.

18   *Kerry Evening Post*, June 1, 1844; *Pennsylvanian*, May 9, 1844; Mahlon A. Sellers and A. I. Sellers, "A Letter Describing the Native American Riots in Philadelphia in 1844," *Records of the American Catholic Historical Society of Philadelphia* 64 (1953): 245.

19   *New-York Tribune*, May 10, 1844; *Brooklyn Evening Star*, May 9, 1844.

20   John M. Campbell, "Biographical Sketch of Hon. James Campbell," *Records of the American Catholic Historical Society of Philadelphia* 5 (1894): 295; Francis Patrick Kenrick, *Diary and Visitation Record of the Rt. Rev. Francis Patrick Kenrick: Administrator and Bishop of Philadelphia, 1830–1851, Later, Archbishop of Baltimore* (Lancaster, PA: Wickersham, 1916), 223; Sister Mary Gonzaga to Mother Xavier, May 9, 1844, "The 'Native American' Riots of 1844," *American Catholic Historical Researches* 8 (1891): 89–90.

21   Charles Wister to Mary Ruschenberger, May 10, 1844, Boston College Collection of Anti-Catholic Documents, MS.2006.059, Archives and Manuscripts Department, John J. Burns Library, Boston College; *DC*, May 9, 1844.

22   *PL*, July 6, 1843, May 9, 1844; *DC*, May 9, 1844; *ST*, May 10, 1844; *USG*, May 9, 1844; Goodman as Lutheran: Historical Society of Pennsylvania, Philadelphia, PA, Historic Pennsylvania Church and Town Records, Reel: 99, available at Ancestry.com; *Journal of the Select Council of the City of Philadelphia for 1841–1842* (Philadelphia: J. Crissy, 1842): 116; Lansing B. Bloom, "Bourke on the Southwest," *New Mexico Historical Review* 8 (January 1933): 25.

23   John Scott to George Cadwalader, May 8, 1844, box 431, folder 2, GC; *NorAm*, May 9, 1844; *DC*, May 9, 1844; *USG*, May 9, 1844; *PL*, May 16, 1844; *Brooklyn Daily Eagle*, May 16, 1844. In February 1844, Fairmount Engine hall had hosted a Native American meeting: *DS*, February 27, 1844.

24   *DC*, May 9, 1844; *NorAm*, May 9, 1844.

CHAPTER 14: THE LORD SEETH

1   *DC*, May 10, 1844.

2   Ovid Johnson to Morton McMichael and John Scott, 1 A.M., May 9, 1844, box 432, folder 1: Suppression of Riots, GC; *DC*, May 9, 1844.

3   George Cadwalader to Horace Binney, March 15, 1834, box 403, folder 5, GC; Hampton Lawrence Carson, *A Sketch of Horace Binney* (n.p., 1907), 33; Charles Chauncey Binney, *The Life of Horace Binney: With Selections from His Letters* (Philadelphia: J. B. Lippincott, 1903), 236.

4   Binney, *Life of Horace Binney*, 237–238; *DC*, May 10, 1844.

5   *DC*, May 10, 1844.

6   *AA*, October 23, 1844; *NatAm*, October 23, 1844; *DC*, May 10, 1844.

7   Morton McMichael and John Scott, broadside, May 9, 1844, box 432, folder 2, GC; *DC*, May 10, 1844.

8   *ST*, May 11, 1844; *DC*, May 10, 1844.

9   *New-York Tribune*, May 10, 1844; *DC*, May 10, 1844.

10 *DC*, May 10, 1844; *American* (South Port, WI), May 25, 1844; *New-York Tribune*, May 11, 1844; *PL*, May 9 1844, May 11, 1844; Appendix to *Journal of the Common Council, of the City of Philadelphia, for 1844–1845* (Philadelphia: J. Van Court, 1845), 24.

11 *New-York Tribune*, May 10, 1844; *DC*, May 10, 1844; *ST*, May 10, 1844, May 11, 1844; *USG*, May 10, 1844; *Baltimore Sun*, May 13, 1844.

12 *DC*, May 10, 1844; *CH*, May 23, 1844.

13 *New-York Tribune*, May 10, 1844; *DC*, May 10, 1844; *NatAm*, May 11, 1844; Sara Trainer Smith, "Sketch of Mary Brackett Willcox, of Ivy Mills, Pa. 1796–1866," *Records of the American Catholic Historical Society of Philadelphia* 7 (1896): 451–452; Francis Patrick Kenrick, *Diary and Visitation Record of the Rt. Rev. Francis Patrick Kenrick: Administrator and Bishop of Philadelphia, 1830–1851, Later, Archbishop of Baltimore* (Lancaster, PA: Wickersham, 1916), 223.

14 *HJCS*, July 17, 1844; *AA*, July 22, 1844; Edwin Wolf and Marie Korey term the plate "Philadelphia's first 'news' photograph," but it is unclear that any city produced an earlier news photo. Edwin Wolf 2nd and Marie Elena Korey, eds., *Quarter of a Millennium: The Library Company of Philadelphia, 1731–1981: A Selection of Books, Manuscripts, Maps, Prints, Drawings, & Paintings* (Philadelphia: Library Company of Philadelphia, 1981), 266.

15 Caroline Mayer to Mary E. Bird, May 10, 1844, box 1, folder 11, Robert Montgomery Bird family correspondence, Ms. Coll. 1074, UP.

16 *DC*, May 10, 1844; *New-York Tribune*, May 10, 1844, May 11, 1844; *PL*, May 10, 1844; Joseph Louis J. Kirlin, *Catholicity in Philadelphia* (Philadelphia: J. J. McVey, 1909), 322; *USG*, May 10, 1844.

17 Headquarters, 1st Division, to George Cadwalader, January 25, 1845, box 432, folder 6, GC; *DC*, May 10, 1844; *ST*, May 10, 1844; *USG*, May 10, 1844; P. A. B., "For the Public Ledger," *PL*, August 31, 1844.

18 *ST*, May 17, 1844; *PL*, May 10, 1844; Roll or List of Volunteer Troops in service during the Riots of 1844 in the County of Philadelphia, box 432, folder 2, GC, lists 1,322 men whose companies were on duty between May 7 and May 10. The document does not distinguish between the numbers present from each brigade or company in May and July, so the number is approximate.

19 *USG*, May 10, 1844; "The Diary of Sidney George Fisher, 1844," *Pennsylvania Magazine of History and Biography* 79 (1955): 492; *DC*, May 10, 1844; *New-York Tribune*, May 10, 1844.

20 Augustus Pleasonton to George Cadwalader, May 20, 1844, box 431, folder 3, GC; 1st Brigade, Brigade Order no. 5, May 9, 1844, box 431, folder 2, GC; *AJP*, May 9 and 10, 1844, 408–409.

21 *New-York Tribune*, May 11, 1844; *NatAm*, May 11, 1844, quoting the *Philadelphia Gazette*; *PL*, May 10, 1844; *DC*, May 10, 1844.

22 *New-York Tribune*, May 11, 1844; Marc Frenaye to Francis Patrick Kenrick, May 10, 1844, in K-F, 54.

23 1st Division Order No. 13, May 10, 1844, and 1st Division, Order no. 7, May 10, 1844, box 431, folder 2, GC; *PL*, May 11, 1844.

24 *PL*, May 10, 1844, May 13, 1844; *ST*, May 17, 1844; *NatAm*, May 11, 1844; *New-York Tribune*, May 11, 1844; *DC*, May 11, 1844; Mahlon A. Sellers and A. I. Sellers, "A Letter Describing the Native American Riots in Philadelphia in 1844," *Records of the American Catholic Historical Society of Philadelphia* 64 (1953): 245; *USG*, May 11, 1844.

25 AJP, May 10, 1844, 409; ST, May 11, 1844; USG, May 11, 1844; PL, May 11, 1844.

26 ST, May 13, 1844, May 17, 1844.

27 PL, May 13, 1844; DC, May 13, 1844, May 14, 1844.

28 Baltimore Sun, May 11, 1844; 1st Div. P.M., General Order, No. 10, May 11, 1844, box 431, folder 2, GC; AJP, May 12, 1844, 410.

29 DC, May 13, 1844; Kenrick, Diary and Visitation Record, 224n464; Gettysburg Compiler, May 20, 1844.

30 Baltimore Sun, May 11, 1844; David A. Wilson, Thomas D'Arcy McGee: Passion, Reason, and Politics, 1825–1857 (Montreal: McGill-Queen's Press, 2008), 79, 373n11; Nation (Dublin, Ireland), June 1, 1844.

31 Sister Gonzaga Grace to Mother Xavier, Ascension Day (May 16, 1844), box 6, folder 11, Philadelphia, PA—St. Joseph's Home/Gonzaga Home Collections, RG 11-4-2, Daughters of Charity Archives, Province of St. Louise, Emmitsburg, MD; Francis Patrick Kenrick to Peter Kenrick, May 15, 1844, ACHS; Sidney George Fisher, A Philadelphia Perspective: The Diary of Sidney George Fisher Covering the Years 1834–1871 (Philadelphia: Historical Society of Pennsylvania, 1967), 165. For this meaning of "angustiis positus," see K. P. Harrington, Medieval Latin, 2nd ed. (Chicago: University of Chicago Press, 2018), 201.

32 PL, May 13, 1844, May 18, 1844; USG, May 13, 1844; 1st Division, P.M., General Order no. 19, May 13, 1844, General Order no. 21, May 13, 1844, W. Heyward Drayton to George Cadwalader, May 13, 1844, box 431, folder 3, GC; 1st Brigade, Brigade Return, May 1844, 1st Brigade, Brigade Order no. 26, June 10, 1844, box 431, folder 4, GC.

33 PL, May 20, 1844, August 6, 1844; ST, May 20, 1844; DC, May 22, 1844; Thomas South Lanard, One Hundred Years with the State Fencibles (Philadelphia: Nields, 1913), 71; College of Physicians of Philadelphia, 257; Augustus Pleasonton to William Rawle, July 27, 1844, box 3, folder 1: Letters, 1st Regiment Artillery, MG7, PSA.

34 PL, May 23, 1844; College of Physicians of Philadelphia, 252, 254, 258–261; NatAm, May 23, 1844; USG, May 8, 1844.

35 NorAm, May 27, 1844; NatAm, May 18, 1844, May 21, 1844, May 27, 1844, June 4, 1844; PL, May 23, 1844, May 27, 1844; Saturday Courier, June 8, 1844; New-York Tribune, May 20, 1844; DS, November 27, 1844.

36 College of Physicians of Philadelphia, 254; PL, May 13, 1844; Pennsylvanian, May 14, 1844; Saturday Courier, May 18, 1844; Hannah Morton testimony, PL, September 14, 1844; NatAm, May 15, 1844.

37 Saturday Courier, June 8, 1844; Jacob Powell, FHL Film Number 1906032, Philadelphia, Pennsylvania, Death Certificates Index, 1803–1915, available at Ancestry.com.

CHAPTER 15: HUMANITY WEEPS

1   Saturday Courier, June 21, 1844; NatAm, June 11, 1844; CH, May 30, 1844; Brooklyn Evening Star, May 22, 1844; PL, June 17, 1844, November 8, 1844; William Young testimony, PL, September 10, 1844.

2   DC, May 20, 1844, June 1, 1844; Francis Patrick Kenrick to Peter Kenrick, May 29, 1844, in K-F, 188; CH, June 6, 1844; Francis Patrick Kenrick, Diary and Visitation Record of the Rt. Rev. Francis Patrick Kenrick: Administrator and Bishop of Philadelphia, 1830–1851, Later, Archbishop of Baltimore (Lancaster, PA: Wickersham, 1916), 224.

3   Cynthia A. Kierner, *Inventing Disaster: The Culture of Calamity from the Jamestown Colony to the Johnstown Flood*, chap. 6 (Chapel Hill: University of North Carolina Press, 2019); *PL*, July 6, 1843; On the importance of storytelling, see Charles Tilly, "Contentious Conversation," *Social Research* 65, no. 3 (1998): 491–510, and Avishai Margalit, "The Exemplary Pogrom," *New York Review of Books*, May 23, 2019.

4   *PL*, July 2, 1844; *Pennsylvanian*, May 9, 1844.

5   *NatAm*, May 15, 1844; *New York Freeman's Journal and Catholic Register*, May 11, 1844, May 25, 1844; *Tralee Chronicle and Killarney Echo*, June 15, 1844; *Connaught Telegraph*, June 5, 1844.

6   John H. Warland, "Philadelphia Riots" (1844), Harris Broadsides, Brown Digital Repository, Brown University Library, https://repository.library.brown.edu/studio/item/bdr:285903/; *New-York Tribune*, May 25, 1844.

7   *NorAm*, May 9, 1844; *ST*, May 11, 1844; *Pennsylvanian*, May 21, 1844.

8   *NatAm*, May 18, 1844; *Evening Post* (New York), May 11, 1844, 2; *Freeman's Journal* (Dublin, Ireland), June 20, 1844 (quoting *Boston Atlas*); Edwin Hubbell Chapin, *A Discourse: Preached in the Universalist Church, Charlestown, on Sunday, May 12, 1844: in Reference to the Recent Riots in Philadelphia* (Boston: A. Tompkins, 1844), 13–14.

9   *PL*, June 12, 1844; "The Philadelphia Riots," *New World* 8 (June 29, 1844): 822; *Kerry Evening Post*, June 1, 1844; "The State of Siege," *Littell's Living Age* 23 (October 20, 1849): 134.

10 Mary Bird to Freddy Bird, May 8, 1844, box 27, folder 338, Robert Montgomery Bird papers, MS Coll. 108, UP; Caroline Mayer to Mary E. Bird, May 10, 1844, box 1, folder 11, Robert Montgomery Bird family correspondence, Ms. Coll. 1074, UP; *Diary of Isaac Mickle*, 447.

11 *PL*, May 13, 1844, June 11, 1844; *DC*, June 11, 1844; While not mentioning Levin's name, the *Ledger* referred to "the editor of the Sun." *PL*, June 17, 1844.

12 Neil Longley York, "Rival Truths, Political Accommodation, and the Boston 'Massacre,'" *Massachusetts Historical Review* 11 (2009): 66; *NatAm*, May 14, 1844.

13 *NatAm*, May 7, 1844; Washington Peale, *The Three Days of May 1844: Columbia Mourns Her Citizens Slain*), 1844, lithograph, 35.2 x 27.4 cm, Library of Congress, https://www.loc.gov/item/2008661451/; *Verses Composed on the Slaughter of Native Americans, in Kensington, Philadelphia, May 1844*, (Philadelphia, 1844), Library of Congress, https://www.loc.gov/resource/rbpe.1540150a/.

14 *DC*, May 7, 1844; *NatAm*, May 7, 1844, May 10, 1844, May 13, 1844, June 1, 1844; *CH*, May 23, 1844. The *Pennsylvanian* (May 7, 1844) mentioned both Shiffler (identified as Shiffley) and the flag, but did not suggest that Shiffler had been holding it.

15 *New York Herald*, May 9, 1844; *Germantown Telegraph*, May 15, 1844; *NatAm*, May 13, 1844, May 15, 1844, June 7, 1844; *WS*, May 11, 1844.

16 *New World*, May 18, 1844, 633; John Hancock Lee, *The Origin and Progress of the American Party in Politics* (Philadelphia: Elliott & Gihon, 1855), 105; B. (Joseph Berg), "False Sympathy," *Protestant Banner* (Philadelphia), June 6, 1844.

17 Joseph Sill, diary extracts, May 8, 1844, in Raymond F. Schmandt, "A Selection of Sources Dealing with the Nativist Riots of 1844," *Records of the American Catholic Historical Society* 80 (June and September 1969): 84; *ST*, June 5, 1844.

18 William Quarter to Francis Patrick Kenrick, May 20, 1844, in K-F, 81; "The Philadelphia Anticatholic Riots," *United States Catholic Magazine* 3 (June 1844): 380.

19 *CH*, May 16, 1844, May 30, 1844.

20 Mary Gonzaga to Xavier, May 9, 1844, 90; *Freeman's Journal* (Dublin, Ireland), May 30, 1844; A Catholic Native American, "Origin of the Late Riots," *New York Freeman's Journal and Catholic Register*, May 18, 1844; *CH*, May 30, 1844.

21 *CH*, May 23, 1844; Justus E. Moore, "On the Ruins of St. Augustine's Church," *CH*, July 11, 1844.

22 Nolan, *Kenrick*, 324; *PL*, June 17, 1844; Francis Patrick Kenrick to Peter Kenrick, June 17, 1844, in K-F, 193.

23 Thomas Roland, ed., "Between Riots in 1844," *Records of the American Catholic Historical Society of Philadelphia* 62 (1951): 64–65; *Address of the Catholic Lay Citizens of the City and County of Philadelphia, to Their Fellow-citizens* (Philadelphia: M. Fithian, 1844), 4; Howard A. Kelly, *A Cyclopedia of American Medical Biography* (Philadelphia: W. B. Saunders, 1912), 214; Charles Houston Goudiss and Joseph Walsh, "Notes on the Life of Dr. William Edmonds Horner: A.D. 1793–1853," *Records of the American Catholic Historical Society of Philadelphia* 14 (1903): 425.

24 *Address of the Catholic Lay Citizens*, 10.

25 Caroline Mayer to Mary E. Bird, May 10, 1844; An Old Citizen, "Mobs," *PL*, May 16, 1844.

26 *NatAm*, June 3, 1844; Morton McMichael to Robert Bird, May 17, 1844, box 2, folder 93, Robert Montgomery Bird Papers, MS Coll. 108, UP; Sidney George Fisher, *A Philadelphia Perspective: The Diary of Sidney George Fisher Covering the Years 1834–1871* (Philadelphia: Historical Society of Pennsylvania, 1967), 165; Sidney George Fisher, *Diaries*, HSP, May 15, 1844.

27 *USG*, May 13, 1844; P. A. B., "To the People of the City and County of Philadelphia," *PL*, May 14, 1844; *PL*, May 15, 1844; *ST*, May 15, 1844.

28 George Cadwalader to J. R. Ingersoll, May 24, 1844, and George Cadwalader to John (?) McCain, May 17, 1844, box 431, folder 3, GC; Augustus Pleasonton to Mayor John Scott, May 12. 1844, box 3, folder 1: Letters, 1st Regiment Artillery, MG7, PSA.

29 The reference was to Napoleon's actions against a Paris mob in 1795, popularized in 1837 by author Thomas Carlyle as a "whiff of grapeshot." Thomas Carlyle, *The French Revolution: A History* (London: Chapman and Hall, 1896), 3:320; *PL*, May 13, 1844, May 16, 1844.

30 *PL*, May 15, 1844; *Freeman's Journal* (Dublin, Ireland), May 30, 1844.

31 *PL*, May 16, 1844, May 18, 1844, May 20, 1844.

32 *USG*, July 2, 1844.

CHAPTER 16: WON'T WE GIVE IT TO YOU ON THE FOURTH OF JULY?

1 *NatAm*, May 28, 1844; *PL*, May 21, 1844, May 28, 1844; Pennsylvania Hospital Historic Collections, Meteorological Records, May 27, 1844; *Cork Examiner*, July 3, 1844.

2 *ST*, June 25, 1844, July 1, 1844; *PL*, July 3, 1844, December 18, 1844; *AA*, December 18, 1844; Chas. Wm. Carroll testimony, *PL*, December 19, 1844.

3 *New-York Tribune*, May 20, 1844; *McElroy's Philadelphia Directory for 1844*; *DC*, June 14, 1844; *PL*, June 14, 1844; *NatAm*, June 15, 1844; C. J. Jack to Captain George Ramsey, June 14, 1844, ACHS; Capt. George D. Ramsay to Morton McMichael, June 14, 1844, in Raymond F. Schmandt, "A Selection of Sources Dealing with the Nativist Riots of 1844," *Records of the American Catholic Historical Society* 80 (June and September 1969): 73; *New York Herald*, June 14, 1844.

4   *NatAm*, June 8, 1844, June 10, 1844; *NorAm*, June 8, 1844; *PL*, June 8, 1844.

5   *NatAm*, June 18, 1844; *Weekly Economist* (Buffalo, NY), June 26, 1844; *PL*, June 18, 1844.

6   W. S. Archer to Elihu D. Tarr, June 14, 1844, in *NatAm*, June 20, 1844; *NatAm*, June 6, 1844, Jume 24, 1844; *Alton Telegraph* (Illinois), June 22, 1844.

7   *PL*, January 21, 1842; *Saturday Courier*, April 16, 1842; *PL*, May 13, 1844, May 18, 1844; *ST*, May 17, 1844; *USG*, May 13, 1844; Bruce Laurie, "Fire Companies and Gangs in Southwark: The 1840s," in *The Peoples of Philadelphia: A History of Ethnic Groups and Lower-Class Life, 1790–1940*, ed. Allen Freeman Davis and Mark H. Haller (Philadelphia: University of Pennsylvania Press, 1998), 75. Laurie states that the Weccacoe Hose included Irishmen but provides no evidence for this claim. Given Hose members' later involvement in the Southwark riots, this seems unlikely.

8   *New-York Tribune*, June 26, 1844; *NatAm*, June 25, 1844; *PL*, June 28, 1844.

9   Chas. M. Sandgram to Morton McMichael, June 27, 1844, Morton McMichael papers, LC; Morton McMichael to Fairlamb, June 26, 1844, ACHS; *DC*, July 1, 1844; Morton McMichael to Robert Patterson, June 29, 1844, ACHS.

10 Susan G. Davis, *Parades and Power: Street Theatre in Nineteenth-Century Philadelphia* (Philadelphia: Temple University Press, 1986), 42–44; Michael Meranze, *Laboratories of Virtue: Punishment, Revolution, and Authority in Philadelphia, 1760–1835* (Chapel Hill: University of North Carolina Press, 1996), 235; *DC*, July 6, 1843; *PL*, July 1, 1844.

11 Adam Criblez, *Parading Patriotism: Independence Day Celebrations in the Urban Midwest, 1826–1876* (DeKalb: Northern Illinois University Press, 2013); *DC*, June 15, 1843; Davis, *Parades and Power*, 46; Frederick Marryat, *A Diary in America*, Second Series (Philadelphia: T. K. and P. G. Collins, 1840), 50.

12 Dan Horner, *Taking to the Streets: Crowds, Politics, and the Urban Experience in Mid-Nineteenth-Century Montreal* (Montreal: McGill-Queen's Press, 2020), 84; *TALR*, April 23, 1842; John F. Quinn, "The Rise and Fall of Repeal: Slavery and Irish Nationalism in Antebellum Philadelphia," *Pennsylvania Magazine of History and Biography* 130 (January 2006): 53; Ric N. Caric, "From Ordered Buckets to Honored Felons: Fire Companies and Cultural Transformation in Philadelphia, 1785–1850," *Pennsylvania History* 72 (2005): 139; *DC*, July 6, 1843.

13 Lydia Blackmore, "Objects for President!: Campaign Material Culture and Populist Politics, 1828–1848" (master's thesis, University of Delaware, 2013), 17 David Grimsted, *American Mobbing, 1828–1861: Toward Civil War* (New York: Oxford University Press, 1998), 187; "Celebration of the 4th of July," *Saturday Courier*, June 29, 1844.

14 *NatAm*, June 10, 1844, June 11, 1844, June 28, 1844; *ST*, June 26, 1844; *PL*, June 26, 1844; *AA*, July 18, 1844.

15 *AA*, July 24, 1844, July 30, 1844.

16 *PL*, June 19, 1844, August 4, 1842; *Freeman's Journal and Catholic Register* (New York), June 29, 1844; *Freeman's Journal* (Dublin, Ireland), July 15, 1844; *ST*, June 25, 1844.

17 Francis Patrick Kenrick to Peter Kenrick, June 17, 1844, in K-F, 193; *Freeman's Journal and Catholic Register* (New York), June 29, 1844; An Exile, "Letters from America, no. XXXIII," *Nation* (Dublin), July 20, 1844; Francis Kenrick, "Card," *CH*, June 27, 1844; *NorAm*, July 3, 1844.

18 *NatAm*, June 17, 1844; Robert Patterson to George Cadwalader, July 3, 1844, box 431, folder 5, GC; Morton McMichael, printed form letter, June 28, 1844, in Raymond F. Schmandt,

"A Selection of Sources Dealing with the Nativist Riots of 1844," *Records of the American Catholic Historical Society* 80 (June and September 1969): 74–75.

19 *NatAm*, July 6, 1844; Pennsylvania Hospital Historic Collections, Meteorological Records, July 3, 1844, July 4, 1844; *DC*, July 6, 1844; John Hancock Lee, *The Origin and Progress of the American Party in Politics* (Philadelphia: Elliott & Gihon, 1855), 136; *New-York Tribune*, July 9, 1844; *AJP*, July 4, 1844, 417; *Philadelphia Gazette*, July 6, 1844; *PL*, July 4, 1844.

20 *PL*, June 24, 1844, June 26, 1844, July 4, 1844; *Baltimore Sun*, July 1, 1844; *Philadelphia Gazette*, July 6, 1844; *NatAm*, June 26, 1844.

21 *AA*, July 13, 1844; *NatAm*, June 17, 1844; *Evening Post* (New York), April 1, 1844; *ST*, July 20, 1844. Author's count of symbols mentioned in the descriptions of banners in Lee, *Origin and Progress*, 140–156.

22 *Times* (London), April 28, 1829; "Covenanting Relics," *Sunday at Home* 31 (1884): 88–90; "Banner Headline for Covenanters," *Scotsman*, February 19, 2002; Michael Augustine Corrigan, "Register of the Clergy Laboring in the Archdiocese of New York from Early Missionary Times to 1885," *United States Catholic Historical Society, Historical Studies and Records* 2 (1900): 232; David Morgan, *Protestants and Pictures: Religion, Visual Culture, and the Age of American Mass Production* (New York: Oxford University Press, 1999), 30–32; *Address of the Board of Managers of the American Protestant Association* (Philadelphia, 1843), 5.

23 *DC*, July 6, 1844; *USG*, July 8, 1844; *AJP*, July 4, 1844.

24 *DC*, June 27, 1844; *ST*, July 4, 1844; *PL*, July 4, 1844; *Philadelphia Gazette*, July 5, 1845; *DC*, July 6, 1844; *NatAm*, July 8, 1844. The route of the 1832 procession is given in *DC*, February 17, 1832, and the route for the 1844 procession is given in *DC*, July 6, 1844. I calculated the distance of each route using Google Maps.

25 *DC*, July 4, 1844, July 6, 1844; *PL*, July 4, 1844; Thomas South Lanard, *One Hundred Years with the State Fencibles* (Philadelphia: Nields, 1913), 72; *AA*, July 13, 1844. The *Daily Chronicle* described Snyder's Woods as "back of Fountain Green," a name preserved in today's Fountain Green Drive in Fairmount Park.

26 Lee, *Origin and Progress*, 161; *PL*, July 4, 1844; *DC*, July 6, 1844; *Baltimore Sun*, July 8, 1844.

27 *DC*, July 6, 1844; Captain Douglass testimony, *PL*, July 15, 1844; *AA*, July 19, 1844; *PL*, July 6, 1844; *NatAm*, July 8, 1844.

28 *AJP*, July 5, 1844.

CHAPTER 17: ARE THERE ANY GUNS IN THE CHURCH?

1 *PL*, July 11, 1844, 418; *AA*, July 18, 1844; Morton McMichael testimony, *PL*, July 15, 1844.

2 Joseph Louis J. Kirlin, *Catholicity in Philadelphia* (Philadelphia: J. J. McVey, 1909), 295; dimensions from June 30, 1840, Southwark District Surveyor, Surveys & Regulations, 1786–1841, RG 221.3, PCA; Southwark, Ward 2, Tax Assessor's Ledger: Southwark 1, 2, & 3, 1841, 5–8, PCA.

3 Samuel John Klingensmith, "The Architecture of Napoleon LeBrun: The Philadelphia Churches" (master's thesis, University of Virginia, 1976), 1–7, 38–39, 42–43, 57; *CH*, July 7, 1842.

4 *Pennsylvanian*, July 13, 1836; John M. Campbell, "Biographical Sketch of Hon. James Campbell," *Records of the American Catholic Historical Society of Philadelphia* 5 (1894): 273; John F. Coleman, "The Public Career of James Campbell," *Pennsylvania History* 29 (January 1962): 27; *NorAm*, October 20, 1841; *PL*, October 14, 1842; *PL*, June 26, 1844.

5 *AA*, August 28, 1844; W. L. McCalla, letter to the editor, *Protestant Banner* (Philadelphia), October 14, 1842; *DC*, January 13, 1844.

6 George Rogers Taylor, "'Philadelphia in Slices' by George G. Foster," *Pennsylvania Magazine of History and Biography* 93, no. 1 (January 1969): 35; *American Sentinel*, May 6, 1844; *DC*, November 2, 1843.

7 *NorAm*, March 12, 1844, May 6, 1844; *Protestant Banner* (Philadelphia), May 2, 1844; *NatAm*, April 25, 1844, June 15, 1844; *New-York Tribune*, June 26, 1844.

8 *Freeman's Journal* (Dublin, Ireland), May 30, 1844; P. Aloysius Jordan, "St. Joseph's Church, Philadelphia," *Woodstock Letters* 3 (1874): 182, 200; John Patrick Dunn, letter to the editor, *Protestant Banner* (Philadelphia), September 2, 1842.

9 *WS*, May 11, 1844; *PL*, June 26, 1844; Thomas S. Harris testimony, *PL*, September 14, 1844.

10 William H. Dunn testimony, *PL*, September 21, 1844; *NatAm*, May 30, 1844; *WS*, May 11, 1844; *McElroy's Philadelphia Directory for 1844*, 240; *ST*, May 10, 1844; *PL*, April 20, 1844; *Baltimore Sun*, May 11, 1844; 1st Division, Order no. 3, May 9, 1844, box 431, folder 2, GC; *Daily Atlas* (Boston, MA), May 13, 1844.

11 *USG*, May 11, 1844, May13, 1844; *ST*, May 13, 1844; Marc Frenaye to Francis Patrick Kenrick, May 11, 1844, 4:30 A.M., in K-F, 53; *Evening Post* (New York), May 13, 1844; J. R. McGleason to General George Cadwalader, May 10, 1844, box 431, folder 2, GC.

12 *NatAm*, May 30, 1844; 1st Division Order no. 3, May 9, 1844, box 431, folder 2, GC; *CH*, August 1, 1844.

13 Francis W. Hoeber, "Drama in the Courtroom, Theater in the Streets: Philadelphia's Irish Riot of 1831," *Pennsylvania Magazine of History and Biography* 125 (2001): 200, 217; *PL*, October 7, 1843; Gen. H. Hubbell testimony, *PL*, July 20, 1844; *CH*, August 1, 1844; "Wm. H. Dunn to Gen. H. Hubbell," *PL*, July 26, 1844.

14 Adam Diller testimony, *PL*, July 22, 1844; Gen. H. Hubbell testimony, *PL*, July 20, 1844; David Porter to Adam Diller, June 13, 1844, Militia Letter Book, 1839–1861, series 26.22, PSA; William Dunn, letter to the editor, *DC*, July 26, 1844.

15 John Patrick Dunn, "The Search," *CH*, August 1, 1844; "The Southwark Riots," *Republic: A Magazine for the Defence of Civil and Religious Liberty* 1 (1845): 14; Isaiah Robbins account, *AA*, February 13, 1845; Grover testimony *PL*, July 18, 1844; John W. Smith et al., "To the Public," *AA*, July 15, 1844. Robbins dialogue reconstructed from paraphrase.

16 *NatAm*, July 4, 1844; John Hancock Lee, *The Origin and Progress of the American Party in Politics* (Philadelphia: Elliott & Gihon, 1855), 143–144; *CH*, July 11, 1844; *DC*, July 4, 1844; Smith et al., "To the Public"; *AJP*, July 4, 1844, 417. The total number of Southwark marchers is the author's calculation from Lee, chap. 17, *Origin and Progress*.

17 Charles Ivar McGrath, "Securing the Protestant Interest: The Origins and Purpose of the Penal Laws of 1695," *Irish Historical Studies* 30 (May 1996): 25–46; Samuel Hazard, ed., *Colonial Records of Pennsylvania* (Harrisburg: T. Fenn, 1851), 6:503; Francis Jennings, *Empire of Fortune: Crowns, Colonies, and Tribes in the Seven Years War in America* (1988; repr., New York: W. W. Norton, 1990), 245.

18 *NatAm*, May 7, 1844; *American* (South Port, WI), May 25, 1844; *AA*, August 6, 1844.

19 Isaiah Robbins account, "Astounding Disclosures," *AA*, February 13, 1845; "Southwark Riots," *Republic*, 14; AJP, July 6, 1844, 418.

20 Thomas Grover testimony, *PL*, July 18, 1844; Alderman Sanders testimony, *PL*, July 15, 1844;

NatAm, July 6, 1844; *Philadelphia Gazette*, August 2, 1844; *PL*, July 15, 1844; George Merrick testimony, *PL*, November 15, 1844; J. N. J. Douglass testimony, *New York Herald*, July 14, 1844.

21 Morton McMichael testimony, *PL*, June 26, 1844; *HJCS*, July 10, 1844; *AA*, December 27, 1844; *USG*, July 15, 1844; Alderman Charles Hortz, "Testimony of the Southwark Magistrates, Police &c.," *AA*, July 16, 1844; Thomas A. Roe, "Southwark Affair," *AA*, July 17, 1844; Clayton McMichael passport application, May 25, 1895, US Passport Applications, 1795–1925, National Archives, available at Ancestry.com; Morton McMichael testimony, *PL*, July 15, 1844; Morton McMichael testimony, *PL*, November 14, 1844; "Riot Cases," *PL*, November 14, 1844.

22 *DC*, July 16, 1844; "Charles Hortz," Thompson Westcott, *Biographies of Philadelphians*, HSP; Morton McMichael, sworn, OB, 39; William Heysham testimony, *PL*, July 15, 1844.

23 McMichael testimony, *PL*, July 15, 1844; McMichael, sworn, OB, 39; Statement No. 2: John Greaves, "Astounding Disclosures," *AA*, February 14, 1845; J. N. J. Douglass testimony, *New York Herald*, July 14, 1844. In 1848, Hortz would win election to the state Assembly as a Native American.

24 Thomas A. Roe, "Southwark Affair," *AA*, July 17, 1844; Morton McMichael testimony, *PL*, July 15, 1844; *NatAm*, June 3, 1844.

25 "Town Meeting—Riots," *Hazard's Register of Pennsylvania* 14 (September 1834): 202; Elliott Drago, "Neither Northern Nor Southern: The Politics of Slavery and Freedom in Philadelphia, 1820–1847" (PhD diss., Temple University, 2017), 174–176; Morton McMichael testimony, *PL*, July 15, 1844. A similar search of a Catholic institution took place in Baltimore in 1839; the mayor and two other notables inspected a convent to assure an angry crowd that no evils were taking place out of sight. Joseph G. Mannard, "The 1839 Baltimore Nunnery Riot: An Episode in Jacksonian Nativism and Social Violence," *Maryland Historian* 11 (June 1980): 14.

26 *PL*, August 15, 1844; *DC*, May 8, 1844; *College of Physicians of Philadelphia*, 261–262; George Young testimony, *PL*, September 13, 1844; *AA*, August 28, 1844; *PL*, July 7, 1844; *McElroy's Philadelphia Directory for 1844*, 186, 268.

27 Roe, "Southwark Affair"; "Statement of David Ford," *AA*, July 25, 1844; Morton McMichael testimony, *PL*, July 15, 1844; Smith et al., "To the Public"; Statement No. 2: John Greaves, "Astounding Disclosures."

28 Smith et al., "To the Public"; "Statement of David Ford"; Dunn, "The Search," *CH*, August 1, 1844.

29 Isaiah Robbins account, "Astounding Disclosures"; "Statement of David Ford," *AA*, July 25, 1844; J. N. J. Douglass testimony, *New York Herald*, July 14, 1844.

30 John Dutton testimony, *PL*, July 20, 1844; Smith et al., "To the Public"; Dunn, "The Search"; David Ford, "Conclusion of David Ford's Statement," *AA*, July 26, 1844; Roe, "Southwark Affair," *AA*, July 17, 1844.

31 Alderman Saunders testimony, *AA*, July 16, 1844; Smith et al., "To the Public"; Ford, "Conclusion of David Ford's Statement," *AA*, July 26, 1844.

32 Smith et al., "To the Public"; David Ford testimony, *PL*, November 16, 1844.

33 *USG*, July 6, 1844; *DC*, July 6, 1844.

34 *AA*, February 14, 1845; McMichael, sworn, OB, 40; AJP, July 6, 1844, 418; Morton McMichael testimony, *PL*, July 15, 1844.

35   Smith et al., "To the Public," *AA*, July 15, 1844; J. N. J. Douglass testimony, *New York Herald*, July 14, 1844; McMichael, sworn, OB, 41; *PL*, July 6, 1844; *USG*, July 8, 1844; John Dutton testimony, *PL*, July 20, 1844.

CHAPTER 18: DON'T YOU FIRE!

1   Captain Joseph Hill testimony, *PL*, July 19, 1844; Thomas A. Roe, "Southwark Affair," *AA*, July 17, 1844; David Ford, "Conclusion of David Ford's Statement," *AA*, July 26, 1844.

2   C. J., letter to the editor, *NatAm*, July 6, 1844; *NatAm*, July 6, 1844; Penrose Ash testimony, *PL*, July 24, 1844; *DC*, July 8, 1844.

3   Isaiah Robbins account, "Astounding Disclosures," *AA*, February 13, 1845; *Christian Observer*, July 12, 1844; *ST*, August 29, 1844.

4   Morton McMichael, sworn, OB, 41–42; George Cadwalader testimony, *PL*, July 19, 1844; George Cadwalader to Judah Spencer, July 3, 1844, vol. 187, George Cadwalader Letterbook, 1841–1848, GC; George Cadwalader to Robert Patterson, July 17, 1844, "Military Report in Relation to the Southwark Riot," *NorAm*, July 25, 1844; *PL*, November 14, 1844; Morton McMichael testimony, *PL*, July 15, 1844; Morton McMichael testimony, *PL*, November 14, 1844.

5   George Cadwalader testimony, *PL*, July 19, 1844; *PL*, July 8, 1844.

6   Susan G. Davis, *Parades and Power: Street Theatre in Nineteenth-Century Philadelphia* (Philadelphia: Temple University Press, 1986), 44; Jonas P. Fairlamb testimony, *PL*, July 24, 1844; *DC*, July 11, 1844; George Cadwalader testimony, *PL*, July 19, 1844.

7   George Cadwalader testimony, *PL*, July 19, 1844; *WS*, May 11, 1844.

8   Mr. Kelly testimony, *PL*, July 15, 1844; Statement No. 10: Franklin L. Jones, "Astounding Disclosures," *AA*, March 1, 1845; McMichael, sworn, OB, 42; *NatAm*, July 8, 1844.

9   William Dickerson testimony, *PL*, July 15, 1844.

10   *DC*, July 8, 1844; Hugh Cassady testimony, *PL*, July 15, 1844; Alderman Saunders testimony, *AA*, July 16, 1844; William Bradford testimony, *PL*, July 15, 1844; *ST*, July 9, 1844, reprinted from July 8, 1844; Fanny Cadwalader to George Cadwalader, July 11, 1845, box 404, folder 7, GC; George Cadwalader testimony, *PL*, July 19, 1844.

11   *USG*, July 8, 1844; *DC*, July 8, 1844; *HJCS*, July 10, 1844.

12   *PL*, July 8, 1844; *DC*, July 8, 1844; *Ordnance Manual for the Use of the Officers of the United States Army* (Washington: Gideon, 1841), 27, 194; Charles M. Haecker and Jeffrey Gm. Mauck, *On the Prairie of Palo Alto: Historical Archaeology of the U.S.–Mexican War Battlefield* (College Station: Texas A&M University Press, 1997), 80; AJP, July 6, 1844, 419.

13   AJP, July 6, 1844, 419–425; *DC*, June 17, 1844; Augustus Pleasonton to George Cadwalader, October 21, 1844, box 431, folder 9, GC.

14   AJP, July 6, 1844, 421; George Cadwalader to Robert Patterson, "Important Documents," *PL*, July 25, 1844.

15   AJP, July 6, 1844, 422.

16   Charles Naylor, *Speech of Charles Naylor, of Pennsylvania, on the Bill Imposing Additional Duties as Depositaries, in Certain Cases, on Public Officers* (Lancaster, PA, 1838); US House of Representatives, *Contested Election—Naylor and Ingersoll*, 26th Cong., 1st sess., H.R. Rep. 588, 1840; *NG*, March 21, 1840; Charles Naylor, "To the Citizens of the Third Congressional District," *NG*, March 23, 1840; *PL*, March 25, 1840.

17   Charles Naylor, "A Card," *PL*, July 27, 1844; *NG*, October 16, 1840.

18   Naylor, "A Card."

19   Statement No. 2: John Greaves, "Astounding Disclosures," *AA*, February 14, 1845; Naylor, "A Card" *PL*; Madison Mills diary, Filson Historical Society, quoted in Timothy D. Johnson, *A Gallant Little Army: The Mexico City Campaign* (Lawrence: University Press of Kansas, 2007), 139; Edward G. Leffingwell, "'A Fine Animal': Portraits of General George Cadwalader of Philadelphia" (master's thesis, University of Cincinnati, 1985), 36; William Dickerson testimony, *PL*, July 15, 1844; Samuel McFate testimony, *PL*, July 26, 1844.

20   George Cadwalader testimony, *PL*, July 19, 1844; Naylor, "A Card."

21   William Bradford testimony, *PL*, July 15, 1844; Cadwalader to Robert Patterson, "Important Documents"; *PL*, July 8, 1844; Naylor, "A Card"; George Cadwalader testimony, *PL*, July 19, 1844.

22   AJP, July 6, 1844, 422–423.

23   McMichael, sworn, OB, 42; Naylor, "A Card"; AJP, July 6, 1844, 422; Statement No. 2: John Greaves, "Astounding Disclosures."

24   George Cadwalader testimony, *PL*, July 19, 1844; McMichael, sworn, OB, 42; Thomas D. Dougherty testimony, *PL*, July 18, 1844.

25   McMichael, sworn, OB, 42; George Cadwalader testimony, *PL*, July 19, 1844; AJP, July 6, 1844, 418–425. Pleasonton began a July 7 entry but got no further than writing the place and date. Address from *McElroy's Philadelphia Directory for 1844*.

CHAPTER 19: BY JESUS CHRIST WE'LL HAVE HIM OUT!

1   John B. Colahan, "To Joseph R. Chandler, Esq.," *CH*, July 25, 1844. A copy of this narrative in Colahan's handwriting exists as John B. Colahan to George Cadwalader, July 18, 1844, box 431, folder 7, GC. The letter also appeared in *USG* and *PL* on July 22, 1844. I have cited the *CH* version because that is the most easily accessible.

2   Muster Roll, Montgomery Hibernia Greens, July 7, 1844, box 431, folder 5, GC; Thomas H. O'Connor, *The Boston Irish: A Political History* (Boston: Northeastern University Press, 1995), 50; *PL*, March 13, 1841.

3   "The Montgomery Hibernia Greens," *Military Magazine and Record of the Volunteers of the City and County of Philadelphia*, May 1839, 9; Leo Hershkowitz, "The Native American Democratic Association in New York City, 1835–1836," *New-York Historical Society Quarterly* 46 (1962): 49–50; Tyler Anbinder, *Five Points: The 19th-Century New York City Neighborhood That Invented Tap Dance, Stole Elections, and Became the World's Most Notorious Slum* (New York: Simon and Schuster, 2001), 29–31.

4   O'Connor, *Boston Irish*, 50–52; AJP, December 11, 1838, 274; W. L. McCalla, letter to the editor, *Protestant Banner*, October 14, 1842.

5   Joseph Louis J. Kirlin, *Catholicity in Philadelphia* (Philadelphia: J. J. McVey, 1909), 324; "Montgomery Hibernia Greens," 10; Jenny Franchot, *Roads to Rome: The Antebellum Protestant Encounter with Catholicism* (Berkeley: University of California Press, 1994), 88; Joseph G. Mannard, "The 1839 Baltimore Nunnery Riot: An Episode in Jacksonian Nativism and Social Violence," *Maryland Historian* 11 (June 1980): 16.

6   D. B., "The Southwark Riot," *DS*, August 3, 1844; Charles Naylor, "A Card," *PL*, July 27, 1844; Franchot, *Roads to Rome*, 128.

7 *CH*, December 29, 1842; John Hugh Campbell, *History of the Friendly Sons of St. Patrick and of the Hibernian Society for the Relief of Emigrants from Ireland* (Philadelphia: Hibernian Society, 1892), 380; *PL*, July 6, 1843; *DC*, April 19, 1843, July 6, 1843; Charles Morris, ed., *Makers of Philadelphia* (Philadelphia: L. R. Hamersley, 1894), 70.

8 *Freeman's Journal* (Dublin, Ireland), September 8, 1843; *DC*, July 22, 1843, November 10, 1843; *PL*, February 15, 1843.

9 Colahan, "To Joseph R. Chandler, Esq."; *PL*, June 29, 1844; *USG*, July 1, 1844; T. L. Saunders, "To the Editors of the Public Ledger," *PL*, July 24, 1844.

10 George Cadwalader testimony, *PL*, July 19, 1844; Thomas D. Dougherty testimony, *PL*, July 18, 1844.

11 Colahan, "To Joseph R. Chandler, Esq."; McMichael, sworn, OB, 42. Colahan's account describes his initial command as "50 men—none of whom had been supplied with ammunition," but later states that he had "scarcely any ammunition." This suggests that some of the men had cartridges, but that he was hoping for a greater supply.

12 William J. Price testimony, *PL*, July 27, 1844. Price eventually found a merchant willing to sell him the cartridges, but only with the mayor's approval. The mayor sent him to General Patterson. By the time Price had secured signatures from both officials as well as the cartridges, he was unable to get through the mob to the soldiers inside the church.

13 John B. Colahan, "For the Public Ledger," *PL*, July 22, 1844; George S. Roberts, affidavit, *PL*, July 23, 1844; Colahan, "To Joseph R. Chandler, Esq."; Mark David Luccioni, "'Fire and Be Damned': Philadelphia Volunteers and the Use of Force in the Riots of 1844" (PhD diss., Temple University, 1996), 155; D. B., "The Southwark Riot," *DS*, August 3, 1844.

14 Colahan, "To Joseph R. Chandler, Esq."; John B. Colahan to George Cadwalader, July 7, 1844, and George Cadwalader to John B. Colahan, July 7, 1844, box 431, folder 5, GC.

15 George S. Roberts testimony, *CH*, August 1, 1844.

16 *Pennsylvania Freeman*, quoted in, *CH*, August 1, 1844.

17 George S. Roberts testimony, *CH*, August 1, 1844; Colahan, "To Joseph R. Chandler, Esq."; George O'Neil testimony, *PL*, November 14, 1844.

18 Alderman M'Kinley testimony, *AA*, July 16, 1844; Abraham Vanarsdale testimony, *PL*, November 14, 1844; "For Sale," *Evening Post* (New York), May 17, 1842; *PL*, November 9, 1837, June 18, 1844; "Brutality," *PL*, June 19, 1844; "Fleming v. Berman," *Robert M. Barr Pennsylvania State Reports* 2 (1846): 408; *Sydney Morning Herald*, April 15, 1841; *AA*, August 31, 1844; John Dunham testimony, *PL*, November 15, 1844; Robert Greenhalgh Albion and Jennie Barnes Pope, *Sea Lanes in Wartime; the American Experience* (1942; repr., London: George Allen & Unwin, 1943), 147.

19 John Dunham testimony, *PL*, November 15, 1844; John Denham testimony, *NorAm*, November 15, 1844 (these are variant spellings of the same witness's name); Michael Cavanaugh testimony, *NorAm*, November 15, 1844; Alderman M'Kinley testimony, *AA*, July 16, 1844; *Sunbury* (PA) *American*, July 20, 1844; George S. Roberts testimony, *CH*, August 1, 1844; Abraham Vanarsdale testimony, *PL*, November 14, 1844; James McGlathery, testimony, *NorAm*, November 15, 1844; Robert Irvine testimony, *PL*, November 16, 1844; *NatAm*, July 8, 1844.

20 Colahan, "To Joseph R. Chandler, Esq."; John B. Colahan to George Cadwalader, July 7, 1844; Naylor, "A Card."

21 *New-York Tribune*, July 8, 1844; *DC*, July 16, 1844; *DS*, March 7, 1844; C. J. Jack, "Col. Jack's Statement," *AA*, August 2, 1844.

22 Charles Hortz testimony, *PL*, July 15, 1844; *DC*, July 17, 1844; Alderman Hortz testimony, *AA*, July 16, 1844; *PL*, September 21, 1844; Lemuel Paynter testimony, *PL*, July 15, 1844; Statement No. 5: Matthew W. Berreman, "Astounding Disclosures," *AA*, February 18, 1845; Isaiah Robbins account, "Astounding Disclosures," *AA*, February 13, 1845.

23 William Crans testimony, *PL*, July 15, 1844; James McGlathery testimony, *NorAm*, November 15, 1844; Statement No. 9: Lucius Webb, "Astounding Disclosures," *AA*, February 22, 1845; Thomas Grover testimony, *PL*, July 18, 1844; deposition of William Macready, *DS*, August 7, 1844; *PL*, July 8, 1844; *DC*, July 8, 1844; *USG*, July 8, 1844; J. N. J. Douglass testimony, *New York Herald*, July 14, 1844; Statement No. 2: John Greaves, "Astounding Disclosures," *AA*, February 14, 1845; Statement No. 4, George N. Nutz, "Astounding Disclosures," *AA*, February 17, 1845; Statement No. 6: Nathaniel Gates, "Astounding Disclosures," *AA*, February 19, 1845; Statement No. 7: John H. Scott, "Astounding Disclosures," *AA*, February 20, 1845; Hugh Cassidy [sic] testimony, *NorAm*, November 15, 1844; Statement No. 9: Lucius Webb, "Astounding Disclosures," *AA*, February 22, 1845; *New York Herald*, July 8, 1844. For John McCoy, see *PL*, June 26, 1844, and Philadelphia, Pennsylvania, Death Certificates Index, 1803–1915, available at Ancestry.com. Witnesses did not agree about when the cannon was first fired, or the sequence in which events took place, but McGlathery, Webb, and Grover were all confident the cannon was first fired just before or after noon.

24 Colahan, "To Joseph R. Chandler, Esq."; Statement No. 2: John Greaves, "Astounding Disclosures," *AA*, February 14, 1845.

25 "A Statement by Capt. Saunders," *PI*, July 24, 1844; *NatAm*, July 12, 1844, July 20, 1844; *AA*, July 31, 1844.

26 "Statement by Capt. Saunders"; Colahan, "To Joseph R. Chandler, Esq."

27 "Statement by Capt. Saunders"; Charles Naylor testimony, *PL*, November 16, 1844.

28 Charles Hortz testimony, *PL*, July 15, 1844; Charles Naylor testimony, *PL*, 16 November 1844; *New-York Tribune*, July 8, 1844; *PL*, July 8, 1844; *DC*, July 8, 1844; Morton McMichael testimony, *PL*, July 15, 1844; Colahan, "To Joseph R. Chandler, Esq."; Thomas A. Roe, "Southwark Affair," *AA*, July 17, 1844. Dialogue reconstructed from paraphrase; Naylor lived at Fifth and Prune, now Locust.

29 Thomas Grover testimony, *PL*, July 18, 1844; James McGlathery testimony, *NorAm*, November 15, 1844; *PL*, July 8, 1844; Colahan, "To Joseph R. Chandler, Esq."

30 "Statement by Capt. Saunders"; Colahan, "To Joseph R. Chandler, Esq."

31 Mr. Kelly testimony, *PL*, July 15, 1844; Thomas Grover testimony, *AA*, July 19, 1844; Thomas Grover testimony, *PL*, July 18, 1844. *McElroy's Philadelphia Directory for 1844* lists Levin's address as 205 S 4th Street, and his New Market Ward residence is established by "The Native American State Convention," *PL*, February 24, 1845. That puts him on Fourth Street between Pine and Cedar, about a half-mile walk to St. Philip's.

32 Thomas Grover testimony, *PL*, July 18, 1844; Thomas Grover testimony, *AA*, July 19, 1844; *DS*, July 12, 1844; *Christian Observer*, July 12, 1844; *PL*, July 8, 1844; Colahan, "To Joseph R. Chandler, Esq."; Statement No. 9: Lucius Webb, "Astounding Disclosures," *AA*, February 22, 1845.

33 Colahan, "To Joseph R. Chandler, Esq."; Captain Saunders testimony, *PL*, July 25, 1844; "Statement by Capt. Saunders"; "The Montgomery Hibernia Greens," 10.

34 Statement No. 9: Lucius Webb, "Astounding Disclosures," *AA*, February 22, 1845; "Statement by Capt. Saunders"; Colahan, "To Joseph R. Chandler, Esq."; *Christian Observer*, July 12, 1844.

35 *DC*, July 8, 1844; "Statement by Capt. Saunders"; *Christian Observer*, July 12, 1844; *CH*, July 11, 1844; *Liberator*, July 12, 1844; Colahan, "To Joseph R. Chandler, Esq."

36 *New-York Tribune*, July 8, 1844; *DC*, July 27, 1844; *PI*, July 8, 1844; *Christian Observer*, July 12, 1844; *NatAm*, July 8, 1844; *CH*, August 1, 1844; *Liberator*, July 12, 1844; *PL*, July 9, 1844.

37 *USG*, July 9, 1844; *ST*, July 9, 1844, reprinted from July 8, 1844; *PL*, July 25, 1844.

CHAPTER 20: A FIGHT MUST COME OFF SOME TIME

1 *DC*, July 8, 1844; Alderman Saunders testimony, *AA*, July 16, 1844; Mr. Kelly testimony, *PL*, July 15, 1844; *New York Herald*, July 7, 1844; C. J. Jack, "Col. Jack's Statement," *AA*, August 2, 1844.

2 *DC*, July 16, 1844; Jack, "Col. Jack's Statement."

3 Alderman M'Kinley testimony, *AA*, July 16, 1844; Thomas A. Roe, "Southwark Affair," *AA*, July 17, 1844; *Buffalo Daily Gazette* (Buffalo, NY), July 20, 1844; Thomas Grover testimony, *PL*, July 18, 1844; Thomas Grover testimony, *AA*, July 19, 1844; *Christian Observer*, July 12, 1844. For John Neal's first name, see Southwark, Ward 2, United States Census, 1850.

4 *Christian Observer*, July 12, 1844; Thomas Grover testimony, *AA*, July 19, 1844; *USG*, July 8, 1844; *DS*, July 12, 1844.

5 *DS*, July 12, 1844; *NG*, January 14, 1840; *PL*, March 21, 1845; *New York Herald*, July 8, 1844.

6 Thomas Grover testimony, *AA*, July 19, 1844; *Catholic Telegraph* (Cincinnati), July 13, 1844; deposition of Thomas A. Warham, *DS*, August 6, 1844; deposition of Jeffry Chew, *DS*, August 8, 1844.

7 Deposition of Robert M'Ewen, *DS*, August 6, 1844; Penrose Ash testimony, *PL*, July 24, 1844; deposition of Jeffry Chew, *DS*, August 8, 1844; Thomas Grover testimony, *AA*, July 19, 1844; Roe, "Southwark Affair"; *New York Herald*, July 9, 1844. Dialogue reconstructed from paraphrase.

8 *PL*, August 5, 1844; *DC*, August 5, 1844; *USG*, July 8, 1844; deposition of William Macready, *DS*, August 7, 1844.

9 Deposition of Jeffry Chew, *DS*, August 8, 1844; Roe, "Southwark Affair"; David Ford, "Conclusion of David Ford's Statement," *AA*, July 26, 1844; John Towell testimony, *PL*, July 15, 1844; Statement No. 8: James Stevenson, "Astounding Disclosures," *AA*, February 21, 1845; deposition of Thomas A. Warham, *DS*, August 6, 1844; Statement No. 16: Samuel Rhinedollar, "Astounding Disclosures," *AA*, March 3, 1845.

10 George Bird testimony, *PL*, July 25, 1844; Ford, "Conclusion of David Ford's Statement"; Thomas Grover testimony, *PL*, July 18, 1844; Isaiah Robbins account, "Astounding Disclosures," *AA*, February 13, 1845.

11 *ST*, July 9, 1844; *New York Herald*, July 9, 1844; Statement No. 8: James Stevenson, "Astounding Disclosures," *AA*, February 21, 1845; Deposition of Thomas A. Warham, *DS*, August 6, 1844; *Diary of Isaac Mickle*, 458.

12 Deposition of Thomas A. Warham, *DS*, August 6, 1844; Thomas R. Fisher testimony, "Investigation—Southwark Riots," *PL*, July 24, 1844; *DS*, July 12, 1844; *DC*, July 15, 1844; *New York Herald*, July 8, 1844; The *Herald* credits its information to an extra edition of the *Sun*, but it does not give a date, and I have not found an extant copy. Since Levin boasted that he observed the Sabbath by refraining from printing extras on Sunday, perhaps he printed the extra early Monday morning, in time for it to make the morning newspapers in New York. "Extras on Sunday," *DS*, November 4, 1844.

13 Thomas Grover testimony, *PL*, July 18, 1844; Statement No. 8: James Stevenson, "Astounding Disclosures," *AA*, February 21, 1845; Truth, "For the American Advocate," *AA*, July 24, 1844; Joseph A. Read, "For the American Advocate," *AA*, August 7, 1844; Statement No. 11: James Slocomb, "Astounding Disclosures," *AA*, February 25, 1845; John Graves testimony, *PL*, November 16, 1844.

14 William J. Price testimony, *PL*, July 27, 1844; Jack, "Col. Jack's Statement."

15 McMichael, sworn, OB, 42; Ford, "Conclusion of David Ford's Statement."

16 Morton McMichael testimony, *PL*, July 15, 1844; George Cadwalader testimony, *PL*, July 19, 1844; William Bradford testimony, *PL*, July 15, 1844; George Cadwalader to Robert Patterson, *PL*, July 25, 1844.

17 Jack, "Col. Jack's Statement."

18 McMichael, sworn, OB, 43–44; A. J. Pleasonton, "To Jos. R. Chandler," *USG*, July 20, 1844.

19 *PL*, July 16, 1844.

20 George Cadwalader testimony, *PL*, July 19, 1844, July 20, 1844; Robert Patterson to David R. Porter, July 22, 1844, "Military Report in Relation to the Southwark Riot," *NorAm*, July 25, 1844.

21 "Official Statements of Gen. Cadwalader and Col. Page," *PL*, July 16, 1844. Despite the headline, Cadwalader insisted that the statement had "no official character," though he did not dispute his authorship. Cadwalader to Mallory, July 16, 1844, *PL*, July 18, 1844; Captain Joseph Hill testimony, *PL*, July 19, 1844; Augustus Pleasonton testimony, *PL*, November 16, 1844.

22 Pleasonton, "To Jos. R. Chandler"; George Cadwalader testimony, *PL*, July 19, 1844; Pleasonton to R. K. Scott, July 13, 1844, box 3, folder 1: Letters, 1st Regiment Artillery, MG7, PSA.

23 Pleasonton, "To Jos. R. Chandler"; muster roll, box 430, folder 6, GC; Report of 1st Sergt of Washington Blues, July 7 1844, July 8, 1844, box 431, folder 5, GC; "A Statement by Capt. Saunders," *PI*, July 24, 1844; W. R. Palmer to George Cadwalader, July 7, 1844, box 431, folder 5, GC; George Cadwalader to Robert Patterson, *PL*, July 25, 1844; *PL*, September 11, 1838; John Butler to George Cadwalader, July 20, 1844, box 431, folder 7, GC.

24 Brigade Order no. 33, box 431, folder 5, GC; *DC*, July 16, 1844; *PL*, September 11, 1844; *DS*, September 7, 1844; John Hancock Lee, *The Origin and Progress of the American Party in Politics* (Philadelphia: Elliott & Gihon, 1855), 137–156.

25 *Germantown Telegraph*, October 9, 1844; *New-York Tribune*, July 10, 1844; Henry Mallory to George Cadwalader, July 13, 1844, box 431, folder 6, GC; *NatAm*, July 8, 1844; *ST*, July 17, 1844.

26 Adam Malka, *The Men of Mobtown: Policing Baltimore in the Age of Slavery and Emancipation, Justice, Power, and Politics* (Chapel Hill: University of North Carolina Press, 2018), 46–51.

27 *DC*, July 8, 1844; *New-York Tribune*, July 8, 1844.

28 McMichael, sworn, OB, 43; *PI*, September 16, 1867; General Adam Diller testimony, *PL*, July 22, 1844; 1st Division Order No. 13, May 10, 1844, box 431, folder 2, GC; George Cadwalader testimony, *PL*, July 19, 1844; *DC*, July 8, 1844.

29 Pleasonton, "To Jos. R. Chandler," Dialogue reconstructed from paraphrase.

30 AJP, December 11, 1838; "Official Statements of Gen. Cadwalader and Col. Page," *PL*, July 16, 1844.

31 George Cadwalader to Robert Patterson, "Important Documents," *PL*, July 25, 1844; Augustus Pleasonton testimony, *PL*, November 16, 1844; Augustus Pleasonton to George Cadwalader, October 21, 1844, box 431, folder 9, GC; Andrew Banner to George Cadwalader, September 9, 1845, box 431, folder 8, GC; Col. Cephas G. Childs testimony, *PL*, July 20, 1844.

CHAPTER 21: YOU BLOODY SONS OF BITCHES!

1 Augustus Pleasonton testimony, *PL*, November 16, 1844; Statement no. 3: Mills. B. Espy, "Astounding Disclosures," *AA*, February 15, 1845; Deposition of Thomas A. Warham, *DS*, August 6, 1844.

2 *USG*, July 8, 1844; Thomas D. Dougherty testimony, *AA*, July 19, 1844; *A True Statement of the First Fire on Sunday Evening, July 7, 1844* (Philadelphia, 1844), 4; *New York Herald*, July 9, 1844; William Bradford testimony, *PL*, November 16, 1844; George Cadwalader testimony, *PL*, July 20, 1844; William Bradford testimony, *PL*, July 15, 1844; A. J. Pleasonton, "To Jos. R. Chandler," *USG*, July 20, 1844; *HJCS*, July 10, 1844.

3 Deposition of Thomas A. Warham, *DS*, August 6, 1844; *AA*, July 17, 1844; *New York Herald*, July 9, 1844; Joseph A. Read, "For the American Advocate," *AA*, August 7, 1844; Isaiah Robbins account, "Astounding Disclosures," *AA*, February 13, 1845.

4 George Cadwalader to Robert Patterson, July 17, 1844, "Military Report in Relation to the Southwark Riot," *NorAm*, July 25, 1844; Muster Roll, State Fencibles, July 7, 1844, July 8, 1844, box 431, folder 5, GC; Statement of Colonel James Page, *PL*, July 16, 1844; George S. Roberts testimony, *CH*, August 1, 1844; George Cadwalader testimony, *PL*, July 20, 1844; George Cadwalader to Robert Patterson, "Important Documents," *PL*, July 25, 1844. For positions of the guns, see *Untitled*, hand-drawn map of Queen Street, box 431, folder 7, GC.

5 Report of the First Regiment of Infantry, 102nd of the Line, July 6–9, 1844, box 431, folder 5, GC; deposition of John Ashcraft Jr., *DS*, August 8, 1844; Statement no. 3: Mills. B. Espy, "Astounding Disclosures," *AA*, February 15, 1845; W. Heyward Drayton to John K. Murphy, July 16, 1844, box 431, folder 6, GC.

6 Statement no. 3: Mills. B. Espy, "Astounding Disclosures," *AA*, February 15, 1845; Statement No. 10: Joseph J. Bishop, "Astounding Disclosures," *AA*, February 24, 1845; Thomas Grover testimony, *AA*, July 19, 1844; Col. Cephas G. Childs testimony, *PL*, July 20, 1844.

7 Statement No. 5: Matthew W. Berreman, "Astounding Disclosures," *AA*, February 18, 1845; Statement No. 10: Franklin L. Jones, "Astounding Disclosures," *AA*, March 1, 1845.

8 Statement No. 4, George N. Nutz, "Astounding Disclosures," *AA*, February 17, 1845; Thomas Grover testimony, *AA*, July 19, 1844; Thomas Grover testimony, *PL*, July 18, 1844; C. J. Jack, "Col. Jack's Statement," *AA*, August 2, 1844.

9 Col. Cephas G. Childs testimony, *PL*, July 20, 1844; *DC*, July 10, 1844, July 16, 1844;

Statement No. 5: Matthew W. Berreman, "Astounding Disclosures," *AA*, February 18, 1845; Thomas Grover testimony, *PL*, July 18, 1844; George Cadwalader testimony, *PL*, July 20, 1844; *HJCS*, July 10, 1844. As late as February 1843, Childs was listed as the brigade major of the First Brigade. *PL*, February 18, 1843. By the time of the May 1844 riots, however, Edward Hurst was acting brigade major. General & Staff return May 1844, box 431, folder 4, GC. While Childs was present in Southwark in July, he seems to have acted only in a civilian capacity.

10 "Official Statements of Gen. Cadwalader and Col. Page," *PL*, July 16, 1844; Thomas Dougherty testimony, *PL*, July 18, 1844.

11 George Cadwalader to Robert Patterson, July 17, 1844, "Military Report in Relation to the Southwark Riot," *NorAm*, July 25, 1844; George Cadwalader testimony, *PL*, July 20, 1844; *HJCS*, July 10, 1844; "Official Statements of Gen. Cadwalader and Col. Page," *PL*, July 16, 1844; George Cadwalader to Robert Patterson, "Important Documents," *PL*, July 25, 1844; "Official Statements of Gen. Cadwalader and Col. Page," *PL*, July 16, 1844.

12 Nathan McKinley testimony, *PL*, July 15, 1844; Col. Cephas G. Childs testimony, *PL*, July 20, 1844; D. P. O'Donnell testimony, *PL*, November 16, 1844.

13 Oliver Hopkinson testimony, *PL*, July 15, 1844; Statement No. 10: Joseph J. Bishop, "Astounding Disclosures," *AA*, February 24, 1845; Edwin Booth testimony, *PL*, July 29, 1844.

14 For First Brigade company strengths, see Report of the First Regiment of Infantry, 102nd of the Line, July 6–9, 1844, box 431, folder 5, GC; Augustus Pleasonton to George Cadwalader, October 21, 1844, box 431, folder 9, GC; Captain Joseph Hill testimony, *PL*, July 19, 1844; Statement No. 5: Matthew W. Berreman, "Astounding Disclosures," *AA*, February 18, 1845.

15 Moses R. Williams account, "Astounding Disclosures," *AA*, February 27, 1845; Deposition of Rev. D. H. Kollock, *DS*, August 7, 1844; Statement No. 4, George N. Nutz, "Astounding Disclosures," *AA*, February 17, 1845; Statement No. 12: Lewis Fayette, "Astounding Disclosures," *AA*, February 26, 1845.

16 Captain Joseph Hill testimony, *PL*, July 19, 1844; Report of the First Regiment of Infantry, 102nd of the Line, July 6–9, 1844, box 431, folder 5, GC; Augustus Pleasonton to George Cadwalader, October 21, 1844, box 431, folder 9, GC; Dougherty testimony, *PL*, July 18, 1844; *AA*, July 26, 1844; Robert Solts testimony, *PL*, July 29, 1844. In later months, nativists would insist that the gunshots came only minutes after Cadwalader's arrival on Queen Street, suggesting that Cadwalader had fired at his fellow citizens before even assessing the situation or considering alternatives. (See the "Astounding Disclosures" clippings from the *AA*, box 432, folder 5, GC.) A more thorough, and therefore plausible, account comes from Lieutenant Thomas Dougherty, who had time to arrive at the church, take possession of the frame house at gunpoint, search the house thoroughly, bring his men back to the street, and form up behind Captain Hill before the first shots, which he believed took place sometime close to eight o'clock, nearly an hour after his arrival on Queen Street. Thomas Grover did not estimate the interval, but his extended negotiations with Cadwalader and his own committee in the church suggest a significant passage of time between Cadwalader's arrival and the first fire. Another witness, Robert Solts, left Queen Street while Cadwalader was addressing the mob, spent ten minutes walking home and another fifteen minutes at home

before he heard the gunfire. That places an interval of at least twenty-five minutes between Cadwalader's arrival and the first gunfire, and a longer interval would still be consistent with Solts's testimony.

17 A Citizen, "The Issue Made—Who Will Meet It?" *Pennsylvanian*, July 10, 1844; *True Statement*, 4; Jack, "Col. Jack's Statement," *DC*, July 8, 1844; Thomas Grover testimony, *PL*, July 18, 1844; Statement No. 8: James Stevenson, "Astounding Disclosures," *AA*, February 21, 1845; Statement No. 11: James Slocomb, "Astounding Disclosures," *AA*, February 25, 1845.

18 *ST*, May 17, 1844; Statement No. 2: John Greaves, "Astounding Disclosures," *AA*, February 14, 1845; Captain Hill testimony, *PL*, July 19, 1844; Samuel Rhinedollar account, "Astounding Disclosures," *AA*, March 3, 1845; William Bradford testimony, *PL*, July 15, 1844; Patrick Starr testimony, *PL*, July 15, 1844; *DC*, July 16, 1844; George Cadwalader's statement, *PL*, July 16, 1844.

19 Oliver Hopkinson testimony, *PL*, July 15, 1844; Pleasonton, "To Jos. R. Chandler"; *DC*, July 16, 1844.

20 George Cadwalader testimony, *PL*, July 20, 1844; Captain Joseph Hill testimony, *PL*, July 19, 1844; Thomas Grover testimony, *PL*, July 18, 1844; "Official Statements of Gen. Cadwalader and Col. Page," *PL*, July 16, 1844; Thomas Grover testimony, *PL*, July 18, 1844; Statement No. 13: Moses R. Williams, "Astounding Disclosures," *AA*, February 27, 1845; Statement No. 5: Matthew W. Berreman, "Astounding Disclosures," *AA*, February 18, 1845; *AA*, July 15, 1844; Statement No. 6: Nathaniel Gates, "Astounding Disclosures," *AA*, February 19, 1845.

21 *HJCS*, July 10, 1844; George Cadwalader to Robert Patterson, "Important Documents," *PL*, July 25, 1844.

22 Captain Joseph Hill testimony, *PL*, July 19, 1844; *Christian Observer*, July 12, 1844; *PL*, July 18, 1844, February 1, 1845; *ST*, July 9, 1844, reprinted from extra of July 8; Lemuel Paynter testimony, *PL*, July 15, 1844; "Official Statements of Gen. Cadwalader and Col. Page," *PL*, July 16, 1844; *DC*, July 8, 1844. Dougherty was buried in St. Mary's Roman Catholic Burial Ground. Philadelphia, Pennsylvania, Death Certificates Index, 1803–1915, available at Ancestry.com.

23 Lemuel Paynter testimony, *PL*, July 15, 1844; William Bradford testimony, *PL*, July 15, 1844; *AA*, July 15, 1844; George Cadwalader testimony, *PL*, July 20, 1844; Statement no. 3: Mills. B. Espy, "Astounding Disclosures," *AA*, February 15, 1845; *PL*, July 8, 1844, July 10, 1844; *A Full and Complete Account of the Late Awful Riots in Philadelphia: Embellished with Ten Engravings* (Philadelphia: John B. Perry, 1844), D-14; *PL*, February 1, 1845; Joseph A. Read, "For the American Advocate," *AA*, August 7, 1844.

24 Nathaniel Gates testimony, *PL*, July 24, 1844; Statement No. 6: Nathaniel Gates, "Astounding Disclosures," *AA*, February 19, 1845.

25 Statement No. 5: Matthew W. Berreman, "Astounding Disclosures," *AA*, February 18, 1845; Deposition of Thomas A. Warham, *DS*, August 6, 1844; Jack, "Col. Jack's Statement"; Morton McMichael, sworn, OB, 44.

26 *AA*, December 6, 1844; J. N. J. Douglass testimony, *New York Herald*, July 14, 1844; Statement No. 11: James Slocomb, "Astounding Disclosures," *AA*, February 25, 1845; *PL*, February 1, 1845; William Bradford testimony, *PL*, July 15, 1844; *AA*, July 15, 1844; Jack, "Col. Jack's Statement."

27   *USG*, July 8, 1844; *Philadelphia Inquirer*, October 16, 1874; *DC*, July 8, 1844; *College of Physicians of Philadelphia*, 252–253.

28   George P. Mercer testimony, *PL*, November 16, 1844; Statement No. 16: Samuel Rhinedollar, "Astounding Disclosures," *AA*, March 3, 1845; Statement No. 11: James Slocomb, "Astounding Disclosures," *AA*, February 25, 1845. The 1850 census shows Slocomb living with females who would have been ages twenty-two and two at the time of the shooting, and a six-year-old who would have been an infant in July 1844.

29   George Cadwalader to Robert Patterson, "Important Documents," *PL*, July 25, 1844; Charles J. Jack testimony, *PL*, November 16, 1844; *PL*, May 2, 1839, September 17, 1844; *AA*, July 17, 1844; *DC*, July 8, 1844, July 17, 1844; Alexander H. Wands testimony, *PL*, November 15, 1844; Thomas Dougherty testimony, *PL*, November 15, 1844.

30   George Cadwalader testimony, *PL*, July 20, 1844.

31   A Full Private, "An Incident of the Battle," *HJCS*, September 4, 1844; Statement No. 2: John Greaves, "Astounding Disclosures," *AA*, February 14, 1845.

32   George Cadwalader to Robert Patterson, "Important Documents," *PL*, July 25, 1844; George Cadwalader to Robert Patterson, July 17, 1844; A. L. Roumfort, "Military Report in Relation to the Southwark Riot," *NorAm*, July 25, 1844.

33   *DC*, July 8, 1844; Statement no. 3: Mills. B. Espy, "Astounding Disclosures," *AA*, February 15, 1845; Alexander Major testimony, *PL*, February 7, 1845.

34   Thomas Grover testimony, *PL*, July 18, 1844; Thomas Grover testimony, *AA*, July 19, 1844; Jack, "Col. Jack's Statement"; James McGlathery testimony, *NorAm*, November 15, 1844; Francis S. Johnson testimony, *PL*, November 16, 1844; C. J. Jack testimony, *PL*, February 7, 1845.

35   *DC*, July 18, 1844; William Tunnier testimony, *PL*, November 16, 1844; Jack, "Col. Jack's Statement"; John Siddons testimony, *PL*, November 15, 1844; *PL*, July 19, 1844; Charles Jack testimony, *PL*, November 16, 1844; *HJCS*, September 11, 1844.

36   John J. N. Douglass testimony, *PL*, February 7, 1845; *HJCS*, July 10, 1844; Capt. W. H. Drayton testimony, *NorAm*, November 15, 1844; W. Heyward Drayton to John K. Murphy, July 16, 1844, box 431, folder 6, GC; *True Statement*, 4. Pleasonton's report lists only ten Junior Artillerists: Augustus Pleasonton to George Cadwalader, October 21, 1844, box 431, folder 9, GC.

37   P. C. Ellmaker testimony, *PL*, February 7, 1845; J. N. J. Douglass testimony, *New York Herald*, July 14, 1844; W. Heyward Drayton to John K. Murphy, July 16, 1844, GC; George Merrick testimony, *PL*, February 7, 1845; Alexander Major testimony, *PL*, February 7, 1845.

38   J. N. J. Douglass testimony, *New York Herald*, July 14, 1844; P. C. Ellmaker testimony, *PL*, February 7, 1845; George Cadwalader to Robert Patterson, July 17, 1844, "Military Report in Relation to the Southwark Riot," *NorAm*, July 25, 1844; Capt. W. H. Drayton testimony, *NorAm*, November 15, 1844; *DC*, July 18, 1844.

39   Thomas Byrnes testimony, *PL*, July 15, 1844; *CH*, August 1, 1844, reprinted from the *Pennsylvania Freeman*.

40   *DC*, July 10, 1844, July 18, 1844; Alexander Major testimony, *NorAm*, November 15, 1844; William Martin testimony, *PL*, November 15, 1844.

41   Statement No. 2: John Greaves, "Astounding Disclosures," *AA*, February 14, 1845; David Ford, "Conclusion of David Ford's Statement," *AA*, July 26, 1844; William Bradford

testimony, *PL*, July 15, 1844; Statement No. 9: Lucius Webb, "Astounding Disclosures," *AA*, February 22, 1845. According to Cephas Childs, one of Grover's committee, most of the committee had left Queen Street before the troops' first volley: Col. Cephas G. Childs testimony, *PL*, July 20, 1844.

42   Alexander Henry testimony, *PL*, July 15, 1844; Thomas South Lanard, *One Hundred Years with the State Fencibles* (Philadelphia: Nields, 1913), 76; Pleasonton, "To Jos. R. Chandler"; Charges and specifications preferred against Third Lieutenant Frederick Bowers, box 432, folder 2, GC, and others in that folder; Augustus Pleasonton to George Cadwalader, October 8, 1844, box 431, folder 9, GC; Jack, "Col. Jack's Statement."

CHAPTER 22: SECRET, COVERT, MURDEROUS

1   A. J. Pleasonton, "To Jos. R. Chandler," *USG*, July 20, 1844; Thomas D. Dougherty testimony, *AA*, July 19, 1844. Note: the newspaper misidentified Dougherty as Thomas D. Dunn. See *PL*, July 18, 1844, for the correct identification.

2   *CH*, August 29, 1844; *PL*, July 9, 1844; *DC*, July 10, 1844; Oliver Hopkinson testimony, *PL*, July 15, 1844; *Philadelphia Gazette*, July 13, 1844.

3   *AA*, July 19, 1844; *CH*, August 29, 1844; *PL*, July 9, 1844.

4   *PL*, July 19, 1844; Pleasonton, "To Jos. R. Chandler"; *DC*, July 8, 1844, July 18, 1844; George Cadwalader to Robert Patterson, "Important Documents," *PL*, July 25, 1844; William Bradford testimony, *NorAm*, November 15, 1844. Location of hospital is shown on *Untitled*, hand-drawn map of Queen Street, box 431, folder 7, GC.

5   George Cadwalader testimony, *PL*, July 20, 1844; *ST*, July 17, 1844; Henry Mallory testimony, *NorAm*, November 14, 1844; Lieut. Edmund Bockius testimony, *Philadelphia Gazette*, November 14, 1844; also *PL* versions of same dates; McMichael testimony, *PL*, November 14, 1844; *Untitled*, hand-drawn map of Queen Street, box 431, folder 7, GC; Muster Roll, State Fencibles, July 7, 1844, July 8, 1844, box 431, folder 5, GC.

6   *DC*, July 9, 1844, July 10, 1844; Mallory to George Cadwalader, July 13, 1844, box 431, folder 6, GC; Edmund Bockius testimony, *PL*, November 14, 1844; *Germantown Telegraph*, July 10, 1844; *USG*, July 9, 1844, July 10, 1844; *ST*, July 9, 1844, reprinted from extra of July 8, 1844; *PL*, July 9, 1844; "Official Statements of Gen. Cadwalader and Col. Page," *PL*, July 16, 1844.

7   Statement of Colonel James Page, "Official Statements of Gen. Cadwalader and Col. Page," *PL*, July 16, 1844; Thomas South Lanard, *One Hundred Years with the State Fencibles* (Philadelphia: Nields, 1913), 76; John Palmer Garber, Naaman Henry Keyser, C. Henry Kain, Horace Ferdinand McCann, eds., *History of Old Germantown* (Germantown, PA: H. F. McCann, 1907), 1:191; Mallory testimony, *NorAm*, November 14, 1844; *PL*, November 14, 1844; *HJCS*, July 17, 1844; *DC*, August 24, 1843; Return of Members of the Wayne Artillery, July 7, 1844, July 8, 1844, box 431, folder 5, GC; Mallory to George Cadwalader, July 13, 1844, box 431, folder 6, GC.

8   *PL*, February 1, 1845; *ST*, July 17, 1844; "Remarks of Mr. J. R. Ingersoll," *Appendix to the Congressional Globe*, December 30, 1845, 335–337; Statement of Colonel James Page, "Official Statements of Gen. Cadwalader and Col. Page," *PL*, July 16, 1844. Of eleven civilian dead listed eventually by the coroner, all were male, and only one, Isaac Freed, was over forty. Most were ages fifteen to thirty.

9   *Untitled*, hand-drawn map of Queen Street, box 431, folder 7, GC; Pleasonton, "To Jos. R. Chandler," *USG*, July 20, 1844; J. Sydney Jones, "For the Public Ledger," *PL*, July 10, 1844; *College of Physicians of Philadelphia*, 252–253.

10 "Official Statements of Gen. Cadwalader and Col. Page," *PL*, July 16, 1844; George Cadwalader, "To Capt. Mallory," *PL*, July 18, 1844; *New York Herald*, July 9, 1844; *USG*, July 9, 1844; *PL*, April 17, 1845; *DC*, July 9, 1844; "Correspondence of the Pittsburgh Chronicle," *Catholic Telegraph* (Cincinnati), July 13, 1844.

11 *Philadelphia Gazette*, July 10, 1844; *DC*, July 9, 1844; William Bradford testimony, *PL*, July 15, 1844; A Citizen, "The Issue Made—Who Will Meet It?" *Pennsylvanian*, July 10, 1844; Statement of Colonel James Page, "Official Statements of Gen. Cadwalader and Col. Page," *PL*, July 16, 1844; George S. Roberts affidavit, *PL*, July 23, 1844.

12 George Cadwalader to Robert Patterson, "Important Documents," *PL*, July 25, 1844; John Butler to George Cadwalader, July 20, 1844, box 431, folder 7, GC.

13 R. Patterson to David R. Porter, July 22, 1844, "Important Documents," *PL*, July 25, 1844; Cephas G. Childs testimony, *PL*, July 20, 1844; *HJCS*, July 17, 1844. Patterson's order to Hubbell was apparently less formal than his to Roumfort's. Hubbell later wrote that "I only acted as a volunteer," and did not submit a brigade report to Patterson: Horatio Hubbell to George Cadwalader, August 24, 1844, box 431, folder 8, GC.

14 A. L. Roumfort to Robert Patterson, July 17, 1844, "Military Report in Relation to the Southwark Riot," *NorAm*, July 25, 1844; George Cadwalader to Robert Patterson, "Important Documents," *PL*, July 25, 1844; John D. Miles, *PL*, November 14, 1844; A. L. Roumfort to George Cadwalader, June 1, 1843, box 430, folder 7, GC; George Cadwalader to A. L. Roumfort, June 2, 1843, box 430, folder 7, GC; Robert Patterson to George Cadwalader, July 16, 1844, box 431, folder 6, GC; Without instruction: George Cadwalader to Robert Patterson, draft, July 15, 1844, box 431, folder 6, GC.

15 George Cadwalader to Robert Patterson, July 17, 1844, A. L. Roumfort, "Military Report in Relation to the Southwark Riot," *NorAm*, July 25, 1844; John D. Miles, *PL*, November 14, 1844; *ST*, July 10, 1844.

16 *PL*, July 8, 1844; "Official Statements of Gen. Cadwalader and Col. Page," *PL*, July 16, 1844; *Daily Picayune* (New Orleans), July 14, 1844; *ST*, July 9, 1844, reprinted from extra of July 8.

17 "A Statement by Capt. Saunders," *PI*, July 24, 1844; *Daily Picayune* (New Orleans), July 14, 1844; Jonas P. Fairlamb testimony, *PL*, July 24, 1844; George Cadwalader to Robert Patterson, "Important Documents," *PL*, July 25, 1844; *New York Herald*, July 28, 1844; return of Members of the Wayne Artillery, July 7, 1844, July 8, 1844, box 431, folder 5, GC.

18 *HJCS*, December 4, 1844; *Germantown Telegraph*, September 13, 1837, June 12, 1844; J. Sydney Jones, "For the Public Ledger," *PL*, July 10, 1844; *USG*, July 9, 1844.

19 *PI*, July 8, 1844; *USG*, July 8, 1844; *DC*, July 9, 1844; *DS*, July 11, 1844. Dialogue reconstructed from paraphrase.

20 John Matheys testimony, *PL*, July 15, 1844; *NatAm*, July 10, 1844; "Statement of George S. Neath," *AA*, July 29, 1844; 1850 census shows three girls ages eleven to eighteen; *New York Herald*, July 28, 1844.

21 *AA*, July 16, 1844; George Cadwalader testimony, *PL*, July 20, 1844; *ST*, August 1, 1844.

22 *ST*, August 1, 1844, August 2, 1844; *HJCS*, July 17, 1844; *McElroy's Philadelphia Directory for 1844* lists Hubbell's home as Tenth above Shippen, today's Bainbridge Street; Hubbell

testimony, *PL*, July 20, 1844; Jonas P. Fairlamb testimony, *PL*, July 24, 1844; Justice, "The Rioters, Murderers of Each Other," *PL*, July 19, 1844.

23 *PI*, July 8, 1844; John Butler to George Cadwalader, July 20, 1844, box 431, folder 7, GC; M. Antonia Lynch, "The Old District of Southwark," in *Philadelphia History: Consisting of Papers Read Before the City History Society of Philadelphia* (Philadelphia: The Society, 1917), 113; *USG*, July 8, 1844, July 9, 1844; *ST*, July 9, 1844, reprinted from July 8, 1844; *PI*, July 8, 1844; *College of Physicians of Philadelphia*, 254.

24 *CH*, August 29, 1844, 277; George Cadwalader to Robert Patterson, "Important Documents," *PL*, July 25, 1844; *NorAm*, July 10, 1844; "Statement of George S. Neath," *AA*, July 29, 1844, A. L. Roumfort to Robert Patterson, July 17, 1844, "Military Report in Relation to the Southwark Riot," *NorAm*, July 25, 1844.

25 *PL*, July 9, 1844; A. L. Roumfort to Robert Patterson, July 17, 1844, "Important Documents," *PL*, July 25, 1844; George Cadwalader testimony, *PL*, July 20, 1844; *Germantown Telegraph*, July 17, 1844; "Statement of George S. Neath," *AA*, July 29, 1844; *USG*, July 8, 1844.

26 *CH*, August 29, 1844, 277; George Cadwalader testimony, *PL*, July 20, 1844; "NOAA Solar Calculator," NOAA Earth System Research Laboratories, https://www.esrl.noaa.gov/gmd /grad/solcalc/ ; Lanard, *One Hundred Years with the State Fencibles*, 77; *McElroy's Philadelphia Directory for 1844*; George Esler Jr. to George Cadwalader, July 8, 1844, GC.

CHAPTER 23: THE MOB IS NOW SUPREME

1 *USG*, July 9, 1844; *PI*, July 9, 1844; *Christian Observer*, July 12, 1844; *DC*, July 9, 1844; *ST*, July 9, 1844, reprinted from extra of July 8.

2 George Cadwalader testimony, *PL*, July 20, 1844; George Cadwalader testimony, *ST*, July 20, 1844; twenty-four hours: *Diary of Isaac Mickle*, 459; Thomas South Lanard, *One Hundred Years with the State Fencibles* (Philadelphia: Nields, 1913), 78; *PL*, July 30, 1844; Col. John S. Jones testimony, *PL*, July 22, 1844.

3 R. Patterson, report in *Reports of the Heads of Departments to the Governor of Pennsylvania, in Pursuance of the Law for the Fiscal Year Ending November 30, 1844* (Harrisburg, PA: J. M. G. Lescure, 1845), 14; Robert Patterson to George Cadwalader, July 8, 1844, box 431, folder 5, GC.

4 J. M. Scott to Robert Patterson, July 8, 1844, box 431, folder 5, GC; George Cadwalader to Robert Patterson, draft, July 15, 1844, box 431, folder 6, GC; A. J. Pleasonton, "To Jos. R. Chandler," *USG*, July 20, 1844; *PL*, July 9, 1844; Patterson, *Reports of the Heads of Departments*, 15; Statement of Colonel James Page, "Official Statements of Gen. Cadwalader and Col. Page," *PL*, July 16, 1844; *USG*, July 8, 1844; Thomas Bradford to George Cadwalader, July 8, 1844, box 431, folder 5, GC; W. Darrach to George Cadwalader, July 8, 1844, box 431, folder 5, GC.

5 *DS*, July 9, 1844, reprinted from the extra of July 8; *NatAm*, July 8, 1844; *Philadelphia Inquirer*, October 16, 1874; *A Full and Complete Account of the Late Awful Riots in Philadelphia: Embellished with Ten Engravings* (Philadelphia: John B. Perry, 1844), D-26; *DC*, July 9, 1844; *ST*, July 9, 1844, reprinted from extra of July 8.

6 *College of Physicians of Philadelphia*, 253–258; *USG*, July 8, 1844; *AA*, August 5, 1844.

7 *College of Physicians of Philadelphia*, 252–253; *USG*, July 9, 1844; "Lex Talionis," *CH*, August 1, 1844; *DC*, July 18, 1844; Justice, "The Rioters, Murderers of Each Other," *PL*, July 19, 1844.

8   Morton McMichael, sworn, OB, 44; *USG*, July 11, 1844.

9   Morton McMichael to George Ramsay, July 8, 1844, ACHS; David R. Porter to Lt. Col. G. Talcott, October 30, 1844, Militia Letter Book, 1839–1861, series 26.22, PSA. The Villanova University library lists the date of McMichael's note as September 8, 1844. Schmandt, "Selection of Sources," explains this as reflecting "the Sheriff's state of mind when he wrote the letter." Since the document in the archives is a copy, it could be that someone other than McMichael wrote the date. It is also possible, given the indistinct handwriting, that the date in fact reads "July 8." Schmandt transcribes the warning as "Americanist mob," but I concur with Villanova transcriber Susan Ottignon, who reads it as "an armed mob."

10   C. J. Jack, "Col. Jack's Statement," *AA*, August 2, 1844; McMichael, sworn, OB, 44–45; Raymond F. Schmandt, "Selection of Sources Dealing with the Nativist Riots of 1844," *Records of the American Catholic Historical Society* 80 (June and September 1969): 75.

11   Jack, "Col. Jack's Statement"; Pennsylvania Hospital Historic Collections, Meteorological Records, July 8, 1844; *DC*, July 10, 1844.

12   *Christian Observer*, July 12, 1844; *DS*, July 9, 1844, reprinted from extra of July 8; George S. Roberts testimony, *CH*, August 1, 1844; William Crans testimony, *PL*, July 15, 1844; John Shannon testimony, *NorAm*, November 15, 1844.

13   George S. Roberts testimony, *CH*, August 1, 1844; Untitled document with correspondence between Robert Patterson and Southwark Commissioners, box 431, folder 5, GC; Jack, "Col. Jack's Statement."

14   *DC*, July 9, 1844; George Cadwalader to Robert Patterson, July 17, 1844, "Military Report in Relation to the Southwark Riot," *NorAm*, July 25, 1844; Untitled document with correspondence between Robert Patterson and Southwark Commissioners, box 431, folder 5, GC; Peter Sken Smith, "Correspondence of the AA," *AA*, July 25, 1844; *ST*, July 9, 1844, reprinted from extra of July 8; *USG*, July 9, 1844; David Ford, "Conclusion of David Ford's Statement," *AA*, July 26, 1844; *DS*, July 9, 1844.

15   *DC*, July 9, 1844; *Daily Picayune* (New Orleans), July 14, 1844; George Cadwalader to Robert Patterson, July 17, 1844, "Military Report in Relation to the Southwark Riot," *NorAm*, July 25, 1844,

16   *DC*, July 9, 1844, July 11, 1844; *USG*, July 9, 1844; Thomas A. Roe, "Southwark Affair," *AA*, July 17, 1844.

17   *Nation* (Dublin, Ireland), August 3, 1844; *PL*, July 10, 1844; *New York Herald*, July 9, 1844; *DC*, July 9, 1844.

18   *ST*, July 9, 1844, reprinted from extra of July 8; Pauline Louise Lagosse, Philadelphia, Pennsylvania, Death Certificates Index, 1803–1915, available at Ancestry.com; *Philadelphia Inquirer*, May 10, 1861; Mordecai Cullen testimony, *PL*, July 15, 1844; *Christian Observer*, July 12, 1844; *DC*, July 10, 1844; *ST*, July 10, 1844.

19   *DC*, July 9, 1844, July 10, 1844; *USG*, July 9, 1844, July 15, 1844; *DS*, July 9, 1844; *ST*, July 9, 1844, reprinted from extra of July 8; Memoranda, July 1845, respecting persons engaged in, or encouraging the Southwark Rioters, box 432, folder 8, GC; *CH*, August 29, 1844; William H. Everly testimony, *PL*, July 15, 1844; *Liberator*, July 19, 1844; *PL*, September 5, 1844.

20   Ford, "Conclusion of David Ford's Statement"; Nathan McKinley testimony, *PL*, July 15, 1844; William Crans testimony, *PL*, July 15, 1844; *DC*, July 9, 1844.

21   *DC*, July 9, 1844, July 11, 1844; *PL*, July 11, 1844, July 19, 1844; *HJCS*, August 7, 1844.

22 *NatAm,* July 10, 1844; *AA,* July 22, 1844; *DC,* July 11, 1844, July 15, 1844; Division Order no. 38, July 10, 1844, box 431, folder 5, GC; J. M., "Citizen Soldiery," *PL,* July 16, 1844; *HJCS,* July 17, 1844.

23 *New-York Tribune,* July 10, 1844; *PL,* July 11, 1844; *USG,* July 10, 1844; *HJCS,* July 17, 1844, February 5, 1845; *Liberator,* July 19, 1844; *ST,* July 10, 1844, July 11, 1844, July 12, 1844.

24 George Cadwalader to Robert Patterson, draft, July 15, 1844, box 431, folder 6, GC; John Colahan to George Cadwalader, July 18, 1844, box 431, folder 7, GC.

25 Maj. Gen. Patterson's Report, in *Reports of the Heads of Departments to the Governor of Pennsylvania, in Pursuance of the Law for the Fiscal Year Ending November 20, 1844* (Harrisburg: Isaac G. M'Kinley, 1844), 14; *Nation* (Dublin, Ireland), August 3, 1844; *USG,* July 12, 1844; *AA,* July 15, 1844; *HJCS,* July 17, 1844.

26 *PL,* August 3, 1844; *AA,* July 16, 1844, July 30, 1844.

27 *DC,* July 10, 1844, July 11, 1844, July 12, 1844; Penrose Ash testimony, *PL,* July 24, 1844; *CH,* July 11, 1844.

28 M. Antonia Lynch, "The Old District of Southwark," in *Philadelphia History: Consisting of Papers Read Before the City History Society of Philadelphia* (Philadelphia: The Society, 1917) 118; Francis Patrick Kenrick to Peter Kenrick, July 10, 1844, in K-F, 195; *CH,* July 18, 1844.

29 *DC,* July 11, 1844; *New-York Tribune,* July 10, 1844; *AA,* August 6, 1844; *AA,* July 13, 1844, July 18, 1844, August 1, 1844, August 6, 1844.

30 *PL,* July 11, 1844, February 1, 1845; *College of Physicians of Philadelphia,* 252–254; *USG,* July 13, 1844; *ST,* July 9, 1844, reprinted from extra of July 8; *Germantown Telegraph,* July 17, 1844.

31 *DC,* July 18, 1844, July 22, 1844; Augustus Pleasonton to George Cadwalader, July 9, 1844, box 431, folder 5, GC; Augustus Pleasonton to the Officers, noncommissioned officers, and privates of the 1st Regiment of Artillery in Southwark, on Sunday night, July 7, 1844, July 13, 1844, box 3, folder 1: Letters, 1st Regiment Artillery, MG7, PSA; AJP, July 7, 1844, 425; *ST,* August 26, 1844.

32 John Quincy Adams and Charles Francis Adams, *Memoirs of John Quincy Adams,* (Philadelphia: J. B. Lippincott & Co, 1874), 70; *PL,* July 16, 1844; *USG,* July 11, 1844; *DC,* July 11, 1844; *PL,* September 18, 1844; Theobald Mathew, qtd. in John F. Quinn, "The Rise and Fall of Repeal: Slavery and Irish Nationalism in Antebellum Philadelphia," *Pennsylvania Magazine of History and Biography* 130 (January 2006): 76.

33 *DC,* July 16, 1844; Robert Patterson letters to David R. Porter, July 10, 1844, July 15, 1844, July 16, 1844, and Report of the Select Committee of the House of Representatives of Pennsylvania, February 7, 1845, all in box 3, folder 1: Letters, 1st Regiment Artillery, MG7, PSA; *PL,* July 19, 1844, August 2, 1844; *NatAm,* July 17, 1844, July 18, 1844, July 25, 1844; R. Patterson to David R. Porter, July 22, 1844, "Important Documents," *PL,* July 25, 1844; Robert Patterson to George Cadwalader, July 24, 1844, box 431, folder 7, GC.

34 *New York Daily Herald,* July 16, 1844; *AA,* August 1, 1844.

35 *AA,* July 31, 1844, August 1, 1844.

36 *HJCS,* August 7, 1844.

CHAPTER 24: SAVIORS OF THE HOMESTEAD AND HEARTHSTONE

1 George Cadwalader to Robert Patterson, "Important Documents," *PL,* July 25, 1844; *NatAm,* July 1, 1844; *PL,* July 15, 1844.

2   Cecil, "The Riots," *Philadelphia Gazette*, July 19, 1844; Sidney George Fisher, *Diaries*, HSP, July 24, 1844; *Baptist Advocate*, qtd. in "Mob Principles," *CH*, August 1, 1844; "The Spirit of Misrule," *Law Reporter* 7 (September 1844): 216, 221.

3   *Liberator*, July 19, 1844; *Practical Christian* (Milford, MA), July 6, 1844; *NatAm*, July 19, 1844; *Illustrated London News*, August 3, 1844.

4   *Freeman's Journal* (Dublin, Ireland), July 31, 1844; Francis Patrick Kenrick to George Cadwalader, July 29, 1844, and George Cadwalader to Francis Patrick Kenrick, July 30, 1844, both in Raymond F. Schmandt, "A Selection of Sources Dealing with the Nativist Riots of 1844," *Records of the American Catholic Historical Society* 80 (June and September 1969): 107–108.

5   *HJCS*, September 4, 1844, September 11, 1844; *AA*, July 15, 1844; *DC*, July 11, 1844; M. L. M., "Lines Suggested by the Conflict between the Military and the Mob on Sunday Evening, July 7th, 1844," *DC*, July 16, 1844.

6   William Roderfield to George Cadwalader, July 16, 1844, box 431, folder 6, GC; *Journal of the Common Council, of the City of Philadelphia, for 1843–1844* (Philadelphia, 1844), 149; *DC*, July 17, 1844.

7   *HJCS*, August 28, 1844, October 9, 1844; *Catholic Telegraph* (Cincinnati), November 9, 1844; *PL*, December 11, 1844; 1st Regiment of Artillery, Order no. 68, January 24, 1845, box 432, folder 6, GC; *DC*, July 29, 1844.

8   *HJCS*, June 4, 1845; Henry Ducachet to Mrs. General Cadwalader, July 30, 1844, box 404, folder 5, GC; *NorAm*, August 1, 1844.

9   *HJCS*, September 25, 1844; Thomas L. Saunders, "A Card," *DC*, July 27, 1844; T. L. Saunders, "To the Editors of the Public Ledger," *PL*, July 24, 1844.

10 *AA*, July 20, 1844; Jonas P. Fairlamb testimony, *PL*, July 24, 1844; Saunders, "To the Editors of the Public Ledger"; Captain Thomas Saunders, testimony, *PL*, July 25, 1844.

11 *AA*, August 12, 1844, October 29, 1844; *PL*, August 9, 1844, September 5, 1844; *Germantown Telegraph*, September 13, 1837; "Col. John H. Bringhurst," in *Biographies of Philadelphians*, Thompson Westcott, 2:292, HSP.

12 C. J. Jack, "Col. Jack's Statement," *AA*, August 2, 1844; C. J. Jack, "A Card," *AA*, August 5, 1844; *PL*, August 3, 1844, August 8, 1844; *NatAm*, August 8, 1844; *AA*, August 8, 1844, August 12, 1844.

13 Charles Chauncey Binney, *The Life of Horace Binney: With Selections from His Letters* (Philadelphia: J. B. Lippincott, 1903), 239; *PL*, July 12, 1844.

14 *HJCS*, July 10, 1844; *PL*, July 12, 1844, July 20, 1844, July 23, 1844; *DC*, July 10, 1844; *Philadelphia Gazette*, July 9, 1844.

15 *New-York Tribune*, July 8, 1844, July 9, 1844; *A True Statement of the First Fire on Sunday Evening, July 7, 1844* (Philadelphia, 1844), 7; James L. Hewitt to George Cadwalader, July 17, 1844, box 431, folder 6, GC; *Brooklyn Evening Star*, July 11, 1844.

16 *Courrier de la Louisiane* (New Orleans), July 17, 1844; *PL*, July 13, 1844.

17 John Thomas Scharf, *The Chronicles of Baltimore* (Baltimore: Turnbull Brothers, 1874), 457; *HJCS*, July 24, 1844.

18 James Morrow, letter to John B. and Sarah Bull, July 18, 1844, James Morrow Papers, South Caroliniana Library, University of South Carolina.

19 *HJCS*, August 7, 1844; *AA*, July 15, 1844, July 26, 1844, August 12, 1844; C. S., "To the Editors of the Native American," *NatAm*, July 13, 1844.

20 *AA*, September 24, 1844, October 11, 1844, November 28, 1844; *AA*, December 10, 1844; *DC*, September 28, 1844.

21 "Statement of George S. Neath," *AA*, July 29, 1844; *American Woman*, December 14, 1844.

22 Thomas Grover testimony, *PL*, July 18, 1844; John Dutton testimony, *PL*, July 20, 1844; *AA*, July 25, 1844; Lieut. Col. James Gruff Charcoal [pseud.] to George Cadwalader, July 28, 1844, box 431, folder 10, GC.

23 *HJCS*, July 10, 1844, August 7, 1844.

24 *NatAm*, July 12, 1844, July 22, 1844; D. B., "The Southwark Riot," *DS*, August 3, 1844.

25 *DS*, July 22, 1844; *AA*, July 20, 1844, August 1, 1844, August 8, 1844, August 12, 1844, September 25, 1844; *DC*, June 29, 1844.

26 *NatAm*, May 18, 1844; John Hancock Lee, *The Origin and Progress of the American Party in Politics* (Philadelphia: Elliott & Gihon, 1855), 144; *AA*, July 26, 1844; *PL*, September 17, 1844.

27 Another Officer of the Brigade, "The 11th July Ordinance," *HJCS*, November 6, 1844.

28 *Journal of the Select Council of the City of Philadelphia for 1843–1844* (Philadelphia: J. Crissy, 1844), 138–140; *Street Talk About an Ordinance of Councils Passed the 11th July, 1844, Organizing a Military Force for the Government of Philadelphia* (Philadelphia, 1844).

29 Augustus Pleasonton to George Cadwalader, July 13, 1844, box 431, folder 6, GC; List of Volunteer Companies attached to the First Brigade, First Division P.M., 1844, box 431, folder 7, GC; Appendix, No. LXXIII, George Cadwalader to Select and Common Councils, September 26, 1844, *Journal of the Select Council*, 179–180; Augustus Pleasonton to George Cadwalader, September 23, 1844, box 431, folder 8, GC.

30 John W. Purdon and George MacDowell Stroud, eds., *A Digest of the Laws of Pennsylvania* (Philadelphia: M'Carty & Davis, 1841), 757; *HJCS*, July 24, 1844, August 21, 1844, October 9, 1844; Undated, untitled draft, ca. October 1844, box 431, folder 5, GC.

31 *HJCS*, September 11, 1844; *Dollar Newspaper* (Philadelphia), March 20, 1844; *AA*, September 7, 1844.

32 *HJCS*, February 19, 1845; *Street Talk About an Ordinance*, 18; A Cadwalader Gray," "The 11th of July Ordinance," *HJCS*, October 2, 1844; Another Volunteer, "For the Public Ledger," *PL*, November 8, 1844; *PL*, September 12, 1844.

33 Newspaper clipping with George Cadwalader to Select and Common Councils, September 26, 1844, box 431, folder 5, GC; *PL*, October 28, 1844; *HJCS*, October 2, 1844, February 26, 1845; George Cadwalader to Select and Common Councils, September 12, 1844, box 431, folder 8, GC; Undated, untitled draft, c. October 1844, box 431, folder 5, GC.

34 Undated, untitled draft, ca. October 1844, box 431, folder 5, GC; List of Volunteer Companies attached to the First Brigade, First Division P.M., 1844, box 431, folder 7, GC; *HJCS*, November 13, 1844, February 26, 1845. The Hibernia Greens became the Patterson Guard.

CHAPTER 25: CONGRESS OR THE PENITENTIARY

1 *HJCS*, September 11, 1844; X., "Capt. H. S. Mallory," *PL*, September 11, 1844.

2 *NatAm*, July 17, 1844; *ST*, August 26, 1844; A Yankee, "America," *Freeman's Journal* (Dublin, Ireland), August 15, 1844.

3 *DC*, July 24, 1844; *PL*, July 26, 1844; Sidney George Fisher, *Diaries*, HSP, October 20, 1844; Eliza Cope Harrison, ed., *Philadelphia Merchant: The Diary of Thomas P. Cope, 1800–1851* (South Bend: Gateway Editions, 1978), 446.

4   *AA*, July 15, 1844; Russell Jarvis, "For the Public Ledger," *PL*, August 15, 1844; *NatAm*,
    August 1, 1844.

5   *AA*, September 4, 1844; *PL*, October 10, 1844; Jeffrey L. Pasley, "Printers, Editors, and
    Publishers of Political Journals Elected to the U.S. Congress, 1789–1861," 2007, http://
    pasleybrothers.com/newspols/images/Editors_in_Congress.pdf ; *NatAm*, August 27, 1844,
    August 28, 1844. *McElroy's Philadelphia Directory for 1844* gives Levin's home address as 205
    S 4th Street. In 1845, Levin attended the Native American State Convention as a delegate
    from the New Market Ward. *PL*, February 24, 1845.

6   *NatAm*, August 5, 1844; *DS*, July 9, 1844.

7   *PL*, July 12, 1844; *NatAm*, July 11, 1844; *DS*, July 12, 1844; *DC*, July 12, 1844; *AA*, July 20,
    1844. Dialogue reconstructed from paraphrase.

8   *DC*, August 30, 1844, September 19, 1844; *ST*, September 10, 1844, September 14, 1844.

9   *DS*, September 13, 1844; Leonard Tabachnik, "Origins of the Know-Nothing Party: A
    Study of the Native American Party in Philadelphia, 1844–1852" (PhD diss., Columbia
    University, 1973), 90; *American Woman*, September 7, 1844; Bruce Dorsey, Reforming Men
    and Women: Gender in the Antebellum City (Cornell University Press, 2002), 218.

10 *AA*, September 11, 1844, September 16, 1844.

11 *AA*, September 12, 1844, September 23, 1844.

12 *AA*, September 11, 1844, September 20, 1844, November 29 1844; *PL*, September 21, 1844;
    NatAm, September 18, 1844.

13 Justus E. Moore, *The Warning of Thomas Jefferson* (Philadelphia: Wm. J. Cunningham,
    1844), 3, 21; *McElroy's Philadelphia Directory for 1844*, 223; *ST*, September 11, 1844, October
    4, 1844; *New-York Tribune*, September 23, 1844; *AA*, September 10, 1844. *New York Herald*,
    October 6, 1844, suggests that Moore's pamphlet seems to have been published in late
    September or early October, shortly before the election.

14 *AA*, October 1, 1844, October 7, 1844; *DS*, October 1, 1844; *DC*, October 8, 1844.

15 Pennsylvania Hospital Historic Collections, Meteorological Records, October 8, 1844; *PL*,
    October 9, 1844; *AA*, October 9, 1844; *DC*, October 9, 1844; Sidney George Fisher, *Diaries*,
    HSP, October 20, 1844.

16 Firth to George Cadwalader, November 29, 1844, box 432, folder 4, GC; *DC*, October 8,
    1844; *Jeffersonian* (Stroudsburg, PA), November 7, 1844.

17 *Journal of the Select Council of the City of Philadelphia for 1844–1845* (Philadelphia: J. Crissy,
    1845), 5.

18 Michael Feldberg, *The Philadelphia Riots of 1844: A Study of Ethnic Conflict* (Westport, CT:
    Greenwood Press, 1975), 166; *DS*, October 16, 1844; *AA*, October 14, 1844, October 15, 1844.

19 Mary Bird to Robert Bird, October 11, 1844, box 1, folder 6, Robert Montgomery Bird
    papers, MS Coll. 108, UP; *PL*, October 9, 1844; *Protestant Banner* (Philadelphia), October
    17, 1844; John Hughes to Terence Donaghoe, October 10, 1844, in Jane Coogan, "A
    Study of the John Hughes–Terence Donaghoe Friendship," *Records of the American Catholic
    Historical Society of Philadelphia* 93 (1982): 56.

20 *PL*, September 14, 1844, August 30, 1852; "Anniversaries of Societies Connected with the
    American Education Society," *American Quarterly Register* 14 (August 1841): 101; *ST*, July 27, 1844.

21 *PL*, November 6, 1844, August 30, 1852; Alan M. Kraut and Phyllis F. Field, "Politics
    Versus Principles: The Partisan Response to 'Bible Politics' in New York State," *Civil War*

History 25 (June 1979): 102; Michael F. Holt, *The Rise and Fall of the American Whig Party: Jacksonian Politics and the Onset of the Civil War* (New York: Oxford University Press, 2003), 205–206; *New-York Tribune*, March 19, 1845; John F. Quinn, "The Rise and Fall of Repeal: Slavery and Irish Nationalism in Antebellum Philadelphia," *Pennsylvania Magazine of History and Biography* 130 (January 2006): 77.

EPILOGUE

1   *ST*, September 12, 1844, July 12, 1845; A Catholic Citizen, "Things in Philadelphia," *New-York Tribune*, October 26, 1844; *DC*, October 23, 1844; Joseph Louis J. Kirlin, *Catholicity in Philadelphia* (Philadelphia: J. J. McVey, 1909), 342; *Pennsylvanian*, September 17, 1844; *Nation* (Dublin, Ireland), August 17, 1844; *CH*, December 5, 1844, cited in K-F, 199; Louis A. Rongione, "Sister to the Liberty Bell," *Records of the American Catholic Historical Society of Philadelphia* 87 (1976): 25–26; Hermits of St. Augustine v. The County of Philadelphia, and St. Michael's Church v. The County, *Reports of Cases Decided by the Judges of the Supreme Court of Pennsylvania* (Philadelphia: James Kay, Jun. & Brother, 1851), 116–120, 122.

2   Francis Patrick Kenrick to Peter Kenrick, January 1, 1845, and Francis Patrick Kenrick to Peter Kenrick, December 16, 1846, in K-F, 199, 239; Francis Patrick Kenrick to Tobias Kirby, July 12, 1845, and August 21, 1845, "Papers Relating to the Church in America," *Records of the American Catholic Historical Society of Philadelphia* 7 (1896): 316, 320.

3   *Pennsylvanian*, September 17, 1844; *ST*, September 17, 1847; *Boston Pilot*, August 29, 1846; "The Great Havana Hurricane of 1846," *New England Historical Society* (blog), October 14, 2016, newenglandhistoricalsociety.com; *PL*, October 14, 1846; *CH*, February 11, 1847; Thomas C. Middleton, "Some Memoirs of Our Lady's Shrine," *Records of the American Catholic Historical Society of Philadelphia* 12 (1901): 405; Joseph Jackson, "Building Philadelphia's Cathedral," *Records of the American Catholic Historical Society of Philadelphia* 56 (1845): 173–175; "About The Cathedral," Cathedral Basilica of Saints Peter and Paul, http ://cathedralphila.org/about/about-the-cathedral/.

4   *PL*, September 21, 1844; P. M. Austin Bourke, "Emergence of Potato Blight, 1843–46," *Nature* 203 (August 1964): 808; Cormac Ó Gráda, *Black '47 and Beyond: The Great Irish Famine in History, Economy, and Memory* (Princeton: Princeton University Press, 2000), 17, 38–39; *ST*, January 27, 1847; James Matthew Gallman, *Receiving Erin's Children: Philadelphia, Liverpool, and the Irish Famine Migration, 1845–1855* (Chapel Hill: University of North Carolina Press, 2000), 2.

5   Gallman, *Receiving Erin's Children*, 2–3, 32, 158–161; *PL*, May 12, 1848.

6   Francis Patrick Kenrick to Peter Kenrick, April 10, 1849, in K-F, 307; Gerald P. Fogarty, "American Catholic Translations of the Bible," in *The Bible and Bibles in America*, ed. Ernest S. Frerichs (Atlanta: Scholars Press, 1988), 126.

7   *AA*, September 25, 1844; *NatAm*, September 12, 1844; *Protestant Banner* (Philadelphia), December 5, 1844.

8   Thomas J. Donaghy, *Philadelphia's Finest: A History of Education in the Catholic Archdiocese, 1692–1970* (Philadelphia: American Catholic Historical Society, 1972), 88, 103, 111.

9   School Dist. of Abington Tp. v. Schempp, 374 U.S. 203 (1963); Anthony Lewis, "Kennedy's Inauguration Today," *New York Times*, January 20, 1961.

10   *PI*, August 22, 1846; John Hill Martin, *Martin's Bench and Bar of Philadelphia* (Philadelphia: Rees Welsh, 1883), 99; *Pennsylvanian*, November 26, 1846; Robert L. Bloom, "Morton McMichael's North American," *Pennsylvania Magazine of History and Biography* 77 (April 1953): 165n4.

11   Robert L. Bloom, "The Philadelphia 'North American': A History, 1839–1925" (PhD diss., Columbia University, 1952), 64–65; *NorAm*, March 4, 1847, October 8, 1850.

12   *USG*, February 8, 1845.

13   *PL*, October 10, 1849; Howard O. Sprogle, *The Philadelphia Police, Past and Present* (Philadelphia, 1887), 91–93; *Star and Banner* (Gettysburg, PA), October 19, 1849; Michael Feldberg, *The Philadelphia Riots of 1844: A Study of Ethnic Conflict* (Westport, CT: Greenwood Press, 1975), 170.

14   *PI*, November 30, 1850; Allen Steinberg, *The Transformation of Criminal Justice, Philadelphia, 1800–1880* (Chapel Hill: University of North Carolina Press, 1989), 151–153.

15   Andrew Heath, *In Union There Is Strength: Philadelphia in the Age of Urban Consolidation* (Philadelphia: University of Pennsylvania Press, 2019), 97–101; *NorAm*, March 13, 1854.

16   *NorAm*, July 1, 1847, May 31, 1854, June 14, 1854; Michael P. McCarthy, "The Philadelphia Consolidation of 1854: A Reappraisal," *Pennsylvania Magazine of History and Biography* 110 (1986): 538; Russell F. Weigley, "'A Peaceful City': Public Order in Philadelphia from Consolidation Through the Civil War," in *The Peoples of Philadelphia: A History of Ethnic Groups and Lower-Class Life, 1790–1940*, ed. Allen Freeman Davis and Mark H. Haller (Philadelphia: University of Pennsylvania Press, 1998), 157.

17   Russell F. Weigley, "The Border City in Civil War, 1854–1865," in *Philadelphia: A 300 Year History*, ed. Russell Frank Weigley, Nicholas B. Wainwright, and Edwin Wolf (New York: W. W. Norton, 1982), 372; Steinberg, *Transformation of Criminal Justice*, 147–149; Ali Watkins, "An Unprepared N.Y.P.D. Badly Mishandled Floyd Protests, Watchdog Says," *New York Times*, December 18, 2020.

18   Alexander Kelly McClure, *Old Time Notes of Pennsylvania* (Philadelphia: John C. Winston, 1905), 342; *Pittsburgh Daily Post*, July 16, 1858; Bloom, "Morton McMichael's North American," 173.

19   *Evening Telegraph* (Philadelphia), January 1, 1866; Heath, *In Union There Is Strength*, 173.

20   *DS*, October 14, 1844, February 6, 1845.

21   *DS*, March 22, 1845; *PI*, October 15, 1845; *PL*, October 20, 1846; *ST*, October 8, 1845, October 11, 1845, October 16, 1845, October 22, 1845; Feldberg, *Philadelphia Riots*, 168.

22   "Naturalization Laws: Speech of Hon. Lewis C. Levin," *Congressional Globe*, December 18, 1845, 49; A. H. Craig, ed., *Pieces for Prize Speaking Contests: A Collection of Over One Hundred Pieces Which Have Taken Prizes in Prize Speaking Contests* (New York: Hinds, Hayden & Eldredge, 1899), 123–125; *Shoemaker's Best Selections for Readings and Recitations* (Philadelphia: Penn Publishing, 1909), 179.

23   *The Papers of Jefferson Davis: Volume 2, June 1841–July 1846* (Baton Rouge: Louisiana State University Press, 1974), 389; "House of Representatives," *Congressional Globe*, December 5, 1846, 113; "Speech of Mr. James Dixon," *Appendix to the Congressional Globe*, December 30, 1845; Alpha, "Washington," *Boston Pilot*, August 8, 1846; Martin H. Quitt, *Stephen A. Douglas and Antebellum Democracy* (New York: Cambridge University Press, 2012), 94.

24   "House of Representatives," *Congressional Globe*, April 8, 1846, 624; Henry G. Wheeler, *History of Congress, Biographical and Political* (New York: Harper & Brothers, 1848), 1:359; "The Proposed Mission to Rome," *Appendix to the Congressional Globe*, 1848, 438.

25   *Lewisburg Chronicle* (PA), October 3, 1856; Henry Richard Mueller, "The Whig Party in Pennsylvania," *Columbia Studies in History, Economics and Public Law* 101 (1922): 163; *Brooklyn Daily Eagle*, February 9, 1850; *Tioga Eagle* (Wellsboro, PA), February 20, 1850.

26   *Boston Pilot*, October 24, 1846; "Party Divisions of the House of Representatives," Office of the Historian, US House of Representatives, http://history.house.gov/Institution/Party-Divisions/Party-Divisions/; Richard Yates, *Lincoln* (Washington, DC: Government Printing Office, 1921), 9; "The Only Correct Report: Mr. Levin's Great Speech on the Pope of Rome," *John-Donkey* 1 (January 1, 1848), 207; Mueller, "The Whig Party in Pennsylvania," 155; *ST*, July 3, 1848; *PL*, October 10, 1850; *Evening Post* (New York), May 13, 1844; *New York Herald*, August 21, 1850; *Adams Sentinel* (Gettysburg), October 21, 1850.

27   US House of Representatives, Select Committee on Colt's Patent, *Extension of Colt's Patent*, 33rd Cong., 1st sess., 744 H.R. Rep. 353, 1854; "Reports of Joint Committee Appointed to Investigate the Charges of Improper Influences in the Election of U.S. Senator, Doc. No. 64," in *Legislative Documents: Miscellaneous Documents Read in the Legislature of the Commonwealth of Pennsylvania* (Pennsylvania), 614, 653.

28   Allison O'Mahen Malcom, "Loyal Orangemen and Republican Nativists: Anti-Catholicism and Historical Memory in Upper Canada and the United States, 1837–1867," in *The Loyal Atlantic: Remaking the British Atlantic in the Revolutionary Era*, ed. Jerry Bannister and Liam Riordan (Toronto: University of Toronto Press, 2012), 219; Edward S. Deemer, ed., *Official History of the Junior Order United American Mechanics* (Boston: Fraternity Publishing, 1897), 18; Dale T. Knobel, *"America for the Americans": The Nativist Movement in the United States* (New York: Twayne, 1996), 67 Leonard Tabachnik, "Origins of the Know-Nothing Party: A Study of the Native American Party in Philadelphia, 1844–1852" (PhD diss., Columbia University, 1973), 233; Tyler Anbinder, *Nativism and Slavery: The Northern Know Nothings and the Politics of the 1850s* (New York: Oxford University Press, 1992), 20.

29   *Daily American Organ* (Washington, DC), January 24, 1856; Henry De Courcy, *The Catholic Church in the United States*, trans. John Gilmary Shea (New York: Edward Dunigan and Brother, 1856), 256; Charles E. Deusner, "The Know Nothing Riots in Louisville," *Register of the Kentucky Historical Society* 61 (1963): 122–147; Francis Patrick Kenrick to John Patrick Spaulding, August 17, 1855, 34 J24, Associated Archives at St. Mary's Seminary and University, cited in Chris Beneke, "The 'Catholic Spirit Prevailing in Our Country': America's Moderate Religious Revolution," in *The First Prejudice: Religious Tolerance and Intolerance in Early America*, ed. Chris Beneke and Christopher S. Grenda (Philadelphia: University of Pennsylvania Press, 2011), 283.

30   Tabachnik, "Origins of the Know-Nothing Party," 263; William E. Gienapp, *The Origins of the Republican Party, 1852–1856* (New York: Oxford University Press, 1988), 405–408; *Daily Journal* (Wilmington, NC), September 20, 1856; *PL*, September 17, 1856; *Evening Star* (Washington, DC), September 17, 1856; Lewis C. Levin, "To the Editors of the Ledger," *PL*, September 17, 1856.

31   *New York Times*, September 27, 1856; J. Forsyth Meigs, *A History of the First Quarter of the Second Century of the Pennsylvania Hospital* (Philadelphia: Board of Managers of

the Pennsylvania Hospital, 1877); Thomas G. Morton and Frank Woodbury, *History of the Pennsylvania Hospital: 1751–1895, Revised Edition* (Philadelphia: Contributors to the Pennsylvania Hospital, 1897); *Sunbury American* (Sunbury, PA), October 4, 1856; "Correction," *Charleston Courier* (SC), October 3, 1856.

32 John Philip Sanderson, *Republican Landmarks* (Philadelphia: J. B. Lippincott, 1856), 80; *Pittsburgh Daily Post*, March 17, 1860.

33 Tabachnik, "Origins of the Know-Nothing Party," 262; Anbinder, *Nativism and Slavery*, chap. 10; Erika Lee, *America for Americans: A History of Xenophobia in the United States* (New York: Basic Books, 2019). One account suggests that Charles Naylor proposed the name for the new party in an 1852 meeting in Pittsburgh, drawing on his favorable view of Philadelphia's American Republicans, but others downplay that claim. Charles H. Dahlinger, "The Republican Party Originated in Pittsburgh," *Western Pennsylvania Historical Magazine* 9 (January 1921): 5–7; Gienapp, *The Origins of the Republican Party*, 105.

34 Fanny Cadwalader to George Cadwalader, August 6, 1845, box 404, folder 7, GC; Cadmus M. Wilcox, *History of the Mexican War* (Washington, DC: Church News, 1892), 685; *ST*, December 5, 1846, December 27, 1846.

35 Dahlinger, "Republican Party"; James M. McCaffrey, ed., *Surrounded by Dangers of All Kinds: The Mexican War Letters of Lieutenant Theodore Laidley* (Denton: University of North Texas Press, 1997), 163–164; George W. Hartman, *A Private's Own Journal: Printed by E. Robinson* (Greencastle, PA: E. Robinson, 1849), 23.

36 *ST*, January 18, 1847, June 30, 1847; Robert Van Trombley, "Pennsylvania's Role in the Mexican American War" (master's thesis, Edinboro University of Pennsylvania, 2013), 28–31.

37 Eugene L. Townsend, "George Cadwalader," in *Sketches of Representative Men, North and South*, ed. Augustus C. Rogers (New York: Atlantic Publishing, 1874), 139–140; Timothy D. Johnson, *A Gallant Little Army: The Mexico City Campaign* (Lawrence: University Press of Kansas, 2007), 139, 140, 172.

38 *The Philadelphia Grays' Collection of Official Reports of Brigadier-General George Cadwalader's Services During the Campaign of 1847, in Mexico* (Philadelphia: T. K. and P. G. Collins, 1848), 52–54; "Letter from Gen. Cadwalader," *ST*, July 27, 1848; *ST*, October 26, 1847; Townsend, "George Cadwalader," 139; "The Diaries of Sidney George Fisher, 1844–1849," *Pennsylvania Magazine of History and Biography* 86 (1962): 88.

39 *ST*, May 20, 1848, June 15, 1848, July 4, 1848; *HJCS*, June 4, 1845; *Washington Union* (Washington, DC), February 24, 1847; George Cadwalader testimony, *PL*, July 19, 1844; Jack L. Lindsey, "The Cadwalader Family during the Early Nineteenth Century," *Philadelphia Museum of Art Bulletin* 91 (October 1996): 40; "Checklist of the Exhibition," *Philadelphia Museum of Art Bulletin* 91 (October 1996): 45; "The Cadwalader Vase and Medal," *ST*, July 4, 1848.

40 *PI*, April 16, 1861; Francis Patrick Kenrick to Peter Kenrick, July 15, 1861, in K-F, 459; Townsend, "George Cadwalader," 141–142.

41 Augustus Pleasonton to George Cadwalader, June 8, 1845, box 3, folder 1: Letters, 1st Regiment Artillery, MG7, PSA; A. J. Pleasonton, *Report of Brigadier Gen'l A. J. Pleasonton, Commanding the Home Guard of the City of Philadelphia, to the Hon. Alexander Henry, Mayor* (Philadelphia: King & Baird, 1864), 8, 42, 45, 54–55.

42 Arnold Shankman, "Draft Resistance in Civil War Pennsylvania," *Pennsylvania Magazine of History and Biography* 101 (1977): 195; *New-York Tribune*, July 20, 1863; *NorAm*, July 21, 1863; *PI*, February 4, 1879.

43 *Times* (Philadelphia), February 4, 1879; *PI*, February 7, 1879; *Carbon Advocate* (Leighton, PA), February 8, 1879.

NOTE ON SOURCES

1 *Saturday Courier*, May 11, 1844.

2 Alice M. Hoffman, *Archives of Memory: A Soldier Recalls World War II* (Lexington: University Press of Kentucky, 1990), 3.

3 *NorAm*, May 9, 1844; *USG*, May 9, 1844; *History of the First Troop Philadelphia City Cavalry* (Philadelphia, 1875), 55.

4 Deposition of William Macready, *DS*, August 7, 1844; John B. Colahan, "To Joseph R. Chandler, Esq.," *CH*, July 25, 1844; compare *DS*, September 13, 1844, with *PL*, September 13, 1844; *PI*, July 8, 1844.

5 *NatAm*, June 7, 1844.

6 Mary Mallon testimony, *PL*, September 16, 1844; Captain Hill testimony, *PL*, July 19, 1844. In this I follow Martha Hodes, "Knowledge and Indifference in the New York City Race Riot of 1900: An Argument in Search of a Story," *Rethinking History* 15, no. 1 (March 2011): 81, 85n20.

ILLUSTRATION CREDITS

1   *The Native Flag*, December 14, 1844. The Library Company of Philadelphia.

10   Anonymous, American School, 1801–1850, *Louis C. Levin* [sic], 1834, oil on canvas, 36 × 28 in. Courtesy of the Frick Art Reference Library.

22   John Sartain, *Brigadier General George Cadwalader*, circa 1842, mezzotint. Library of Congress.

35   Thomas D. Grover, *The Will of the Late Thomas D. Grover, Esq., Procured from the Office of the Probate of Wills, with a Short Sketch of His Life* (Southwark [Pa.]: H. B. Pierson, 1849). Library of Congress.

50   *Hon. Morton McMichael*, c. 1848, daguerreotype, ½ plate. The Library Company of Philadelphia.

57   H. R. Robinson, *The City of Brotherly Love*, 1843, lithograph, 32.3 × 47.2 cm. Courtesy of the American Antiquarian Society.

64   John Neagle, *Colonel Augustus James Pleasonton*, 1846, oil on canvas, 91.8 × 74.2 cm (36 ⅛ × 29 ³⁄₁₆ in.). Courtesy of the National Gallery of Art, Washington.

69   *The Tired Soldier* (Philadelphia, 1839). Library of Congress.

73   *The Most Rev. Francis Patrick Kenrick, D.D. Archbishop of Baltimore*, c. 1863, lithograph. Catholic Historical Research Center of the Archdiocese of Philadelphia.

86   *The Native American*, April 11, 1844. Courtesy of the American Antiquarian Society.

102 J. L. Magee, *Death of George Shifler in Kensington. Born Jan 24 1825. Murdered May 6 1844*, 1844, lithograph, hand-colored, 46 × 30 cm.(18 × 11.5). The Library Company of Philadelphia.

110 *Picture Gallery of the New and Old Worlds*, May 18, 1844, Y Period .P538 Oversize. Illustration: The Philadelphia Riots. New-York Historical Society Library, 98377d.

117 Unidentified artist, American, 19th century (R. J. Z.), *Hibernia Hose Company*, about 1842, graphite pencil and watercolor on paper. Sheet: 30.2 × 40.2 cm (11 ⅞ × 15 ¹³⁄₁₆ in.). Museum of Fine Arts, Boston. Gift of Maxim Karolik for the M. and M. Karolik Collection of American Watercolors and Drawings, 1800–1875, 56.449. Photograph © 2021 Museum of Fine Arts, Boston.

121 *Alexander's Express Messenger*, May 15, 1844. Courtesy of the American Antiquarian Society.

133 *Alexander's Express Messenger*, May 15, 1844. Courtesy of the American Antiquarian Society.

144 *Picture Gallery of the New and Old Worlds*, May 18, 1844, Y Period .P538 Oversize. Illustration: Conflagration of St. Augustine's Church. New-York Historical Society Library, 98377d.

153 *Picture Gallery of the New and Old Worlds*, May 18, 1844, Y Period .P538 Oversize. Illustration: Ruins of St. Michael's Church, and the Priest's House. New-York Historical Society Library, 98377d.

158 William and Frederick Langenheim, *North-East Corner Of Third & Dock Street. Girard Bank, at the Time the Latter Was Occupied by the Military During the Riots*, 1844, daguerreotype, ½ plate. The Library Company of Philadelphia.

168 *Pictorial Times* (London), circa May 1844. Author's collection.

174 Washington Peale, *The Three Days of May 1844. Columbia Mourns Her Citizens Slain*, 1844, lithograph, 35.2 × 27.4 cm. Library of Congress.

183 Fourth Ward Spring Garden, Native American Association, parade ribbon, 1844. Old Politicals Auctions, http://oldpoliticals.com/, accessed May 12, 2017.

193 *Native American Grand March*, 1844. Lester S. Levy Sheet Music Collection Sheridan Libraries, Johns Hopkins University.

196 Herbert S. Packard, *Church of St. Philip Neri. Philadelphia, Penna.*, c. 1880, lithograph. Catholic Historical Research Center of the Archdiocese of Philadelphia.

209 *A Full and Complete Account of the Late Awful Riots in Philadelphia: Embellished with Ten Engravings* (Philadelphia: John B. Perry, 1844). Library of Congress.

219 "To the Montgomery Hibernia Greens," *Military Magazine and Record of the Volunteers of the City and County* 1 (1839), plate 9. The Library Company of Philadelphia.

233 *Alexander's Express Messenger*, July 10, 1844. The Library Company of Philadelphia.

245 *Alexander's Express Messenger*, July 17, 1844. Courtesy of the American Antiquarian Society.

259 H. Bucholzer, *Riot in Philadelphia*, 1844, lithograph. Library of Congress.

270 David R. Porter, *General Orders*, July 8, 1844, 56 × 39 cm, #Am 1844 Penn. Gov. 9272.F. The Library Company of Philadelphia.

286 Cadwalader Family papers, collection 1454, series 7, General George Cadwalader papers, box 431, folder 10 - Awful Riots of 1844. Historical Society of Pennsylvania.

300 *Circular of the Native Americans of Philadelphia to the Voters of the City* (Philadelphia, 1844 or 1845), sm # Am 1844 Native 50434.O.19a (Gilpin). The Library Company of Philadelphia.

311 George K. Childs, Presentation Urn, 1848, silver, 30 ¼ × 16 ¼ × 10 ¾ inches (76.8 × 41.3 × 27.3 cm), Accession Number 1998-157-1a,b, gift of John Cadwalader, Jr., 1998. Philadelphia Museum of Art.

INDEX

INDEX